The Hills of Rome

Rome is 'the city of seven hills'. This book examines the need for the 'seven hills' cliché, its origins, development, impact and borrowing. It explores how the cliché relates to Rome's real terrain and how it is fundamental to the way in which we define this. Its chronological remit is capacious: Varro, Virgil and Claudian at one end, and on, through the work of Renaissance antiquarians, to embrace frescoes and nineteenth-century engravings. These artists and authors celebrated the hills, and the views from these hills, in an attempt to capture Rome holistically. By studying their efforts, this book confronts the problems of encapsulating Rome and 'citiness' more broadly and indeed the artificiality of any representation, whether a painting, poem or map. In this sense, it is not a history of the city at any one moment in time, but a history of how the city has been, and has to be, perceived.

CAROLINE VOUT is Senior Lecturer in Classics at the University of Cambridge, and Fellow of Christ's College and the Society of Antiquaries. She is a historian and art historian who publishes on a wide range of topics related to Greek and Roman art and its reception, Latin Literature and Roman history, and is the author of *Power and Eroticism in Imperial Rome* (Cambridge, 2007). In 2008 she was awarded a Philip Leverhulme Prize for her work on Art History, and in 2010 was the Hugh Last Fellow at the British School at Rome.

The Hills of Rome

Signature of an Eternal City

CAROLINE VOUT

CAMBRIDGE
UNIVERSITY PRESS

University Printing House, Cambridge CB2 8BS, United Kingdom

Cambridge University Press is part of the University of Cambridge.

It furthers the University's mission by disseminating knowledge in the pursuit of education, learning and research at the highest international levels of excellence.

www.cambridge.org
Information on this title: www.cambridge.org/9781107678712

© Caroline Vout 2012

First published 2012
First paperback edition 2016

A catalogue record for this publication is available from the British Library

Library of Congress Cataloguing in Publication data
Vout, Caroline.
The hills of Rome : signature of an eternal city / Caroline Vout.
    pages.   cm.
Includes bibliographical references and index.
ISBN 978-1-107-02597-4 (hard back)
1. Rome (Italy) – Description and travel.   2. Rome – History.   I. Title.
DG63.V68   2012
937'.63 – dc23   2012012765

ISBN 978-1-107-02597-4 Hardback
ISBN 978-1-107-67871-2 Paperback

It was *surnamed* Septicollis from its seven hills.

Hazlitt 1851 (1995: 296)

Contents

The colour plates willl be found between pages 174 and 175

Figures

Acknowledgements

This book would have been slower to write, were it not for the generous support of The Leverhulme Trust and the British School at Rome. The receipt of a Philip Leverhulme Prize in 2008 enabled me to enjoy a sabbatical from my teaching and to take up the Hugh Last Fellowship at the British School in 2010. I thank both institutions. I would also like to thank everyone at the School, especially its Director, Christopher Smith, Sue Russell and Valerie Scott for making it such an easy and productive place to work. And I thank my colleagues in the Faculty of Classics and at Christ's College, Cambridge for their generosity, friendship and academic engagement. David Sedley deserves special mention for stepping into my shoes to be Director of Studies.

Many people have helped in the writing of this book. I am particularly indebted to David Larmour and Diana Spencer, who set me off on this journey by inviting me to contribute to their co-edited volume, *The Sites of Rome: Time, Space, Memory* (2007), and to audiences in the Classics Departments of Edinburgh and St Andrew's as well as the Triennial in Cambridge and the British School for giving direction to my initial forays. Mary Beard, Jacopo Benci, Ed Bispham, Nicholas Champkins, Robert Coates-Stephens, Catherine Fletcher, Emily Gowers, Paul Howard, John Patterson, Richard Pollard, David Reynolds, Carol Richardson, Clare Rowan, Amy Russell, Christopher Smith, Michael Squire and Andrew Wallace-Hadrill all contributed more than they will know, either in advice, critical discussion or in their reading of draft chapters, and Torsten Krude, Ann, Colin and Sue Vout provided support throughout. Yet again, Michael Sharp has been a sympathetic editor. I thank him and Cambridge University Press's anonymous readers for challenging me.

The final stages of any project are always harder than one expects. But the process has been made easier by Kathryn Stevens, who cheerily checked all of my translations from the Latin and Greek; Franco Basso and Lucia Prauscello, who did the same with the Italian; by my heroic copy-editor, Jan Chapman; by the Librarians in the Faculty of Classics, Trinity College and the University Library, Cambridge; and by Maria Pia Malvezzi and Lucyna Prochnicka, who helped me in acquiring the picture permissions. I again

thank the Leverhulme Trust, whose grant paid for these permissions and enabled me to publish some of the images in colour.

I could not end these acknowledgements without also expressing my gratitude to Felix Budelmann, Viccy Coltman, Philip Jones, Helen Lovatt, Helen Morales, Maryam Parisaei, Sophie Read and Elizabeth Speller. It would have been a more difficult journey without them. And I thank Robin Osborne. It would be a very different book, were it not for Robin, who read all of it, more than once, and always understood where it was going.

1 | Introduction: the journey to Rome

There is a strong and pleasant memory for hills.

Kevin Lynch (1961: 173)

The map

I was born in a 'city of seven hills'. Durham is one of the hilliest cities in the north of England. Yet even now I am unsure which of its contours add up to seven. It is hard to imagine any of them competing with the dramatic Cathedral peninsula, which gives the city its name (Figure 1.1). In 995 CE, when the monks of Lindisfarne on the Northumbrian coast were looking for a permanent resting place for the body of their bishop, Saint Cuthbert, he appeared to them in a vision directing them towards 'Dunholm' or 'hill island'. Despite the vividness of this name ('dun' means 'hill', and 'holm' means 'island', in Anglo-Saxon), it took a milkmaid and her 'dun cow' to help them find their destination.

Archaeological evidence points to a history of settlement in the Durham area long before the monks' arrival. But it is at this point that the settlement becomes a city. When Durham acquired its seven hills is less clear. Yet knowing that there are seven is, in a sense, sufficient – safe, solid and strangely familiar. The concept underwrites Durham's urban credentials, taking us back to cities as old as Babylon and Jerusalem. As old as Rome. Small wonder that when writer DBC Pierre was describing the faded glories of Durham's Miners' Gala, the best-known and largest meeting of the mining community in England, he found it an obvious way of invoking tradition and summoning regional pride. It was 2004, a decade after the last colliery in the Durham coalfield had closed, yet comfort is gained from 'the men, women and children of the pit villages labouring up and down any number of Durham's seven hills under sizable silver instruments'.[1] Their route is irrelevant; it is the general terrain that makes

---

[1] Pierre 2004. Though Pierre was brought up in Mexico City and considers himself Mexican, his mother was born in Durham, and, like me, he would return there for holidays.

Figure 1.1 The Cathedral, Durham City.

their marching momentous. Seven hills lend *gravitas* to Pierre's account, turning struggle into an image of triumph.

Durham is not the only 'city of seven hills' in Britain. Bath, Bristol, Edinburgh and Sheffield all celebrate as much in their tourist information and university websites, while for Torquay on the South Devonshire coast, its 'famous seven hills provide the backdrop to a waterfront scene that matches anything you'll find on the French Riviera'.[2] The precise

---

[2] For the active myth that is the seven hills of Bath, see, for example, the *Bath Chronicle* on 28 August 2008 and *The Independent* (www.independent.co.uk/travel/uk/winter-walks-and-refreshing-rambles-1845579.html?action=Gallery&ino=2, last accessed 13 August 2011). For Bristol, see the description in *The National Gazetteer of Great Britain and Ireland* (1868): 'The surface is very irregular, so that within the limits of the town, there are, as in ancient Rome, seven hills'; www.bristolviews.co.uk/views-h.htm (last accessed 13 August 2011): 'As with many English towns and cities, Bristol claims, like Rome of old, to be built on seven hills'; and the recent composition by Jolyon Laycock entitled 'Among Seven Hills – Sinfonia Concertante for Piano and Orchestra', which, though about Bath, premiered at Colston Hall, Bristol. For Edinburgh, see Anderson 1922: 136: 'Like ancient Rome, Edinburgh is now a city of seven hills', and the folded map that is *Edinburgh: Seven Hills* (1998). And for Sheffield, the BBC website, also accessed 13 August, www.bbc.co.uk/dna/h2g2/classic/A659847: 'Another feature of Sheffield is the hills. Sheffield, like Rome, is built on seven hills' and, less positively, George Orwell (diary, 3 March 1936; Orwell and Angus 1968: 91): 'I have now traversed almost the whole city. It seems to me, by daylight, one of the most appalling places I have ever seen . . . I

stratigraphy of these places is less important than their aspirations. The fact that even Cambridge, one of the flattest of England's cities, has been known to manipulate its fenland into seven 'hills' highlights how wide the gap can be between image and experience.[3] Leave the British Isles behind, and the list becomes formidable: not only Babylon and Jerusalem, but Bergen, Brussels, Budapest, Istanbul, Lisbon, Moscow, Nijmegen, Nîmes, Prague, Siena, Turku, Seattle, Somerville in Massachusetts, Rio de Janeiro, Kampala in Uganda, Amman in Jordan, Thiruvananthapuram in India . . . [4] This cannot be a coincidence. A visit to any of them reveals that their 'seven hills' are a sales-pitch rather than a reality. The currency of the seven hills goes beyond western culture to imply a universal, or at least transferable, idea of 'citiness'.[5]

This book is about Rome's role in this economy. Rome is the 'city of seven hills' par excellence. What are the names of these hills? The Palatine, Capitoline, Aventine – sites which are as central to Rome's identity and foundation history as the Cathedral peninsula is to Durham. After this, though, the list is harder to compile. Even specialists in classics founder. The modern city sprawls either side of the River Tiber, embracing the Oppian and Cispian spurs of the Esquiline hill, the Caelian, Quirinal, Viminal, the Pincian Hill and Monti Parioli to the north, Monte Mario and the Janiculum to the west, not to mention Monte Testaccio, to the south, an artificial mound made from the sherds of discarded amphorae. This already gives a total of thirteen, with such names as Monte Savello and Montecitorio adding to the confusion. Which of these 'hills' are included in the canon? What counts as a 'hill' in the first place? How and when did *seven* hills come to be

doubt whether there are any architecturally decent buildings in the town. The town is very hilly (said to be built on seven hills, like Rome) and everywhere streets of mean little houses blackened by smoke run up at sharp angles, paved with cobbles which are purposely set unevenly to give horses etc a grip. At night the hilliness creates fine effects because you look across from one hillside to the other and see the lamps twinkling like stars.' The quotation about Torquay is repeated on tens of tourist websites.

[3] Castle Hill, Pound Hill, Honey Hill, Market Hill, Peas Hill, St Andrew's Hill and Senate House Hill. Although rumours have long circulated about the existence of an early map of the city which celebrates this canon, my classics colleague, James Clackson (pers. comm.), assures me that these rumours are false, and that he is the list's inventor. To counter construction with construction, see Iman Wilkens (1991), who has suggested that Troy is in Cambridgeshire.

[4] Some websites now extend these claims to Athens: see http://wikitravel.org/en/Athens (last accessed 13 August 2011). On the question of whether ancient Roman cities ever made the claim, see Chapter 2.

[5] Thucydides (7.77.7), in a sentiment which can be traced back to the Greek lyric poet Alcaeus (fr. 22), reckoned that 'citizens make a city, not walls nor ships devoid of men', but cities remain difficult to define. See de Certeau 1984, Rodwin and Hollister 1984, Middleton 1996, Frey and Zimmer 2001, Amin and Thrift 2002, Mayernik 2003 and Reader 2004. On the city as a work of art, see Calvino 1972 and Olsen 1986, and on Rome itself, Rykwert 1976.

the magic number, and less a description of the scenery than an enviable concept?

These questions demand that we dig through the layers of Rome's geographical and historical landscape – back to its mythological foundation by Romulus. As we dig, some strata will detain us longer than others: the radical interventions made to the urban environment by Mussolini, Napoleon, Sixtus V, Aurelian, Augustus; the ways in which this environment was represented in nineteenth-century engravings, Renaissance maps and painting, late antique, Flavian and Augustan poetry, Republican prose texts . . . But, unlike most books which bring this breadth of material together, the subject of this one is not Rome and its development, but the development of an idea – Rome as a city of seven hills – and how this idea was honed and sustained to give coherence to a chaotic, growing, shifting metropolis. First celebrated in the literature of the late Republic, but with a resonance that hints at a pre-established heritage,[6] 'the seven hills' have withstood major shifts in Rome's topography, and in representational strategy, to become one of the city's chief characteristics, and one which other communities have seen fit to appropriate for themselves. How did this happen? This book tells the story of their status and celebration over time. Unlike Heiken, Funiciello and De Rita's *The Seven Hills of Rome* (2005) or ongoing projects to map the various phases of the ancient city, it is not about land formation, but canon formation; about the written-ness of urban geography.

The 'seven hills' are not the only standard-bearer of what Rome is and was. The Capitoline hill and the Temple of Jupiter Optimus Maximus upon it have a special standing as the 'nucleus of Roman glory, the centre of the universe'.[7] Even in antiquity Livy could claim, 'Here is the Capitol, where once upon a time, upon the discovery of a human head [*caput*, from which the hill is said to take its name], it was foretold that in that place would be the head of the world and the pinnacle of power.'[8] Not all members of the canon are equal. As we shall discover, their jostling for supremacy is part of what keeps the canon a live issue. Apart from the hills – in the valley between the Caelian and Esquiline – the mighty Colosseum vies for attention as an icon of Rome's identity (Figure 1.2). In 80 CE already, the poet Martial celebrated its completion by claiming that it surpassed, or could stand for, the seven wonders of the ancient world.[9] 'Here where the venerable mass of

---

[6] This statement is complicated by the related issue of Rome's 'Septimontium' to which we will return in Chapter 3.

[7] Lady Morgan 1821: 114.

[8] Livy 5.54.7: 'hic Capitolium est, ubi quondam capite humano invento responsum est eo loco caput rerum summamque imperii fore.' See also Livy 1.55.5–6.

[9] Mart. *Spect.* 1 and the discussion by Fitzgerald 2007: 38. For a possible connection between Rome's seven hills and the seven wonders, see Chapter 3.

Figure 1.2 The Colosseum, Rome.

the amphitheatre rises in full view, were Nero's lakes . . . Rome is returned to herself.'[10] The Colosseum too was able to function as a metonym.

Emphasis on one hill or one building inevitably fragments the city. Hence the importance of the idea of 'the seven hills' in lending Rome integrity. It took until the 270s CE and the emperor Aurelian for the capital to be

[10] Mart. *Spect.* 2.5–6 and 11: 'hic ubi conspicui venerabilis Amphitheatri | erigitur moles, stagna Neronis erant . . . reddita Roma sibi est . . . '

fortified by a hefty brick and concrete boundary. Before this, Rome was effectively without defences. The built-up area of the city had long spilt over the Republican walls, out into surrounding territory: 'in other directions, it [Rome] had been secured by lofty walls or precipitous mountains, except that the spread of buildings has added many cities'.[11] The capital was in danger of having multiple personalities. Several definitions of Rome as an administrative entity applied that were not contiguous with these walls: the sacred boundary or 'pomerium', the customs boundary.[12] But in visual terms,

> If someone, by looking at these suburbs, wishes to estimate the size of Rome, he will necessarily be misled and have no secure sign by which to discern up to which point, as it stretches forth, the city is still the city, and from which point it starts not to be the city any longer – to such an extent is the fabric of the city interwoven with the countryside and provides its viewers with the notion of a city stretching to infinity.[13]

The Aurelianic wall provides a commanding circumference or frame for the first time for centuries, and one which is routinely plotted on post-antique representations of the city so as to mark its limits. Renaissance artist Pirro Ligorio's map of the ancient city, first published in 1561, constitutes a good example (Figure 1.3).[14] As Hendrik Dey puts it: 'the Aurelian wall came to dominate physical and mental landscapes of the Eternal City like

---

[11] Plin. *HN* 3.67: 'cetero munita erat praecelsis muris aut abruptis montibus, nisi quod exspatiantia tecta multas addidere urbes'.

[12] Excellent on the problems of definition is Haselberger 2007: 19–22. Also important is Goodman 2007: 7–38. On the 'pomerium' specifically, see also Patterson 2000.

[13] Dion. Hal. *Ant. Rom.* 4.13.4: καὶ εἰ μὲν εἰς ταῦτά τις ὁρῶν τὸ μέγεθος ἐξετάζειν βουλήσεται τῆς Ῥώμης, πλανᾶσθαί τ' ἀναγκασθήσεται καὶ οὐχ ἕξει βέβαιον σημεῖον οὐδέν, ᾧ διαγνώσεται, μέχρι ποῦ προβαίνουσα ἔτι πόλις ἐστὶ καὶ πόθεν ἄρχεται μηκέτ' εἶναι πόλις, οὕτω συνύφανται τὸ ἄστυ τῇ χώρᾳ καὶ εἰς ἄπειρον ἐκμηκυνομένης πόλεως ὑπόληψιν τοῖς θεωμένοις παρέχεται. Also important here are the ways in which jurists distinguished between the 'urbs' (the Servian city) and 'Rome': so P. Alfenus Varus, in the Augustan period, cited by second-century lawyer Ulpius Marcellus (*Dig.* 50.16.87): 'ut Alfenus ait, "urbs" est "Roma", quae muro cingeretur, "Roma" est etiam, qua continentia aedificia essent: nam Romam non muro tenus existimari ex consuetudine cotidiana posse intellegi, cum diceremus Romam nos ire, etiamsi extra urbem habitaremus' ('As Alfenus said, "urbs" is "Roma" which was surrounded by a wall, but "Roma" also extends as far as there are continuous buildings: for it can be understood from daily use that Rome is not considered to extend only as far as the wall, since we say that we are going to Rome, even if we live outside the urbs'). And, similarly, in the third century, Julius Paulus (*Dig.* 50.16.2).

[14] This version was made in 1570 for Braun and Hogenberg 1572–1617: 49, its caption, 'Urbis Romae Situs cum iis quae adhuc Conspiciuntur Veter. Monumet Reliquiis Pyrrho Ligorio Neap. Invent. Romae M.D.LXX'. Braun's accompanying commentary drew attention to the city's river, its gates, its seven hills and the Campus Martius.

Figure 1.3 Bird's-eye view of ancient Rome by Pirro Ligorio, as printed in Braun and Hogenberg 1572–1617. See also colour plate section.

no other manmade feature, ever'.[15] But even this wall can be breached – and not just by marauding invaders.[16] In contrast to Ligorio's image, the *Forma urbis Romae*, or Marble Plan, a map displayed in the hall, or *aula*, of the Temple of Peace from the start of the third century CE, marks neither geographical nor political boundaries and includes buildings *beyond* what will be embraced by Aurelian's perimeter.[17] Although invaluable for anyone studying urban topography, the Marble Plan is not a map as we would understand it, but a monument or exhibit, recently described as 'offering a hyper-abundance of cartographic information designed to overwhelm the viewer'.[18] Its Rome is its buildings, and its buildings are a chequerboard covering a hundred and fifty marble slabs. In recording the ground plans of

---

[15] Dey 2011: 279. Dey is now the standard work on the wall and its impact on the city. Particularly relevant here are pp. 160–95.

[16] Note, however, Dey 2011: 135–7 on the wall's extraordinary effectiveness, at least according to the literary sources.

[17] Goodman 2007: 33–4.

[18] Trimble 2007: 378 in a piece which examines the plan's visual function in its original viewing context in the temple. Also relevant here is Favro 2006: 38: 'The largely illegible individual components shown on the map collectively projected the scale and grandeur of the city, but not its specificity. Alive and always growing, representing time and place, Rome was too complex, too grand for human observers to grasp. The aniconic image of the Forma Urbis

these buildings, this monument achieves in cumulative surface detail what Pliny achieves with the idea of elevation: 'if someone were to add the height of the buildings, he would certainly come up with a worthy estimate and would admit that the magnitude of no other city in the whole world could be compared to it [i.e. to Rome]'.[19]

For Pliny and the Marble Plan, the power of Rome lies in its capacity to spread onwards and upwards, to dominate the landscape, the world even – imperial expansion as expansiveness and order. It is an image of dominion which is of a piece with Roman expertise in road building and in controlling water (whether in bringing fundamental supplies along aqueducts or exploiting its sound and reflections to enliven a grotto or villa-garden). And it is very much an imperial vision, which can potentially accommodate similar *fora*, amphitheatres and bathhouses springing up throughout the provinces. These structures are an obvious part of what made settlements Roman. But what of Rome's natural landscape – the rustic Rome of Evander that these technologies adapted; the geology that made this part of Italy perfect for a city in the first place? What of the seven hills and the valleys between them? The Tiber is the only natural feature to be represented on the Marble Plan, and this, a gap or negative area left by the buildings.

The Marble Plan's decision not to represent the hills does not militate against their importance as an image of Rome in antiquity. As we shall discover, public, and it seems private, art was reticent about representing precise geographical features,[20] preferring to personify Rome and its elements, for example, the Tiber and the Campus Martius (see Figure 5.6 on p. 128).[21] More than this, depictions of *conquered* cities were particularly favoured. None of this detracts from the prolific presence of the seven hills in Latin poetry, or from their prominence in Rome's reception history. If anything, it better explains their function – not as territory but as concept, and one which exceeded the certainties of the Augustan or Flavian landscape, the physical appearance of the city such as one would plot by tracing its wall or measuring its buildings. If 'the seven hills' did reference real

---

Romae was an artefact of the capital's pictorial inconceivability.' For more compendious coverage, see Rodríguez-Almeida 1981 and, for a broader context, 2002, with the review by Najbjerg and Trimble 2004, as well as the Stanford Digital *Forma Urbis* Project (http://formaurbis.stanford.edu/), and the survey on the scholarship by Najbjerg and Trimble 2005.

[19] Plin. *HN* 3.67: 'quod si quis altitudinem tectorum addat, dignam profecto aestimationem concipiat fateaturque nullius urbis magnitudinem in toto orbe potuisse ei comparari'.

[20] For images of cities in Roman painting, see Pappalardo and Capuano 2006, and Goodman 2007: 28–36.

[21] *LIMC s.v.* 'Campus Martius' and 'Tiberis, Tiberinus'.

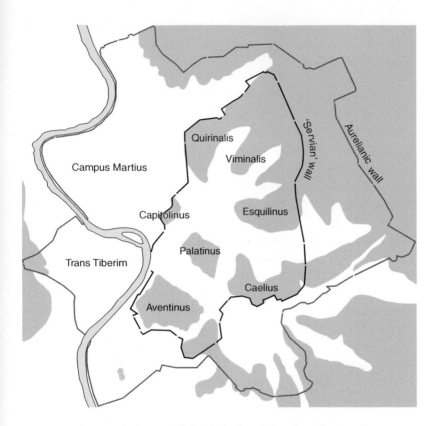

Figure 1.4 The canonical seven hills inside the 'Servian' and Aurelianic wall.

topography, it was that of the sixth-century BCE city, contained within the wall attributed to the early king, Servius Tullius. And we shall be pursuing this possibility in more detail later. But, for all that the canonical seven – the Aventine, Caelian, Capitoline, Esquiline, Palatine, Quirinal and Viminal, as it turns out – were included in its circumference, Servius and his urban reforms are as legendary as Durham's milkmaid (Figure 1.4).

When in 7 BCE the first emperor, Augustus, took the sprawling metropolis by the scruff of the neck, organizing it into fourteen regions which formally recognized the extra-mural settlement as part of Rome, the Servian city was officially engulfed.[22] The Campus Martius, the low-lying plain in the bend of the river beyond the walls, was key to this development. Greek author Strabo, writing under Augustus, observes: 'for the size of the Campus Martius is wondrous'. Such is the intensity of the buildings there that 'they seem to

---

[22] See Sablayrolles 1981, Frézouls 1987, Coarelli 1988, Favro 2005 and Haselberger 2007.

render the rest of the city incidental'.[23] The focus of urban activity had shifted. From this moment, if not before, Rome's status as a city of seven hills was symbolic.

Given this symbolism, what reason was there for Rome's reluctance to personify its hills – especially when the Campus Martius was bodied forth as a strong young man and the Tiber depicted as a reclining, bearded male? The hills of other localities were personified in Greek literature from the fifth century BCE and are sometimes seen in the visual record.[24] For Rome, though, it is the sense of *seven* hills that is crucial. As is the case with each of the porphyry 'tetrarchs' that now grace the sea-facing corner of the south façade of the Basilica of San Marco in Venice (Figure 1.5), to give the hills individualized, charismatic bodies would have been to arm them with sufficient might to compete with one another for supremacy.[25] Jostling for position in the literary record is one thing – it reinforces the canon by making cohesion and membership something worth contesting. But visually, this competition risks fracturing the canon's unity: it gives each member attributes which refer to specific divinities, landmarks, legendary rivalries. Even after Rome's early hilltop settlements had come together as one community, hills had their own identities, with the Aventine, for example, associated in the fifth century BCE with the *plebs*, or poorest inhabitants, in their conflict with the patricians.[26] Personification would give these hills character traits, their own relationship to the river and place in history. Collectively, they could be more amorphous, a-temporal, before time even. They could bring the Rome of Augustus and heirs into dialogue with the Romes of Servius Tullius and of mythical founder, Romulus.

The chapters that follow trace exactly how this dialogue develops. Under Augustus already, the idea of the seven hills enabled the city to enjoy an established identity, a space to occupy which transcended the changes that were happening on the ground. Inevitably, ongoing urban development, including the removal of large mounds of earth to make way for buildings, and raised ground levels elsewhere in Rome led to further changes in the physical fabric, which made the relationship of 'the seven hills' to the land more pressing. It is hardly surprising that by late antiquity, with Old Saint Peter's rivalling the Capitoline as Rome's nucleus, the hills to the west of the river often appear in the canon: for example, the appendices to the late antique regionary catalogues, the *Curiosum* and *Notitia,* substitute the

---

23 Strabo 5.3.8: καὶ γὰρ τὸ μέγεθος τοῦ πεδίου θαυμαστόν . . . ὡς πάρεργον ἂν δόξαιεν ἀποφαίνειν τὴν ἄλλην πόλιν, and Coarelli 1997.

24 *LIMC* supplementum, *s.v.* 'montes'. Also relevant here is Buxton 2009.

25 See Bergmann 1977: 163–79; Rees 1993; and Smith 1997: 179–83.

26 Cornell 1995: 242–71.

Figure 1.5 The 'tetrarchs', St Mark's Square, Venice.

Vatican and Janiculum hills for the Quirinal and Viminal.[27] Even then, the celebration of the seven hills in literature affirms the currency of the concept.

The itinerary

Rome is its seven hills in ways in which it is not its wall, the Colosseum or Capitol. Chapter 2 illustrates why this is so, giving us something of a survey of its seven hills as an idea and unpacking the extent to which this idea does

---

[27] Jordan 1871: vol. II.ii, 539–74. See Arce 1999.

and does not fit the city's changing landscape. Exposing this divergence proves a useful starting point. Today, to be a 'city of seven hills' is a cliché as applicable to Durham and Kampala as to Rome. But what is at the root of this borrowing? I argue that though Jerusalem and Babylon are also ancient cities renowned for their seven summits, Rome is the original of this stereotype. What prior assumptions about Rome do the seven hills carry with them and where do these come from? The answers to these questions reveal that being a city of seven hills was a cliché in antiquity already, and that authors then were almost as unsure of precise membership as we are today. Not that this makes the seven hills meaningless. Rather, their import lies in their capacity to give contours to the palimpsest that is Rome, defining the territory of the city while at the same time turning this city into an abstract idea which rises above its links to the land. For each new politician or poet wanting to make their mark there, and for those who live outside it, 'the seven hills' gave a sense of continuity to what it was they were experiencing. These hills created a template for comparing Rome, past, present and future, and for committing this place to paper. In this way, the glory that was the ancient city is made forever reproducible.

If Chapter 2 presents the end point or overuse of 'the seven hills' concept, Chapters 3 and 4 set out in search of its origins and original effectiveness. I am not the first to do this. Back in the 1970s Remo Gelsomino cut a swathe through a series of arguments and counter-arguments about the minutiae of membership, when he claimed that late Republican author Marcus Terentius Varro (116–27 BCE), whose obsession with the number seven is attested throughout his oeuvre, invented the canon. Up to that point, according to Gelsomino, there was no canon, only communities, which scholars have mistakenly associated with seven 'hills'. This 'error' and correction of this 'error' hinges on 'Septimontium', the name of a festival in which these communities had long taken part.[28] More recently, archaeologist Andrea Carandini has re-established the link between 'Septimontium' and the land, tying the word, and Varro's etymology of it, back to Rome's real peaks and troughs and to earlier phases of the city's development.[29]

The claims on both sides are as complex as they are bold. Attractive as Gelsomino's idea is, my concern in Chapter 3 is less to credit Varro, or anyone else, with 'an invention of tradition'[30] than to understand why

---

[28] Gelsomino 1975, 1976a and 1976b.

[29] Carandini 1997: 269: 'L'insediamento del Septimontium prende nome dall'insieme dei monti che lo compongono . . . I monti non erano infatti sospesi in aria . . . ' ('The settlement of the Septimontium takes its name from all of the *montes* of which it consists . . . the *montes* were not in fact suspended in air . . . ').

[30] Seminal here is Hobsbawm and Ranger 1983.

seven and why then, when the Republic was on its last legs and autocracy was looming. Varro and his friend Cicero presage an investment in Rome as a city of seven hills by Augustan poets Horace, Ovid, Propertius, Tibullus and Virgil, which requires us to think hard about how the idea fits with the urban reforms of the Princeps. Whether or not Servian and pre-Servian Rome had seven hills, why did that number sound so sweet now? What does popularity of the seven hills reveal about how the Romans regarded Augustus and, more broadly, conceptualized the current city and its relationship to previous incarnations? All Romes are relative. Varro himself recognizes this: his is the earliest extant work to link the concept of the seven hills with the ancient festival of the 'Septimontium', with Rome's real terrain. Rather than *inventing* the concept, it seems that Varro too is attempting to understand how the Romans got there.

Varro and the Augustan poets set the ball rolling. Domenico Palombi has recently summarized the evidence for the part that 'the seven hills' and the Tiber played in the updating of the urban imagination engendered by Augustus' adornment of the city.[31] Chapter 4 builds on his survey, reading this poetry closely so as to explicate exactly what it does to the landscape, bringing the city of fourteen regions into alignment with the Servian city of seven hills to rewrite innovation as re-foundation. As we read, we begin to unpick the process by which the Servian city becomes the 'city set high on seven hills which presides over the whole world',[32] a city which remains distinct from the satellite cities of its Empire, yet a city which speaks not only of itself but of urban aspirations everywhere. While scholars such as Paul Zanker, Diane Favro and Lothar Haselberger have done much to understand the impact of Augustan reforms on the city and on the way that its inhabitants experienced the city,[33] the abstraction innate in the hills' cliché makes it easier for us to look forwards as well as back, putting pressure on the extent to which this experience, along with the description it elicited, was peculiarly Augustan. In the Domitianic period and in the fourth and fifth centuries, poets celebrated Rome's seven hills with renewed vigour. By the time when the Christian poet Paulinus of Pella was writing, the Aurelianic walls were complete. But he envisages these walls 'on the world's heights (*culminibus*)', 'culmina' being used of the seven hills by the Flavian poet Statius.[34]

---

[31] Palombi 2006.

[32] Prop. 3.11.57: 'septem urbs alta iugis, toto quae praesidet orbi'.

[33] P. Zanker 1987, Favro 1996 and Haselberger 2007.

[34] Paulinus of Pella, *Eucharisticos* 36–7: 'visurus et orbis | inclita culminibus praeclarae moenia Romae' and Stat. *Silv.* 1.5.23.

Paulinus' Rome is a different world from that of Virgil; and not just in terms of its physical appearance, but in terms of its centrality, domination and influence. Constantine the Great's decision to found a new city, Constantinople, a 'second Rome', on the site of Byzantium in 324 CE, pushed the centre of power eastwards.[35] The emperors were no longer based in Rome. Those who did visit were tourists. Such distance and the demise in Rome's fortunes intensified the sense in which 'the eternal city' was an imaginary city, one whose authority lay not in what it was but in what it stood for. The concept of 'the seven hills' enabled poets to put these rare imperial visits, and the Rome that they came into contact with, on equal, or at least comparable, footing with the Rome of the Flavians, Julio-Claudians, and early kings of the mythological past. The figure of Roma, personified, is imagined as old and grey, but she still has the hills to support her.[36] The final third of Chapter 4 examines what kind of continuum this is. All too often modern scholarship reduces the relationship between late antique panegyric and earlier poetry to literary allusion. The hills flesh out this relationship by highlighting what Claudian and his contemporaries do – not to Virgil or Statius, but to Rome as a city, and model for other cities. In their hands, it is not just Rome's status as a city of seven hills that is symbolic, but Rome itself, as its supremacy shifts from real to notional.

The Renaissance codified Rome's cultural capital. The sixteenth century was the first time, as far as we can tell, that anyone was comfortable in making the canon more than a poetic conceit or, different again, a list of names, and in representing each and every member visually. Up to this point, visualization of the seven hills and of the Rome(s) they piece together had been in the hands of the reader. Now imagination was confronted with concrete images which intruded upon this space, as – following in Varro's footsteps – artists and antiquarians attempted to understand how the concept mapped onto the real terrain. It no longer mattered if the city were atomized in the process: ancient Rome was a foreign country to be mined for valuable fragments. Chapter 5 concentrates most of its attention on two such visual depictions – the first of them a set of sixteenth-century frescoes, and the second a series of engravings made in the nineteenth century as antiquarianism ceded to archaeology and grand teleological narratives – to examine the different ways in which their artists pay homage to the seven hills, and what these artistic choices reveal about the relationship of the ancient and modern city. Neither of these endeavours was about refining

---

[35] Still key reading on the early history of Constantinople is Janin 1950. Also relevant here are C. Kelly 1999 and Bassett 2004.
[36] Claud. *De bello Gildonico* 17–25.

the canon. Like this book, they exploit its value as a vehicle for getting a handle on Rome's constructedness.

'The seven hills' are not the land but a way of seeing the land. In the penultimate chapter, I take this statement at its most literal by tracking how, from antiquity onwards, special premium has been given to the panoramic or bird's-eye view, and to the act of surveying Rome from its summits. Today, a special 'Seven Hills Tour' still takes visitors to the top of the canonical seven in an air-conditioned minivan. More than this, many people enjoy the most memorable vista of the city from the Janiculum or Pincio. What are they looking at?; looking for? Rome's hills were never simply safe havens from possible attacks or from the miasma and malaria of the low-lying areas. They were oases of calm – in the city, yet above the city – on which elite residences were built and nature enhanced with sculpture in formal parkland. An alternative name for the Pincian Hill, for example, is the 'Hill of Gardens'. All of this exploited their importance as viewing platforms, from which auguries could be taken, Rome commanded, and its area delineated, not by real or sacred boundaries, but by the gaze. From the Capitol, it was – as poets have often exploited – Jupiter himself who looked out, turning his temple into a beacon of Empire. What does his particular prominence and the role of the Janiculum and the Pincio do to the idea of the seven hills? How is it that using its hills as tripods has made Rome comprehensible?

These questions allow us to come at Rome's constructedness from a different angle – not Rome as its hills but the antithesis, Rome as the flatland beneath them. Stand on the Janiculum today, and the dome of the Pantheon on the plain that is the Campus Martius rivals the Capitoline for eminence (see Figure 6.8 on p. 206). The Capitoline, meanwhile, has been said to look 'abroad upon a large page, of deeper historical interest, than any other scene can show'.[37] This 'page' is one of many in this book which reveal how the hills have helped centuries of people, both inhabitants and visitors, get a purchase on Rome's complexity.

The destination

The complexity of any city is itself a cliché, and the particular cachet of ancient Rome is fundamental for western culture. Scholars have left few stones unturned: from the city's topography, demography, decline and fall, to its place in the literary and artistic imagination. As far as the hills of

---

[37] Nathaniel Hawthorne [1860] 2007: 127.

Rome are concerned, individually, they have been intensively studied, their history written and rewritten in light of new excavations and geological surveys. There are articles on distinct etymologies, rituals, phases. There are also useful overviews.[38] But putting these hills together is a different matter. Despite, if not because of, the difficulty of reconstructing their ancient elevations,[39] topographical debate dominates, with little questioning of the merging of the real and representational. For example, Funiciello, Heiken and De Rita take 'the seven hills' of their title for granted.

On a parallel track to this research on Rome's land transformation is that of Catharine Edwards, Alexandre Grandazzi, Nicholas Purcell, Peter Wiseman and others, whose interests in written Rome have led to a more self-conscious reading of the ancient literature than is practised by many historians and archaeologists.[40] Edwards focuses on several different themes: how the city's authors related to Rome's own past and to Troy, how they treated the Capitol and Rome's built environment, and finally how exiles and aliens, ancient and more modern, imagined the city. Relationships between Edwards' chosen themes and sources and the material Rome they reference are elucidated throughout to reveal how perceptions of the city are conditioned by texts and images. But the material city remains a city of fragments. 'We must struggle', she writes, 'to imagine a city, or rather a succession of cities, in which different buildings dominated';[41] as indeed people in late antique or Flavian Rome must have struggled. Taking inspiration from what Edwards does – but with, and from, the seven hills – makes overlapping visions possible.

These visions cannot be divorced completely from the natural contours that created them. They do not simply condition perceptions of the city; they are the city, or rather the raw material or bedrock on which the city

---

[38] The most useful starting point for surveys of individual hills and their recent bibliography are the relevant entries in *Lexicon topographicum urbis Romae* (*LTUR*), for the Augustan period, Haselberger 2002, and, for a literary approach, Boyle 2003. Also important is the entry on 'montes' in *LTUR*, and Coarelli 2007. Further to the publications cited in these, one should now also see Giavarini 1998, Cecamore 2002 and Pensabene 2002 on the Palatine; Carandini 2004 on the Palatine and Velia, and 2007 on the Quirinal; Carafa 1993, Palombi 1997 and Carandini 2007 on the Palatine and Esquiline; Coates-Stephens 2004 on the Esquiline, Colini 1944 and Pavolini 2006 on the Caelian; Merlin 1906, Di Gioia 2004 and Mignone 2010 on the Aventine; Paradisi 2004 on the Capitoline, and Steinby 1996 on the Janiculum. On classifying the hills, see Langdon 1999 and on their history, Zolfanelli 1884.

[39] See Ammerman 2006: 300. For the current state of research into the urban imaging of ancient Rome, see Haselberger and Humphrey 2006.

[40] Edwards 1996, Grandazzi 1986 and 1991, Purcell 1992 and T. P. Wiseman 1979.

[41] Edwards 1996: 4.

was created – geo-graphy, the writing of the land.[42] Scholars who work on imaginary Rome sometimes underestimate the ways in which the land shapes conceptualization of the land. Those studying the city's ancient topography can underestimate the ways in which conceptualization of the land shapes the land. Rome's seven hills bind these elements. They were what Rome's poets chose back in the late Republic and Empire, if not before, to give the city then, and from its foundation, a form, content and unity which could transcend aristocratic rivalries, radical revision under Augustus, and expansion into Empire. As an idea, they have withstood its Christianization, collapse and shift to cultural paradigm, tourist capital even, to forge a link between past and present. Still today they epitomize, without shrinking, the eternal city. So strong are they that other communities can challenge them with impunity – even the market town of Morley in West Yorkshire makes a cheeky claim to seven summits.[43]

Interrogating this strength of character, and where it wavers – for Rome, and for town and 'citiness' more broadly (something notoriously difficult to define) – will have us look at not only ancient authors such as Virgil, Varro, Statius and Claudian, but antiquarians, including Fulvio and Fauno, and artists, including Mantegna, Rossini and Palmer, to make us more conscious of what we are doing when we look at Rome and at literary descriptions, maps, engravings and paintings of Rome. The hope is that they will make all of us – classicists, (art) historians, geographers and tourists – see, read and experience the Eternal City differently.

---

[42] Crucial in thinking about the writtenness of landscape is the work of Denis Cosgrove 1984 and 1993 and Cosgrove and Daniels 1988. Also important is J. Duncan and N. Duncan 1988, J. Duncan 1990, Barnes and J. Duncan 1992, Daniels 1993, Rose 1993, who turns 'landscape as a way of seeing' into an exploration of landscape and the gendered gaze, and Olwig 1996. A critical overview of the importance of 'constructedness' in the field of cultural geography is Wylie 2007.

[43] See e.g. www.visitoruk.com/historydetail.php?id=13308&cid=592&f=leeds (accessed 4 April 2010): 'Like Rome, Morley is built on seven hills.'

2 | The lie of the land

> When the Queen of Nations is at length before us; when we enter within the walls of the Seven-hilled City; pass along the ruins of her greatness; or glance with eager gaze on her venerable piles, then, to use the language of Byron, 'full flashes on the soul the light of ages.' The studies of our juvenile days and the labours of our maturer years are conjured 'up by the genius of the spot:' we seem to live and converse with the illustrious dead, whose names are familiar to us from boyhood, and are so intimately associated with the objects and localities around us, ennobling the spot on which we stand – 'A world is at our feet'; 'Our tread is on an Empire's dust.'
>
> Jeremiah Donovan (1842: xi–xii)

This is a book about a cliché. Rome was not built in a day. It takes time to make a city eternal. All roads lead there. As the capital of the Roman Empire and home of the papacy, Rome and its influence on western culture have proved inescapable. Yet how are we to reconcile this mighty reputation with the metropolis in Lazio on the River Tiber? Today, a graffito in the Ghetto reads 'Rome is not a museum.' The city is a living organism, which has survived collapse, occupation and modernization to become one of the most popular tourist destinations in the world and home to some three million residents. What does this built environment have to do with the Rome of Mussolini, the Renaissance, Augustus, Romulus, with the Rome of the imagination? This mismatch of reality and expectation is particularly acute for the many visitors, eager to gaze 'on her venerable piles'. For some, there is pleasure, for others, disappointment, for many, puzzlement. Those who are impressed tend, like the very Reverend Jeremiah Donovan, whose aim it was to offer 'a more accurate and comprehensive study' of ancient and modern Rome than had thus far been undertaken in English, to draw on existing authorities to articulate their admiration.[1]

Such inherited wisdom does more than lend weight to personal opinion. It recognizes that the Rome that one is looking at has a history, and that it is this history that makes the city more than a city – a veritable Queen of

---

[1] Donovan 1842: i.

Nations. Donovan's recourse to Lord Byron, and later to Pliny, turns him from a tourist to a traveller in a more visionary sense, tying past and present together in such a way that the ruins rise again from the ashes.[2] Any one of us who has stood on the Palatine is familiar with the frisson of feeling the genius of the spot and of standing on an empire's dust. It is an experience which is extremely evocative. Centuries of response find focus in the view of the Forum which transports us back through the Romes of romanticism, classicism and the Renaissance, back to antiquity and to the greatness of a culture which could build such foundations, further back to the origins of the city and to Romulus, Evander, Aeneas. But these Romes do not exist – they are cultural capital as opposed to concrete cities with populations, prosperity and perimeters. Where did these Romes begin and end? Where did the city stop and the suburbs and countryside start? What is Rome when defined as a single urban intervention?

The geographical remit of Donovan's Rome is alluded to on the title page already in a couplet by the poet Martial (Figure 2.1). At the end of the first century CE, he wrote:

hinc septem dominos videre montis,
et totam licet aestimare Romam

From here it is possible to see the seven sovereign hills and to get the measure of the whole of Rome.[3]

It is a couplet which is picked up in the preface as Donovan enters 'within the walls of the Seven-hilled city'. The image immediately gives form to the city, taking the reader from Italy into Rome itself – not a Rome of the mind, but a physical Rome, which is not simply built environment nor faded glory, but shelves of tufa; a Rome that is and always will be; that has been since volcanic activity in the Alban Hills formed these shelves tens of thousands of years ago.[4] Donovan continues: 'The seven-hilled city has become a marble wilderness.' But the implication is that its ruins are surface decoration; the hills are its substance as well as its bedrock. For all of the changes that man has made to these hills, 'Rome, city of seven hills' is a cliché which enables the city's universal significance to speak to the natural terrain that it occupies.

This cliché pervades high and low culture. For example, *The Seven Hills of Rome* is the English title of Italian tenor Mario Lanza's penultimate film,

---

[2] Excellent on the difference between the response of a tourist and a traveller to a new place is Buzard 1993.
[3] Mart. 4.64.11–12.   [4] Heiken *et al.* 2005.

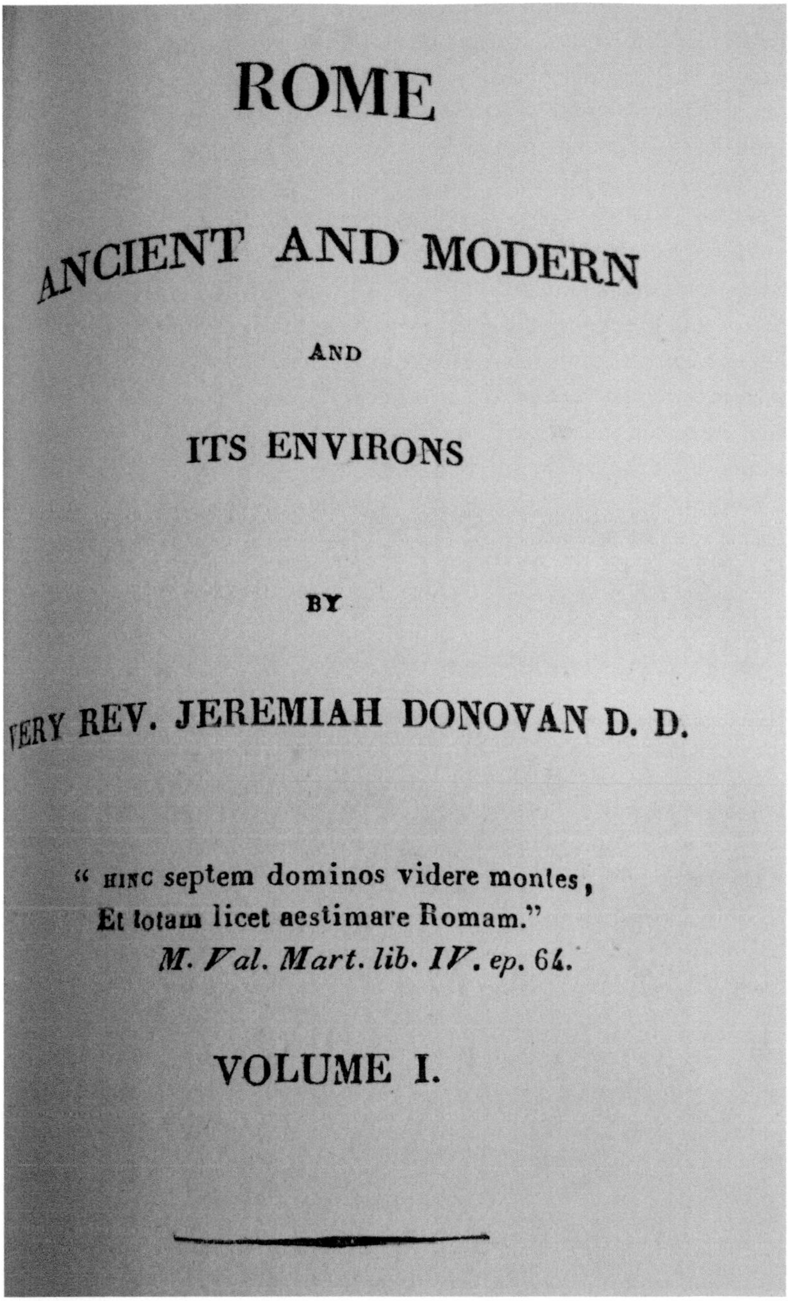

ROME

ANCIENT AND MODERN

AND

ITS ENVIRONS

BY

VERY REV. JEREMIAH DONOVAN D. D.

" HINC septem dominos videre montes,
Et totam licet aestimare Romam."
M. Val. Mart. lib. IV. ep. 64.

VOLUME I.

Figure 2.1 Title page of Jeremiah Donovan's *Rome, Ancient and Modern and its Environs*, 1842.

Arrivederci Roma, released by MGM in 1958. *Madonna of the Seven Hills* is Jean Plaidy's recently reissued historical novel of the young Lucrezia Borgia,[5] and *The Seven Hills* is John Maddox Roberts' 2005 alternative account of the Punic Wars. Today, the 'Sette Colli Giallorossi' is a prize, awarded by football club A. S. Roma on the eve of their annual derby with local rivals, Lazio (Roma's colours being red with a yellow trim).[6] What kind of space do the seven hills connote? Is it still a Rome that fits within the walls as Donovan's does? And if so, which walls: those attributed to Servius Tullius or to Aurelian? How do the natural and built environments, and Rome's real terrain and the seven-hills shorthand relate? This chapter sketches a history of these relationships, accenting key moments of evolution, on the ground in Rome and in terms of Rome's reception history. Its vision is deliberately *longue durée*, introducing the territory of ensuing chapters and establishing some ground rules. 'Septicollis' never was a straight description. Like every place, 'Rome' is crystallized in experiences of the land which have impressed themselves on the imagination.

The seven hills of Rome, Republic and Empire

Can Queen Victoria eat cold apple pie?[7]

Tradition has it that the sixth king of Rome, Servius Tullius (conventionally dated to 578–535 BCE), was the first to build a wall which embraced the canonical seven summits. We shall be examining the texts that underpin this tradition in the next chapter. But Dionysius of Halicarnassus, writing in the second half of the first century BCE, states the case succinctly: 'after Tullius had surrounded the seven hills with one wall, he divided the city into four regions'.[8] Although the best-known stretches of the 'Servian Wall' are now known to be fourth century BCE in date, archaeology confirms earlier phases of construction.[9] Follow the line of this wall, and we find it embracing the Aventine, Caelian, Capitoline, Esquiline, Palatine, Quirinal and Viminal, and excluding the Pincian Hill and those across the river.

---

[5] Plaidy 1958. See also the books about Rome and its mythology which carry the seven hills in their titles, for example, Harding and Harding 1898 and Hastings and Hodder 1936.

[6] For more details, see e.g. (last accessed on 15 March 2010): www.ccsnews.it/ipusher/dettaglio. asp?id=a5150588&titolo=PREMIO%20SETTE%20COLLI%20GIALLOROSSI.

[7] A well-known mnemonic for remembering the members of Rome's now canonical seven hills.

[8] Dion. Hal. *Ant. Rom.* 4.14.1: Ὁ δὲ Τύλλιος, ἐπειδὴ τοὺς ἑπτὰ λόφους ἑνὶ τείχει περιέλαβεν, εἰς τέτταρας μοίρας διελὼν τὴν πόλιν . . .

[9] Cornell 1995: 198–202.

But this 'discovery' begs a greater suspension of disbelief than maps like Figure 1.4 acknowledge. First there is the question of the Velia, which Dionysius describes as 'a relatively high and steep hill commanding the Forum'.[10] Why was it ignored, when it too was inside the perimeter? The fire of Rome in 64 CE, ambitious building projects by the Roman emperor, Nero, and his successors, and the construction of the Via dei Fori Imperiali by Benito Mussolini in 1932 have so changed this region as to make reconstruction difficult. Consensus now downgrades the Velia as a 'ridge' which joined the Esquiline and Palatine.[11] But if the Velia is a ridge, then what about the Quirinal, Viminal and Esquiline, which, like fingers on a hand, are promontories of one volcanic plateau? Conversely, the Esquiline is made up of two fingers or spurs, the Oppian and the Cispian – why were these not taken separately? One Renaissance humanist was so struck by its summits as to compare it to the many-headed monster, the Hydra.[12] One could ask the same of the Capitoline, with its two summits, the northern 'arx', or 'citadel', and the southern Capitolium with its temple to Jupiter, separated by the 'asylum', or saddle, which now accommodates Michelangelo's piazza;[13] or indeed of the largest of the hills, the Aventine, which again has two heights, only one of which, the north-western point, was definitely always known by this name.[14] Even the Caelian is made up of a 'Caelius Minor' and 'Caelius Maior'.[15] Getting seven from these contours requires creative counting.

Already this raises the question of what an incline has to look like to qualify as a 'hill'. For Dionysius, the Velia was a 'λόφος', a noun that he and other Greek authors use for the canonical seven (more often than they use the alternative 'ὄρος').[16] In Latin, a hill could be a 'mons' or a 'collis'. Although there is a tendency in English to translate the former as 'mountain', for Rome's authors the two are regularly coterminous. For Martial, Varro, Tibullus and Ovid, the seven hills are 'montes', for Horace and Claudian, 'colles', and for Virgil, 'arces', the plural of 'arx', or 'citadel', and a word which carries with it an idea of defence or powerbase, in contrast to its more natural counterparts. Propertius, meanwhile, refers to them as

---

[10] Dion. Hal. *Ant. Rom.* 5.19.1: ... λόφον ὑπερκείμενον τῆς ἀγορᾶς ὑψηλὸν ἐπιεικῶς καὶ περίτομον, ὃν καλοῦσι Ῥωμαῖοι Οὐελίαν, ἐκλεξάμενος.

[11] Steinby 1993–2000: vol. V, 109: 'La posizione della collina non si ricava con chiarezza dalle testimonianze antiche' ('The position of the hill cannot be determined with clarity from ancient sources'). On its early importance in ancient Rome, see Fraschetti 2002: 57. Also important are Rebert 1925, Terrenato 1992, Tomei 1994, Palombi 1997, Carandini 2004 and Capanna and Amoroso 2006.

[12] Fulvio 1513: bk 1: 'Hinc mons Exquilinus cunctis Spatiosor unus | in plures apices velut hydra attollitur altos.'

[13] On the 'arx' between myth and reality, see Tucci 2006.

[14] See, for example, Skutsch 1961: 254 with bibliography.

[15] Mart. 12.18.6; Cic. *Har. resp.* 15.32; and Varro, *Ling.* 5.46.   [16] Langdon 1999.

'iuga', or 'ridges', which potentially opens the door to the Velia, Oppian and Cispian.[17] Beyond poetry, in the epigraphic record, a stronger separation is maintained between the terms 'collis' and 'mons', with the Quirinal and Viminal routinely referred to as 'colles' as distinct from the other members of the now traditional canon, and the Oppian and Cispian, all of which are 'montes'.[18] 'Tarpeius mons' (Tarpeian hill) is also found in the literature and in inscriptions, sometimes used as an early synonym for the whole of the Capitoline and sometimes, even in late antiquity, for part of it.[19] As Richard Buxton writes in 'Imaginary Greek Mountains', 'a mountain is in the eye of the beholder'.[20]

Some of Rome's canonical seven are, and always were, more vulnerable in their membership than others. A 'mons' it may be, but the Aventine, though within the 'Servian wall' and fundamental to Rome's foundation mythology, remained outside the city's sacred boundary, or 'pomerium' (again usually attributed to Servius), until the reign of Claudius (emperor, 41–54 CE) – and this, despite the fact that across the city, the Campus Esquilinus or burial grounds beyond the wall's Esquiline Gate had been included in the late Republic under Sulla.[21] Aulus Gellius, writing in the second century CE, notes, 'it has been asked and even now is the subject of inquiry, why only the Aventine, which is neither a remote nor a thinly populated quarter, is outside the *pomerium*, when the other six are inside it'.[22] His answer, based on an Augustan source, is that this was because Remus had taken his auspices there, making the hill inauspicious. There is also, as I have already mentioned, the hill's early history as public land (*ager publicus*), which was taken over unlawfully and then throughout the Republic associated with

---

[17] For these poets and their manipulation of the concept, see Chapter 4.

[18] See Fridh 1993, and with an emphasis on Greek authors, Langdon 1999. Also crucial here are Poucet 1967 and Fraschetti 1996. Poucet 1985: 83 explains that the Viminal and Quirinal are 'colles' because they belonged to a part of the city which was originally called 'colles' or 'Collina' (Varro, *Ling.* 5.45), a more marginal community than that embraced within the 'Septimontium'. That said, there were exceptions to this norm: Flor. 1.7.16 and Eutr. 1.7 and the tradition that the Quirinal was first called 'Mons Agonus' (Festus 304L).

[19] See Varro, *Ling.* 5.41; Livy 1.55.1; Dion. Hal. *Ant. Rom.* 4.60.3–61.1, 7.35.4; Prop. 4.4.93–4; Suet. *Iul.* 44.1; Plut. *Num.* 7.2; *CIL* VI 37170 = *ILS* 4438 and *Cataloghi regionari Notitia e curiosum, appendix* in Valentini and Zucchetti 1940: 294–6.

[20] Buxton 1992: 2, revisited in 2009: 81–96.

[21] L. Richardson 1992: 294. On the Campus Esquilinus, Hor. *Sat.* 1.8.14–16: 'Now it is possible to live on a health-giving Esquiline and to stroll on the sunny rampart where recently people, miserable, used to gaze at ground ugly with white bones' and T. P. Wiseman 1998 and Edmunds 2009. And on the stinking pits and mass graves of its former incarnation, Lanciani 1889a: 14 and 1899b: 64–5 and Hopkins 1983: 208–11.

[22] Aul. Gell. 13.14.4: 'propterea quaesitum est, ac nunc etiam in quaestione est, quam ob causam ex septem urbis montibus, cum ceteri sex intra pomerium sint, Aventinus solum, quae pars non longinqua nec infrequens est, extra pomerium sit'.

the *plebs*, to consider.[23] On the other side of the river, the highest of Rome's hills not to make it, the Janiculum (the only one more often referred to as an ὄρος in Greek), mounted a challenge: it is said to have been walled by Ancus Marcius, the fourth of the early kings, and joined to the city already by the Pons Sublicius.[24]

In time, the Viminal and Quirinal prove the most precarious members of the list (perhaps because of their unusual colline status), although even the Capitoline can be excluded in favour of the Janiculum.[25] Before late antiquity, when that particular list was compiled, no one seems to have worried very much about which hills were included – so much so that Theodor Mommsen could claim, rather too strenuously, that 'no ancient author knows the to us familiar seven (Servian) hills'.[26] Instead, in the late Republic and early Empire when the seven hills became a modish way of referring to the city, poets were content simply to celebrate the concept; and prose writers, to explore how Rome had grown from one hill to seven and thereby reached maturity. Of these authors, Varro causes most problems by claiming that 'where Rome now is was called Septimontium after the same number of hills which afterwards the city surrounded by its walls',[27] and by thus conflating a festival celebrated on 11 December and its associated rituals with the city's territorial remit. It is a move which has introduced other names to the list of contenders – the collis Latiaris, collis Mucialis, and collis Salutaris, not to mention the Fagutal and Cermalus as well as the Velia – and has led some scholars to commit to a second canon of earlier hills (more of which later). For the moment, however, our subject is the now traditional canon and its growth into a cliché that had to be carefully managed from the outset. It is this management that makes Rome's seven hills more than a fact – a calculated formula or concise way of expressing the city's complexities and making this city potentially navigable. Rome equals . . . What follows builds on the introduction to explore how this general relationship between qualities (Rome and the hills, soil and symbol) works out. In this way, the land becomes landscape, 'a cultural image, a pictorial way of representing, structuring or symbolizing surroundings'. 'Landscape is not merely the world we see, but rather a way of seeing the world. It is an ideological concept

---

23 Cornell 1995: 242–71.

24 Livy 1.33.6; Plut. *Num.* 9.2–3; and Dion. Hal. *Ant. Rom.* 3.45.2.

25 Serv. *ad Aen.* 6.783. Although note D'Anna (1992: 155–7), who claims that the Janiculum referred to here is part of the Capitoline. See below, p. 213.

26 As cited in Jordan 1871: 206: 'die uns geläufigen sieben (servianischen) Hügel kein alter Schriftsteller kenne'.

27 Varro, *Ling.* 5.41: 'ubi nunc est Roma, Septimontium nominatum ab tot montibus quos postea urbs muris comprehendit'.

that represents how specific classes of people have signified themselves and their world through their imagined relationships with nature.'[28]

'After the high Roman fashion'[29]

Cities are, above all, places whose analysis requires a sense of spatial and physical structure.[30]

Rome is not unique in seeking circumscription. Nor is it unique in claiming seven summits. As Spiro Kostof observes in his book *The City Assembled*, defining a city and belonging to a city ask for delineation of its span and circumference.[31] And as we have already established, cities the world over have found 'seven hills' a possible solution. Their competing claims to the accolade have given it universal value. But what does this do for them and to the 'Rome equals' formula? A closer look at a few of these cities reveals that their celebration of a seven-hills status is less ancient than one might think – a phenomenon which seems to depend, to a large extent, on Rome's Renaissance standing. As Rome, the model western city, becomes more paradigmatic by lending its attributes, these attributes become a more essential mark of what Rome is, turning it from capital of the Empire into the ideal urban centre into 'Urbild'. Constantinople's strategic position on the Bosphorus Strait is not enough to ensure success. Only seven hills give it the geography to be a world-leading city.[32]

The most famous reference to seven hills outside the classical canon is in the Bible. In the Book of Revelation, written in the first century CE, an allegorical 'whore of Babylon' in purple and scarlet and adorned with gold, jewels and pearls is pictured seated on a scarlet beast with seven heads, which are interpreted by an angel as 'seven mountains' and seven kings.[33] Although opinion is divided over whether these hills point to Rome or Jerusalem, there is a rationale to the former, and only one explicit mention of Jerusalem as a city of seven hills in the whole of the *Talmud*, this being late antique.[34] It is likely that Rome is at the root of both passages and is in

[28] Meskell and Preucel 2004: 219 on the work of Denis Cosgrove. See Chapter 1 above, n. 42.
[29] Cleopatra in Shakespeare, *Antony and Cleopatra* Act 4, scene 15: 'What's brave, what's noble, Let's do it after the high Roman fashion, And make death proud to take us.'
[30] C. Tilly 1984: 120.   [31] Kostof 1992: 11.
[32] For Constantinople as a city of seven hills, see e.g. Janin 1950: 4 and Baldovin 1987: 168.
[33] Book of Revelation 17.9. For a careful weighing of Rome and Jerusalem's candidature in this passage, see Biguzzi 2006; also, Aune 1998: 944–5.
[34] Bialik and Rawnitzky 1992: 371 citing the *Pirke de-Rabbi Eliezer*, 71. I thank Simon Goldhill for help with this point. Also important here are the rash of references to Rome as a city of seven

Figure 2.2 Copy of the Capitoline Lupa.

the New Testament the antithesis of the model city, the acme of a decadent metropolis.

In Constantinople, Rome's reputation and Christianity enjoyed a more positive relationship. Founded by the first Christian emperor, Constantine, on the site of an existing city, Constantinople was perhaps always destined to be a rival. Although it is not, at least as far as the existing literature is concerned, called 'new Rome' until after his death in 337 CE,[35] there can be little doubt that this nomenclature is what Constantine would have wanted: the city was soon crowded with artefacts from all over the Empire, including a bronze sculpture of Romulus and Remus being suckled by the she-wolf (Figure 2.2) and the Palladion (the cult statue of Pallas Athena which had been stolen from Troy, taken to Rome by Aeneas and

hills in the later *Sibylline Oracles* and apocalyptic literature, so: *Or. Sib.* 2.18, 11.112, 13.45 and 14.08 (see Lightfoot's commentary on the first and second books (2007: esp. 447)), ps.-John Chrysostom's *Visio Danielis* p. 37, l. 8 (ed. Vassiliev) and Oecumenius, *Comm. in Apocalypsin* p. 188, l. 9 (ed. Hoskier).

[35] Them. *Or.* 3.42, delivered in 357 CE, under Constantius II, is the first to be explicit in its comparison of new and 'old' Rome. But the city was 'altera Roma' already in a poem by Porphyry Optazianus in 326 CE (*Carmina* 4.6 and 18.34) and Socrates Scholasticus, writing in the fifth century (*Hist. eccl.* 1.16), claimed that Constantine had established it by law that it should be called 'second Rome'. Still classic here is Dölger 1937.

kept for centuries in the Temple of Vesta in the Forum); both of these were images intimately connected to Rome's foundation. Constantinople was also divided into fourteen regions as Augustan Rome had been. It was only a matter of time before it boasted seven hills too, making its situation more providential.[36] When this happened is less easy to reconstruct. While it is tempting to give the credit to Constantine, not all of the seven hills lay inside his new wall. This did not happen until the fifth century when, under Theodosius II, the praetorian prefect Anthemius built another circuit, recognizing the city's spread westwards. And none of the literary sources or regionary catalogues to survive from the fourth or fifth centuries, or the later *Chronicon Pascale, Parastaseis* or *Book of Ceremonies* mention them. Although apocalyptic literature of the eighth to tenth centuries sows the seeds,[37] we have to wait until the sixteenth century and the publication of Pierre Gilles' *De topographia Constantinopoleos* for these really to germinate. He starts his 'general description' of the city thus, 'Constantinople occupies a peninsula embracing seven hills'.[38] Whereas 'it is easy to distinguish Rome's hills, which Nature made discrete from their valleys', it is harder to do justice to Constantinople.[39] A detailed description of each of the hills and corresponding valleys follows. It is a project that owes much to the Renaissance rediscovery of Rome and attempts to document that city.[40]

After the fall of Byzantium to the Turks in 1453, Moscow assumed the religious and imperial mantle of the patriarchy to which it had been attached and wasted little time in declaring itself successor. Again ritual and writing combined to celebrate the cities' comparison. In 1492 already, in a charter of Zosimius, Metropolitan of Moscow Ivan III was referred to as 'the new Emperor Constantine of the new Constantinople-Moscow'; and by the start

---

[36] For the Lupa, see Niketas Choniates, *De signis* 650–1, and on the Palladion, Alan Cameron 1983 and C. Kelly 1999. Note that the famous Lupa Capitolina statue, mentioned as standing near the Lateran Palace in Rome in the twelfth century already, is now not thought ancient, but mediaeval in date. For a summary of the arguments, see Mazzoni 2010: 35–9. For a detailed list of the sculptures that were said to have adorned Constantinople, see Bassett 2004. However, this should be read with caution. Many of these sources, like Niketas Choniates, are very late in date, and even earlier ones, including Christodoros of Koptos' poem about the Baths of Zeuxippos, ekphrastic in nature. See Kaldellis 2007. The fourteen regions are first mentioned in the Theodosian *Notitia urbis Constantinopolitanae* of 425 CE.

[37] Relevant here is the Rome of the apocalyptic tradition: see above, n. 34.

[38] Gilles 1561: 24: 'Constantinopolis occupat peninsulam septem colles complectentem'.

[39] Gilles 1561: 26: 'Romanos colles facile est decernere, quos Natura secrevit vallibus'.

[40] Lønstrup 2009 (I thank Gavin Kelly for this reference). Important on the later development of the story is Brandes 2003. By the nineteenth century Constantinople's 'seven romantic hills' make it an attractive destination: see e.g. the *Morning Chronicle* 25 September 1839.

of the sixteenth century the 'new Constantinople', as 'the third Rome'.[41] A monk from Pskov, Philotheus, was amongst the most energetic proponents of this image: 'So be aware, lover of God and Christ, that all Christian empires have come to an end and are gathered together in the singular empire of our sovereign in accordance to the books of prophecy, and this is the Russian Empire: because two Romes have fallen, and a third stands, and a fourth there shall not be.'[42] As the recipient of the baton in a relay that went Rome – Constantinople – Moscow, it is only natural that this city too should have seven summits. It needed them as much as a Caesar or 'Tsar' to declare itself the centre of Christian Empire.

Where does this leave the remaining cities in the list – for example Siena, Kampala, Sheffield, Durham? Where does it leave Rome? Siena had at least been a Roman city and one which, from the fifteenth century onwards, invested heavily in the mythology of its foundation by Remus' son, Senio, twin brother of Aschio.[43] It was keen to be a clone. Uganda's capital, Kampala, was assimilated for other reasons. It became a city of seven hills under the British who arrived there in 1890 – an example of colonialism and the classics underpinning it, of a piece with images in accounts by Jesuit missionaries of native Americans wearing togas.[44] In 1962, the year of its independence, it was reinscribed as 'far more than a "Rome of Seven Hills"'.[45] For the others, the relationship with Rome is less obviously political and the rationale for borrowing more opaque, sometimes pretentious, often twee, occasionally droll. But with each invocation, Rome is remembered ('Sheffield, like Rome, is built on seven hills'), and the age-old formula is tested. The result is that Rome is solved all over again, and its rival (wherever it is) is accorded a value. In the process, the natural is made cultural, and the cultural or cultivated is made natural.

The seven hills were always meant to have us weigh Rome against other cities and prior incarnations of itself. Some scholars think that back in antiquity Rome's colonies had seven hills in homage to the mothership.[46] Much of their evidence pertains to the number and the names of their 'vici',

---

[41] Stremooukhoff 1953: 91 and M. Poe 2001. Related to this is Balina (2007: 331–3), who discusses the importance of Rome and its hills for Peter the Great and the creation of St Petersburg.

[42] 'Poslanie o zlykh dnekh i chasekh', ed. Vladimir V. Kolesov, in *Pamiatniki literatury drevnei Rusi. Konets XV – pervaia polovina XVI veka*, ed. Lev A. Dmitriev and Dmitri S. Likhachev (Moscow: 'Khudozhestvennaia literatura', 1984), 452, as cited by M. Poe 2001.

[43] This was, in part, a response to Biondo's *Italia illustrata* of 1474, which claimed that the city was a post-antique foundation. See Nevola 2007: 147–56 and Jacks 1993: 86–9.

[44] E.g. Lafitau 1724.   [45] Weeks 1962: 7.

[46] Levick 1967: 77: 'There may have been only seven *vici* [in Pisidian Antioch], one to correspond to each of the seven hills on which the colony was built' with an accompanying footnote which states that 'Ariminum, Nemausus, and Constantinople shared this feature.'

or neighbourhoods: so Ariminum (Rimini), which became a Latin colony in 268 BCE, was divided into seven *vici*,[47] the names of five of which are known (*vicus Cermalus, vicus Velab(rensis), vicus Aventinus, vicus Dianensis* and *vicus For[tunae?]*), and the Augustan colony of Pisidian Antioch in Turkey into at least seven (*vicus Venerius, Aedilicius, Velaber, Patricius, Tuscus, Cermalus* and *Salutaris*). In Cales, north of Naples, a Latin colony since 334 BCE, inscriptions record a *vicus Palatius* and *vicus Esquilinus*.[48] Of these names, many that do not refer to hills *per se* refer to Roman *vici* in their vicinity: even apparently less auspicious ones such as Patricius and Salutaris recall *vici* in the northern part of Rome between the Viminal and Quirinal.[49] We would do well, writes Filippo Coarelli, to recognize the relationship of these names 'with the canon of the seven hills' of that city 'in the various versions of it which have come down to us, starting from the Septimontium to the definitive Varronian crystallization'.[50] But either they form a recognizable canon of seven or they do not. Not all of Antioch's names (e.g. Venerius and Aedilicius) are easy to associate with Rome's topography, let alone the topography as it is handled by Varro in his discussion of the Septimontium,[51] nor can we say categorically that there were only seven *vici*,[52] and, what is more, as we shall soon discover, seven was a widely significant number.[53] Borrowing toponyms is different from what Constantinople did in arming itself with the seven-hills concept.

---

[47] *CIL* XI 377, 379, 418 and 419.

[48] Ariminum: *CIL* XI 404, 417, 419, 421; Antioch: *CIL* III 68111–2, 6835–6837; and Cales: *CIL* I²
416 and *CIL* X 4641. See Mommsen 1887: 114, no. 4; Mansuelli 1941: 47–9; Levick 1967: 76–8;
Palmer 1970: 129; Tarpin 2002; and Bispham 2006.

[49] Coarelli 1995: 177.

[50] Coarelli 1995: 176: 'Come già da tempo è stato proposto, si deve piuttosto [*contra* Bormann
(*CIL* XI. i. p. 77) and the idea that Ariminum's seven *vici* represented half of the fourteen
regions of Rome] riconoscere in questa divisione un rapporto con il canone dei "sette colli" di
Roma, nelle varie redazioni che di questo ci sono pervenute, dal Septimontium alla definitive
cristallizzazione varroniana.' Coarelli argues that the seven *vici* predate this, describing the
colony's original organizatory structure, but how exceptional is Ariminum? Bispham 2006: 87
and 90–2: 'Strikingly, Cales and Ariminum between them produce (under the Empire) most of
the Roman or Romanizing urban (or presumably urban) toponyms known from Italy . . . '; 'It
should not surprise us that Cales, and perhaps Ariminum too, in their exposed positions on
the edge of a very un-Roman, un-Latin, world, should have Romanizing toponyms of this sort
as early as the third century, and in the case of Cales, perhaps earlier.' For more on this issue
and the controversies surrounding it, see Tarpin 2002: 87, n. 2.

[51] Varro, *Ling.* 5.41–54.

[52] There were at least ten *vici* at Alexandria Troas (*ILS* 1018) and possibly twelve at Lystra, both of
these made Roman colonies by Augustus; Levick 1967: 77, n. 3.

[53] See e.g. Den Boer 1954: 171 for the suggestion that the number of Spartan districts or 'obes'
was seven.

'Nîmes', however, 'like the eternal city, would have been able to display its seven hills.'[54] Nemausus, to give it its Roman name, enclosed seven hills within its wall and boasts its status as such today.[55] In the Antonine Square, for example, inaugurated in 1874, on the base of a statue of the Roman emperor Antoninus Pius, are lines by local poet, Jean Réboul (1796–1864). But when did this kind of self-promotion start?

Le Nîmois est à demi Romain
Sa ville fut aussi la ville aux sept collines.
Un beau soleil luit sur de grandes ruines.
Et l'un de ses enfants se nommait Antonin.

Someone from Nîmes is half Roman,
His city was also a city of seven hills.
Beautiful sun shines on grand ruins
And one of its children was called Antoninus.[56]

Although it is attractive to trace it back to the Augustan period when Nîmes became 'colonia Augusta Nemausus' and, according to many modern scholars, an 'image of Rome in conquered territory',[57] neither Pliny nor Strabo, whose descriptions are contemporary and not insubstantial, mentions its seven hills,[58] and indeed the text which is often cited as the earliest evidence, by Carolingian Bishop Theodulf of Orléans, turns out not to read 'inde Nemausiacas septem properamus ad arces' ('from where we hurry to the seven hills of Nemausus') but 'inde Nemausiacas sensim properamus ad arces' ('from where we hurry little by little to the hills of Nemausus' – 'sensim' being an adverb meaning 'softly' or 'by degrees', and 'arces' a noun

---

[54] Jullian 1920: 48: 'Nîmes, comme la Ville Éternelle, aurait pu montrer ses sept collines.'

[55] *RE* XVI 2295 claims that Nîmes was a city of seven hills even before the Roman period, but being able to list Latin names for seven hills is not the same as saying that it celebrated itself as such. See also Levick 1965: 57; Picard 1902; Igolen 1935; and Célié *et al.* 1994.

[56] Also English writer, Sabine Baring-Gould 1897: 7:

> Seven are the hills on which old Rome is founded,
> Seven are the hills engirdling thy fountain,
> Seven are the planets set in heaven ruling,
> Father Nemausus.

[57] 'Image de Rome en territoire conquis' – J.-C. Balty 1960. Aul. Gell. 16.13.8 had described Roman colonies as 'little effigies' or 'replicas' of Rome, the word for the latter, 'simulacra' being the same as Tacitus uses for the models of defeated cities, carried in the Triumph, and, on this basis, scholars have been quick to understand them accordingly. In contrast, Bispham 2006: 92 prefers that the names of these *vici* 'are *not* the Roman names of districts of Rome, but the re-application of place-names from Rome to colonial geography to produce new toponyms: Roman topography acted as a matrix, from which *new names*, and inevitably new associations, were generated. Our colonial toponyms are *Romanizing*, not Roman.'

[58] Strabo 4.1.12; Plin. *HN* 3.37; and for a survey of the ancient sources, Christol 1996: 58–60.

which is as applicable to the towers of its wall as to its hills).[59] Again, the implication is that we have to wait until the fall of Rome, and its fetishization by antiquarians, for other cities actively to promote the concept for their own ends. Roman cities were satellites of Rome with imperial statuary, bathhouses, *fora*, temples and *vici*: these features contributed to their feeling Roman. But imitation is one thing, identity theft another.[60] It is not really until the early Renaissance that the hills shift from being the skeleton of Rome, the capital of the Empire, into an essential element of the ideal city.

The Renaissance of the seven hills

Fulvius a septem describit montibus Urbem. (Francesco Arsilli (1524: line 241))[61]

The Renaissance injects new life into the canon and its relationship with Rome's real contours. In antiquity these hills had been graced not only with important temples but with elite housing and gardens. They were the site of foundation myths, prodigies and auguries. Being closer to the gods on high had practical advantages: Livy has the Roman general Marcus Furius Camillus explain: 'not without reason did gods and men choose this place for founding a city – the hills are extremely health-giving . . . '[62] They offered protection against invasion, and cooler air, away from malaria and flooding.[63] They also offered vistas, and vistas offered power, as we shall explore in Chapter 6. In the Republic the augurs ordered a new apartment block built on the densely populated Caelian Hill to be demolished for impeding their view from the Capitoline.[64]

Even a cursory glance at the Palatine and Capitoline exposes something of this intensity. The former hill is inhabited by the shades of Romulus, Evander

---

[59] *Contra iudices* 131 as cited in Jullian 1920: 48: n. 5. Also Varène (1992: 107, n. 2), whose work on the wall is now the standard reference and who chooses not to treat the theme of the seven hills because it 'relève à l'évidence de l'ethnographie et du folklore et non de la recherché archéologique'.

[60] Bispham 2006: 124 on colonization in the middle Republic: 'Certainly the Latin *comitia* might be *symbolic* evocations of the Roman *comitium*, but in the present state of research it looks unlikely that they were intended to be close copies of it. Detailed evocations of the micro-topography of the Roman *comitium* are scarcely easier to see than those of the Roman *arx*.'

[61] Ijsewijn 1997: 353.

[62] Livy 5.54.4 (drawing on Cic. *Rep.* 2.5–10): 'Non sine causa di hominesque hunc urbi condendae locum elegerunt, saluberrimos colles . . . '

[63] On malaria, see Sallares 2002 and on flooding, Aldrete 2007.

[64] Cic. *Off.* 3.66 and Val. Max. 8.2.1.

and Aeneas, not to mention emperors from Augustus to the Severans, and beyond, to Theoderic. These imperial residences were preceded by Republican houses, including those of Cicero, Clodius and Marcus Aemilius Scaurus, accompanied by sanctuaries to Jupiter Victor, Victoria and the Great Mother goddess Cybele, and damaged by fire in 192 CE.[65] On the Capitoline, the Temple of Jupiter was merely the crowning glory of a profile that hailed it as the *caput* of the skeleton.[66] There were numerous other temples, including that of Juno Moneta, built on the *arx* in 344 BCE, that of Veiovis, dedicated in 192 BCE in the saddle of the hill and excavated by Mussolini during digging beneath the Piazza del Campidoglio, and the small temple to Jupiter Tonans, dedicated by Augustus in 22 BCE. And there were masses of dedications inside and out – so many that some were periodically removed.[67] Among the largest of these were statues of Apollo and Jupiter, the latter made from the weaponry of defeated Samnites, so large as to have been visible from the Alban Mount some ten miles from the city.[68] As we have already noted with the Aventine, each of the seven hills had a distinct character and different residents. But each hill was a hive of activity.

In the mediaeval period, however, Rome's population plummeted,[69] and the damage done to the aqueducts by the Ostrogoths in 537 CE made the hills less habitable.[70] Although several aqueducts were maintained at least

[65]   On Cicero and Clodius' houses, see Cic. *Dom.* 103 and 114–16; and on Scaurus' house, Cic. *Scaur.* 27 and Plin. *HN* 17.5–6 and 36.6. The last of these has recently been identified archaeologically: Papi 1995: 26 (in *LTUR* II). These merely scratch the surface of the hill's housing stock and its reuse: see e.g. the entries under 'domus' in L. Richardson 1992. For recent rethinking of the temples on the Magna Mater end of the hill, Cecamore 2002.

[66]   As already observed in Chapter 1, the Capitoline is supposed to take its name from a human head that was discovered there: Livy 1.55.50–6, 5.54.7; Dion. Hal. *Ant. Rom.* 4.59.2; and, for discussion, Bourgeaud 1987. For Rome as 'caput mundi', see Luc. 2.655, and less explicitly Livy, whose head signals that Rome will be the head of everything and the seat of Empire. The emphasis that both he and Dionysius put on the humanness of the face contrasts sharply to stories about the foundation of rival city, Carthage, and the discovery of an animal head.

[67]   See Livy 40.51.3. Useful here are Mellor 1978, Stamper 2005: 125–6 and P. C. N. Stewart 2003: 128–36.

[68]   Colossal statue of Apollo, brought from Apollonia in Pontus by Marcus Lucullus, Plin. *HN* 34.39; and the Roman-commissioned statue of Jupiter, Plin. *HN* 34.43: 'fecit et Sp. Carvilius Iovem, qui est in Capitolio, victis Samnitibus sacrata lege pugnantibus e pectoralibus eorum ocreisque et galeis. amplitudo tanta est, ut conspiciatur a Latiari Iove. e reliquis limae suam statuam fecit, quae est ante pedes simulacri eius.' Statues so large that they can be seen from far away are a familiar trope: see the Athena Promachos statue on the Athenian acropolis, which could supposedly be seen from Cape Sounion (Paus. 1.28.2).

[69]   Estimates of the population of early mediaeval Rome vary wildly. For the eighth and ninth centuries, the best estimate on evidence currently available is probably 50,000–60,000 (Meneghini and Santangeli Valenzani 2004: 22–3). See Dey 2011: 196, n. 119.

[70]   For the damage done to the aqueducts by Vitigis, see Procop. *Goth.* 1.19. Whereas the traditional view is that the settlement on the hills was abandoned at this point

through the ninth century, and there is some elite housing on the Esquiline, Aventine and the foot of the Caelian in the tenth century, with more diffuse occupation of the city than scholars have traditionally assumed, it is still fair to say that settlement 'contracted into the low land on either side of the Tiber'.[71] The Capitoline assumed the name 'Monte Caprino' (Goat Hill) and, like the Forum or 'Campo Vaccino' (Cow Meadow) below it, was largely given over to grazing land. There was also the attraction and supporting infrastructure of Old Saint Peter's. Richard Krautheimer concludes that as the city moved westwards towards Trastevere, Ponte Sant' Angelo and the Borgo, 'the hills no longer counted'.[72] It is a strong statement and one borne out by contemporary literature. Although the so-called 'Einsiedeln Itinerary', a late eighth- or early ninth-century circuit for pilgrims arranged in eleven crossings of the city from gate to gate, does draw attention to the Palatine, Capitoline and Aventine, its emphasis on Rome's churches obviously affects its subject matter.[73] And an appendix in the same codex, but in a different hand, offers a description not of the seven hills but of the Aurelianic wall, which had, to Bryan Ward-Perkins' mind, long 'freed the inhabitants from the pressures of danger that elsewhere were to encourage settlement on the hills'.[74] By then the wall was in a sorry state after centuries of neglect but from the start of the eighth century it underwent a series of major repair works on the orders of the Popes.[75]

By the twelfth century the much-copied guidebook for pilgrims known as the *Mirabilia urbis Romae* (*Marvels of the City of Rome*) began to put more weight on Rome's ruins and vital statistics, and on recounting the traditions of the ancient city. Now the 'montes' were an important component of urban organization as they had been in the appendices of the late antique regionary catalogues, the *Notitia* and the *Curiosum*, which listed them as a defining feature of the city after its six obelisks and eight bridges.[76]

(e.g. Krautheimer 1980: 68), Coates-Stephens 1996 has finessed this view somewhat. Also important here is Hubert 1990, Santangeli Valenzani 2000 and 2004, and Christie 2006: 237–40, whose summary up to 800 CE builds on the work of Guidobaldi (1986, 1999).

[71] Ward-Perkins 1984: 125.

[72] Krautheimer 1980: 237 and 243: 'the Capitol was merely a cartographic landmark'.

[73] *Einsiedeln*, Bibliotheca Monasterii Ordinis Sancti Benedicti, 326: edition by del Lungo 2004: 66–73.

[74] Ward-Perkins 1984: 125.

[75] *Liber Pontificalis* 89.2, 91.2 and 92.15. See Dey 2011: 247–8 and Coates-Stephens 1998: 167–71.

[76] Note that by now the *disabitato* was also changing, the slopes of the hills now fortified with the strongholds of Rome's leading families; Krautheimer 1980: 317–18.

hii sunt montes infra urbem: Ianiculus; Aventinus qui et Quirinalis dicitur; Celius mons; Capitolium; Pallanteum; Exquilinus; Viminalis.

These are the hills inside the city: the Janiculum, Aventine which is also called the Quirinal, the Caelian Mount, the Capitoline, Palatine, Esquiline and Viminal.[77]

In the *Mirabilia*, Rome's hills are described as being 'infra', 'within' or 'beneath' the city. They literally underpin it. The Janiculum may have muscled its way in but – unlike in the regionary catalogues, which substitute the Vatican and Janiculum hills for the Quirinal and Viminal – the traditional seven are still there in a sleight of hand that makes the Aventine and Quirinal one and the same. Later versions of the text credit the hills with new mythologies, claiming that the Janiculum took its name from Janus, son of Noah, and that the Viminal was 'where Virgil, taken captive by the Romans, escaped invisibly and went to Naples'.[78] Stories like these began to invest the hills with renewed symbolism. For Rome to be reborn, its hills had to be re-excavated.

The *Mirabilia* remained the standard guide to Rome until the publications of Renaissance humanists, Flavio Biondo, whose three-volume *Roma instaurata* of 1444–6 is often described as 'the first scientific study of the city', and Andrea Fulvio. Paving the way for them was Petrarch (1304–74) and his engagement with authors such as Virgil, Livy and Varro.[79] He crammed his letters to friends with references from their work and wrote others to heroes,

---

[77] *Mirabilia urbis Romae* 4. See Lanzillotta 1996: 47 for the view that 'qui et Quirinalis dicitur' is probably a later addition by the scribe. Compare the *Cataloghi regionari Notitia e curiosum*, *appendix* in Valentini and Zucchetti 1940: 294–6.

[78] The Noah material is from the *Graphia aureae urbis* (Nichols 1887: 1–3), which omits the hills chapter but associates Janus with the Janiculum hill and with the Palatine; and the Virgil material is from Nicolás Rossell's *De mirabilibus civitatis Romae* – 'ubi Virgilius captus a Romanis, invisibiliter exiens, ivit Neapolim, unde dicitur: "Vado ad Napolum"'. For the various versions of the *Mirabilia*, see Lanzillotta 1996: 13–27 and 48.

[79] Note too the famous twelfth-century lament of Hildebert of Lavardin (as cited by Sassoli 2000: 18), which already talks of time destroying Rome's arrogance and of the 'arces' of Caesar and the temples of the proud falling into the marsh; the *Polistoria* by Ioannes Caballinus, secretary at the papal court of Avignon (d. 1349), which devotes book 7 to the seven hills, often citing several sources, and starting with the Janiculum and ending the section with the passage from the Book of Revelation (critical edition by Laureys 1995: 188–201 and his article 1997); and Fazio degli Uberti's *Dittamondo* of 1347, an unfinished poem about his travels through Europe, Asia and Africa. In book 1, chapter 11, the author asks Solinus where earthly Paradise is and then meets a Claudian-inspired Roma in a sad and tattered state, who recounts her history including (book 2, chapter 31) all the things that bear witness to how beautiful she was – her walls, the baths of Diocletian, her hills (the Quirinal and its link to Numa, the Velia and Tullus Hostilius, the Esquiline, and the Capitoline, which he calls 'the height and time-piece of the whole world').

including Cicero, Livy, Virgil and Horace: to the last of these, he confides: 'sweet is it now to follow thee through secluded woodlands, to gaze upon the spring water bubbling up in the dimly lighted dales, to admire the purple hills and the verdant meadows, the cool lakes and the dewy grottos'.[80] These hopes for continuity were particularly pertinent now: the papacy had recently moved to Avignon, attracted by the French king and powerful French cardinals. 'If the Roman empire is not at Rome, where can it be?', asked Petrarch.[81] Antiquity was essential to his effort to entice Benedict XII and successors back again.

'Could you not guess how greatly I would want to see the walls of the city and the hills and, as Virgil says, "the Etruscan Tiber and the Roman Palatine"?'[82] Far from being disappointed by what meets him on his first visit to Rome in 1337, Petrarch is inspired to pen an epic poem, the *Africa*. Written in Latin hexameters, the epic tells of Scipio Africanus' victory over the Carthaginians, incorporating visions of the future and views of Rome which owe much to Virgil and Claudian.[83] But it is Republican poet Ennius who stars and, in the final book, accompanies the victor to the Capitoline to be crowned with laurel. The scene rehearses the triumph of poetry that Petrarch celebrates when in 1341 he is similarly acknowledged in the audience hall of Rome's Palazzo Senatorio, his poem little more than a fragment. Its Ennius prophesies, 'he will call his poem *Africa* ... At last in tardy triumph he will climb the Capitol.'[84]

Rome's seven hills and the view from the hills are an intrinsic part of the *Africa*'s vision. When Scipio's friend Gaius Laelius is asked by the Numidian King Syphax about the history of Rome, one of the exemplary stories he tells is of Marcus Curtius, who sacrifices himself for his fellow Romans by riding into a chasm which had opened in the middle of the Forum. Stones, beams and baskets of earth had been insufficient to fill the gap: 'Not if the Tarpeian Rock and the other six hills in order sank down into the void and heavy Apennine and Etna lay on top, would there be an end; it is the things which are dear to you that the yawning ditch craves. Filled with a few

---

[80] *Familiarum rerum libri* (*Fam.*) 24.10 to Horace, written in minor asclepiads, as one of Horace's favourite lyric metres, as translated by Costenza 1910: 124. On his letter writing more broadly, see Kirkham and Maggi 2009: 277–332.

[81] As cited in Coogan 1983: 56.

[82] Petrarch to Giacomo Colonna, *Fam.* 2.9.24 (ed. Dotti 2002): 'quanti demum extimaturum reris menia Urbis et colles et, ut ait Virgilius, "tuscum Tyberim et romana palatia" cernere?'

[83] See Hardie 2007: 137.

[84] See the Bergin and Wilson translation of the *Africa* (1977: 237 and 231); and for Petrarch's coronation oration, E. H. Wilkins 1953, Looney 2009 and Regn and Huss 2009. Also relevant here are *Fam.* 4.7 and 4.8.

(of these things), the gap will come together.'[85] Later, in book 8, when the Carthaginian envoys see the city for themselves, the names of the canonical seven are used to navigate:[86] first they go to the Palatine, 'the first famous place of the newly born city',[87] then between the Caelian and Aventine, after that to the top of the Capitoline, with its temple to Jupiter, statuary and spoils, then to the Esquiline, and 'the "collis" called after the willow' ('vimen' in Latin, so Viminal),[88] to the summit of Mons Quirinalis. After that, they descend towards the Flaminian Gate, before heading across the Campus Martius, by the river, and then over to the foot of the Janiculum. The description blends observation (the 'naked giants' on the Quirinal 'a work worthy of famous Praxiteles or Phidias' – statues of Castor and Pollux which still grace the piazza and which are thought to have stood there since antiquity)[89] with details drawn from Livy, Virgil and Festus (the human skull on the Capitoline, the story of Hercules and Cacus, the etymology of the Viminal).[90] In so doing, it has a lot in common with the work of Fulvio and Biondo, who systematically sieve ancient authors for stories about Rome's surface. But it also boosts the hills' literary significance – a significance which they had last had in the poetry of Claudian.[91] As was the case for him, whose subject, Honorius, was only briefly in Rome from Ravenna, the seven hills are specially comforting when the power base is elsewhere.

The Avignon papacy was short-lived. In 1420 the papal seat moved back to Rome, though by the middle of the century the popes were living largely

---

[85] Livy 7.6 and Petrarch (edition by Pingaud 1872) 3.559–63:

> ... non si Tarpeius in imas
> sexque alii latebras descendant ordine colles,
> ac super incumbat grauis Apenninus et Aetna,
> finis erit; sunt quae uobis pretiosa dehiscens
> fossa petit, paucis plenus concurret hiatus.

[86] Compare, however, the chaos of Petrarch's description of his own walking of the city with Colonna: *Fam.* 6.2.

[87] *Africa* 8.865: ... primusque nouae locus inclitus urbis.

[88] *Africa* 8.906: ... dictum a uimine collem.

[89] *Africa* 8.907–10:

> inde Quirinalem superato uertice montem
> transierant, nudoque duos astare gigantes
> corpore conspiciunt. En quot certamina famae
> Praxitelis opus Phidiaeque insigne supremi ...

For the historiography of these statues, see Haskell and Penny (1981: 136–41) who title them Alexander and Bucephalus.

[90] On the etymology of the Viminal, see Festus 516–17L and Juv. 3.71, and with a related but different explanation, Varro, *Ling.* 5.51.

[91] Claudian's poetry will be discussed in detail in Chapters 4 and 5.

in the Vatican rather than the Lateran Palace, where they had been based before.[92] This relocation put more emphasis on Saint Peter's and greater pressure on keeping the ancient city in the picture. Throughout the fifteenth century, measures were put in place to promote the preservation of antiquity throughout the capital – measures which were both influenced by and formative of humanist inquiry.[93] Biondo's work is exemplary: after a brief account of that city's situation, its gates, Christian character and obelisks, he is into the hills: 'De montibus urbis in genere', then the seven, 'Capitolium', 'Aventinus', 'Palatinus', 'Celius', 'Exquiliae', 'Quirinalis & Viminalis'.[94] 'As a consequence, I sometimes reach various views about what can be apprehended about the rest of Rome from those three hills, the first and only ones to have been contained by Romulus in the early city. Now if the ruins are absent, we see them almost as they were, stripped of their buildings, as though Rome had not yet been founded.'[95] So too with Fulvio's two-volume verse text, the *Antiquaria urbis* of 1513 (Figure 2.3), in which a history of each of the seven hills and of the 'Hill of Gardens', or Pincian Hill, Vatican and Janiculum follows a brief introduction to the city, its early kings and later emperors, gates and paths. Dedicated to the pope as Biondo's book had been, the *Antiquaria* is careful to blend antiquarian investigation with Christian, sometimes contemporary, history. Yet as with Petrarch, it is the hills that offer a path through the city, taking up over half of the first book to its conclusion. In book 2, we are into specific buildings.

Such was the weight of the hills here that when the poet and physician Francesco Arsilli published his *De poetis urbanis* in 1524, celebrating the names and characterizing the works of a number of Latin poets then resident in Rome, it captured Fulvio thus:

Fulvius a septem describit montibus Urbem
    reddit et antiquis nomina prisca locis.

Fulvio described the city of Rome by its seven hills and restored former names to ancient places.[96]

[92] Note that though Gregory XI had moved to Rome already in 1377, the Great Schism (1378–1417) followed when several 'popes' claimed office.
[93] Karmon 2011: 47–76; and on the 'renovatio urbis' of Martin V who moves the papacy back to Rome, Rinne 2010: 42–5.
[94] Biondo 1510: book 1, lxv–lxxvii.
[95] Biondo 1510: book 1, lxxvi: 'qua ex re aliquando varias cogitationes venimus quid de caetera liceat Roma suspicari cum tres illos montes qui primi et soli in prima urbe a Romulo compraehensi fuerint: nunc si absunt ruinae videmus pene adeam deductos aedificiorum nuditate: quam Roma nondum condita habuerunt.'
[96] Ijsewijn 1997: 353. See Laureys 2006: 201 and Ceresa 2004.

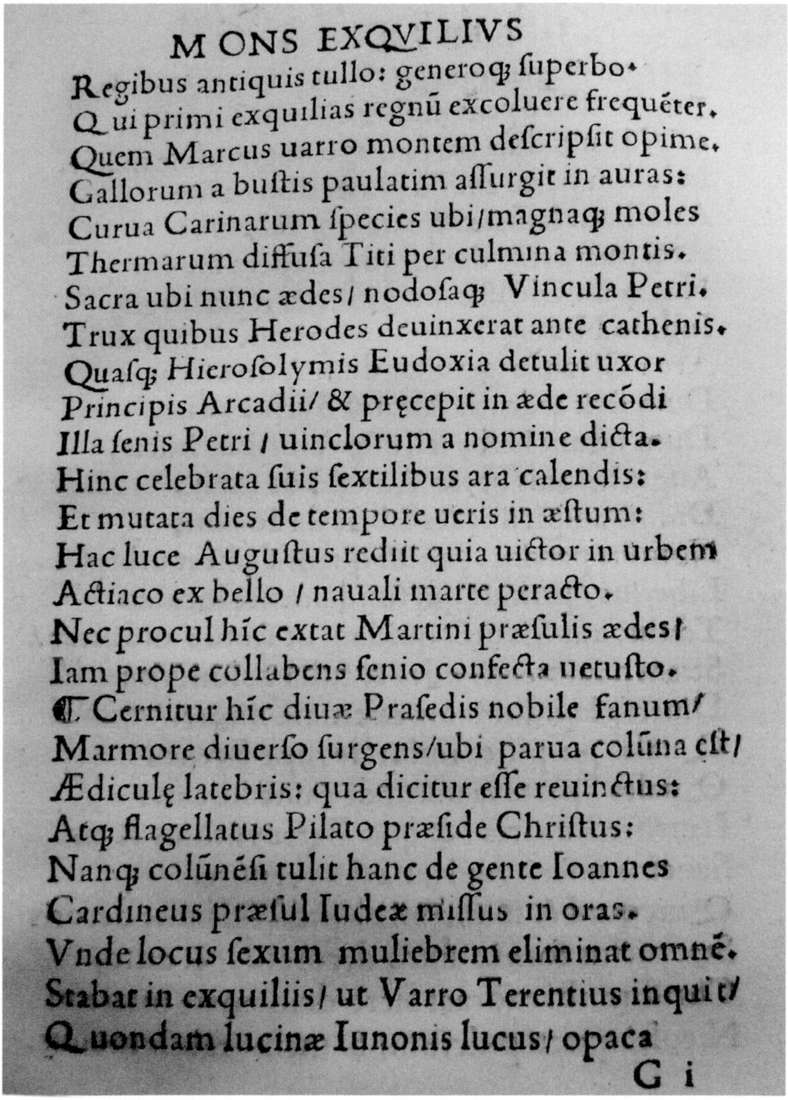

MONS EXQVILIVS

Regibus antiquis tullo: generoq; superbo*
Qui primi exquilias regnū excoluere frequéter.
Quem Marcus uarro montem descripsit opime.
Gallorum a bustis paulatim assurgit in auras:
Curua Carinarum species ubi/magnaq; moles
Thermarum diffusa Titi per culmina montis.
Sacra ubi nunc ædes/ nodosaq; Vincula Petri.
Trux quibus Herodes deuinxerat ante cathenis.
Quasq; Hierosolymis Eudoxia detulit uxor
Principis Arcadii/ & precepit in æde recódi
Illa senis Petri / uinclorum a nomine dicta.
Hinc celebrata suis sextilibus ara calendis:
Et mutata dies de tempore ueris in æstum:
Hac luce Augustus rediit quia uictor in urbem
Actiaco ex bello / nauali marte peracto.
Nec procul hic extat Martini præsulis ædes/
Iam prope collabens senio confecta uetusto.
℃ Cernitur hic diuæ Prasedis nobile fanum/
Marmore diuerso surgens/ubi parua colūna est/
Ædiculę latebris: qua dicitur esse reuinctus:
Atq; flagellatus Pilato præside Christus:
Nanq; colūnesi tulit hanc de gente Ioannes
Cardineus præsul Iudeæ missus in oras.
Vnde locus sexum muliebrem eliminat omnē.
Stabat in exquiliis/ ut Varro Terentius inquit/
Quondam lucinæ Iunonis lucus/ opaca
                                          G i

Figure 2.3 Page of Andrea Fulvio's *Antiquaria urbis*, 1513.

Three years later Fulvio published an expanded prose version of his description, the *Antiquitates urbis*, book 1 of which dealt with Rome's foundation,
Romulus, walls, gates, roads and regions; and book 2, the hills: first, 'the
seven hills where ancient Rome was first founded', then the Pincian Hill,

Montecitorio, the Vatican and Janiculum.[97] The loss of antiquities and other precious objects in the sack of Rome by the mutinous troops of the Holy Roman Emperor, Charles V, in the same year made the book's contents all the more momentous, and soon Giovanni Bartolomeo Marliani, Lucio Fauno, Lucio Mauro and Bernardo Gamucci were using the hills to structure their discussions of the city.[98] Diplomat Thomas Hoby (1530–66), translator of Baldassare Castiglione's *Il Cortegiano* (*The Courtier*) and a man whose tour of Italy was the most ambitious undertaken from sixteenth-century England, was certainly aware of their importance. If anything, they were too important to be summarized by an amateur.

The better half of the city within the walles is desert and not inhabited, and especiallie the seven hilles, Campidoglio, Palatino, Celio, Aventino, Squille, Viminale, Quirinale ... Upon these vij hilles was wont in the olde time to consist all the majesty of the citie, as it may well appere by the ruines upon them ... And the ruines abowt the seven hilles the whiche I passe over all: and the particuliarities thereof I leave to the searchers owt of them of the instructions of Lucias Faunus, Martian, and Biondo, which all have written verie diligentlie of the antiquities of the citie of Roome. And by probable reason have ghessed upon manie things for the whiche no certaintie is to bee alleged. Bicause in times past the citie hathe oftentimes bine enlarged and taken in again as occasion served.[99]

By the time of Hoby's travels, the seven hills had regained their prominence: they were a tried and tested means of ordering and defining antiquarian knowledge.

Fulvio worked together with physician and philologist Fabio Calvo in advising the artist Raphael in his efforts to map Rome's ruins onto an

[97] Fulvio 1527, table of contents: book 2, 'De septem montibus ubi prisca Roma prius condita fuit'. It is only in book 3 that the author turns to the Tiber. Book 2 opens: 'montes urbis, in quibus Roma prius condita fuit, septem memorantur, unde Septimontium dicta, ut tradit Antistius Labeo & hisce montibus feriae'. For Labeo's link between the seven hills and Septimontium, see Chapter 3.

[98] Marliani's *Urbis Romae topographia* was first published as *Topographia antiquae Romae: libri septem* in 1534 and then expanded in an illustrated edition of 1544; he begins his journey through Rome at the Capitol, using the hills as signposts (in the 1544 edition, the Capitoline (p. 18), the Palatine (33), the Aventine (65), the Caelian (71), the Esquiline (79), the Viminal (87), the Quirinal (88) and the 'Hill of Gardens' (i.e. the Pincio) (91)). Fauno's *Delle antichità della città di Roma* (1548) and his *De antiquitatibus urbis Romae ab antiquis novisq[ue] auctoribus exceptis, et summa brevitate ordineq[ue] dispositis per Lucium Faunum* (1549) both devote their first book to gates, before turning to the hills in book 2. His *Compendio di Roma antica* (1552) again uses hills as orientation, as does Mauro (1558). In Gamucci's illustrated *Libri quattro dell'antichità della città di Roma* (1565), the Capitoline is p. 11, the Palatine, 56, the Aventine, 88, the Caelius and Caeliolus, 91, the Esquiline, 97, the Viminal, 113 and the Quirinal and the Hill of Gardens, 120.

[99] Hoby 1902: 24–5 (written in 1547–64).

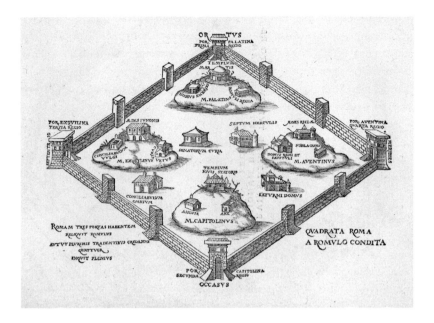

Figure 2.4 Fabio Calvo, 'Roma Quadrata', *Antiquae urbis Romae cum regionibus simulachrum*, 1527.

archaeological plan divided by regions.[100] Calvo had been prevailed upon by Raphael to translate Vitruvius' *De architectura* for him and drew on this experience to publish, again in 1527, a slim volume of some twenty-four woodcuts, the *Antiquae urbis Romae cum regionibus simulachrum*. Whereas Fulvio's text had viewed itself as a historical work, which was not just geographical but etymological, Calvo's was closer to Raphael's aims and objectives, its core made up of individual plans of the fourteen regions. Before this, there were images of ancient Rome in four key phases: under mythical founder, Romulus, Servius Tullius, and Augustus, and – finally, when the city was at its height in the time of Pliny the Elder, and – after these – a bird's-eye view of the Capitoline with a separate wall and gates and the *arx* further fortified by its own wall inside it. The hills play a crucial role in all but the image of the Augustan city. In the first icon, representing Romulean Rome (Figure 2.4), there are only four of them (the Palatine, Aventine, Capitoline and Esquiline) and a smattering of buildings.[101] In the second, the Servian city (Figure 2.5), the canonical seven are arranged in

---

[100] Jacks 1990.

[101] For example, on the Capitoline, Calvo represents only the asylum, *arx* and, erroneously, the Temple of Jupiter Stator, which Romulus was supposed to have vowed during the battle

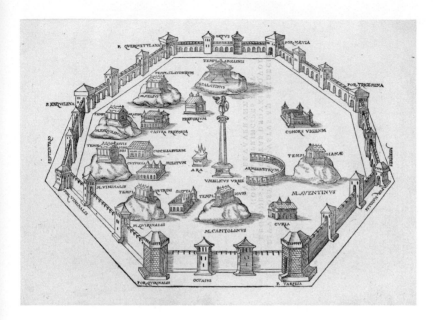

Figure 2.5 Fabio Calvo, 'Rome in the reign of Servius Tullius', *Antiquae urbis Romae cum regionibus simulachrum*, 1527.

neat semi-circle formation. In both, the Tiber is absent. Rome is defined by the hills which are depicted as distinct mounds of equal size, each topped with a temple. Whereas the Temple of Diana on the Aventine had supposedly been dedicated by Servius Tullius, others in the second image, like that of Apollo on the Palatine, are imperial (in this case, founded by Augustus). Such conflation reinforces the sense in which the seven hills make Rome an eternal city. That said, the image of Augustan Rome is without geological features (Figure 2.6). Instead, the Rome it represents is more abstract, laid out on a radial pattern, not with fourteen regions as we would expect, but sixteen, a spurious 'Regio Campus Martius Maior' and 'Regio Vaticana' augmenting the total. Their presence again raises the question of how any organizatory principle relates to the built environment. In the final phase of urban development, under Pliny (Figure 2.7), the Tiber does make an appearance, integrating the port at Ostia, the Mons Vaticanus and the Janiculum. But there are still only seven summits as both of these hills are brought together into one, long promontory, and the Viminal is excluded.

between the Romans and the Sabines (Livy 1.13.3–6; Ov. *Fast.* 6.793–4; Dion. Hal. *Ant. Rom.* 2.50.3), but which was not built until the middle Republic, and then at the foot of the Palatine.

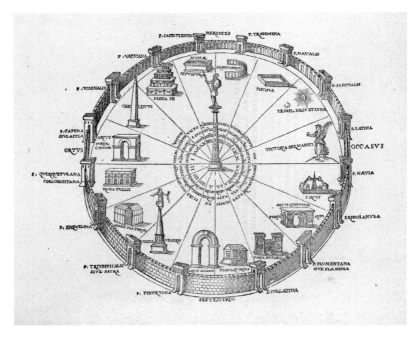

Figure 2.6 Fabio Calvo, 'Augustan Rome', *Antiquae urbis Romae cum regionibus simulachrum*, 1527.

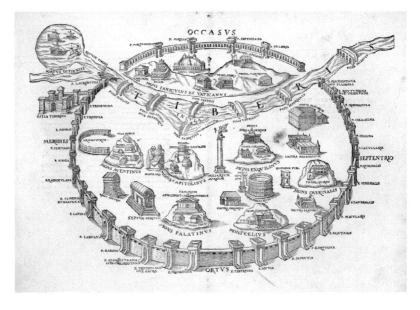

Figure 2.7 Fabio Calvo, 'Rome at the time of Pliny the elder', *Antiquae urbis Romae cum regionibus simulachrum*, 1527.

'It seems that Calvo's intention was less to dissect the topography of Classical Rome in scientific terms than to offer a series of facsimiles, or "simulachra", of the ancient city.'[102]

All topography is a 'simulacrum'. These simulacra and others like them, tied the literary concept of the seven hills more resolutely to the land than ever before, forging a path for those who followed. A fourteenth-century map of Rome drawn in the manuscript of Solinus' *Polyhistor* in Milan's Biblioteca Ambrosiana renders only two hills, the Aventine and the misspelled Viminal (Figure 2.8).[103] But by the sixteenth century such errors were less excusable. For example, the expanded, illustrated version of Marliani's topographical text, published in 1544, included a figure of the imperial city with the canonical seven clearly marked, and not as discrete mounds as in Calvo's woodcuts but as something more akin to landforms, defined by cross and parallel hatching (Figure 2.9).[104] And it was not the only one. Seven years later, military engineer Leonardo Bufalini produced the first printed map of the city with the hills again carefully delineated. Although idealizing, with reconstructed ancient structures next to modern ones, this was not a 'view map', but the first ichnographic map of Rome since the *Forma urbis Romae*, its buildings plotted in ground plan.[105]

The hills, which in antiquity were above representation on the Marble Plan, were now chartable territory. Understanding ancient Rome meant understanding what it looked like, and what Rome looked like was something that popes as early as Nicholas V and Sixtus IV in the fifteenth century were keen to emulate.[106] With Leon Battista Alberti and other architects already at work cutting streets and building bridges, simulacra of the ancient city were hearty fodder for contemporary town planning.[107] One of Sixtus'

[102] Jacks 1990: 480.

[103] Solinus, *Collectanea rerum memorabilium*, Milan, Biblioteca Ambrosiana, Cod. Pinelli, Inf. C. 246, fol. 4r.

[104] Bartolomeo Marliani's *Urbis Romae topographia* of 1544. Bernardo Gamucci's *Libri quattro dell' antichità della città di Roma, raccolte sotto brevità da diversi antichi et moderni scrittori* of 1565 contains a similar map. For the idea that Bufalini may have helped Marliani with this earlier map, see Maier 2007: 6–7.

[105] Maier 2007 and on ithnographic city plans more broadly, Pinto 1976. It takes some time, however, for there to be anything like a mapping standard: compare, for example, the engraving by Christoph Stimmer, *Veduta di Roma* (1549–50), 362 x 455 mm, Rome, ING FN 39562 (3824), which marks the Esquiline's two prongs and the Velia as part of the Palatine promontory (Sassoli 2000: 141) and Sebastiano del Re, *Pianta di Roma* (1557), 355 x 470mm, Rome, ING FC 36644, which singles out the Capitoline for special treatment by flattening it completely so as to make it a space or circle rather than an elevation (Sassoli 2000: 146).

[106] Grundmann 2007: 13 and Blondin 2005.

[107] On Alberti's *Descriptio urbis Romae*, written sometime in the middle of the fifteenth century but not published until the nineteenth, see Hicks 2003 and the critical edition of the text by

Figure 2.8 Rome as depicted in the codex of Solinus' *Polyhistor* in the Biblioteca Ambrosiana, Milan, fourteenth century.

contemporaries wrote 'For you [Sixtus] are repairing churches which for all this time were deformed in ugly ruins. You are laying paving on new bridges and on those very roads from which Agrippa had removed the paving, roads which Augustus paid attention to from then on! You also repair the flow of

Furno and Carpo 2000. Also helpful is the review by Marsh 2002. The *Descriptio* uses polar co-ordinates based on the Capitoline Hill.

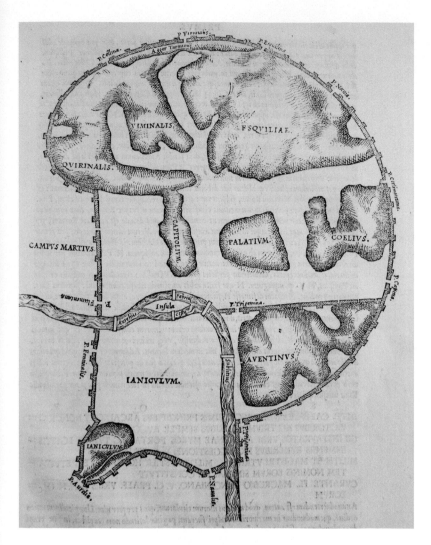

Figure 2.9 Map of the city of Rome under the emperors, from Marliani's *Urbis Romae topographia*, 1544.

the Aqua Virgo.'[108] Rome was establishing itself as the centre and paradigm of Renaissance architecture. It does not take long before the 'seven hills' became good for other cities to think with.

[108] Ludovico Lazzarelli, *Fasti Christianae religionis*, Biblioteca Apostolica Vaticana, *Cod. Vat. Lat.* 2853, fol. 255r: 'turpibus enim reparas iam deformata ruinis Templa, | novos Pontes sternis et ecce vias. | quas Agrippa tulit, quas dehinc Augustus adrexit! | Virginei reparas tu quoque fontis aquas.'

Towards the end of the sixteenth century with Rome's population on the increase, Pope Sixtus V (1585–90), took an even more ambitious view of town planning, bringing the whole city into play and ploughing the renewed significance of the seven hills back into Rome's real topography.[109] Predecessors of his, Julius II (1503–13) for example, had built streets on both sides of the river. But Sixtus reclaimed the depopulated hills as habitable space, repairing portions of the Aqua Alexandrina and Aqua Marcia aqueducts to supply the Quirinal, Viminal, Esquiline and Caelian.[110] He unified the city across its peaks and troughs by building wide, straight roads such as the Strada Felice (today, the Via Agostino Depretis and the Via delle Quattro Fontane) and crowned these achievements by placing obelisks at intersections.[111] Sigfried Giedion writes: 'It was these hills of ancient Rome, open to the winds of the Campagna, and stretching from the Pincio in the north-east to the Esquiline, Quirinal, Viminal and Caelian, that Sixtus wanted to make more accessible.'[112] Not that this recognition made them more noticeable. Sixtus' architect, Domenico Fontana explains:

> Sixtus has extended these streets from one end of the city to the other without concern for either the hills or the valleys which they crossed: but causing the former to be leveled and the latter to be filled, has reduced them to most gentle plains and charming sites, revealing in several places which they pass, the lowest portions of the city with various and diverse perspectives, so that aside from the devotions, they also nourish with their charm the senses of the body.[113]

But his projects did begin to produce a coherent urban framework which his successors would develop.

This moderated, undulating city is closer to the city we encounter today. And yet despite this, if not because of this, the seven hills remain as important and enigmatic as ever. Although the seven pilgrim churches offered Renaissance writers an alternative set of beacons for navigating Rome (see Figure 3.1 on p. 63), they never trump them entirely.[114] In 1666 Famiano

---

[109] Grundmann 2007: 14–16.

[110] The Acqua Felice (after his family name) was the result: Rinne 2010: 3 and 122–54.

[111] Giedion 1982: 82–91, and, on the Quirinal, Marder 1978.   [112] Giedion 1982: 94.

[113] From *Della Trasportatione dell' Obelisco Vaticano et delle Fabriche di Nostro Signore Papa Sisto V, fatto dal Cav. Domenico Fontana, Architetto di Sua Santita*, book 1, 1590, as cited in Giedion 1982: 94.

[114] The tour of the seven pilgrim churches is a sixteenth-century phenomenon, propagated by Saint Philip Neri (1515–95). See, for example, Palladio (1554), whose *Descritione de le chiese, stationi, indulgenze e reliquie de Corpi Sancti, che sono in la città di Roma* was companion piece to his *Le antichità romane* of the same year, Panvinio 1570, Francino 1588, the first chapter of which is dedicated to the seven churches, and Piazza 1694. In the engraving by Étienne Dupérac, printed by Antonio Lafréry in 1575 the seven churches stand like pseudo-hills,

Nardini began his *Roma antica* with the city's founding, walls and gates, before moving to the 'seven hills and the Septimontium'.[115] Over a century later Bonnie Prince Charlie's secretary, Andrew Lumsden, followed suit. 'Having thus examined the gates and walls of Rome, and the antiquities to be seen in its environs, I shall now enter the city', writes Lumsden as he turns to a lengthy discussion of its hills.[116] Rome's seven hills had become a primary point of access.

Nineteenth- and twentieth-century encounters

Students who visit Rome for the first time would do well to take at once a general survey of the seven hills.[117]

Early in the nineteenth century Giovanni Battista Brocchi built on Giambattista Nolli's famous topographical plan to produce the first geological map of the city, his *Carta fisica del suolo di Roma*.[118] This publication was less concerned with reconstructing the grandeur that was Rome than with surveying its original surface as it existed beneath the man-made structures of the historical city. It paved the way for studies that include Heiken, Funiciello and De Rita's *The Seven Hills of Rome* and for the digital modelling that today aims to provide a more accurate image of the stratigraphy of archaic Rome than was available to Livy and other Augustan authors.[119]

defining Rome's identity. They also play a part in Sixtus V's thinking: his architect (above, n. 113) also claims, 'Our Lord [Sixtus], now wishing to ease the way for those who, prompted by devotion or by vows, are accustomed to visit frequently the most holy places in the city of Rome, and in particular the seven churches to be celebrated for their indulgences and relics, opened many most commodious and straight streets in many places.'

[115] Nardini 1666: 45–51.   [116] Lumsden 1797: 135.

[117] Lanciani 1897: 4. Note that Homo's guide to the city also opens with 'les collines' 1921: 1, while W. Smith's *Dictionary of Greek and Roman Geography* 1854: 719–20 starts its long entry on Rome with 'the celebrated group of seven hills – the site on which the eternal city itself was destined to stand'.

[118] The map and explanatory notes were published in 1820: see Funiciello and Caputo 2006. Nolli's *La pianta grande* of 1748 is widely regarded as one of the most important documents about the city: see Ceen 1989 and 2000.

[119] See, for example, Bernie Frischer's ongoing *Rome Reborn* project (http://www.romereborn. virginia.edu/; Google Rome: http://earth.google.com/rome/), an international initiative, based at the Institute of Advanced Technology in the Humanities at the University of Virginia, and one which owes its title to Biondo's *Roma instaurata*, and the CD produced by the University of Caen-Basse Normandie (Fleury 2005). Also in progress are more traditional mapping projects, for example, the *Nuova Forma Urbis Romae* Project of the archaeological superintendancy of the Comune di Roma, the German *AIS* Roma Project (C. Häuber 2005 and Häuber and Schütz 2006), and the *Imago Urbis* Project of the University of Rome, La Sapienza.

And it confirmed how far the ground level had risen in some parts and been cut away in others. But it also downplayed Rome's literary layering, turning away from antiquarian interest in the written-ness of the ancient city, the etymologies and mythologies of the hills, and the significance of the number seven. For all that Renaissance humanists had sought to reconstruct ancient Rome, they had been conscious that these reconstructions were a way of seeing the city. Sixtus V's development of the hills had as much to do with their conceptual significance as it did with their value as underexploited territory. Fulvio's modern counterparts, by contrast, combine geophysical data with 'facts' from ancient and Renaissance texts with barely a nod towards the weight of representation.

When in 1897 Italian archaeologist Rodolfo Lanciani advised his readers to survey the seven hills, it was with Brocchi's map and works by his successors in hand. But his instructions, prior to the bibliographical information he gives, repay closer reading.

Students who visit Rome for the first time would do well to take at once a general survey of the seven hills, of the plain, of its border of mountains and sea, from the dome of S. Peter's, from the campanile of S. Maria Maggiore, or from the tower of the Capitol, which is easier of access and has a more interesting foreground (open every day from ten to three).[120]

For Lanciani, the number seven is important and the seven hills, as they were for Martial, are emblematic of the ancient city. More than this though, his preferred vantage point – the Capitoline – offers a history of viewing which stretches back in time to bring the Rome of the present into dialogue with Romes of the past, and to turn each of these from objective reality into subjective response. 'The ascent of the tower is well repaid by the view from the summit, which embraces not only the hills of Rome, but the various towns and villages of the neighbouring campagna and mountains which successively fell under her dominion' explains English writer Augustus Hare in his *Walks in Rome* of 1871.[121] It was from the Capitoline in the fifteenth century that Poggio Bracciolini contemplated Rome's desolation and, following in his footsteps three centuries later, that the historian Edward Gibbon was inspired to write about the 'decline and fall of the city'.[122] In 1838 artist

---

[120] Lanciani 1897: 4.   [121] Hare 1923: 84.

[122] Gibbon's story about his moment of inspiration on the Capitoline survives in three different versions and is revisited in the concluding chapter of the *Decline and Fall* itself. See Carnochan 1987; Craddock 1984: 63–82; Edwards 1996: 72–4; and O'Brien 1997. In this final chapter he has his readers visit the Capitoline with Poggio Bracciolini. Bracciolini's *De varietate fortunae* dates to 1430; a good Latin edition of the text was published in 1993. Georgina Masson (1965: 24) continues the trope: 'it is quite possible that Poggio [Bracciolini]

Samuel Palmer, again, made for the tower of the Capitol, from where he saw 'everything', 'the whole of the grand ruins'.[123]

The force of Lanciani's prose depends on this heritage. His seven hills are reminiscence and rock, as they are for anyone who visits Rome; as they should be for anyone who studies Rome. Take diplomat Antonio Loschi's description of the Capitoline in the fifteenth century: 'golden once, now neglected, crammed with thorns and brambles'.[124] It is a picture coloured as much by Virgil's Capitoline as it is by what he sees – the inverse of the *Aeneid*'s 'golden now, but once upon a time, bristling with woodland brambles'.[125] Such conceits had been honed from a young age. Michel de Montaigne explains, 'I knew the Capitol and its plan before I knew the Louvre, the Tiber before the Seine' (the verb is 'savoir' as opposed to 'connaître' – not to be familiar or become acquainted with; simply 'to know'). He continues, 'the qualities and fortunes of Lucullus, Metellus and Scipio have ever run more in my head than those of my own country'.[126] His was a Rome founded on classical literature.

When Montaigne eventually visited Rome in 1580, he could not understand how the seven hills, especially the Palatine and Capitoline, could have held the buildings ascribed to them.[127] And he was not alone in this consternation: so prominent were the hills in written Rome that they often left people frustrated. Henry James writes:

> The Capitol – that long inclined plane . . . is the unfailing disappointment, I believe, of tourists primed for retrospective raptures . . . The hill is so low, the ascent so narrow, Michel Angelo's architecture in the quadrangle at the top so meagre, the whole place somehow so much more of a mole-hill than a mountain, that for the first ten minutes of your standing there Roman history seems suddenly to have sunk through a trap-door.[128]

And the disenchantment is not confined to the literary visitor. In the 1960s, urban planner Kevin Lynch captured the experience of countless others

---

stood on almost exactly the same spot as we'. And it extends back even before Bracciolini: Petrarch's letter to Cardinal Colonna concerning his first impressions of Rome (above, n. 82) was composed on the Ides of March, on the Capitol.

[123] Palmer 7 June 1838; Lister 1974: vol. I, 146.

[124] *Op.* fol. 50ʳ: 'aurea quondam, nunc squalida, spinetis vepribusque referta'.

[125] Virg. *Aen.* 8.348: 'aurea nunc, olim silvestribus horrida dumis'.

[126] Montaigne 2003, *De la vanité* 3.9: 'je sçavois le Capitole et son plant avant que je sceusse le Louvre, et le Tibre avant la Seine. J'ay eu plus en teste, les conditions et fortunes de Lucullus, Metellus, et Scipion, que je n'ay d'aucuns hommes des nostres.'

[127] As cited in Ammerman 2006: 300. For Montaigne's vision of Rome, see McGowan 1990.

[128] James 1995: 126 (written in 1873). On James' response to Rome, see Tolliver 2000: 136–45 and Foeller-Pituch 2003. Hawthorne [1860] 2002: 127 called the Capitoline 'that renowned hillock'.

Figure 2.10 James Barry, *The Tarpeian Rock*, 1769.

when he confessed: 'the hills are not prominent as I had thought, but buried in the buildings'.[129]

We have already acknowledged that 'the soil has risen from rubbish at least fifteen feet, so that no wonder the hills look lower than they used to do, having been never very considerable at the first'.[130] As far as the Capitoline is concerned, the infilling of its saddle in the mediaeval period and its reorientation by Michelangelo had a striking effect. 'Part of the primitive fortress wall of the Capitol remains at the edge of the perpendicular rock. The rock as seen here is the best exposed remnant of the cliffs which were characteristic of the hills of ancient Rome, as they still are of Ardea, Veii, and many other ancient sites in her neighbourhood.'[131] But most of the hill was unrecognizable (Figure 2.10). Nathaniel Hawthorne is one of the most evocative witnesses:

[129] Lynch 1961: 129 and Zeleznikar 2002: 18: 'Rome's famous hills are a little disappointing. A few of them are difficult to recognize as the bluffs they are, let alone as hills.'

[130] Thomas Arnold 1827, as cited by Hare 1923: 145. In his *History of Rome* 1840: 33, Arnold admits that 'the hills of Rome are such that we rarely see in England, low in height but with steep and rocky sides'. See also Coxe 1818: 196: 'These hills are much reduced since the valleys have been filled up with enormous quantities of rubbish'; Lanciani 1897: 2: 'It is difficult to reconstruct in one's mind the former aspect of the site of Rome, as hills have been lowered, valleys filled up, and cliffs turned into gentle slopes'; and de Staël [1807] 1998: 64.

[131] Hare 1923: 199.

Not that it was still the natural, shaggy front of the original precipice; for it appeared to be cased in ancient stonework, through which the primeval rock showed its face here and there grimly and doubtfully. The mosses grew on the slight projections, and little shrubs sprouted out of the crevices, but could not much soften the stern aspect of the cliff. Brightly as the Italian moonlight fell adown the height, it scarcely showed what portion of it was man's work and what was nature's, but left it all in very much the same kind of ambiguity and half-knowledge in which antiquarians generally leave the identity of Roman remains.[132]

Fulvio and Biondo's progress notwithstanding, no amount of scientific analysis can transport us back there. The Capitoline's reputation and the reputation of the other six hills demands that they were higher in antiquity. It also demands that they are tamed. Rome has to be in a different league from subject cities such as Ardea and Veii.

Such dissatisfaction sends the imagination into overdrive. English surgeon, Samuel Sharp, anticipates Hawthorne by a century, plugging the gap with gallows humour:

The surface of modern Rome is certainly more elevated than it was in ancient times; such an alteration must happen in the course of ages to every city . . . The Tarpeian rock is still of such a height, that should a man be thrown from it, his bones would be in the greatest danger, though there would certainly be no break to the neck; nor indeed would it be certain, though the rock were ten or fifteen feet higher, as some have supposed in the time of the Romans, when this kind of execution was in vogue: I should imagine, therefore, they had some method of dispatching the delinquent, when death did not immediately ensue from the fall; perhaps an executioner was at the foot of the rock, ready to give the coup-de-grace in case of that event, which, I imagine, would often happen, though the rock had been of twice its present height.[133]

Twice the height or not, the hill is certainly larger than life in Piranesi's engraving, part of volume I of his *Le antichità romane*, first published in 1756, in which the saddle has been lowered and modern building cleared (Figure 2.11).[134] So too the Palatine, if that is what it is, in the background of Andrea Mantegna's *St Sebastian* in the Louvre, and the hills in the ambulatory fresco of Nero persecuting the Christians from Santo Stefano

---

[132] Hawthorne [1860] 2002: 130.

[133] Sharp 1766: 52. Lending a little more flesh to Sharp and to eighteenth-century history painter James Barry, whose image of the Tarpeian Rock (1769) is reproduced (Fitzwilliam Museum, Cambridge, Paintings, Drawings and Prints, 2280) is Pressly 1995.

[134] Piranesi 1756: plate 107. See Ficacci's edition of the etchings, 2006. Note here, however, that Piranesi often exaggerates scale with the result that many buildings too appear bigger.

Figure 2.11 Piranesi's engraving of the Capitoline, *Le antichità romane*, 1756.

Rotondo in Rome, and in Bartolomeo di Giovanni's *Rape of the Sabines*, in Galleria Colonna (Figures 2.12, 2.13 and 2.14).[135] One would need crampons to climb these Renaissance cliff faces. When did the seven hills last look like this? However authentic di Giovanni's vision, his mountains have a lot in common with those in his *Procession of Thetis and Peleus*, signalling each landscape as mythological.[136]

The seven hills are an enduring part of Rome's mythology, and – unlike many myths about Rome – something that defines not the Empire but the city. It is in recognition of this mythology that Mussolini's Master Plan promised to reveal the seven hills 'currently submerged under the chaotic constructions of past centuries'.[137] He saw that they were as

[135] Andrea Mantegna, *St Sebastian* (*c.* 1480), Louvre, Paris, R. F. 1766. Although the Louvre prefer to see the backdrop as metaphorical, Augenti 1996: 94 identifies the hill as the Palatine. For the late sixteenth-century Jesuit-sponsored martyrdom-cycle, see Monssen 1982 and 1983. My third example is Bartolomeo di Giovanni (active *c.* 1475–1501) *Rape of the Sabines* (1488), *cassone* panel, tempora on wood, Galleria Colonna, Rome, inv. no. 12.

[136] *The Procession of Thetis and Peleus* (1490–1500), *cassone* panel, Louvre, Paris, R. F. 1347.

[137] Mussolini 1930: 269–70 – Baxa 2004 and 2010: 54–75. So extensive was Mussolini's remodelling of the city that one contemporary noted that if the current rate of destruction were anything to go by, Rome would disappear altogether: *AsC, Gov. di Roma: Del Governatorato, anno 1932, terzo semestre: Delib. no. 7405. Ric. AMALIA DOMINICI ved. RONCI, domiciliata al Lungotevere Mellini 17, scala 2e, interno 10.* For Mussolini as successor to Sixtus V and his urban development, see Anker 1996.

Figure 2.12 Section of Andrea Mantegna's *Martyrdom of St Sebastian*, 1480. See also colour plate section.

Figure 2.13 Fresco of Nero persecuting the Christians, Santo Stefano Rotondo, Rome. See also colour plate section.

Figure 2.14 Bartolomeo di Giovanni, *Rape of the Subines*, 1488. See also colour plate section.

fundamental a link back to ancient Rome (Augustan Rome in particular) as the artefacts in his exhibition, the *Mostra Augustea della Romanità* of 1937–8.

The Italian people have created the Empire with their blood, will make it fertile with their labour, and will defend it against whomever with their arms. In this certain hope, raise high, legionaries, your standards, your weapons and your hearts, and salute after fifteen centuries, the reappearance of the empire on the predestined hills of Rome.[138]

Much of this urban development was about ensuring that the hills and the views from the hills could be best captured by a new lens – the motor car.[139] Today a company, selling Vespa tours of the city, puffs:

enjoy the fabulous sites from the legendary peaks of the Seven Hills of Rome while whizzing along by a two-wheel vintage Vespa. Cruise along the ridges of this *Caput Mundi* (Capital of the world) and stop along the way to admire the breathtaking views. With the aid of a knowledgeable guide, you will learn about the importance of these hills in the mythical origins of the city as well as be able to identify the principal historical monuments and districts of the ancient city.[140]

It is as attractive a prospect as it is contrived: as though Mussolini's clearance ensures that Lanciani's hopes are realized and the hills again able to give visitors the measure of all of Rome. As Madame de Staël's Corinne makes clear, 'The top of the Capitol as it is today is the place from which we can easily have a view of the seven hills. Then we shall explore all of them, one after the other. There is not one of them which does not preserve some traces of history.'[141]

This chapter has begun to unpack what kind of history this is – not history as a study of the past, the city's lumps, bumps and soil levels, but history as a way of perceiving these features. We might be foolish to treat Piranesi's engraving or Giovanni's painting as evidence for early Rome, but what about the poetry of Fulvio, Propertius and Virgil, or the prose of Dionysius of Halicarnassus (even the Rome of Servius Tullius is not irrefutably a city of seven hills)? Their visions of the Capitoline shaped, and responded to, the

---

[138] Mussolini 1936, in a speech reproduced in part in *Il Popolo d' Italia* (*The People of Italy*) 11 May, p. 1: Minor 1999: 154. On the *Mostra* and Mussolini's cult of *Romanità* more broadly, see Scriba 1995, Visser 1992 and Stone 1999.

[139] See Baxa: 2004.

[140] See www.isango.com/italy-tours/rome-tours/the-seven-hills-of-rome_6233 (accessed 20 August 2011).

[141] De Staël [1807] 1998: 62.

'Rome equals its seven hills' equation. This equation has long wrestled with the land to make mountains out of molehills and continues to dictate how we witness Rome today. It has also given ballast to other cities – a common language with which to compete in an international arena. But when did the seven hills become a formula? Next we return to its origins and to Rome of the late Republic and early Empire. Why does the city need to celebrate its contours in this way then? Why the urgency to work out where it is and what it is made of?

3 | Seven is the magic number

A prime number like 7 is especially hard to manage and therefore very significant; and here an additional psychological factor is at work – it is easy to picture in one's mind a group of six or a hexagon, but much harder to imagine a heptagon. Thus many kinds of threads join to compose this complicated fabric.

Walter Burkert (1972: 473)

Rome was not born a city of seven hills. It grew into them. This is not simply a story of Servius Tullius constructing a wall to enclose all seven for the first time, but a story of gradual accretion as each of Rome's early kings is credited with embracing an additional hill or hills within the city. Which king embraced which hills proves to be as contentious as membership of the canon, and the contention is evidence of the importance of the land for realizing the role of each ruler. It is also evidence of the fact that the value of Rome's territory was not a given. As Strabo acknowledges, Rome is 'in a place which was fit for purpose not through choice but through necessity. For the ground was not strong nor did the site possess enough of the surrounding land to be capable of supporting a city, nor people to form a community.'[1] Rather Rome was a commodity that accrued interest by being disputed – not only in quarrels between brothers, in competing legends (Romulus versus the Trojan Aeneas), or in wars with the Sabines, but by posterity, centuries later. Compared with Mycenae or Athens, Rome was a latecomer to the international stage,[2] and its founder Romulus was not autochthonous like Athenian king Erechtheus, but exposed and miraculously saved by a she-wolf. Years of fighting and uneasy alliances followed. The seven hills became building blocks which lent longevity to Rome and made its haphazard expansion deliberate. Their 'acquisition' was an early model for imperial expansion.

---

[1] Strabo 5.3.2: ἐν τόποις οὐ πρὸς αἵρεσιν μᾶλλον ἢ πρὸς ἀνάγκην ἐπιτηδείοις· οὔτε γὰρ ἐρυμνὸν τὸ ἔδαφος οὔτε χώραν οἰκείαν ἔχον τὴν πέριξ ὅση πόλει πρόσφορος, ἀλλ' οὐδ' ἀνθρώπους τοὺς συνοικήσοντας.

[2] See Cic. *Rep.* 1.37.58.

The earliest extant authors to use the seven hills in this way, as the logical conclusion to something that was predestined from the start, indicative of Rome's arrival as a fully-fledged city, were late Republican or Augustan. But were they the first to do this, or was Rome already known as a city of seven hills in the poetry of Ennius (d. 169 BCE),[3] whose work was so influential not only on Petrarch, but on Cicero, Livy and Virgil? Or even earlier? Was it that the city's location had always been talked about in these terms? For Virgil, whose *Aeneid* and *Georgics* are often credited with fuelling the process of popularization which makes the concept a cliché,[4] the seven hills predate Servius Tullius: as we shall discover, they stand for the unified, perfect city which resulted from the removal of Romulus' twin brother.[5]

Whatever the answers to these questions, the seven hills of this literary/oral culture can be described as an 'invention of tradition'. Historian Eric Hobsbawm writes:

'Invented tradition' is taken to mean a set of practices, normally governed by overtly or tacitly accepted rules and of a ritual or symbolic nature, which seek to inculcate certain values and norms of behaviour by repetition, which automatically implies continuity with the past. In fact, where possible, they normally attempt to establish continuity with a suitable historic past . . . However, insofar as there is such reference to a historic past, the peculiarity of 'invented' traditions is that the continuity with it is largely fictitious. In short, they are responses to novel situations which take the form of reference to old situations, or which establish their own past by quasi-obligatory repetition. It is the contrast between the constant change and innovation of the modern world and the attempt to structure at least some parts of social life within it as unchanging and invariant, that makes the 'invention of tradition' so interesting.[6]

Chapter 4 will unpick the ways in which Virgil, Horace, Ovid, Tibullus and Propertius hit upon the hills as a means of managing the novelty of Augustus' urban reforms, and how in doing this they imbue the hills with meaning which still makes cities borrow them. But it is late Republican writer Varro more than Virgil who is behind the Renaissance fascination with the hills, and he and other prose writers of the period — Livy, Dionysius of Halicarnassus and Strabo – who, together with the poets, cement them as

---

[3] Paratore 1975: 192 uses Varro's own citation of Ennius (*Ann.* 25 Vahlen) at *Ling.* 5.42 ('They report that this *mons* (the Capitoline) used to be called the Saturnian Hill, and that from it Latium was called the Saturnian land, as indeed Ennius calls it') and Virgil's reference to 'Saturnia tellus' (*Aen.* 8.329) to suggest that Ennius may already have been engaged with the seven hills.

[4] See e.g. Holland 1953: 33–4 and R. F. Thomas 2011: 64.

[5] Morgan 1999: 117–18 and for the idea of the perfect city, Carandini 1997: 271.

[6] Hobsbawm and Ranger 1983: 1–2.

a set with a symbolic nature which establishes continuity with the past. As Richard Buxton observes, 'mountains are before. They were believed to be humanity's place of first habitation. In the *Laws* (677b–c) Plato's Athenian speculates about a time after a prehistoric flood, when life was preserved on the tops of mountains among herdsmen . . . Before also, because they are the location of the early lives of the gods.'[7] Our ancient authors exploit this potential, making myth and history merge in and on Rome's 'montes'. Their arguments about the binding of the hills or, in Varro's case, his analysis of their names, lend a *raison-d'être* to the city.

An invention of tradition

ubi nunc est Roma, Septimontium nominatum ab tot montibus quos postea urbs muris comprehendit. (Varro, *De lingua Latina* 5.41)

The present chapter is about this invention of tradition. If the next chapter is about the fleshing out of the seven-hills skeleton, this one is about its growth phases. There are scholars, most notably in recent years archaeologist Andrea Carandini, who believe that Rome had 'seven hills' from the start (hence the possibility that mid-Republican colonies might have emulated them),[8] even prior to its traditional foundation as a city.[9] The claim is that when Varro explains, 'where Rome now is was called Septimontium after the same number of "montes", which the city afterwards surrounded by its walls', he is transmitting 'living memory' of a proto-urban phase of development in the ninth century which had its own seven 'montes' and a parallel group of 'colles'. The names of these 'montes' – the Cermalus, Velia and Palatium (part of the Palatine), the Oppius, Cispius and Fagutal (or Subura, if you are Carandini, who defines it as the north-west slope of the Velia and Fagutal and counts the Fagutal as part of the Oppian) and the Caelian – are then derived from Sextus Pompeius Festus (most probably second century CE),[10] whom we shall be discussing later.[11] But Carandini does not stop

---

[7] Buxton 1992: 8.   [8] See above, Chapter 2.

[9] Carandini 1997: 267–79, with reviews by Fentress and Giudi 1999 and T. P. Wiseman 2000; and, in an abbreviated English version (without the degree of emphasis he gives to seven on pp. 270–3), Carandini 2011: 18, 22–5 and 46–7. See also De Sanctis 1907: 185; Gjerstad 1962: 23–4; Momigliano 1963: 99; Paratore 1975; D'Anna 1992; and Cornell 1995: 74.

[10] Glinister *et al.* 2007: 1–2.

[11] The main problem stems, as we shall discover later in this chapter, from the fact that Festus records not seven names but eight. In the nineteenth century it was usually the Subura that was dropped because it is a valley, but Carandini 1997: 316 is cleverer, creating hills where there are no hills: 'Ma se il termine *mons* significa in quest'epoca non una unità orografica intera,

there as, in the spirit of Dionysius of Halicarnassus and Strabo, he maps the story of Rome's maturation onto its 'montes': so before the 'Septimontium' phase one and two, he gives us the five-part 'Quinquimontium' (Palatium, Velia, Fagutal, Subura, and Cermalus) and prior to this, a 'Trimontium' (Palatium, Velia and Cermalus), neither of which features in the ancient literature.[12]

Although 'Septimontium' is attested as an ancient entity, it was highly contested even then. Varro uses the word in two different ways – first to identify a certain tract of land, and secondly to refer to a religious festival, involving, so he claims, the people who lived on the 'montes', the 'montani'.[13] It is this second meaning, as a festival held in December, that is most common: Suetonius, for example, describes how Domitian (emperor 81–96 CE) threw a banquet in celebration of the Septimontium, distributing large baskets of food to the senators and *equites* and smaller ones to the people.[14] At roughly the same time, Plutarch claims that this festival commemorated the allotting of the seventh hill to the city, by which Rome became seven hilled.[15] But overall, the Septimontium and Rome's seven hills, real or conceptual, are harder to reconcile than his confidence suggests: Louise Adams Holland makes the point that the word more probably derives from 'saepti montes', meaning 'enclosed or fortified montes' rather than 'septem montes'.[16] Might Varro's history of the word 'Septimontium' be an etymological fiction responsible for further mythologies?

comme abbiamo già visto, ma una contrada ospitante uno o piú rioni o curie, che può essere accolta su qualsiasi lobo o pendio, quindi su una parte anche singola di un rilievo, ogni difficoltà viene a cadere' ('But if the title *mons* signifies at this time [of the Quinquimontium] not an entire orographic unit, as we have seen, but a single living quarter or several regions or *curiae* that can be accommodated on either a lobe or a slope, so also on a discrete part of an elevation, every difficulty comes to fall away'). Also, Gjerstad 1962: 23, n. 2: 'Subura cannot be the notorious quarter in Rome with that name, because it was no hill but a part of the valley between the Quirinal, Viminal and Esquiline. As one of the seven hills, Subura stands for Succusa, a summit on the Caelian.'

[12] C. J. Smith 2006: 361.   [13] Varro, *Ling.* 6.24: see Ampolo 1981 and Fraschetti 1984.
[14] Suet. *Dom.* 4.5.
[15] Plut. *Quaest. Rom.* 69: τὸ δὲ Σεπτιμούντιον ἄγουσιν ἐτὶ τῷ τὸν ἕβδομον λόφον τῇ πόλει προσκατανεμηθῆναι καὶ τὴν Ῥώμην ἑπτάλοφον γενέσθαι.
[16] Holland 1953, rebutted aggressively by Carandini 1997: 270, n. 13. Also C. J. Smith 1996: 155 and Coarelli 1999, with bibliography, who judiciously claims that the term 'septimontium' sembra definire in origine una festa dei *montes*, intesi come entità preurbane e poi extraurbane: è perciò errata la teoria ottocentesca che vi riconosce una fase della città, anteriore a quella serviana delle quattro *regiones*': ('Septimontium seems to define in origin a festival of the *montes*, understood as an entity pre-urban and then extra-urban: the nineteenth-century theory that it identifies a phase of the city, prior to that of the Servian city of four regions is, therefore, wrong').

For Remo Gelsomino, Varro's emphasis on the 'septem' and 'montes' in Septimontium, and his tying it so strongly to Rome's territory and identity, makes him author of the 'seven hills' concept and creator of the canon. While I am keen to resist apportioning this kind of credit, Varro's complex, fragmentary text has certainly muddied the waters – a fact which is exacerbated by the loss of his *Antiquitates rerum humanarum et divinarum*, an encyclopaedia of Roman religious and cultural practices, which may well have had more to say on the subject. The seven hills need rescuing from his thrall, and his observations need reinstating into a broader contemporary framework. 'It is the contrast between the constant change and innovation of the modern world and the attempt to structure at least some parts of social life within it as unchanging and invariant, that makes the "invention of tradition" so interesting.' As Gelsomino himself recognized, Cicero too (106–43 BCE) refers to Rome as the 'city of seven hills'. The important question is less when Rome first acquired this status than why a special investment in its seven summits was made late in the Republic?

The potency and possibility of the number seven

That in many natural phenomena a certain potency and possibility of the number seven has been observed, about which Marcus Varro discourses at length in his *Hebdomades*.[17]

According to Aulus Gellius, Varro suffered from a bad case of 'heptophilia'. He saw sevens everywhere, from the sublime to the ridiculous. In the first book of his *Hebdomades*, or *De imaginibus*, a lost work which Pliny the Elder tells us consisted of portraits of seven hundred celebrities, organized on some sevenly principle,[18] and which inspired Renaissance pocket books such as Andrea Fulvio's *Illustrium imagines*,[19] seven is central to everything from the cosmos and the zodiac, birth, health, death and disease to human stature and 'piffling things' like circus races.[20] Censorinus' *De die natali*, written in the third century CE and influenced by Varro, especially his Logistoricus, *Tubero de origine humana*, again sees seven as key to embryology.[21]

---

[17] Aul. Gell. 3.10: 'quod est quaedam septenarii numeri vis et facultas in multis naturae rebus animadversa, de qua M. Varro in Hebdomadibus disserit copiose.'

[18] Plin. *HN* 35.2.11. Arguments rage over the arrangement and content: see Ritschl 1877: 508–22; delle Corte 1970: 190–3; Norden 1990 and Geiger 1998.

[19] Fulvio 1517 and Pelc 2002.

[20] Aul. Gell. 3.10 including (3.10.16), the 'piffling', or 'frigidiuscula'.

[21] Censorinus, *De die natali* 9.1, for explicit mention of Varro, and his Chapter 7 for embryology.

This theory about development of the embryo is explicitly Pythagorean. For the Pythagoreans, seven was 'καιρός', meaning 'due measure' or 'opportunity',[22] and for Philo in the first half of the first century CE, 'τελεσφόρος', or 'perfection-bringing'.[23] It was not only Varro who deemed it significant. As he himself acknowledges in his *Hebdomades*, it was the limiting factor of many an ancient list: the seven sages, seven against Thebes, seven wonders of the world.[24] And we could add the seven gates of Thebes, the seven early kings, the 'septemviri' or 'seven men' (an urban priestly college, founded in Rome in 196 BCE by resolution of the people), the 'septem iugera', or 'seven measures of land' (the size of the allotments traditionally granted to each Roman citizen at the founding moment of the Republic), and the 'septem pagi' or 'seven villages' (the name given by Dionysius of Halicarnassus and Plutarch to an area close to Rome on the right bank of the Tiber which Romulus supposedly took from the Veientes).[25] Some ancient sources even claim that there were seven Muses, Cyclopes and Titans. Although Aristotle would have us believe, contrary to the Pythagoreans, that the ubiquity of the number seven in such formulae as the seven against Thebes or seven Pleiads is accidental, even he goes to some considerable effort in his *De sensu* to make the number of both colours and flavours come out as seven and claims that the mind is fully developed at the age of forty-nine (seven multiplied by seven).[26] His pupil, Theophrastus is even more enthusiastic: for him, in his work on plants, seven is 'the most apposite and natural'.[27]

It is unimaginable that this venerable heritage does not intersect with and underpin the 'seven hills' canon. It certainly begins to explain its ongoing success: not only does seven remain important for Christianity (seven deadly sins, seven pilgrim churches (Figure 3.1), seven sleepers of Ephesus, who are said to have hidden inside a cave to escape persecution, only to awake years later...), but it is also cross-cultural, writ large in Babylonian, Egyptian

---

[22] Alexander, *Comm. on Aristotle's Metaph.* (p. 38.16–20 ed. Hayduck). See Riedweg 2002: 81.
[23] Philo, *De mundi opificio* 102 (Arnaldez 1961) in a section on seven, 89–128. The fullest survey of seven in antiquity, with specific reference to ancient Greek literature, is Roscher 1904. Also important are Robbins 1921, Hartnell 1964, Grilli 1979 and Giora 1988.
[24] Aul. Gell. 3.10.16.
[25] For the seven gates of Thebes, see below (n. 33); on the 'septemviri', Cornell 1995: 252; and on the 'septem pagi' (seven villages), Dion. Hal. *Ant. Rom.* 2.55.5, 5.31.4, 5.36.4 and Plut. *Rom.* 25. For a full discussion of the 'septem iugera' and the complexities of the evidence, see T. P. Wiseman 2009: 46–9. The earliest source for these is Varr. *Rust.* 1.2.9.
[26] Arist. *Metaph.* 1039a, *Sens.* 4 and *Rh.* 1390b9–11. I thank David Sedley for his help here.
[27] Theophr. *Caus. pl.* 6.4.2: καιριώτατος καὶ φυσικώτατος.

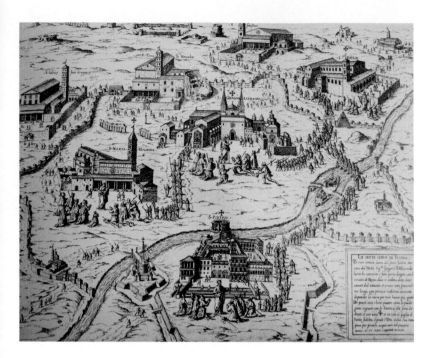

Figure 3.1 Stefano Dupérac, *Veduta delle sette chiese di Roma*, 1575.

and Jewish traditions,[28] and on into our own psyche. When scientists in the 1970s asked children to write down a number between zero and nine, and adults to repeat the first that came to mind, the most popular response in each case was seven.[29] The number's association with Rome's landscape puts the city at the centre of the universe. Philo makes the point very well: 'for what part of the universe is not enamoured of seven, overcome by desire and longing for the number seven?'[30]

A closer look at these other heptads helps us understand not only the origins of the 'seven hills' as an influential idea, but also the uncertainty

[28] On the 'completeness' that seven implies in the early Christian, Jewish and Babylonian traditions, see Yarbro Collins 1984: 1276, and on the seven sages in the Babylonian tradition, Martin 1993: 121. Also important here is Riehm in Grimm and Grimm 1854–1960: vol. X, 785–6.

[29] Simon and Primavera 1972 and Kobovy and Psotka 1976. Also important here, for the reactions it elicited, is George Miller's classic 1956 paper on the number seven and working memory capacity.

[30] Philo, *De mundi opificio* 111: Τί γὰρ οὐ φιλέβδομον τῶν ἐν τῷ κόσμῳ μέρος, ἔρωτι καὶ πόθῳ δαμασθὲν ἑβδομάδος. Also important is his discussion of the Sabbath in *De specialibus legibus* 2.39–59: see Leonhardt 2001: 54–63.

concerning the specific membership of the canon. Take the seven sages, a canonical set of archaic Greek wise men which German historian Detlev Fehling would have us believe was invented by Plato.[31] The accumulation of lists to survive from antiquity offers at least seventeen contenders, with some versions unsurprisingly favouring local intellectuals over more established superstars.[32] But even the site-specific seven gates of Thebes are unstable, with authors as diverse as Aeschylus, Hyginus, Statius and Nonnus proposing different candidates.[33] Why is there this need to itemize, and refine the formula, if not to play a part in the handing down of history? For it is this handing down that injects information with life, turning it into 'tradition'. As with Chinese whispers, the value lies in the divergence between original and variants. Accuracy is secondary.

Similar questions of membership and authorship plague the seven wonders of the ancient world, which were not finally fixed until the Renaissance.[34] Antipater, writing as early as the second century BCE, is the first extant author to supply a full list of seven, these being the walls of Babylon, the statue of Zeus at Olympia, the Hanging Gardens of Babylon, the Colossus of Rhodes, the pyramids, the Mausoleum of Halicarnassus and the Temple of Artemis at Ephesus.[35] Eventually, the lighthouse at Alexandria ousts the first of Babylon's entries, but not before Martial has inserted the Colosseum,[36] and a work commonly attributed to the Venerable Bede, the

---

[31] Fehling 1985, who gives the credit to the *Protagoras* 343a with Callimachus, the first to modify Plato's list. And, in opposition to this, Martin 1993, Bollansée 1999 and Busine 2002, who argue for an older, evolving tradition which begins in the late sixth century and is committed to writing soon after. Elsewhere in Plato, there are seven celestial orbits (*Tim.* 38e), seven kinds of motion (*Tim.* 34e) and some sevens in the myth at the end of the *Republic*. That said, we must concede that it is also easy to find other recurrent numbers.

[32] Martin 1993: 109. For visual testimony of the seven sages, see Chéhab 1958–9 (Baalbek), J. Balty 1977: 78–9 (Apamea, Sicily), and for their relationship, Jones Hall 2004: 239. Also relevant here is a mosaic from Emerita in Spain, Dunbabin 1999: 152, and the wall painting from the Baths of the Seven Sages in Ostia, Mols 1997 and Clarke 2003: 171–5.

[33] On the seven gates of Thebes, Hom. *Od.* 11.263; Pind. *Pyth.* 3.90–91, 8.39–40, 9.80, 11.11, *Nem.* 9.18, *Isth.* 1.66–7; Hyg. *Fab.* 69.7; Stat. *Thebaid*; Nonnus, *Dionysiaca*; and Aeschylus throughout the *Seven against Thebes*. And on the various possible names, Wilamowitz-Möllendorff 1891: 210–20 and Berman 2002: 75–6. Using the archaeology to tie these 'seven gates' to a historical phase of the real city is Symeonoglou 1985 (reviewed by Snodgrass 1985).

[34] On the seven wonders or 'θαύματα', see Dombart 1967, Clayton and Price 1988, Ekschmitt 1984 and, on their *Nachleben*, Kunze 2003. Roscher 1904: 188–9 records twenty-two contenders in eighteen wonder lists, though he omits Martial.

[35] *Anth. Pal.* 9.58. It is still undecided whether the author is Antipater of Sidon, and the poem, second century BCE; or Antipater of Thessalonica, and the poem, Augustan: see Gow–Page 1965: vol. II, 20–1. Note too a papyrus from Abusir-el-Melek, the 'Laterculi Alexandrini', which probably also dates to the second century BCE: see Diels 1904.

[36] Mart. *Spect.* 1. See Coleman 2006: 1–13.

Capitol.[37] Neither of these has any staying power. But it is in Rome that the seven wonders become a popular cliché – they are the sum total of man's genius elsewhere.

Rome versus the rest of civilization. Not only does Varro refer to the seven wonders in his *Hebdomades* but, at about the same time, Greek historian Diodorus Siculus, who is also based in Rome, mentions them in passing three times and, a little later, a graffito from Pompeii confirms them as part of popular culture.[38] It would be naïve of us not to set the celebration of the seven hills in the late Republic and early Empire against them. It is tempting even to see the seven hills as a local response, which substitutes Rome for the world, and brings with it a crucial sense of cohesion – particularly at that moment. Rome was a city under strain, pulled apart by rival aristocrats. Civil war between Caesar and Pompey and Octavian and Antony followed Sulla's bloody struggle with Marius and the Catilinarian conspiracy. What Rome was, and might become, was being radically reformulated. At the same time, the city was at war with external forces, first with other cities in Italy in the Social War,[39] then with the provinces of Spain under Sertorius, and finally with Cleopatra and Egypt. These threats added to the urgency to define its territory, and to acquire a visible, defensible boundary.[40] Walls could be breached, as the Gallic sack of Rome early in the fourth century forcefully demonstrated. Livy underlines this when he writes that what was left of the Roman legions after the Battle of the Allia in around 390 BCE took refuge on the Capitol without closing the gates.[41] What was needed was a more 'complicated fabric', to which and from which to signal devotion and exclusion.

It was Octavian's victory that stimulated this vision. Were he to succeed where his adoptive father, Julius Caesar, had failed, he would have to bring the city together and have its image speak to his identity and vice versa, and

---

[37] Bohn 1845: 156: 'of the seven wonders of the world, made by the hand of man, the first is the Capitol at Rome, the very salvation of the inhabitants, and greater than a whole city'.

[38] Diod. Sic. 1.63.2, 11.5 and 18.4.5 and *CIL* IV 1111. Also interesting is Plin. *HN* 36.101, whose 'wonders (miracula) of our city [Rome]' turn out to total seven (Jordan 1871: 142–3). Note too Barton (1994: 62–3), who identifies a special engagement in astrology in particular in late Republican Rome, linked to legitimation of the Principate.

[39] Note that there are some ancient commentators who present the Social War as a kind of proto-civil war.

[40] Note, for example, the emphasis on the visible boundary of the city, its walls and its innards, in Cic. *Cat.* I and II (new edition by Dyck 2008). Relevant here are Vasaly 1993: 40–87 and Edwards 1996: 20–3.

[41] Livy 5.41.4: 'Galli . . . ingressi postero die urbem patente Collina porta in forum perveniunt' ('the Gauls entered the city on the following day by the Colline Gate which was open, and made their way to the forum').

to the rest of the Empire. This did not happen overnight: building had a large part to play, as did urban landscaping more broadly. Horace reminds his readers how the cemetery on the Esquiline was turned into gardens as Rome took on the appearance of a Hellenistic capital.[42] By 7 BCE the new Princeps had divided Rome into its fourteen regions. Although the case is never made explicit in the ancient literature, this number was a graphic way of suggesting that he was doubling the Servian city of seven summits.[43]

It makes sense, given the radical nature of Rome's facelift, that Augustan poets should have clung to the seven hills as a means of ensuring continuity. 'Augustus changed the city of Rome to a degree that was never seen before or after.'[44] Some of the most important monuments – the Mausoleum, Ara Pacis, Pantheon – were on the Campus Martius beyond Servius' wall. Lothar Haselberger explains: 'The visible image of Rome and the narrowly defined area of the Urbs were not identical.'[45] As we have seen in Chapter 1, this disparity threatened to blow old Rome out of the water. So spectacular was Strabo's Campus Martius that the rest of the city seemed almost incidental. How to quell this competition and ensure that Rome's growth did not demand cell division; or indeed that the pre-Augustan Rome should not be condemned as a chaotic rehearsal by comparison? The answer was the seven hills. They lent the city a meaningful, indelible shape that conferred intricacy and grandeur.

By the time that Martial is writing, the seven hills do not belong solely to the walled *urbs* but to the whole of Rome ('et totam licet aestimare Romam'). But already in Ovid's *Tristia*, the exiled poet writes that he is not from Dulichium, Ithaca or Samos but from Rome, 'the place of empire and the gods, that surveys the whole world from its seven hills'.[46] He uses the seven hills not of the *urbs* but of a bigger place than that, his home, the same Rome as had been founded by Romulus and walled by Servius, Rome, capital of the Empire. In a sense, it was always thus, the seven hills

---

[42] On the urgency in this period for the *locus* of Rome to become a world city, and on the tensions inherent within this, see Favro 1996: 116–21.

[43] Favro 1996: 136–7.

[44] Hölscher 2000: 248: 'Augustus hat die Stadt Rom in einem Ausmaß verändert wie niemand vor und nach ihm.'

[45] Haselberger 2007: 22.

[46] Ov. *Tr.* 1.5.67–70:

> nec mihi Dulichium domus est Ithaceve Samosve,
>   poena quibus non est grandis abesse locis,
> sed quae de septem totum circumspicit orbem
>   montibus, imperii Roma deumque locus.

See Spentzou 2005.

circumventing the jurists' ongoing problems of defining the *urbs* to bring Rome's disparate parts together,[47] just as they did the hilltop communities of the early city – to give circumference to Augustus' 'città aperta'. Mid-second-century CE sophist Aelius Aristides wrote: 'to place walls around the city itself... you have considered to be base and not in keeping with your other purpose... you certainly have not neglected walls – rather, you have placed them around your empire, not around your city'.[48]

The seven hills also worked to make Rome, capital city, distinct from its Empire. As Greek art flowed in and was displayed in the city's temples, and obelisks were imported into the Campus Martius and Circus Maximus, the city began to look radically different, alien even.[49] There had to be a counterweight to offer a stable footprint; to make Augustan Rome, Servian Rome and beyond into the same country, different from its conquered territory. Once Rome acquired its seventh hill, it had a full set, the magic number: seven sages, gates of Thebes, wonders of the ancient world, seven hills. Whatever their identity, it was impossible to improve on perfection.

Varro's contribution to the story

Varro's confusion seems fundamental and complete.[50]

So what are we to make of Varro's contribution? In a speech delivered in the Forum on the second day of January 63 BCE against the agrarian legislation proposed by the tribune P. Servilius Rullus, Cicero draws attention to the danger Rome will face from Capua if the law is passed. Capua is painted as an alternative or anti-Rome which will only grow more arrogant if home to five hundred colonists. 'They will laugh at and despise Rome', warns Cicero, situated as it is 'in mountains and enclosed valleys, raised up by, and suspended in, garrets, without the best roads and with the narrowest paths, compared to their own Capua, which is spread out on the flattest of

---

[47] See above, p. 6.

[48] Aristides, *Roman Oration* 80: αὐτῇ μὲν γὰρ τῇ πόλει περιβαλεῖν τὰ τείχη, οἷον ἀποκρύπτοντες αὐτὴν ἢ φεύγοντες τοὺς ὑπηκόους, ἀγεννές τε εἶναι καὶ οὐ πρὸς τῆς ἄλλης διανοίας ἐνομίσατε, οἷον εἴ τις δεσπότης δεικνύοιτο τοὺς ἑαυτοῦ δούλους φοβούμενος. τειχῶν γε μὴν οὐκ ἠμελήσατε, ταῦτα δὲ τῇ ἀρχῇ περιεβάλετε, οὐ τῇ πόλει. See edition by Fontanella 2007.

[49] On the influx of Greek art, see Walker 2000, Miles 2008 and K. E. Welch 2006, with reviews by Vout 2009a and 2009b, and on obelisks, and incorporating the alien, Edwards 2003.

[50] Holland 1953: 22.

sites and most splendidly situated'.[51] Ten years or so later, his take is more positive, making the most of the highs and lows of a settlement site still being criticized by Strabo:

urbis autem ipsius nativa praesidia quis est tam neglegens qui non habeat animo notata planeque cognita? cuius is est tractus ductusque muri cum Romuli, tum etiam reliquorum regum sapientia definitus ex omne parte arduis praeruptisque montibus, ut unus aditus, qui esset inter Esquilinum Quirinalemque montem, maximo aggere obiecto fossa cingeretur vastissima, atque ut ita munita arx circumiectu arduo et quasi circumciso saxo niteretur, ut etiam in illa tempestate horribili Gallici adventus incolumnis atque intacta permanserit. locumque delegit et fontibus abundantem et in regione pestilenti salubrem; colles enim sunt, qui cum perflantur ipsi tum adferunt umbram vallibus.

As far as the natural defences of the city are concerned, who is so unobservant as not to have them marked in his memory, thoroughly known? The course and structure of the wall were fixed by the wisdom of both Romulus and the kings who followed him – on the hills which were in all parts steep and rugged – so that the one approach, which was between the Esquiline and the Quirinal *montes*, was surrounded by an extremely large rampart and the widest ditch and so that the fortified *arx* was supported to such an extent by the high rocks surrounding it and by the rock which looks as though it has been rent apart on all sides that it remained safe and intact even at that terrible time that saw the approach of the Gauls. And he chose a place abundant in springs and healthy, though in a disease-ridden region; for there are hills (*colles*) which are both breezy in themselves and provide shade to the valleys.[52]

In revisiting the foundation of Rome, Cicero rescues Romulus from his Palatine crib and makes him and his successors as strategic as Durham's monks in his decision to found his city. This Rome has 'montes' and 'colles'; the former affording immediate security, and the latter, life-enhancing sanctuary. It paves the way for Livy's 'health-giving hills' and is grounded in wisdom not serendipity. As he explains earlier in book 2, founding a city demands 'foresight', and Rome's founder has chosen sensibly.[53]

The *Republic* was published in 51 BCE, before Cicero started for Cilicia. In a letter addressed to his friend Atticus on 26 June 50 BCE, Cicero refers to

[51] Cic. *Leg. agr.* 2.96: 'Romam in montibus positam et convallibus, cenaculis sublatam atque suspensam, non optumis viis, angustissimis semitis prae sua Capua planissimo in loco explicata ac praeclarissime sita irridebunt atque contemnent.' See Bell 1997: 14.
[52] Cic. *Rep.* 2.6.11.
[53] *Rep.* 2.3.5: 'quod est ei, qui diuturnam rem publicam serere conatur diligentissime providendum, incredibili oportunitate delegit'.

Rome as the 'city of seven hills' (ἐξ ἄστεως ἑπταλόφου).[54] Why now, when the formulation would have served him well in his account of Romulus' prescience, and why in Greek? For Gelsomino, there is only one answer: Varro tells Cicero his new idea in 52–51 BCE before going public with it in the *De lingua Latina* several years later, dedicating the relevant book to him.[55] Or might the influence have gone the other way, and Varro have caught the ball and run with it? But it is also possible that the concept was already so familiar as to be implicit in the earlier passages, just as it is in Livy some twenty-five years later. Livy's Marcus Furius Camillus speaks fondly of his native Rome, 'the hills and the fields and the Tiber and the region familiar to my eyes'.[56] Is the absence of the number seven evidence of his ignorance too? Or might there be contexts which call for explicit mention of it more than others? Might Cicero be reinforcing an existing idea by imagining the *decemvirs* of Capua mocking Rome in these terms? Seen like this, his 'code-switching' into Greek is evidence not only of conspiratorial chatter amongst friends, but of the seven-hills gaining rhetorical significance.[57]

---

[54] Cic. *Att.* 6.5.11. The only other usages of ἑπταλόφον are in Plutarch's passage on the Septimontium (see above, n. 15); *Or. Sib.* 14.108: Ῥώμη ἑπταλόφος (Chapter 2, n. 34); and *Anth. Pal.* 14.121:

> Ἑπτάλοφον ποτὶ ἄστυ Γαδειρόθεν, ἕκτον ὁδοῖο
> Βαίτιος εὐμύκους ἄχρις ἐς ἠιόνας
> κεῖθεν δ' αὖ πέμπτον Πυλάδου μετὰ Φώκιον οὖδας
> Ταύρη χθών βοέης οὔνομ' ἀπ' εὐετίης·
> Πυρήνην δέ τοι ἔνθεν ἐπ' ὀρθόκραιρον ἰόντι
> ὄγδοον ἠδὲ μιῆς δωδέκατον δεκάτης.
> Πυρήνης δὲ μεσηγὺ καὶ Ἄλπιος ὑψικαρήνου
> τέτρατον· Αὐσονίης αἶψα δυωδέκατον
> ἀρχομένης ἤλεκτρα φαείνεται Ἡριδανοῖο.
> ὦ μάκαρ, ὃς δισσὰς ἤνυσα χιλιάδας,
> πρὸς δ' ἔτι πέντ' ἐπὶ ταῖς ἑκατοντάδας ἔνθεν ἐλαύνων·
> ἡ γὰρ Ταρπείη μέμβλετ' ἀνακτορίη.

This poem is one of forty-six numerical problems or mathematical verse compositions in the form of riddles, compiled by the grammarian Metrodorus in late antiquity, but perhaps dating from earlier. Here too (Lightfoot 2007: 447) it is 'in the riddling, oracular, and apocalyptic manner'. Some of the epigrams in the series celebrate links to the *Arithmetiká* of Diophantus, whose dates are controversial but who is generally assumed to have been active in Alexandria in the third century CE. See Cuomo 2001: 244–6 and Dalby 2000: 82–3. I thank Richard Hunter for advice on this point.

[55] Gelsomino 1975 and 1976b. Note the attack by Paratore 1975 and Gelsomino's defence, 1976a. While Ogilvie 1977 is largely positive, he too worries about Cicero.

[56] Livy 5.54.3: 'colles campique et Tiberis et adsueta oculis regio...'

[57] See Adams (2003: esp. 329–30), who suggests that Cicero's use of Greek at this point is due to conspiracy of a different kind, so as to prevent the letter and its claims about the fraud of his wife's freedman being read en route.

It is likely, then, that Rome was a city of seven hills before Varro. Attribution to a particular inventor gives an otherwise random and unstable list authority, but as is the case with Plato and the seven sages, the irretrievability of most ancient literature, not to mention the importance of oral tradition, makes his authorship an act of faith. Some acts of faith demand more devotion than others. Unlike Plato's *Protagoras*, which provides a neat seven names for its seven wise men, Varro's text is a meandering, frustrating read and gives no immediate justification for doing what Gelsomino does in interpreting its ensuing analysis as a commentary on the statement 'Ubi nunc est Roma, Septimontium nominatum ab tot montibus quos postea urbs muris comprehendit.' In fact, the subject of book 5 is not the city but place names: the origins not of Rome, but of words as diverse as 'locus' (place) and 'caelum' (sky) through to 'rura' (countryside), 'praedia' (estates), 'Septimontium', 'Capitoline', and beyond, to 'pretium' (price), 'tributum' (tribute) and 'stipendium' (stipend). It is etymology, not topography.[58] But its emphasis on definition makes it different from our other ancient evidence for the seven hills – the histories, poems, later lists – and thus highly significant. In the origins it offers for 'Septimontium', it is the first to pin the concept to specific terrain. As we follow it, we are led on a journey which turns Rome and its constituent parts from location to lexis and back again. It brings the present into dialogue with the past, blazing a trail for Fulvio and Petrarch.

Looked at again, Varro's claim is indeed radical: Rome had seven hills before it had walls, before it was Rome. So significant were these seven hills that they gave the early settlement a name, and one which dictated the template of the Servian city. Whether or not this statement is fanciful is a different question from whether or not Rome was already being celebrated as a city of seven summits. The relevant section of his text (5.41) opens in the present ('ubi *nunc* est Roma') before transporting its reader back in time to explain how the different parts of the city come to have their names.[59] First is the Capitoline, called after the human head or 'caput' that was found there, and previously known as the 'Mons Tarpeia', after Tarpeia, the Vestal Virgin who was killed by the Sabines with their shields and buried on it. Her name is still preserved, Varro reminds us, in the part of the hill called the Tarpeian Rock. He continues (5.42): before Tarpeia and Romulean Rome,

---

[58] For criticism of Varro's etymologies, see R. Harris 1997: 47; and for these passages of the *Ling.*, Fraschetti 1990: 134–54 and 1996 and Wallace-Hadrill 2008: 261–2, with review by Osborne and Vout 2010.

[59] Helpful here is the edition by Collart 1954, with notes.

the Mons Tarpeia was already a 'mons' – 'montem Saturnium' – after an early settlement to Jupiter's father, Saturn.

Next to be interrogated is the Aventine (5.43), for which Varro favours the root 'advectus', as its earliest inhabitants had to be ferried there across swamps and streams. This gives him the opportunity to discourse on the derivation of Velabrum (the low-lying area between the Forum Romanum and the Forum Boarium), a word which he would have us believe comes from 'vehere', 'to carry', the implication being again by boat. After this, we would be justified in expecting the five other 'montes', but instead we are told that the 'rest of the city' ('reliqua urbis loca') was long ago divided when the 'shrines of the Argei' were distributed among the four Servian regions, the Suburan, Esquiline, Colline and Palatine (5.45).[60] Little is known about these Argei except that every year in mid-May all of them were visited, and straw puppets were collected which were then thrown into the Tiber by the Vestal Virgins in some sort of purificatory ritual.[61] Varro exploits our expectation: 'reliqua urbis loca olim discreta, cum Argeorum sacraria septem . . . ' ('the remaining regions were long ago divided, when the seven . . . '). It takes the rest of the sentence to determine that there are not seven shrines, but twenty-seven.[62]

After this, it is these regions and ancient shrines, and not the hills, that are the stage posts for our journey. Shrine one is at least on the 'Caelius mons' (5.46) but we have etymologies of the Vicus Tuscus, the main route between the Forum and the lower Forum Boarium, the Carinae and the Subura to get through[63] before we reach the Esquiline, only to be told that this is 'two *montes*' as far as the sacrifices of the Argei are concerned, called by their old names, the Oppian and Cispian. That these are now one *mons* remains implicit, and we are soon into the third region (5.51–2), which, as its name – Colline – suggests, is introduced with a claim about its 'colles', five of them to be precise, two of which are said to be well known ('nobiles'). Unsurprisingly, these turn out to be the Viminal, named, according to Varro, not after its willow trees but after the altar to Jupiter Viminius, and the Quirinal, both of which were 'colles' in the epigraphic record. He concludes: the names of the adjoining regions – the Collis Salutaris, Collis Mucialis and Collis Latiarus – have since been forgotten.

---

[60]   Livy 1.21.5 attributes the foundation of these shrines to Romulus.
[61]   Varro, *Ling.* 7.44; Ov. *Fast.* 3.791 and 5.621; and Dion. Hal. *Ant. Rom.* 1.38.3. See Holland 1961, Nagy 1985, Coarelli 1993, Graf 2000 with bibliography, and C. J. Smith 2006: 356–62.
[62]   Although, as scholars have been keen to point out, Varro goes on to give only twenty-four.
[63]   For the Carinae, see Terrenato 1992, Rodríguez-Almeida 1993, Tomei 1994 and Palombi 1997.

Region four finally gets us to the Palatine (5.53–4) and to the etymology of it, the Cermalus, and the infamous Velia.[64] None of these is qualified as either a 'mons' or a 'collis', but Varro's claim that the last two were joined to the Palatine does give seven summits, allowing the canon to emerge, albeit subtly, without any of the special pleading about their number or their designation as 'montes' that the etymology of Septimontium might stipulate. Before we can take stock, we are into the names of the tribes, and places pertaining to mortals and gods. Although several of the hills reappear, the Septimontium and the seven montes do not re-emerge until book 6 and Varro's discussion of Rome's festivals (6.24). He writes, 'Septimontium Day took its name from these "septem montes", on which the city was situated; it is a holiday not of the people as a whole, but of the *montani* only, in the same way as there is the Paganalia for those who are members of some *pagus*.'[65] This only causes further problems as far as the traditional canon is concerned. When other ancient sources refer to 'montani', they link them to the Palatine, Oppian, Cermalus and Velia, only one of which belongs to these seven.[66]

Whether confused or ingenious, Varro is straining to tie the word 'Septimontium', and the communities it embraced, to the canon of the Servian city as we have come to know it. This sense of strain is compounded by testimony in the work of Sextus Pompeius Festus, 'a dictionary of a kind, with an abundance of etymologics and grammatical explanations'.[67] It derived mainly from the *De verborum significatu* (*On the Meaning of Words*) written by Augustan grammarian Marcus Verrius Flaccus, who was himself indebted to Varro.[68] In the relevant section, Festus' authorities are explicitly stated as Varro and Augustan lawyer Marcus Antistius Labeo:

Septimontio, ut ait Antistius Labeo, hisce montibus feriae: Palatio, cui sacrificium quod fit, Palatuar dicitur; Veliae, cui item sacrificium; Fagu<t>ali, Suburae, Cermalo, Oppio, Caelio monti, Cispio monti. Oppius autem appellatus est, ut ait Varro Rerum humanarum lib. VIII., ab Opitre Oppio Tusculano, qui cum praesidio Tusculanorum missus ad Romam tuendam...

On the Septimontium, as Antistius Labeo says, there is a festival for these 'montes': for the Palatine, the sacrifice offered to which is called Palatuar; for the Velia, to which there is a similar sacrifice; for the Fagutal, for the Subura, for the Cermalus, for the Oppian, for Mons Caelius, for Mons Cispius. Yet the Oppian was called, as

---

[64] The location of the Cermalus is not uncontroversial: see Coarelli 1993.

[65] Varro, *Ling.* 6.24: 'Dies Septimontium nominatus ab his septem montibus, in quis sita Urbs est; feriae non populi, sed montanorum modo, ut Paganalibus, qui sunt alicuius pagi.'

[66] Wissowa 1904 and *CIL* VI 32455.   [67] Glinister *et al.* 2007: 1.

[68] Glinister *et al.* 2007 and Lhommé 2007.

Varro says in book 8 of his *Antiquitates*, after the Tusculan Opiter Oppius, who was sent with a garrison of Tusculans to support Rome . . . [69]

Here the Septimontium is a festival for the listed 'montes', the names of which correspond to those of the *montani* above and not to the hills of the Servian city. There are also eight of them; an idiosyncrasy which an epitome of Festus' text made by Carolingian cleric Paul the Deacon, in the eighth century, makes more glaring by repeating the same list and, in the same sentence, saying that they add up to seven:

Septimontium appellabant diem festum, quod in septem locis faciebant sacrificium: Palatio, Velia, Fagutali[a], Subura, Cermalo, Caelio, Oppio et Cispio.

They called the festival day the Septimontium because they performed a sacrifice in seven locations: on the Palatine, Velia, Fagutal, Subura, Cermalus, Caelian, Oppian and Cispian.[70]

Scholars, including Carandini, have been quick to dispense with one of these 'hills',[71] but is this not to give Varro too much credit? Who is to say that Festus (or Verrius) is not responding to Varro,[72] struggling, as we still struggle, with Varro's 'Septimontium equals seven hills equals Rome' equation; that Varro is not so much the *inventor* of the seven-hills concept as the first to confuse it with the archaic festival? Think like this, and the rituals associated with the Septimontium can originally and unproblematically have embraced eight places, and these not necessarily 'hills' but communities of a different kind (recently, for example, Michel Tarpin has argued that the opposition in antiquity between 'montes' and another division, 'pagi', did not rest on the relative elevation of the land but on its relationship to the *pomerium*).[73] 'Mons' versus 'pagus' as opposed to 'mons' versus 'valles' (valley) makes for a different entity.

Varro deserves credit for rather different reasons – not for what he tells us about early Rome but for how he tells it. Even if Rome had long been

---

[69]   474.36F.

[70]   459.1P. Note also a further highly fragmentary, heavily restored section of Festus (458.1F): 'Septimontium ———— ap>pellatur mense <Decembri . . . post eum, qui dicitur in> Fastis Agonalia <quod eo die in septem m>ontibus fiunt sa<crificia: Palatio, Velia, F>agutali, Subura, <Cermalo, Caelio, Oppio.,> et Cispio' (note that the edition by Müller suppresses the Caelian). See Lhommé 2007: 44.

[71]   The Subura: Wissowa 1904, De Sanctis 1907, Poucet 1960, J. P. Poe 1978, Erkell 1981 and 1985 and response by Fridh 1987: 123 and 1990. Caelian: Wissowa 1904, Lugli 1943, Pallotino 1960 and J. P. Poe 1978. Fagutal: Fridh 1987 and Carandini 1997.

[72]   Note too Gelsomino's suggestion (1975: 30) that Antistius Labeo might represent a 'timely polemic against Varro'. That said, Labeo's work on pontifical law might also draw on priestly records which predate Varro.

[73]   Tarpin 2002: 187 with bibliography. Also Fraschetti 1996.

a city of seven hills, it is Varro, writing in the final throes of the Republic, who turns this from a fact into something far more resonant, making it worthy of questioning and imbuing it with a sense of religiosity that is nigh on antediluvian. Using the shrines of the Argei to enable his reader to walk the ancient landscape with him, he establishes the Septimontium as an official growth stage of Rome, and its *montes* and those of the modern city as equivalents. The impact of this is considerable, responsible ultimately for Plutarch's claim that the festival commemorated the addition of the seventh hill to the city. Indeed it makes sense to think that Domitian's festival, which involved all of the people, divided by rank, rather than just the *montani*, built on Virgil and his successors' celebration of the canon.[74] It is also responsible for considerable confusion. In the fourth century CE, for example, the grammarian Servius wrote a commentary on the *Aeneid*, glossing its reference to the seven hills as follows:[75]

bene urbem Romam dicit septem inclusisse montes. et medium tenuit: nam grandis est inde dubitatio. et alii dicunt breves septem colliculos a Romulo inclusos, qui tamen aliis nominibus appellabantur. alii volunt hos ipsos, qui nunc sunt, a Romulo inclusos, id est Palatinum, Quirinalem, Aventinum, Caelium, Viminalem, Esquilinum, Ianicularem. alii vero volunt hos quidem fuisse, aliis tamen nominibus appellatos: quae mutata sunt postea, ut de multis locis et fluminibus legimus, ut (VIII 329) *saepius et nomen posuit Saturnia tellus*.

[Virgil] says rightly that Rome embraced seven hills. And he holds a middle course: for after that there is great uncertainty. Some say that seven small hills were enclosed by Romulus, which nevertheless were called by other names. Others wish it that these very hills which are here today, were enclosed by Romulus: i.e. the Palatine, Quirinal, Aventine, Caelian, Viminal, Esquiline, Janiculum. Yet others venture that these were indeed the hills, but called by other names, and these names were changed later, as we read is the case for many places and rivers, as (VIII 329) 'the Saturnian land often changed its name'.

It is a point of contention which is still live today, and one which makes Virgil's text all the more momentous: how old are these hills? Are they, and the Rome they represent, the same, or different from how they were in the beginning? As scholars search for answers, the modern and archaic city, even the proto-city, are brought together, and the early settlement on the Palatine, Esquiline and Caelian made commensurate with the Servian city. Varro's influence now, in the Renaissance, and in the early Roman Empire,

---

[74] Coarelli 1999.
[75] Serv. *ad Aen.* 6.783. Also John Lydus, writing in the sixth century CE (*De mens.* 4.155), mentions two lists with some strange alternative names making an appearance.

should not be underestimated.[76] Post Varro, it is not simply that Rome is a seven-hilled city, but that Rome cannot be Rome without them.

'Before the mountains were settled'[77]

See! Under his auspices, my son, that famous Rome will make her empire equal to the earth's ends and her ambitions to Olympus, and she will surround for herself seven hills with a wall.[78]

Anchises' prophecy to Aeneas in book 6 of Virgil's *Aeneid* represents the realization of Rome. Under Romulus the city will assume its familiar shape by encircling seven 'arces' within a single set of fortifications: seven hills, one unified capital. A few lines later and the new Romulus, Augustus, will appear, who will 'extend his empire beyond even the Garamantes and Indians'.[79] But though Rome will be re-founded, the implication is that the city will not change. This Rome is his, and his Rome, our final destination. With the circle complete, Anchises goes back in time to Romulus' immediate successors, pointing out the early kings, Numa, Tullus Hostilius, Ancus Marcius, and the Tarquins, then key figures of Republican history, ending up with Marcellus the elder and Augustus' tragic heir of the same name. Only then, once the trajectory has been traced, does Virgil move in book 8 to colour in the detail, first in a tour of Rome with Evander, then in the images on the famous shield. We will return to these passages in more detail in Chapters 4 and 6, but the tour makes similar moves to those made by Varro to relate past and present: so Evander points out 'the Carmental Gate, as the Romans call it, ancient honour of the Nymph Carmentis . . . he shows too the wood of holy Argiletum, and . . . tells of the death of his guest, Argus'.[80] Again, Rome's intrinsic value lies not in its land, but in its geography.

---

[76] For Varro's influence on the poets discussed in Chapter 4, see O'Hara 1996: 48–9; Bartelink 1965: 19–25; and the entries under 'Varrone' in the *Enciclopedia virgiliana* (Virgil). For his influence on Tibullus, see Cairns 1979: 90–9; and on Ovid, see Ahl 1985: 22–31; Porte 1985; and Baier 1997. For Varro as 'originator of the formula *ubi nunc Roma est . . .* (where Rome now is . . .) to introduce a comparison of Rome past and present', see Fox 1996: 237–8.

[77] Proverbs 8.25.

[78] Virg. *Aen.* 6.781–3:

> en huius, nate, auspiciis illa incluta Roma
> imperium terris, animos aequabit Olympo,
> septemque una sibi muro circumdabit arces.

[79] Virg. *Aen.* 6.794–5.

[80] Virg. *Aen.* 8.337–9 and 345–6.

If the city of Rome has to have seven hills, then it makes sense that its getting there, whether by expansion or synoecism, should be measured in hills – hence Carandini's desire to see a Trimontium and Quinquimontium prior to the Septimontium. And indeed archaeological excavations leave no doubt that there was human habitation on the Palatine and elsewhere in Rome in the Bronze Age. But archaeology and geography, and habitation and urbanism, are different things. For Virgil, the city of Rome is conceived and gets its DNA under Romulus. Only then, when Rome, a single city, enclosed the seven hills with one wall was it 'most beautiful of all things'.[81]

Attributing Rome's seven hills and wall to Romulus is more unusual than we might imagine. As we have already seen, it is more often Servius Tullius who is credited, while Pliny implicates his own imperial patrons: 'Romulus left the city possessing three, or – to accept the highest figure passed down to us – four, gates. When the Vespasiani were emperors and censors in 73 CE, the city walls comprised in circumference an area of 13 miles and 200 yards and embraced seven hills.'[82] Romulus' Rome was a square peg in a round hole. So Dionysius of Halicarnassus:

ἐπεὶ δὲ πᾶν, ὅσον ἦν ἐκ λογισμοῦ θεοῖς φίλον, ᾤετο πεπρᾶχθαι καλέσας ἅπαντας εἰς τὸν ἀποδειχθέντα τόπον περιγράφει τετράγωνον σχῆμα τῷ λόφῳ, βοὸς ἄρρενος ἅμα θηλείᾳ ζευχθέντος ὑπ᾽ ἄροτρον ἑλκύσας αὔλακα διηνεκῆ τὴν μέλλουσαν ὑποδέξεσθαι τὸ τεῖχος· ἐξ οὗ Ῥωμαίοις τὸ ἔθος τοῦτο τῆς περιαρόσεως τῶν χωρίων ἐν οἰκισμοῖς πόλεων παραμένει.

When he [Romulus] thought everything had been done which according to reasoning would be dear to the gods, he called everyone to the appointed place and drew a square-shaped figure around the hill [the Palatine], tracing with a plough drawn by a bull and a cow yoked together an unbroken furrow intended to admit the wall; and from that time this custom of ploughing a furrow around sites for the foundation of cities persists among Romans.[83]

The dimensions of Romulus' new city – his 'Roma Quadrata' as it came to be called – are open to question: according to Tacitus, it stretched from the two ends of the Circus Maximus (the Ara Maxima and the Altar of Consus) to the eastern fringes of the Palatine, and on the other side, to the Shrine

---

[81] Virg. *G.* 2.534–5:

> scilicet et rerum facta est pulcherrima Roma,
> septemque una sibi muro circumdedit arces.

[82] Plin. *HN* 3.66–7: 'urbem III portas habentem Romulus reliquit, ut plurimas tradentibus credamus, IV. moenia eius collegere ambitu imperatoribus censoribusque Vespasianis anno conditae DCCCXXVI m. p. XIII·CC, complexa montes septem.'

[83] Dion. Hal. *Ant. Rom.* 1.88.2.

of the Lares.[84] But regardless of its remit, the presence of the furrow, or *pomerium*, makes it an *urbs*, and one which establishes the rules for future city building.[85] Such is its paradigmatic status that a highly fragmentary papyrus from Oxyrhynchus, commonly dated to the second century CE, associates it with, if not also attributes it to, the later king, Servius Tullius.[86]

Servius Tullius gives Rome the formal definition that one would expect of a self-conscious community.[87] He divides the city 'according to its inhabited regions and "colles" into four parts',[88] holds a census[89] and extends the urban perimeter so as to 'increase the state by the magnitude of the city'.[90] He is as much a proto-Augustus as he is a latter-day Romulus. 'It was obvious', explains Livy, 'that the city also had to be extended for this population. He added two hills, the Quirinal and Viminal; after this he then enlarged the Esquiline and lived there himself so that dignity might be conferred on the place. He surrounded the city with a rampart, trenches and a wall and in this way extended the *pomerium*.'[91] We have already noted how Dionysius tells a similar story: 'after Tullius had surrounded the seven hills with one wall, he divided the city into four regions'.[92] Before this, he too explains the process:

τῇ τε πόλει προσέθηκε δύο λόφους, τόν τε Οὐιμινάλιον καλούμενον καὶ τὸ Ἰσκυλῖνον, ὧν ἑκάτερος ἀξιολόγου πόλεως ἔχει μέγεθος, καὶ διένειμεν αὐτοὺς τοῖς ἀνεστίοις Ῥωμαίων οἰκίας κατασκευάσασθαι· ἔνθα καὶ αὐτὸς ἐποιήσατο τὴν οἴκησιν ἐν τῷ κρατίστῳ τῆς Ἰσκυλίας τόπῳ. οὗτος ὁ βασιλεὺς τελευταῖος ηὔξησε τὸν περίβολον τῆς πόλεως τοὺς δύο τοῖς πέντε προσθεὶς λόφοις, ὀρνιθευσάμενός τε ὡς νόμος ἦν καὶ τἆλλα τὰ πρὸς θεοὺς ὅσια διαπραξάμενος. προσωτέρω δ᾽ οὐκέτι προῆλθεν ἡ καρασκευὴ τῆς πόλεως, οὐκ ἐῶντος, ὥς φασι, τοῦ δαιμονίου.

He also added two hills to the city, the one called the Viminal and the Esquiline, each of which has the size of a noteworthy city, and he apportioned them to the homeless among the Romans for them to build houses. And he himself also made his home there on the most superior part of the Esquiline. This king was the last to increase the city's perimeter, by adding these two hills to the other five, after he had taken the auspices as law dictated and performed the other holy rites for the gods.

---

[84] Tac. *Ann.* 12.24.

[85] Fraschetti 2005: 35–8; Castagnoli 1951; Grandazzi 1993; Mastrocinque 1993; and Zawadzka 2002.

[86] *P. Oxy.* 17.2088.14ff. See Grandazzi 1993 and 1997: 206–8 and, for a new reconstruction and reading of the text, Ammannati 2011.

[87] Cornell 1995: 202–4.   [88] Livy 1.43.13.   [89] Livy 1.43.13–44.1.

[90] Livy 1.45.1: 'aucta civitate magnitudine urbis'.

[91] Livy 1.44.3–4: 'ad eam multitudinem urbs quoque amplificanda visa est. addit duos colles, Quirinalem Viminalemque; inde deinceps auget Esquilias, ibique ipse, ut loco dignitas fieret, habitat. aggere et fossis et muro circumdat urbem; ita pomerium profert.'

[92] See above, Chapter 2, n. 8.

Construction of the city has still not gone any further, since the gods, or so they say, have not allowed it.[93]

Once Rome reaches the grand total of seven hills, its urban footprint is fixed for ever.

Comparison of Livy and Dionysius exemplifies how the gestation period is not easy to reconstruct: 'in this respect, the ambition and glory of the kings is variously reported'.[94] From the moment that Romulus fortifies the Palatine,[95] Livy has the city grow, reaching out with its defences to include more and more territory 'with an eye to the size of population they hoped to have in the future rather than the number of people there actually were'.[96] Dionysius explicitly states that soon Romulus secured the hills adjacent to the Palatine – the Aventine and Capitoline – for fear of attack, only to lose the latter to the Sabines under leader Titus Tatius. After their reconciliation, both men then enlarged the city by adding the Quirinal and Caelian to it, Romulus occupying the Palatine and Caelian, and Titus Tatius occupying the Capitoline and Quirinal.[97] After Tatius died, his son-in-law, and Romulus' eventual successor, Numa, 'increased the city's circuit with the Quirinal hill (for up until that time, it was still without a wall)', having a house there and at the foot of the Palatine.[98]

Later on in his text, Dionysius prefers to credit Numa's successor, Tullus Hostilius, with including the Caelian within the city and building a palace there, and his successor, Ancus Marcius, with enclosing the Aventine.[99] The former is a sentiment that finds sympathy in Livy, but with few other authors.[100] Varro is quoted as saying that Tullus had lived on the Velia;[101]

---

[93] Dion. Hal. *Ant. Rom.* 4.13.2–14.13.3.

[94] Tac. *Ann.* 12.24: 'regum in eo ambitio vel gloria varie vulgata'.   [95] Livy 1.7.3.

[96] Livy 1.8.4: 'crescebat interim urbs munitionibus alia atque alia adpetendo loca, cum in spem magis futurae multitudinis quam ad id quod tum hominum erat munirent'.

[97] Dion. Hal. *Ant. Rom.* 2.37.1 and 2.50.1–2: Οἱ δὲ περὶ τὸν Ῥωμύλον καὶ Τάτιον τήν τε πόλιν εὐθὺς ἐποίουν μείζονα προσθέντες ἑτέρους αὐτῇ δύο λόφους . . . Also, Tac. *Ann.* 12.14: 'forumque et Capitolium non a Romulo, sed a Tito Tatio additum urbi credidere' ('both the forum and Capitoline were believed to have been added to the city not by Romulus but by Titus Tatius').

[98] Dion. Hal. *Ant. Rom.* 2.62.5: καὶ τῆς πόλεως τὸν περίβολον αὐξήσας τῷ Κυρινίῳ λόφῳ (τέως γὰρ ἔτι ἀτείχιστος ἦν) . . . and Plut. *Num.* 14.1.

[99] Dion. Hal. *Ant. Rom.* 3.1.5: ἵνα δὲ μηδὲ οἰκίας ἄμοιρος εἴη τις προσετείχισε τῇ πόλει τὸν καλούμενον Καίλιον λόφον, ἔνθα ὅσοι Ῥωμαίων ἦσαν ἀνέστιοι λαχόντες τοῦ χωρίου τὸ ἀρκοῦν κατεσκευάσαντ' οἰκίας, καὶ αὐτὸς ἐν τούτῳ τῷ τόπῳ τὴν οἴκησιν εἶχεν and Dion. Hal. *Ant. Rom.* 3.43.1.

[100] Livy 1.30: 'duplicatur civium numerus; Caelius additur urbi mons, et quo frequentius habitaretur, eam sedem Tullus regiae capit ibique deinde habitavit.' Also Aur. Vict. *De vir. ill.* 4.4.

[101] As cited in Nonius 531 and Solinus I.22.

and Strabo and Cicero, that it was rather Ancus Marcius who embraced the Caelian, together with the Aventine, turning it from fortified enclosure to part of the city proper.[102] Strabo writes:

Ancus Marcius took in the Caelian hill and the Aventine hill and the plain between them, which were separate from both one another and from the regions that were already walled, adding them out of necessity. For neither was it a good idea to leave such naturally fortified hills outside the walls for those seeking to build enemy strongholds, nor did he have the power to complete the whole circle as far as the Quirinal. But Servius recognized the defect and plugged it by adding both the Esquiline Hill and the Viminal.[103]

'Defect', 'omission' or 'failing' (ἔκλειψις) is a strong word which implies that Rome was incomplete before Servius; that despite the 'additions' of the others, only he knew what was missing. The seven hills gave these writers a formula for calculating the contribution of Rome's early kings by means of creative retrospection.

This process of retrospection injects the Rome of Ancus Marcius, Tullus Hostilius, Numa and Romulus with an authenticity worth arguing over. It turns their world into a valuable, understandable space: 'Roman' racing 'Roman', then, and again now – in writing – under Augustus, to put the building blocks in place to create the capital.[104] Other visual markers of Rome's distant past, such as Romulus' competing huts on the Palatine and Capitoline, claimed to be his alone. They often had to be rebuilt, taking them further and further from their inception.[105] In contrast, the hills add real weight to Rome's history, enabling its kings not only to make their mark, but to speak to each other. They are neither 'museum pieces' nor tawdry reconstructions. In fact, they are not about the then and the now, but about the links in between, the duration. They are also about the before:

---

[102] Cic. *Rep.* 2.18: 'atque idem Aventinam et Caelium montem adiuxit urbi'. For the early history and topography of the Caelian, see Colini 1944. Also note Tac. *Ann.* 4.64, who is undecided whether the man responsible for receiving the district as a settlement is not in fact Tarquinius Priscus or another king, and *CIL* XIII 1668, which links Caeles Vibenna, after whom the hill is supposedly named (Varro, *Ling.* 5.46), with Servius Tullius rather than Romulus.

[103] Strabo 5.3.7: Ἄγκος δὲ Μάρκιος προσλαβὼν τὸ Καίλιον ὄρος καὶ τὸ Ἀβεντῖνον ὄρος καὶ τὸ μεταξὺ τούτων πεδίον, διῃρημένα καὶ ἀπ' ἀλλήλων καὶ ἀπὸ τῶν προτετειχισμένων, προσέθηκεν ἀναγκαίως· οὔτε γὰρ οὕτως ἐρυμνοὺς λόφους ἔξω τείχους ἐᾶσαι τοῖς βουλομένοις ἐπιτειχίσματα καλῶς εἶχεν, οὔθ' ὅλον ἐκπληρῶσαι τὸν κύκλον ἴσχυσε τὸν μέχρι τοῦ Κουρίνου. ἤλεγξε δὲ Σέρουιος τὴν ἔκλειψιν, ἀνεπλήρωσε γὰρ προσθεὶς τόν τε Ἠσκυλῖνον λόφον καὶ τὸν Ὀυιμίναλιν.

[104] Intriguing here is Pais 1898: especially 375–408, which sees the seven kings as entirely mythical, personifications no less of the seven hills and the religious rites associated with them. See review by A. S. Wilkins 1898 and the article by Cassola 2002.

[105] See Balland 1984 and Edwards 1996: 31–43.

about the Capitoline's Saturnian past and the Palatine's colonization by the Arcadian king Evander. Dionysius describes Evander's colony as follows, 'And the Arcadians, as Themis, inspired by the gods, kept telling them, chose a hill, not far from the Tiber, which is now very much in the centre of the city of Rome.'[106] There was need for a finite group of hills to pull disparate decisions, communities and legends together, and to make the *arx* the only citadel. After Varro, 'adding' a hill could never again be read as a random act. It becomes a crucial cog in urban development. Once the city is made whole, seven endures to give Rome an exportable image no matter how great its future expansion.

In this way, the Romans are given a reason for being, a place they can call their own, with a profile that they can foster and bring to maturity. Only a few paragraphs after praising Servius Tullius' completion of the city in a passage which in full gives the names of all seven of the canonical summits, Strabo turns to its ongoing Augustan adornment. After enumerating the wonders of the Campus Martius and the risk that they might make the rest of Rome seem secondary,[107] he pauses: 'But, there again, if someone, going on to the old Forum, saw one forum after another parallel to it, and basilicas and temples, and saw also the Capitoline and the works of art there and those on the Palatine and at the Portico of Livia, he would easily forget the things outside. Such is Rome.'[108] The two centres, one old, with the Palatine and Capitoline at its core, and the other new, vie with each other for attention. If Augustan Rome is to be an improved Rome rather than a different, Hellenistic-styled city, and the Princeps, a new Servius Tullius, a new Romulus, then the Campus Martius cannot win. In this battle, the seven hills will prove fundamental. This chapter has established them as Rome's contents. It is now time to see how poets interpret them.

---

[106] Dion. Hal. *Ant. Rom.* 1.31.3: οἱ δὲ Ἀρκάδες, ὡς ἡ Θέμις αὐτοῖς ἐπιθειάζουσα ἔφραζεν, αἱροῦνται λόφον ὀλίγον ἀπέχοντα τοῦ Τεβέριος, ὅς ἐστι νῦν ἐν μέσῳ μάλιστα τῆς Ῥωμαίων πόλεως.

[107] See above, Chapter 1, n. 23.

[108] Strabo 5.3.8: πάλιν δ' εἴ τις εἰς τὴν ἀγορὰν παρελθὼν τὴν ἀρχαίαν ἄλλην ἐξ ἄλλης ἴδοι παραβεβλημένην ταύτῃ καὶ βασιλικὰς στοὰς καὶ ναούς, ἴδοι δὲ καὶ τὸ Καπιτώλιον καὶ τὰ ἐνταῦθα ἔργα καὶ τὰ ἐν τῷ Παλατίῳ καὶ τῷ τῆς Λιβίας περιπάτῳ, ῥᾳδίως ἐκλάθοιτ' ἂν τῶν ἔξωθεν. τοιαύτη μὲν ἡ Ῥώμη.

4 | Rome, *la città eterna*

> It is through the opportunity they offer to shore up rich silences and
> wordless stories, or rather through their capacity to create cellars and
> garrets everywhere, that local legends (*legenda*: what is *to be read*, but
> also what *can be read*) permit exits, ways of going out and coming back,
> and thus habitable spaces.
>
> Michel de Certeau, 'Walking in the City',
> from *The Practice of Everyday Life* (1984: 106)

Hills attract foundation myths. Local legends create dimensions which allow
worlds and experiences of the world to collide. They energize environments,
making locations extraordinary, and creating more permanent sanctuaries
than anything built from bricks and mortar. From these 'cellars and garrets' the present is made mysterious, and the past accessible, with door-
ways for encountering heroes, kings and milkmaids. Daily lives are left
behind and imagined landscapes navigated. In the process, places develop
personalities – they become not just 'habitable' but lived in.

Unsurprisingly, work done on Rome's local legends has privileged the
Palatine and Capitoline. Jennifer Rea writes, 'Vergil, Tibullus and Propertius all explore in detail the moral and political significance of both the
Palatine and Capitoline hills. The poets confirm the sites' primacy as a
religious and political focal point for the city during the development of
Rome's early origins.'[1] But the primacy of these sites, not to mention their
competition with each other (after Augustus, they both boasted a hut of
Romulus),[2] threatens the cohesion cemented by the fourteen regions, and
the reorganization that comes with it. The *urbs* risks seeming smaller, if more
glorious, than even its Servian self, at the same time as it must incorporate
a larger territory.

Authors who have privileged the Capitoline as a 'metonymy of Rome
itself' or seen it standing for 'the city by synecdoche'[3] run similar risks
to Rea. Not that this hill was not always symbolically head and shoulders
above the rest, but because the city had a body, the skeleton of which

---

[1] Rea 2007: 136.   [2] See above, p. 79.   [3] Edwards 1996: 87 and Jaeger 1998: 7.

had the other six hills as its vertebrae. And because, as Vitruvius implies, from any one citadel one could see most of a city's defences, but not the entire circumference.[4] Only Jupiter could see that.[5] Calling the Capitoline a 'metonymy' assumes that we know what Rome is. So too with 'synecdoche', a figure of speech which works by substituting a part for the whole. The seven hills are metonymous in a different sense, lending the city a shape which brings its various regions together as a unit, enabling it to be more than the sum of its parts, giving it an edge. By the end of the first century CE 'the seven hills' were being established as a figure of speech which allowed Rome to remain true to itself. Julius Caesar's plans to increase the city ('de urbe augenda') had met with criticism: Cicero carped to Atticus that Caesar thought Rome too small, when Rome's only problem was containing his ego.[6] In contrast, cultivation of the hills meant that Augustus could tidy and titivate, as opposed to increase, the city without either of them seeming bloated.

The present chapter studies this cultivation in detail. As we are about to discover, the authors who magnified the prestige of the Palatine and Capitoline were also the ones who celebrated the city's seven-hilled status and used these hills to offer a controlled environment for the many spaces afforded by Rome's local legends. Too many 'cellars and garrets', and ways in and out, and a navigable city becomes a labyrinth. The hills did more than create a restricted canvas on which, and from which, Rome could be written and read; they created a means of making it a special kind of city. Countless cities had citadels with impressive temples: when Livy's Lucius Aemilius Paullus first encounters Athens, the Acropolis is the first 'must see' he mentions (and the only one mentioned twice), while in 'renowned' Corinth, it is 'the *arx,* rising to a huge height within the city walls' that excites him.[7] At the sanctuary of Olympia he encounters a scene which reminds him of home: 'and there too he saw other things which seemed to him worth seeing; gazing at Jupiter as though the god were present, he was

---

[4] Vitr. 1.7.1: 'aedibus vero sacris, quorum deorum maxime in tutela civitas videtur esse, et Iovi et Iunoni et Minervae, in excelsissimo loco unde moenium maxima pars conspiciatur, areae distribuantur' ('Indeed for the temples of the gods, under whose protection the city most seems to be, for those of both Jupiter, Juno and Minerva, land is to be allotted on the highest spot from which the greatest extent of wall may be seen').

[5] Luc. 1.195–6: 'o magnae qui moenia prospicis urbis | Tarpeia de rupe, tonans...' ('O Jupiter the Thunderer, you, who look out over the walls of the great city from the Tarpeian Rock...').

[6] Cic. *Att.* 13.20, 13.33a and 13.35–6: 'gentilis tuus urbem auget, quam hoc biennio primum vidit, et ei parum magna visa est, quae etiam ipsum carpere potuerit.'

[7] Livy 45.27.11 and 45.28.2: 'arx intra moenia in immanem altitudinem edita...'

moved to the core. And so, just as if he had been about to offer a sacrifice on the Capitoline, he ordered a sacrifice to be made that was larger than usual.[8] What is the difference between these historic Greek places and the capital of the Roman Empire? Is not one citadel, sanctuary, wonder of the world, pretty much like another? Without due acknowledgement of not one but *seven* hills, Rome loses international supremacy.

The seven hills and the ambitions of Empire

This, all this that you see, stranger, where greatest Rome is, before Phrygian Aeneas, was a hill and grass.[9]

When Aeneas meets his father, Anchises, in the Elysian Fields in book 6 of the *Aeneid*, as well as his many descendants who will secure the spectacle that is Rome's future, he is first shown the settlements that they will build, prior to Rome, in Latium. Already Rome's reputation and hills dictate the narrative: 'for you, these men will establish Nomentum and Gabii and the city of Fidenae; these, will place Collatia's citadels on mountains'.[10] Whatever the status of these places in the past, by the time that Virgil is writing and Augustus is building, they are nigh on deserted,[11] 'then, little cities, now but villages, or else holdings of private citizens', writes Strabo.[12] Yet in this context, their destiny is to be proto-*urbes*, which prepare the ground for the main event. We are already familiar with Anchises' image of Rome, but it is worth quoting the passage in full. Only at this point in their meeting does he address Aeneas as 'son', as the founding of Rome converges with his move from Trojan to Roman hero:

---

[8] Livy 45.28.5: 'ubi et alia quidem spectanda ei visa; Iovem velut praesentem intuens motus animo est. Itaque haud secus, quam si in Capitolio immolaturus esset, sacrificium amplius solito apparari iussit.'

[9] Prop. 4.1.1–2:

> hoc quodcumque vides, hospes, qua maxima Roma est,
> ante Phrygem Aenean collis et herba fuit,

[10] Virg. *Aen.* 6.773–4:

> hi tibi Nomentum et Gabios urbemque Fidenam,
> hi Collatinas imponent montibus arces.

[11] Sen. *Ep.* 104.1; Mart. 6.43, 10.44.3 and 12.57.1 (Nomentum); Hor. *Ep.* 1.11.7–8; Cic. *Planc.* 23; Juv. 6.56–7, 10.100; Prop. 4.1.34 and Dion. Hal. *Ant. Rom.* 4.53 (Gabii); and Plin. *HN* 3.68–70 (Collatia and Fidenae). See Gossage 1955: 72–4 and Feeney 1986: 7.

[12] Strabo 5.3.2: τότε μὲν πολίχνια, νῦν δὲ κῶμαι, ἢ κτήσεις ἰδιωτῶν...

en huius, nate, auspiciis illa incluta Roma
imperium terris, animos aequabit Olympo,
septemque una sibi muro circumdabit arces,
felix prole virum: qualis Berecyntia mater
invehitur curru Phrygias turrita per urbes   785
laeta deum partu, centum complexa nepotes,
omnis caelicolas, omnis supera alta tententis.

See! Under his auspices, my son, that famous Rome will make her empire equal to the
earth's ends and her ambitions to Olympus, and she will surround for herself seven
hills with a wall, fortunate in her brood of heroes. Just like this, the Berecynthian
mother rides in her chariot through Phrygian towns, her turreted crown on her head,
delighted by her divine offspring, embracing a hundred grandsons, all dwelling in
heaven, all tenants of the heavenly heights.[13]

Rome will be world-famous, once it has enclosed seven 'arces' within one
wall, extended its Empire to the ends of the earth and its ambition to
the skies. These three actions are synonymous: seven hills – one unified,
successful city. The word order of 'septemque' next to 'una' highlights how
Rome will be one and seven. Like the Christian Trinity, the formulation is
a paradox or, rather, one which holds the paradox of divisible indivisibility
intact. It acknowledges that the city is composed of different elements
(perhaps too that these were once separate defences), the amalgamation
of which brings unparalleled potency; except that the goddess Roma is
somehow still distinct from the city she personifies, embracing its hills
like the Berecynthian mother, Cybele, embraces her divine grandchildren.
Cybele was the Phrygian deity whose cult was officially brought to Rome
in 205–204 BCE and installed in a temple on the Palatine.[14] The Phrygians
and Trojans had long been amalgamated.[15] Her presence underscores how
Rome and Troy are assimilated.

Cybele was primarily a fertility goddess, who demanded castration as a
mark of devotion. But she had also long been worshipped as 'Μήτηρ ὀρεία',
or 'Goddess of Mountains',[16] and she wore the turret-crown, according to
Ovid, because she had given the first cities their 'turres' or defences.[17] In

---

[13] Virg. *Aen.* 6.781–7.   [14] Vermaseren 1977: 38–43.   [15] See E. Hall 1988.
[16] See Eur. *Hipp.* 144, *Hel.* 1301; Schol. in Ar. *Birds* 876, and Kall. fr. 761.1 (Pfeiffer). For
secondary discussion: Gasparro 1985: 84–6.
[17] Ov. *Fast.* 4.219–21:

    'at cur turrifera caput est onerata corona?
     An primis turres urbibus illa dedit?'
    annuit.

Figure 4.1 The goddess Roma as depicted in the Palazzo dei Congressi, EUR, Rome. See also colour plate section.

this sense, she was a model for Roma, gracing the city's coinage in the Republic already in her guise as city protectress.[18] Like her, Roma was peripatetic, her origins reaching back to fifth-century Greek authors who had had her wander the earth with Aeneas (Figure 4.1). By the Hellenistic period she was a fully-fledged personification in the East, and by the second century BCE a deity, who stood not so much for the city of Rome as for the Empire. Worshipped in conjunction with Augustus, she extended her influence west, though not to Rome itself.[19] She was not accorded cult there until the Hadrianic period;[20] not that this prevented the city's poets from celebrating her: 'Roma, goddess of lands and peoples, to whom nothing is equal and nothing even comes close', wrote Martial at the end of the first century CE.[21] When in late antiquity she was paired with the Tyche

[18] See e.g. *BMCRR* Rome 1581 (bust of Cybele in turreted crown, obverse), 2605 (head of Cybele in turreted crown, obverse) and 3179 (in *biga*, with turreted crown, reverse).
[19] Toynbee 1934, Vermeule 1959, Mellor 1981 and Erskine 1995 and, on personifications more broadly, Hughes 2005 and Stafford and Herrin 2005.
[20] The biggest temple in Rome, and supposedly designed by Hadrian himself, the Temple of Venus and Roma on the Velia was vowed in 121 CE, but not finished until later. See Cass. Dio 69.4 and the SHA, *Hadr.* 19.13, Ridley 1989 and Lorenzatti 1990.
[21] Mart. 12.8.1–2:

> terrarum dea gentiumque Roma,
> cui par est nihil et nihil secundum.

of Constantinople, she maintained the upper hand in their Empire-wide remit.[22]

This capaciousness, coquettishness even, called for a restraining order. Ronald Mellor argues, 'Roma had from the first been for "foreigners": Greeks and distant provincials.'[23] She was in danger of belonging to them over and above her own city. She needed to be famous for something other than ubiquity and to embody a capital as well as an empire. Renewed commitment was particularly pressing under the emperors. It was not only that this capital was expanding and incorporating the alien,[24] but that the Empire was expanding, gobbling up Northern Europe, North Africa and Syria as it had done Phrygia and the rest of Asia Minor and Greece. For the city of Rome to remain the progenitor in the face of provincial 'clones', it needed a rooted figurehead. Virgil affects this by having Roma adopt the seven hills, thereby initiating a relationship which later poets will foster in ever more inventive ways. We have already seen Ovid imagine her 'surveying the whole world from the seven hills'.[25] Elsewhere in his exile poetry, he sends his poems to 'gaze on Rome'[26] and plead his case, going first to Caesar's Forum, then along the Sacred Way past the Temple of Vesta and so on, to the House of Augustus on the Palatine and then down to the Theatre of Marcellus: his desire to see the city himself is like that of the elegiac lover for his mistress, fetishizing and fragmenting her.[27] The seven hills bring him back down to earth and the city's topography back together. Unlike his wandering Odysseus, his home is not 'places from which it is no great punishment to be absent', but Rome.[28] There are places and places. From Virgil onwards, the seven hills make Rome more important than other cities, one which controls the Empire and rivals Olympus.[29]

Once Rome has been sketched in this way, Virgil's Aeneas has an arena in which to witness his Romans. Immediately after the image of Cybele, he is directed to look:

huc geminas nunc flecte acies, hanc aspice gentem
Romanosque tuos. hic Caesar et omnis Iuli
progenies magnum caeli ventura sub axem.   790
hic vir, hic est, tibi quem promitti saepius audis,

---

[22] Standard on Roma and Constantinopolis is still Toynbee 1947. On Tyche more generally, see *LIMC* 8.1: 115–40 and Matheson 1994.

[23] Mellor 1981: 1028.   [24] See above, p. 67.

[25] See above, p. 66.   [26] Ov. *Tr.* 1.1.57: 'aspice Romam'.

[27] Ov. *Tr.* 3.1 and the discussion by Edwards 1996: 116–25.

[28] Ov. *Tr.* 1.5.68: 'poena quibus non est grandis abesse locis'.   [29] Virg. *Aen.* 6.781–2.

Augustus Caesar, divi genus, aurea condet
saecula qui rursus Latio regnata per arva
Saturno quondam . . .

Now, turn both eyes this way, and look at this people, your Romans. Here is Caesar and the whole dynasty of Julus which will come under heaven's great axis. This man, this is he whom you so often hear promised you, Augustus Caesar, son of a god, who will again found a golden age in Latium through fields once ruled by Saturn . . .[30]

All roads lead 'huc', 'to this place'. It is a forceful little word with which to start the line, especially when followed closely by 'hanc gentem' ('this people'), 'Romanosque tuos' ('your Romans'), 'hic Caesar' ('here is Caesar'), 'hic vir, hic est' ('this man, this is he'). From his vantage point, on a 'tumulus', mound or proto-hill, which affords the kind of command we shall be exploring in Chapter 6,[31] Aeneas is suddenly bombarded with figures from Virgil's Rome, golden Rome that is being re-founded by Augustus. As the Caesars crowd in, there can be no doubt that we have arrived. The present and the divergent strands of the mythical past are reconciled on this seven-hilled stage set.

Virgil's *Aeneid* was not published until after Virgil's death in Brundisium in 19 BCE but had been known in Maecenas' circle prior to this, influencing the elegies of Tibullus and Propertius as well as Horace's choral hymn, the *Carmen saeculare*, performed on the Palatine and then again on the Capitoline during the Secular Games of 17 BCE.[32] Commissioned by Augustus in honour of his new regime, the hymn is, despite its performance history, explicitly for 'the gods who take pleasure in the *seven* hills': as Richard Thomas notes, 'the seven hills come in the seventh line of a poem highly aware of numbers'.[33] And it is for the son of a god, whose moral legislation is celebrated. Horace is the first extant author to refer to Rome's hills as 'colles', as distinct from Varro's 'montes' and Virgil's 'arces', downplaying as he does so the defensiveness of Virgil's walled city in favour of a more idyllic opening, more attuned with the first line's reference to Diana, ruler of the woods.[34] In the poem's third stanza, the Sun god is imagined looking down from his chariot, 'unable to see anything greater than the city of Rome'.[35] Virgil's underworld vision is now a reality.

---

[30] Virg. *Aen.* 6.788–94.   [31] Virg. *Aen.* 6.754.

[32] For Virgil's influence on Propertius, book 3, see Cairns 2003, and on 4.1, Buchheit 1965 and Fantham 1997, who also discusses Varro and Livy.

[33] Hor. *Carm. saec.* 7. R. F. Thomas 2011: 64.

[34] See Putnam 2001: esp. 56–8. For a succinct summary of the festival of the Secular Games, see Ross Taylor 1934 or R. F. Thomas 2011: 53–60. Much of their information is derived from a fragmentary inscription from near Tarentum: see Sherk 1988: no. 11 = *CIL* VI 32323.

[35] Hor. *Carm. saec.* 11–12: 'possis nihil urbe Roma | visere maius!'

In Ovid's *Fasti,* composed some two decades later, between 2 and 17 CE (Augustus dying in 14, and Tiberius succeeding him), Evander's mother, the nymph Carmentis, whom we have already met in connection with the Carmental Gate, prophesies about Rome's future in lines which bring its 'colles' and the story of its foundation together.

fallor, an hi fient ingentia moenia colles,
    iuraque ab hac terra cetera terra petet?
montibus his olim totus promittitur orbis:
    quis tantum fati credat habere locum?

Am I deceived, or will these hills become huge city-walls,
And will the rest of the earth take its laws from this land?
One day the whole world is promised to these mountains.
Who would believe that a place has such an allocation of good fortune?[36]

In this image the 'colles' become walls in a blink of an eye, and from there, 'montes'. And it is these *montes* that give Rome the clarity to govern the universe. Though seven is not mentioned, it is hard not to hear it. Tibullus' Sibyl had chivvied the cows that grazed on the ancient Palatine – 'eat now, bulls, while you can, the grass of the seven *montes.* Here already is the site of what will be a great city.'[37] And Propertius had described Rome prior to Aeneas' arrival as just one hill, a single 'collis', and the Capitoline as 'bare rock'.[38] Contrary to Varro, Rome had not always benefited from having the power of seven summits at its disposal. Or if it had, they had only been cultivated to stand up and be counted when it had become a city with world ambition.

This ambition was Augustus' to fulfil and would ensure peace and prosperity as long as he remained in power. Propertius, this time in book 3 of his elegies, wrote:

septem urbs alta iugis, toti quae praesidet orbi,

. . .

haec di condiderant, haec di quoque moenia servant:
    vix timeat salvo Caesare Roma Iovem.

---

[36] Ov. *Fast.* 1.515–18.
[37] Tib. 2.5.55–6:

> carpite nunc tauri de septem montibus herbas
> dum licet hic magnae iam locus urbis erit.

[38] Prop. 4.1.1–2 and 4.1.7: 'de nuda rupe'. On the importance of Tib. 2.5 for Prop. 4.1, see La Penna 1951, Solmsen 1961 and Hutchinson 2006: 60. And on reading the 'then' and 'now' in 4.1, Fox 1996: 143–54; Fantham 1997; DeBrohun 2003: 86–117; and T. Welch 2005: 19–34.

The city, high on seven hills, which presides over the whole world . . . These walls the gods had founded, and these the gods also protect: with Caesar safe and well, let Rome scarcely fear Jupiter.[39]

Earlier in the poem Propertius described Cleopatra as having designs on Rome's walls and its senators (line 32), forcing the Tiber to endure the threats of the Nile (42), and seeking to ensnare the Capitoline in Egyptian nets (45). In the heat of the poet's outrage, Rome is atomized; broken down into discrete units. The Capitoline is referred to by one of its summits, the 'Tarpeian Rock',[40] and Cleopatra imagined sitting in judgement 'amidst the statues and arms of Marius'.[41] It is a place which has a violent history, named after the Vestal Virgin Tarpeia, who had been crushed to death for her betrayal; the place where criminals convicted of capital crimes were still executed in similar fashion.[42] Even the spoils and statues of Gaius Marius are contentious, having been pulled down by Sulla and reinstated by Julius Caesar, who had also slept with Cleopatra at the height of civil unrest in Rome. Historian Velleius Paterculus, who was born around the time when Propertius was publishing his poem, writes, 'Then Gaius Marius entered within the city walls in a return ruinous to its citizens.'[43]

Only after Cleopatra's death has been remembered and Augustus' victorious return celebrated (49–56), in other words, once Rome is secure, do the seven hills make their appearance. They are testimony to its integrity. Unlike monuments, which can fall into ruin, be dashed to the ground or removed, or individual *arces* which can be stormed, they endure together, *are* Rome, whatever happens to it. 'The city, high (*alta*) on seven hills (*iugis*)': the adjective 'altus' is from 'alere' meaning 'to nourish' or 'support'; it is as though the city is sustained by its hills. 'Iugis' are 'ridges', 'collars' or 'yokes' and bind the city together. As it presides over the whole world, strengthened by these, rather than by flimsy nets, it has the power to subjugate others.

---

[39] Prop. 3.11.57–9. Propertius' text has been described as 'one of the worst transmitted of the classical Latin authors; any edition must therefore be seen as provisional, a contribution to a continuing debate' (Heyworth 2007b: vii). Line 57 is particularly problematic: see the discussion by Heyworth 2007a: 341–2 and Sandbach (1962: 264), who suggests 'stat non humana deicienda manu'. Throughout this chapter, I use Heyworth's OCT edition.

[40] Prop. 3.11.45: 'foedaque Tarpeio conopia tendere saxo'.

[41] Prop. 3.11.46: 'iura dare statuas inter et arma Mari'.

[42] See Aul. Gell. 20.1.53, Sen. *Controv.* 1.3.6, Livy 6.20.12, Festus 458L, Tacitus, *Ann.* 6.19 and Aur. Vict. *De vir. ill.* 24.6 and 66.8.

[43] Vell. Pat. 2.22.1: 'mox C. Marius pestifero civibus suis reditu intravit moenia.'

The poem is both an elaborate exploration of the effects of civil war and an apology against the charge that Propertius is subservient to his mistress, Cynthia (3–4).[44]

criminaque ignavi capitis mihi turpia fingis,
   quod nequeam fracto rumpere vincla iugo?

And do you make up shameful charges of cowardice against me because I am unable to break the yoke and snap my chains?

The story of Cleopatra's seduction of Antony provides Propertius with the ultimate defence: even Rome was nearly made subordinate to a woman, as were the bulls of Colchis by Medea (9–10, where we find the related phrase, 'sub iuga', meaning 'under the yoke'). In bringing his own fate into alignment with Rome's narrow escape, Propertius does as Virgil does and personifies the city. Are he and Rome alike or not? In the end, it is Rome who does the yoking, with Augustus in the driving seat.

Everywhere these poets looked, the city of Rome was changing – so much so that scholars such as Elaine Fantham have read, if not resentment, then at least 'nostalgic distaste',[45] into Propertius' view of the construction site around him: 'The poet has let his image of Rome be dominated by groves and grottoes and waters that outbid the glitter and luxury of the new Augustan city.'[46] Rome had reached its potential with the Principate but, for all of Horace's Arcadian sentiment, it risked obscuring old Rome for ever. 'See what the Capitol now is', sighs Ovid, 'and what it used to be, and you would say that they belonged to a different Jupiter'; 'what was the Palatine which now glitters under Apollo and our leaders, if not pasture land for oxen who were about to plough?'[47] But read on to Propertius 4.4, back to the primitive Rome of Tarpeia, when 'the *montes* served as its wall',[48] and our protagonist expresses her betrayal as follows: 'Goodbye, hills of Rome and Rome that was added to these hills, and goodbye Vesta who

---

[44] On the shame of civil war, see Gurval 1995: 189–208 and on the connection between history and the morality of different kinds of love, Fox 1996: 161–5.

[45] Fantham 1997: 134.   [46] Fantham 1997.

[47] Ov. *Ars am.* 3.115–6:

> aspice quae nunc sunt Capitolia, quaeque fuerunt:
>   alterius dices illa fuisse Iovis

and 119–20:

> quae nunc sub Phoebo ducibusque Palatia fulgent,
>   quid nisi araturis pascua bubus erant?

See the commentary by Gibson 2003.

[48] Prop. 4.4.13: 'murus erant montes'. Useful on this poem is O'Neill 1995.

must be ashamed of my scandalous behaviour.'[49] Whereas the Capitoline is described as 'thorn-covered' or 'obscured' ('*spinosus*'),[50] the hills, plural, are even then linked to the idea of martial fortifications as they are in the *Aeneid*'s and *Fasti*'s visions of the future. The implication is that they are not primitive, but primordial. They are already Rome, with a cumulative weight to offset the remodelling of individual hills and their building. They defy a link to specific events and people that make single summits monuments.

It is unsurprising that under Tiberius we hear of proposals to rename the Caelian Hill, 'Mons Augustus', after a fire there, the reason being, according to Tacitus, that the only thing to remain unscathed had been one of his portraits.[51] The authority of the hills threatened to overshadow the authority of the emperor. There was a tension between the hills as the centre of Rome's power and the emperor's desire to leave his mark on them or remove them. Their altitude provided 'a rule against which men (for this is a distinctively masculine obsession) would measure the stature of humanity, the reach of empire'.[52] So Suetonius cites Caligula's decision to build a bridge to join the Palatine and Capitoline as one of the acts that defined him as a monster.[53] All hills had long been shaped by human intervention, with both of these heavily terraced and built onto. But tying two of the seven together was too much, akin to putting his head on the statue of Olympian Zeus, turning the Temple of Castor and Pollux into his vestibule and inviting the Moon to sleep with him.[54] It was hubristic, just as Nero's palace was hubristic in uniting the Palatine and Esquiline.[55] 'Rome will become a house; migrate to Veii, citizens, if that house does not also occupy Veii', went one lampoon.[56] Nero's house transgressed even the city limits.

The classic case of this kind of extravagance is provided by Alexander the Great and Mount Athos in the Chalcidic Peninsula of north-eastern Greece. Well known in Rome, this story tells of the monarch's rejection of

---

[49] Prop. 4.4.35–6:

> Romani montes, et montibus addita Roma,
> et valeat probro Vesta pudenda meo:

[50] Prop. 4.4.48. See R. King 1990 and Rothwell 1996: 839, who are keen to dismiss Propertius' topography in this poem as a fiction.

[51] Tac. *Ann.* 4.64 and Suet. *Tib.* 48.   [52] Schama 1995: 396.

[53] Suet. *Cal.* 22.4.   [54] Suet. *Cal.* 22.

[55] Also relevant here are the unrealized plans (1810–11) by architect and hydraulic engineer, Scipione Perosini, for a huge imperial palace for Napoleon, centred on the Capitoline and stretching across the Forum: 'Projet d'un palais impériale à Rome', Archives Nationales de Paris, N/III/Rome/10. See Nicassio 2005: 31–2 and Watkin 2009: 182–3.

[56] Elsner 1994 and Suet. *Ner.* 39.2:

> Roma domus fiet; Veios migrate, Quirites,
> si non et Veios occupat ista domus.

Figure 4.2 Fischer von Erlach, *Entwurff einer historischen Architectur*, 1725.

a scheme to shape the mountain in human form (in some versions, that of Alexander himself), holding a city in one hand, and a bowl to catch its rivers in the other. The reasons given for Alexander's coyness differ, but the story's central tenet is unchanging: that the plans are not realized. Plutarch, at the end of the first century CE, has its architect explain himself:

'Well-carved and configured, it can be called an image of Alexander and that's what it will be. The sea will reach its base and in its left hand it will embrace and bear the weight of a city of ten thousand inhabitants, while with its right, it will pour an eternal stream from a libation bowl into the sea. But let's throw away gold and bronze and ivory and wood and gilding, cheap imitations that can be bought, stolen or melted down.' Alexander listened to these words, wondered at the architect's spirit and courage, and said 'thanks, but no thanks!' 'Let Athos stay as it is. It is enough for it to be a memorial to one hubristic king.'[57]

---

[57] Plut. *Mor. (On the Fortune of Alexander)* 335D–E: ʻδύναται κατεργασθεὶς καὶ σχηματισθεὶς εἰκὼν Ἀλεξάνδρου καλεῖσθαι καὶ εἶναι, ταῖς μὲν βάσεσιν ἁπτομένου τῆς θαλάσσης, τῶν δὲ χειρῶν τῇ μὲν ἐναγκαλιζομένου καὶ φέροντος πόλιν ἐνοικουμένην μυρίανδρον, τῇ δὲ δεξιᾷ ποταμὸν ἀέναον ἐκ φιάλης σπένδοντος εἰς τὴν θάλασσαν ἐκχεόμενον. χρυσὸν δὲ καὶ χαλκὸν

Figure 4.3 Pierre-Henri de Valenciennes, 1750–1819, *Mount Athos Carved as a Monument to Alexander the Great*, 1796. See also colour plate section.

The hubristic king is Xerxes of Persia, whose decisions to cut a canal through the isthmus of the Athos peninsula and to bridge the Hellespont had become synonymous with tyranny (so much so that, in the paragraph prior to his bridging of Palatine and Capitoline, Caligula is said by Suetonius to have bridged the gap between Baiae and Puteoli – some said, 'in emulation of Xerxes').[58] With the Persian monarch in the frame, Plutarch's description of the plan's abortion serves as an object lesson in the proper limits of imperial ambition, underlining how urban development can swamp a city, making it an appendage of something greater – the grand designs of man. If this happens, the landscape is cut from the land to become not geography but art history. Realizations of Athos by later artists Johann Bernhard Fischer von Erlach and Pierre-Henri de Valenciennes (Figures 4.2 and 4.3) capture this nicely, their two-dimensionality able to dare what Alexander's architect could only imagine.[59] In the former, the hill

καὶ ἐλέφαντα καὶ ξύλα καὶ βαφάς, ἐκμαγεῖα μικρὰ καὶ ὠνητὰ καὶ κλεπτόμενα καὶ συγχεόμενα, καταβάλωμεν.' ταῦτ' ἀκούσας Ἀλέξανδρος τὸ μὲν φρόνημα τοῦ τεχνίτου καὶ τὸ θάρσος ἀγασθεὶς ἐπήνεσεν, 'ἔα δὲ κατὰ χώραν' ἔφη 'τὸν Ἄθω μένειν. ἀρκεῖ γὰρ ἑνὸς βασιλέως ἐνυβρίσαντος εἶναι μνημεῖον. Also relevant here are Plut. *Alex.* 72.4; Strabo 14.1.23; and Vitr. 2 *praef*. 2. While Plutarch calls this architect Stasicrates, in Strabo he is Cheirocrates, and in Vitruvius, Deinocrates. Important is the ambiguity about the identity of the sculpted mountain, with Vitruvius saying only, 'statuae virilis figura'. See McEwan 2003: 127–9, and for the development of the myth, Oechslin 1982 and della Dora 2005 and 2008.

58 Suet. *Cal.* 19.
59 Fischer von Erlach (1712) *Entwurff einer historischen Architectur*, plate 18, and Pierre-Henri de Valenciennes, French, 1750–1819, *Mount Athos Carved as a Monument to Alexander the Great*, 1796, oil on canvas, 16 1/2 x 36 in. (41.9 x 91.4 cm), Restricted gift of Mrs Harold T. Martin, 1983.36, The Art Institute of Chicago.

is home to a Harryhausen-style colossus, who stares out at the viewer as he toys with the city – not unlike Ustinov's Nero with the model of his new Rome.[60] The second paints a more harmonious marriage between nature and artifice.[61] But again the mountain is Buddha-esque, belittling of any cult statue.

Augustus quickly realized what he could and could not do to the authority of Rome's hills. His adornment of the city might have risked seeming superficial, the icing on the cake – or excessive. But instead, the investment of his poets ensured that it made the cake whole, writing the Princeps' name on the landscape in ways which tempered his impact. It was not about self-aggrandizement or about extending Rome's boundaries out into Latium. It was about raising the city to its full heights, making it an extreme version of itself. This was imperial Rome and the landscape that later rulers and writers had to work with,[62] Rome, eternal city: Ovid is confident, 'and as long as Martian Rome gazes out, victorious, at the whole conquered world from its (seven) hills, I shall be read'.[63] He has good cause: by the end of the century, Juvenal teases: 'Don't worry, one won't ever lack pathic friends, while these hills stand firm.'[64]

---

[60] Mervyn LeRoy's film, *Quo Vadis* (1951).   [61] Della Dora 2005: 510–12.

[62] Perhaps the most daring statement of imperial intervention is Trajan's Column, the inscription of which claims that the 'Senate and people [dedicate this column] to the emperor Caesar, son of the deified Nerva, Nerva Trajan, Augustus, Germanicus, Dacicus, Pontifex Maximus, with tribunicial power for the seventeenth time, commander in chief for the sixth time, father of his country, in order to declare how deep were the mound (or how high the *mons*) and space excavated by these mighty works'. *CIL* VI 960:

> SENATVS POPVLVSQVE ROMANVS
> IMP CAESARI DIVI NERVAE F NERVAE
> TRAIANO AVG GERM DACICO PONTIF
> MAXIMO TRIB POT XVII IMP VI COS VI P P
> AD DECLARANDVM QVANTAE ALTITVDINIS
> MONS ET LOCVS TANT[is oper]IBVS SIT EGESTVS.

Packer 1997: vol. I, 117–18 and 447–8, with bibliography. A recent alternative restoration of the last line reads, 'mons et locus tan[tis viribus sit egestus'.

[63] Ov. *Tr.* 3.7.51–2:

> dumque suis victrix omnem de montibus orbem
>   prospiciet domitum Martia Roma, legar.

Note, however, how in the Holkham manuscript, 'omnem' is rendered 'septem'.

[64] Juv. 9.130–1:

> ne trepida, numquam pathicus tibi derit amicus
> stantibus et salvis his collibus . . .

Dizzy heights under the Flavians

Let the hills be joyful together.[65]

From then until the abdication of the last western Roman emperor in 476 CE, the seven hills worked like armour to protect the city. When, in the second half of the first century CE, Silius Italicus wrote his epic poem on the second Punic war, the hills were not only the city's core but its shield. As the Carthaginian general, Hannibal, urges his troops to attack Rome's walls, and Rome's women act as though these walls have already been breached, panic ensues and the Romans advance beyond their gates to meet the enemy outside. Seeing the city's vulnerability, Jupiter intervenes:

caelicolis raptim excitis, defendere tecta
Dardana et in septem discurrere iusserat arces.

Quick as a flash, he had summoned the gods and ordered them to defend the Dardan city and to disperse among the seven hills.[66]

Positioned on the Tarpeian Rock, Jupiter orders his fellow Olympians to make for the other summits. From there, they produce a storm so fierce that the city is hidden from view and they are forced to retreat – but only temporarily, until Juno is forced to speak to him. 'Come (for I will briefly remove the cloud from your eyes and allow you to see everything), look at where the apex of the hill, which was called the Palatine by the Arcadian king, rises high into the air – Apollo holds it with a full, rattling quiver and he bends his bow and thinks about battle.'[67] After this she shows him Diana on the Aventine which 'lifts itself above the neighbouring hills',[68] Mars on the Campus Martius, and Janus and Quirinus, 'each god preparing for war on his own hill'.[69] It is a vision that intensifies the investment shown

---

[65] Psalms 98.8.   [66] Sil. *Pun.* 12.605–8.
[67] Sil. *Pun.* 12.707–11:

> en, age (namque, oculis amota nube parumper,
> cernere cuncta dabo) surgit qua celsus ad auras,
> aspice, montis apex, vocitata Palatia regi
> Parrhasio, plena tenet et resonante pharetra
> intenditque arcum et pugnas meditatur Apollo.

[68] Sil. *Pun.* 12.712: 'qua vicinis tollit se collibus...'
[69] Sil. *Pun.* 12.719–20:

> hinc Ianus movet arma, movet inde Quirinus,
> quisque suo de colle deus...

by Horace's deities in the city's 'colles', ramping it up to an epic scale, with fighting not on the plains, as at Troy, but on high. It is too much even for Hannibal, who sees sense, for the moment at least, and leaves. The Romans go to the Capitol, then purify their walls and return to the city.[70]

The latter part of this chapter will determine to what extent this image of the hills endures the decentring and sacking of Rome in late antiquity. But to what extent is it fixed at the start of the first century already, or at the end? What happens to it once Augustus is dead and buried? Silius Italicus, Martial and Statius pepper their poetry with references to the hills but with each reiteration, the cliché shifts slightly. We have already noted how different poets use different signifiers, but even within Statius, the hills are sometimes 'septem montes' or 'septem iuga', sometimes, 'Romulean arces' or 'Ilian citadels of the Tiber', and sometimes, 'septina culmina' (seven-part prominences) or 'septemgeminum iugum' (a seven-part ridge), while Rome itself is also described as 'septemgeminus',[71] an adjective which Catullus and Virgil had used of the seven-mouthed Nile.[72] Are these conceits, and the cities they conjure, similar? Do they extend the remit of the 'seven hills' in challenging, new directions?

By the time that Martial, Statius and Silius are writing, Rome is no longer a budding imperial capital to vie with Alexandria, but an unrivalled cosmopolis.[73] Emperors had come and gone over the course of a century, all of them keen to make their mark on its canvas. Their emperor, Domitian (emperor from 81 to 96 CE), was no exception: he restored the Temple of Jupiter Capitolinus after the structure rebuilt by Vespasian in 69 CE burned down,[74] and he constructed an exceptional palace on the Palatine, which put even the pyramids to shame.[75] Martial praises it accordingly, 'the sun sees nothing more magnificent in the whole world. You would think the *septenos*

---

[70] Sil. *Pun.* 12.741–3 and 752.

[71] *Silv.* 4.1.6–7, 1.2.191, 1.5.23, 2.7.45, 1.2.144–5 and 4.4.4–5. Also pertinent here is 1.1.63–5 where in manuscript M, for 'Martis', we have 'montis':

> ... strepit ardua pulsa
> machina; continuus septem per culmina Martis
> it fragor et magnae vincit vaga murmura Romae.

[72] Virg. *Aen.* 6.800.

[73] On Martial as topographical source for this cosmopolitan city, see Rodríguez-Almeida 2003.

[74] For Vespasian, see e.g. Tac. *Hist.* 4.4, 9, 53; Suet. *Vesp.* 8; and Cass. Dio 65.7.10; and for Domitian, Suet. *Dom.* 5; Plut. *Pub.* 15; and Eutr. 7.23. The latter gilded the bronze roof tiles and commissioned a chryselephantine cult statue to rival that of Zeus at Olympia.

[75] Martial (8.36.1) invites the emperor to laugh at the pyramids. On Statius' version of Domitian's palace (4.2), see Newlands 2002: 260–83.

montes were rising up together. [Mount] Ossa with Thessalian Pelion on top was less tall.'[76]

This heightened sensitivity is not unique to Martial. Whereas the concept of the seven hills had given the innovative Augustus a familiar city to inhabit, this concept was now in long-standing service to the emperor, and the emperor was a god, whose house rivalled the hills for prominence (even if extending upwards was always less controversial than Caesar and Nero's perceived crime of extending Rome outwards):

atque oritur cum sole novo, cum grandibus astris,
clarius ipse nitens et primo maior Eoo.
exsultent leges Latiae, gaudete, curules,
et septemgemino iactantior aethera pulset
Roma iugo, plusque ante alias Evandrius arces
collis ovet.

And he rises with the new sun and with the abundant stars, he himself shining more brightly than them, greater than first light. Let Latium's laws rejoice; be delighted, magistrates, and let Rome knock more proudly on heaven's door with her seven hills; and above the other citadels, let Evander's hill celebrate.[77]

Here Roma is doing more than embrace the hills, she is using them actively, boastfully even ('iactantior'), to strike the heavens in acclamation of her emperor. In so doing, the gods do not make for them, as they did in Silius. The mountains go to Mohemet; they threaten Olympus. The Palatine in particular is asked to rejoice, presumably because of its new palace as well as its occupant. But this premium is unable to shake the solidarity of the seven. Rome needs all of them, not just the Palatine or Capitoline, to qualify as the 'head of empire' ('Who would have founded the walls of seven-hilled Rome, the Latin head of Empire, if the Dardan [Rhea Silvia] had not secretly slept with Mars?', asks Statius in an earlier poem, the adjective used for Rome, 'septemgemina', laying claim to the Nile's special charm, just as real Rome was still commandeering Egypt's obelisks and its gods, Isis and Sarapis).[78]

---

[76] Mart. 8.36.4–6:
> clarius in toto nil videt orbe dies.
> septenos pariter credas adsurgere montes,
> Thessalicum breuior Pelion Ossa tulit.

Interesting on the phrase 'septenos montes' is Schöffel 2002: 332–3.

[77] Stat. *Silv.* 4.1.3–8. See Coleman 1988.

[78] Stat. *Silv.* 1.2.191–3:
> quis septemgeminae posuisset moenia Romae
> imperii Latiale caput, <ni> Dardana furto
> cepisset Martem . . .

The seven hills are no longer just a metaphor. They have become a grand gesture.

For Martial, the seven hills had become 'dominos montis'.[79] This is more than is implied by Propertius' play with the idea of the yoke, or 'iugum'. Although 'dominus' is a common term in Latin, used for the master of slaves or, in its feminine form ('domina'), for the elegiac poet's mistress, it was also a title conferred on Domitian, and one which Augustus and Tiberius had famously refused.[80] It was controversial, and this controversy was regularly exploited by Martial and Statius. To give Rome's hills this accolade at the current time was to dispute openly who the master was.

Martial's vantage point in this epigram – the Janiculum – is something to which we will return in Chapter 6. From here, the 'dominos montis' must mean the Servian city across the Tiber. So too perhaps in Statius, *Silvae* 1.1, where the noise produced in constructing Domitian's equestrian statue in the Forum sends shock waves through 'Mars' seven hills', noise which 'drowns out the vague murmurs of *great* Rome'.[81] But in other poems, the implication is that it is all of the urban sprawl that is referenced: as when a road built by Domitian 'moves the home of Euboea's Sibyl and the folds of Mount Gaurus and bubbling Baiae towards the seven hills'.[82] The allusion to Cumae's famous Sibyl takes the reader back to *Aeneid* 6 and further back to Tarquinius Priscus, who was widely reputed to have bought three books of oracles from her. It ensures that whichever Rome is meant, it is less a familiar place (as Augustan Rome had to be) than a legendary city.

This cementing of the seven hills' concept and the status that it confers on Rome as a renowned and invincible capital contribute to its longevity. Once the hills applaud, as well as delineate, imperial investment in the city, their appeal increases, not only for Claudian and his panegyric of the emperor Honorius, but for Sixtus V and Mussolini. There was nothing random about Martial's and Statius' timing: they were not writing in a vacuum, but responding to initiatives by an emperor who was himself holding Secular Games and celebrating the Septimontium.[83] With Nero's demise in 68 CE

---

[79] Mart. 4.64.11.

[80] Compare Suet. *Aug.* 73, *Tib.* 26–7 and *Dom.* 13. For more on Domitian's appropriation of the term and its exploitation by Martial and Statius, see Thompson 1984 and Vout 2007a: 197.

[81] Stat. *Silv.* 1.1.64–5:

> . . . continuus septem per culmina Martis
> it fragor et magnae vincit vaga murmura Romae.

[82] Stat. *Silv.* 4.3.24–6:

> gaudens Euboicae domum Sibyllae
> Gauranosque sinus et aestuantes
> septem montibus admovere Baias.

[83] See above, Chapter 3.

came the end of the Julio-Claudian dynasty and a year of civil war, after which Domitian and his predecessors, Titus and Vespasian, had to stress Rome's re-foundation: 'the city is restored to itself'.[84] The hills were a crucial part of this as they had been for Augustus: 'with me you shall found a second Age',[85] says Statius' Janus in the poem in which Rome knocks at the sky. They reasserted Rome's shape after its Neronian flattening. Coins were minted under Vespasian which showed Roma seated on seven summits – a rare visual representation to which we shall return in the next chapter – as well as, in the same year, coins with 'Roma resurge(n)s' (the emperor raising kneeling Roma to her feet) and the emperor receiving the palladion from Victory.[86] Such adaptations made Rome more self-conscious of its summits and set the city at the dizzy heights of global supremacy.

The seven hills are also the dizzy heights of poetic aspiration. Statius addresses their divine inhabitants:

vos mihi, quae Latium septenaque culmina, Nymphae,
incolitis Thybrimque novis attollitis undis,
quas praeceps Anien atque exceptura natatus   25
Virgo iuvat Marsasque nives et frigora ducens
Marcia, praecelsis quarum vaga molibus unda
crescit et innumero pendens transmittitur arcu,
vestrum opus aggredimur, vestra est quam carmine molli
pando, domus.   30

But you, Nymphs, who live in Latium and on the seven summits and make the Tiber higher with fresh water; you whom the Anio, flowing downhill, and the Aqua Virgo, destined to accept swimmers, and the Aqua Marcia that brings the cold and the snow, pleases; you whose travelling flow grows stronger on towering masses and is transmitted, suspended, on countless arches – we set about your work; yours is the home which I broadcast with my soft song.[87]

Statius' subject here is the baths of Claudius Etruscus, which are supplied by Rome's aqueducts, in particular the Aqua Virgo, built by Agrippa, and the famous Aqua Marcia, which was originally constructed in the second century BCE but restored in the Augustan period.[88] Their presence in the text reminds us how crucial they were for the inhabitation of the hills,

---

[84] Mart. *Spect.* 2.12: 'reddita Roma sibi est'.
[85] Stat. *Silv.* 4.1.37–8:

> ... mecum altera saecula condes,
> et tibi longaevi renovabitur ara Tarenti.

[86] RIC II², 67, nos. 109–10, 73, nos. 194–5 and 68, no. 131. On the idea of 'Roma resurgens' and 'renascens', see Levick 1999: 66.
[87] Stat. *Silv.* 1.5.23–30.   [88] See Evans 1997: 105–9 and 83–93.

which are here called 'culmina', as though the cupolas of a temple. But their inhabitants are neither gods nor emperors but nymphs, which Statius is cultivating over the Muses. The poem opens: 'my divinely inspired lyre does not strike Helicon with heavy quill', as the hills had knocked ('pulset' again) on heaven's door, 'nor am I invoking the Muses, the powers that have so often been made tired by me'.[89] Archaic Greek poet Hesiod had made the 'great and holy mountain' of Helicon the fount of poetic inspiration and had described how mother earth 'had given birth to great mountains, charming dwellings of the goddesses, the Nymphs, who live on wooded mountains'.[90] His Hellenistic successor Callimachus, who had notoriously rejected epic style to become a major influence on Rome's poets, had conversed with the Muses in a dream on Mount Helicon.[91] Yet, whatever the complexities of Statius' authorial positioning, work on his own epic, the *Thebaid,* is suspended as he conjures instead an 'urban version of a *locus amoenus*'.[92] The problems of writing epic, writing Rome, and writing the emperor, are left behind: the nymphs of the seven hills stimulate a softer song in praise of delicate pleasures.

This is not the only time that Statius uses the hills to speak about his poetry. In 2.7, written to commemorate the birthday of the dead poet Lucan, he again implicates them in well-known stories of poetic inspiration and power. Lucan's epic poem on the civil war between Caesar and Pompey was highly influential on Statius' *Thebaid.* But he is also famed for being forced into suicide by Nero.[93] Statius has Calliope, Muse of Epic Poetry, compare the future of baby Lucan to that of the mythical poet, Orpheus:

[89] Stat. *Silv.* 1.5.1–2:

> non Helicona gravi pulsat chelys enthea plectro
> nec lassata voce totiens mihi numina Musas.

[90] Hes. *Theog.* 2: ὄρος μέγα τε ζάθεόν τε and *Theog.* 129–31:

> γείνατο δ' οὔρεα μακρά, θεᾶν χαρίεντας ἐναύλους
> Νυμφέων, αἳ ναίουσιν ἀν' οὔρεα βησσήεντα.

[91] See Callim. *Aet.* 2 (*The Dream*). See Hunter 2006.

[92] Newlands 2002: 211. Also of interest here is Prop. 4.1.65–8:

> scandentis quisquis cernit de vallibus arces,
>   ingenio muros aestimet ille meo!
> Roma, fave, tibi surgit opus, date candida cives
>   omina, et inceptis dextera cantet avis!

'Whoever sees the citadels rising from the valleys, may he value those walls by my genius. Rome, be well disposed towards me – my work soars for you. Citizens, give me fair omens and let a lucky bird sing for the works I have started.'

    This passage follows Propertius' claim to be a Roman Callimachus and is thought by most scholars (e.g. Fantham 1997: 129; Hutchinson 2006, ad loc.) to refer to the *arces* and *muros* of his home town of Assisi. Given Cic. *Agr.* 2.96 and *Rep.* 2.6.11, we are not far from Rome (Sandbach 1962: 272). Maybe one has to see this potential to get the poet's true measure.

[93] Tac. *Ann.* 15.70. See Ahl 1971.

tum primum posito remissa luctu
longos Orpheos exuit dolores 40
et dixit: 'puer o dicate Musis,
longaevos cito transiture vates,
non tu flumina nec greges ferarum
nec plectro Geticas movebis ornos,
sed septem iuga Martiumque Thybrim 45
et doctos equites et eloquente
cantu purpureum trahes senatum.'

Then recovering for the first time, she set her mourning aside, cast off her lengthy sadness for Orpheus and spoke: 'Boy, dedicated to the Muses, who will soon outdo the bards of old, you will not move rivers or herds of wild animals or Thracian Ash with your quill, but you will draw the seven hills and Martian Tiber and learned *equites* and the purple clad senate with your eloquent singing.'[94]

Just as Orpheus' song can entice rivers, trees and beasts to follow him (rocks too in Ovid's version),[95] so Lucan will move the seven hills of Rome and the River Tiber. Everything invites the reader to measure Statius' skill against this comparison. In the opening lines of the poem he asks those who have drunk from the spring on the 'colles' of Isthmian Dione (the fountain of Peirene behind the Temple of Aphrodite at Corinth, a place whose nymphs were linked by the Romans to poetic inspiration)[96] to join him in celebrating Lucan, and he incites the learned rivers to wander more widely, and the Aonian woods, where Mount Helicon was, to flourish.[97] He too wants to play at being Orpheus. Will he suffer, as Orpheus did, if he fails to honour his patron? And if so, will he still be able to sing, or will he be silenced?[98] We can be fairly optimistic. We have already seen him animating Rome's seven hills in a later poem in praise of Domitian.

---

[94] *Silv.* 2.7.39–47.
[95] Ov. *Met.* 11.1–2:

> carmine dum tali silvas animosque ferarum
> Threicius vates et saxa sequentia ducit.

[96] See Stat. *Silv.* 1.4.27 and Buxton 2009: 198–9.
[97] Stat. *Silv.* 2.7.1–4:

> Lucani proprium diem frequentet
> quisquis collibus Isthmiae Diones
> doctor pectora concitatus oestro
> pendentis bibit ungulae liquorem.

2.7.12–13:

> docti largius evagentur amnes,
> et plus, Aoniae, virete, silvae.

[98] As Statius reminds his readers (*Silv.* 2.7.99), Orpheus' head continues to sing after his death: see Lovatt 2007: 153.

'Roman poets were fond of the idea of an enclosed, often sacral, space, usually away from the city, which served as an image of poetry and its inspiration.'[99] The seven hills fulfil this function, but less away from the city, than above it, closer to the realm of the gods – making their summits a welcome retreat from urban living and throwing its exigencies into relief. This is still the case today. We have already witnessed Edward Gibbon and Samuel Palmer being knowing about the stimulation they found there. French author Jean-Louis Guez de Balzac, writing from Rome to his colleague in the Académie française, sums up these sentiments very nicely:

Certainly I never go up to the Palatine hill or the Capitol without my spirit being refreshed and without thinking thoughts very different from my usual ones because of that air that inspires in me something great and generous that I did not feel before.[100]

These and the other hills are Rome, and transcendent of it, according us the depth and the distance to apprehend not only the city but its vast influence upon us – its 'civilité' (to use Balzac's word), civilizing influence or humanities training (the religion, law, arts and science, war and peace that come with it).[101] It is only apt that when Petrarch was hailed Poet Laureate, this took place on the Capitoline. 'The intimate connection between state power and poetic enterprise is, clearly enough, expressed in the single motif of the triumphal laurel that crowns both imperial victor and poet', writes James Simpson.[102] Empire and Arcadia are part of one utopian vision.

---

[99] Hunter 2006: 16.
[100] Balzac, letter to Nicholas Bourbon the younger, 25 March 1621, published 1665: vol. II, 106–8: 'Il est certain que je ne monte jamais au Mont Palatin, ni au Capitole, que je n'y change d'esprit, et qu'il ne m'y vienne d'autres pensées que les miennes ordinaires: cet air m'inspire quelque chose de grand et de généraux que je n'avois point auparavant.'
[101] Immediately before his section on the Capitoline and Palatine, Balzac writes: 'Rome est cause que vous n'êtes plus ni barbares, ni payens, car elle vous a appris la civilité et la religion; elle vous a donné les loix que vous empêchent de faillir, et les exemples, à qui vous devez les bonnes actions que vous faites; c'est d'ici que vous sont venues les inventions et les arts, et que vous avez reçu la science de la paix et de la guerre. La peinture, la musique, et la comédie sont étrangères en France et naturelles en Italie' ('Rome is the reason that you are no longer barbarians nor pagans, because she taught you civility and religion; she gave you the laws that stop you failing, and the examples to which you owe the good actions that you do. It is from here that inventiveness and the arts have come to you and that you have received the science of peace and of war. Painting, music and comedy are foreign in France and natural in Italy').
[102] Simpson 2005: 498.

The rise and fall of Rome in late antiquity

He saw a city besieged by black clouds in the darkness of obscure night; the thick mist blocked out the clear air from the seven hills.[103]

The growth of the Empire eventually caused it to fracture. At its height, under Hadrian, it stretched south to embrace Libya, east as far as Parthia (modern Iran) and north to Britain and Dacia (Romania). Gibbon wrote:

If a man were called to fix the period in the history of the world during which the condition of the human race was most happy and prosperous, he would, without hesitation, name that which elapsed from the death of Domitian to the accession of Commodus. The vast extent of the Roman Empire was governed by absolute power, under the guidance of virtue and wisdom. The armies were restrained by the firm but gentle hand of four successive emperors, whose characters and authority commanded involuntary respect. The forms of the civil administration were carefully preserved by Nerva, Trajan, Hadrian and the Antonines, who delighted in the image of liberty, and were pleased with considering themselves as the accountable ministers of the laws.[104]

In this predictable climate, it is unsurprising that poets and prose writers are less obsessed with Rome's hills. The situation was stable with little need for reassertion.

Hadrian was the emperor to make travel an imperial virtue. Instead of holing up on the Palatine, like Domitian, he toured the Empire, taking the court with him. The *locus* of imperial power was now wherever he happened to be. Roman might was brought into dialogue with a sense of the past which emphasized local histories, especially Hellenic culture. His extraordinary munificence established Athens as 'the center of a Greco-Roman world',[105] worthy home of the recently instituted league of cities, the Panhellenion. Greek writer Pausanias, who was writing at the time, epitomizes the competition Athens posed: 'In front of the entrance to the sanctuary of Olympian Zeus – Hadrian the Roman emperor, dedicated the temple and the statue – worth seeing – its size is such that all the other

---

[103] Prudentius, *Contra Symmachum* 1.412–14:

nubibus obsessam nigrantibus aspicit urbem
noctis obumbratae caligine; turbibus aer
arcebat liquidum septena ex arce serenum.

[104] Gibbon (ed. Bury) 1896–1900: vol. I, 78.   [105] Boatwright 2000: 144.

statues are left equally wanting, with the exception of the colossi at Rhodes and Rome.'[106]

Hadrian's successor, Antoninus Pius, was less frenetic. But he could afford to be: we have already noted Greek orator Aelius Aristides' remarks about the city walls being redundant at this period. So secure was Rome in its rule as to make maintaining the distinction between city and Empire irrelevant. Earlier in his speech, Aristides notes how praise of something so great is impossible:

Not only is it impossible to speak about her properly, but to see her properly... For who – on looking at so many inhabited summits or on the plains, pasture turned urban development, or so much land brought together under the name of one city – could then accurately contemplate her? What kind of place would they survey her from? For what Homer says of the snow, that, as it falls, it covers 'the summits of the lofty mountains and the highest headlands'... what Homer says is also the case for this city... Moreover she is poured out not (just) on the surface, but truly goes far beyond the example, reaching a great distance up into the air, so that her height cannot be compared to a covering of snow but to the peaks themselves.[107]

For all of the distinction that Rome's seven summits provide (still Aristides speaks of its built environment on the hills), there is a sense in which enumerating them is indulgent. Why the nostalgia for the hills of Servian Rome when the city overruns the planet?

But resting on one's laurels is dangerous. The Antonine dynasty spectacularly self-detonated under Commodus (emperor 180–92 CE),[108] leading yet again to a year of civil war. Septimius Severus (193–211 CE) brought some stability but – despite his mother's Italian origins – remained the African emperor. His empire was a world at war, both internally and on its borders, and Rome, a city of 'barbarous soldiery'.[109] The third century witnessed a

---

[106] Pausanias 1.18.6: πρὶν δὲ ἐς τὸ ἱερὸν ἰέναι τοῦ Διὸς τοῦ Ὀλυμπίου – Ἀδριανὸς ὁ Ῥωμαίων βασιλεὺς τόν τε ναὸν ἀνέθηκε καὶ τὸ ἄγαλμα θέας ἄξιον, οὗ μεγέθει μέν, ὅτι μὴ Ῥοδίοις καὶ Ῥωμαίοις εἰσὶν οἱ κολοσσοί, τὰ λοιπὰ ἀγάλματα ὁμοίως ἀπολείπεται...

[107] Aelius Aristides, *Roman Oration* 6–8: περὶ ἧς μὴ ὅτι εἰπεῖν κατὰ τὴν ἀξίαν ἔστιν, ἀλλ' οὐδ' ἰδεῖν ἀξίως αὐτήν... τίς γὰρ ἂν τοσάυδε ὁρῶν κορυφὰς κατειλημμένας, ἢ πεδίων νομοὺς ἐκπεπολισμένους, ἢ γῆν τοσήνδε εἰς μιᾶς πόλεως ὄνομα συνηγμένην, εἶτα ἀκριβῶς καταθεάσαιτο ἀπὸ ποίας τοιαύτης σκοπιᾶς; ὅπερ γὰρ ἐπὶ τῆς χιόνος Ὅμηρος ἔφη, χυθεῖσαν αὐτὴν 'ὑψηλῶν ὀρέων κορυφὰς καὶ πρώονας ἄκρους' καλύπτειν 'καὶ πεδία λωτεῦντα καὶ ἀνδρῶν πίονα ἔργα, καί τ' ἐφ' ἁλὸς πολιῆς', φησί, 'κέχυται λιμέσιν τε καὶ ἀκταῖς', τοῦτο ἄρα καὶ ἥδ' ἡ πόλις... καὶ μὲν δὴ οὐδ' ἐπιπολῆς γε κέχυται, ἀλλ' ἀτεχνῶς πολὺ ὑπὲρ τὸ παράδειγμα ἐπὶ πλεῖστον ἄνω ἥκει τοῦ ἀέρος, ὡς εἶναι μὴ χιόνος καταλήψει τὸ ὕψος προσεικάσαι, ἀλλὰ μᾶλλον αὐτοῖς τοῖς πρώοσι. See text and commentary by Fontanella 2007 and the English translation and commentary by Oliver 1953.

[108] See Hekster 2002.

[109] Birley 1999: 196. That said, it would be curious if Septimius Severus had not exploited the seven-hills topos, given both his name and his celebration of the Secular Games in 204 CE.

series of 'soldier-emperors', some of them, like their precursor, Macrinus (217–18), never even making it back to the capital. The internal fighting and external pressures were soon so overwhelming that control had to be divided.

Not much of a utopia here. When the Empire was split into four zones in 293 CE, none of the 'tetrarchs', as they are now called, was formally based in Rome, which was downgraded to notional capital. Indeed Diocletian, who instituted this collegiate government, went there only once in 303 CE to celebrate the twentieth anniversary of his accession.[110] Rome's heritage, real and symbolic, made it as impossible for any of them to make it their base as it was for them to have a torso of classical proportions, a sculpted image in the tradition of the Primaporta statue of Augustus.[111] There was only one Rome, just as there could only be one old-style emperor. Neither could be shared without dilution, hence the need for a new imagery without this kind of individual charisma. For the Empire to still be the Roman Empire, it had to seem indivisible.

After Diocletian's abdication in 305 CE, his system of having two Augusti and two Caesars collapsed, and the city of Rome was again in the spotlight as Maxentius, son of Diocletian's Augustus in the West, was overlooked as successor. His response was to make Rome the focus of his ambition, investing his resources into new building projects on the Palatine and, outside the city, on the Via Appia, as well as into repairs to the Aurelianic Wall.[112] But it was not to be. In 312 CE, with, or so it was claimed, the support of the Christian God, Constantine, son of the western Caesar, defeated him at Saxa Rubra, and twelve years later, he reunified the Empire. Rome now belonged to a 'Christian emperor' who endowed a basilica, baptistery and bishop's residence at the Lateran.[113] But soon it had to compete for primacy with Constantine's 'other Rome' on the Bosphorus, Constantinople. This rivalry opened the floodgates for it and other cities eventually to stake a claim to seven contours and their significance.

In the meantime, the accession of brothers Valentinian I and Valens in 364 CE led again to a division of resources between East and West, which was repeated definitively after the death of Theodosius I in 395 CE. Although

Certainly, a passage like Cass. Dio 76.1–2 takes much pleasure in playing with multiples of seven, this time in connection with games associated with his tenth year in power.

[110] A useful overview of the city of Rome in late antiquity is provided by Curran 2000 and Lançon 2000. Also important are W. V. Harris 1999 and Krautheimer 1980 and 1983. For a survey of the history of the period, see Averil Cameron 1993 and *CAH* 1998 and 2000.

[111] See above, pp. 10–11.

[112] See e.g. Rasch 1984, Giavarini 2005 and Dey 2011: esp. 43–6.

[113] Elsner 2006, with bibliography.

wealthy senatorial families still lived in Rome, the emperor was elsewhere and rarely visited. Competition between senators did little to bolster the city's overall standing.[114] And the Goths who had been given asylum by Valens were growing increasingly restless.[115] In 410 CE, with the western emperor, Honorius, based in Ravenna, they sacked the city. Jerome wrote, 'the city which conquered the whole world is conquered'.[116]

These threats to Rome in the fourth and fifth centuries call its hills back into active service. Just as the Greeks in the second century CE had mustered authors such as Homer and Xenophon to help them maintain an identity for themselves at the height of Roman domination, so late antique authors turned to an image of Rome that had been nurtured by earlier poets.[117] The city's value was increasingly seen in terms of symbolic capital. In the fifth century, for example, when in his eighties, Gallo-Roman aristocrat Paulinus of Pella (after his Macedonian birthplace) writes a confessional poem to God in which he describes going to Rome in 379 CE as an infant.

illic, ut didici, ter senis mensibus actis	
sub genitore meo proconsule rursus ad aequor	35
expertasque vias revocor, visurus et orbis	
inclita culminibus praeclarae moenia Romae;	
quae tamen haud etiam sensu agnoscenda tuentis	
subiacuere mihi, sed post comperta relatu	
adsiduo illorum quibus haec tam nota fuere,	40
propositum servans operis subdenda putavi.	

From there, as I have learned, when I had spent eighteen months under the pro-consulship of my father, I was again called back to the sea and to tried and tested paths, soon to see the renowned walls of famous Rome on the world's heights. All things which passed before me, though they were not even to be comprehended by my sense of sight, but learned afterwards by virtue of the careful report of those to whom these matters were so well known, I have thought must be included, preserving as I do so the purpose of my work.[118]

The emphasis is inevitably on learned experience. Paulinus does not see Rome, even in the poem. He is only ever 'about to see it' ('visurus'). His understanding of the famous city comes not from witnessing it, but from

---

[114] See Humphries 2003 and Weisweiler 2010.
[115] See Heather and Moncur 2001: 199–205.
[116] Jerome, *Letter* 127.12: 'capitur urbs, quae totum cepit orbem.'
[117] On the so-called 'Second Sophistic' and its celebration of Greek literary culture, see Swain 1996, Goldhill 2001 and Whitmarsh 2001. Also relevant is Vout 2007a: 213–39.
[118] Paulinus of Pella, *Eucharisticos* 34–41. See Matthews 1990: 70, 78–9 and 324–5; McLynn 1995; and Gärtner 2002.

the testimony of others. His description is a mix of Virgil and Statius, whose work must have formed the mainstay of his classical education.[119] What he remembers are barbarian incursions, as represented in the poem by the burning of Bordeaux in 414 and the seizure of his and his mother's property.[120] Infancy is thus a useful mechanism for evoking a more pervasive sense of nostalgia – that Rome's celebrated walls and hills, and what they stand for, are no longer recognizable by anyone; only by reputation. 'Relatus' has something of the poetry recital about it, while 'adsiduus' means everlasting. Rome, as it was under Servius Tullius, Augustus and Domitian, now only endures in poetry.

A similar message emerges from the elegiac poem of a second Gallic landowner, Rutilius Namatianus, who describes his journey from Rome, where he had briefly been prefect, to Gaul in 417 CE. This time it is the trope of looking back towards the city as he waits in port at Ostia that provides an opportunity for reminiscence:

respectare iuvat vicinam saepius urbem,
   et montes visu deficiente sequi,   190
quaque duces oculi grata regione fruuntur,
   dum se, quod cupiunt, cernere posse putant.
nec locus ille mihi cognoscitur indice fumo,
   qui dominas arces et caput orbis habet;
(quamquam signa levis fumi commendat Homerus,   195
   dilecto quotiens surgit in astra solo)
sed caeli plaga candidior tractusque serenus
   signat septenis culmina clara iugis.
illic perpetui soles, atque ipse videtur
   quem sibi Roma facit purior esse dies.   200
saepius attonitae resonant Circensibus aures;
   nuntiat accensus plena theatra favor.
pulsato notae redduntur ab aethere voces,
   vel quia perveniunt, vel quia fingit amor.

It is a pleasure to look back several times at the city which is still near and to trace its hills as our vision fails, wherever the guiding eyes enjoy the beloved region, for as long as they believe that they can see what they desire to see. Not that that place, which houses sovereign citadels and the world's capital, is known to me by the smoke that marks it out (although Homer commends the signs of thin smoke whenever it rises to the stars from a well-loved land); rather a fairer tract of sky and

---

[119] Paulinus of Pella, *Eucharisticos* 113–17.   [120] Paulinus of Pella, *Eucharisticos* 311ff.

a serene expanse signals the clear summits of the seven hills. There, the sun always shines and the very daylight which Roma makes for herself seems purer. Regularly our surprised ears echo with the noise of circus games and intense applause tells of full theatres. Familiar voices are sent back by the echoing air, whether because they reach us or because love makes it seem so.[121]

As Rutilius strains to see what is already beyond his vision, it is Rome's 'montes' that he searches for. Again the language is a mix of Virgil and Statius, as well as Martial: these 'montes' add up to a Rome which possesses 'sovereign citadels'. It is the 'caput' of the world. And it is rendered recognizable not by signs of human habitation or smoke of the kind that made Homer's Odysseus identify his home,[122] but by the signalling of the seven hills which are doubly marked, as 'iugis' with 'culmina'. They are not visible, so much as alluded to by the brighter, ethereal sky above them. Here at least the sun always shines, but it is a daylight of Rome's own making, self-generating – as real Rome fights for oxygen. Once the hills are conjured up, it is as if the city's inhabitants are enjoying themselves in front of him. 'How great an error or rather insanity is this, that – while as we have heard, people in the East and in the greatest states in the remotest parts of the earth were weeping over your destruction and leading public lamentation and mourning – you made for, entered and packed out the theatres, and did far madder things than you had done before?', asks Augustine at roughly the same time as Rutilius is setting out with the circus ringing in his ears.[123] How long can the seven hills sustain Rome's writers before they must face reality?

Rutilius is more optimistic than Paulinus of the city's recovery,[124] even as book two of his poem utters a damning assessment of Roman general Stilicho's ambition and his incapacity to keep Rome safe: 'while he strove to outlive the Roman people, his cruel frenzy turned the world upside down'.[125] As adviser of the emperor Theodosius and then regent to the young Honorius who ruled the West from 395 CE, Stilicho was initially a

---

[121] Rut. Namat. *De reditu suo* 1.189 204. See editions by Martinez 2002 and Wolff 2007 and articles by M. Roberts 1988 and Wolfgang 1988. On Rutilius and Virgil, see Filoche 2007.

[122] Hom. *Od.* 1.57–9.

[123] Aug. *De civ. D.* 1.33: 'quis est hic tantus non error, sed furor, ut exitium vestrum, sicut audivimus, plangentibus orientalibus populis et maximis civitatibus in remotissimis terris publicum luctum maeroremque ducentibus vos theatra quaerentis intraretis impleretis et multo insaniora quam fuerant antea faceretis?'

[124] Rut. Namat. 1.120 and 140. See Matthews 1990: 325–8.

[125] Rut. Namat. 2.43–4:

> Romano generi dum nititur esse superstes,
> crudelis summis miscuit ima furor.

key player in keeping Alaric's forces at bay with, as we are about to discover, a starring role in court poet Claudian's imperial panegyric. Soon after Claudian's arrival in Italy from Alexandria in around 394 CE, his praise of his young patrons, the consuls, Probinus and Olybrius, elicited admiration and attention. He expresses his joy at their election to office the following year in proverbial terms:

extemplo strepuere chori collesque canoris
plausibus impulsi septena voce resultant.

Immediately the choirs broke into singing and the hills resounded in sevenfold voice their tuneful applause.[126]

Claudian's bundling of 'seven' into the phrase 'septena voce' allows him to keep 'collesque resultant' as it is in book 8 of the *Aeneid*, where it refers to what happens to the woods when the priests of Mars sing of the glorious deeds of Hercules. It also enables him to keep the 'strep-' of Virgil's 'strepitu' in the same line.[127] The difference is that Roma, in the guise of the goddess Minerva, has had to beg this favour from Theodosius.[128] 'Her right side is bare and her snow-white shoulders are uncovered. A gem pins her dress, holding the loose material together and daringly reveals a breast. The belt which supports her sword divides her white chest with its strip of brilliant purple.'[129] In her shield 'are depicted Romulus and Remus, the love of father Mars and his offspring. The reverent river is in there and their animal-nurse'.[130] Like a refugee, the goddess leaves Rome behind and heads for the Alps, taking the symbols so fundamental to the city's foundation with her. When she meets the emperor, he sits like Mars before her, the grass rising

---

[126] Claud. *Panegyricus dictus Probino et Olybrio* (*Cons. Olyb. et Prob.*) 175–6.

[127] Virg. *Aen.* 8.305–7:

> consonat omne nemus strepitu collesque resultant.
>   exim se cuncti divinis rebus ad urbem
>   perfectis referunt . . .

[128] Not that this is the first time in Latin literature that Roma is imagined petitioning Caesar: see Luc. 1.190–2, where the goddess pleads with Caesar as he is about to cross the Rubicon, and Ash 2007: 212.

[129] Claud. *Cons. Olyb. et Prob.* 87–90:

> dextrum nuda latus, niveos exerta lacertos,
> audacem retegit mammam, laxumque coercens
> mordet gemma sinum; nodus, qui sublevat ensem,
> album puniceo pectus discriminat ostro.

[130] Claud. *Cons. Olyb. et Prob.* 96–7:

> hic patrius Mavortis amor fetusque notantur
> Romulei; pius amnis inest et belua nutrix.

from higher banks around him.[131] Close by, the deepest valley is said to have been made equal with the hills ('iugis'), but this time owing to the corpses of those who died in Theodosius' recent victory against the usurper, Flavius Eugenius.[132] The Rome of the *Aeneid* is a million miles away: Virgilian echoes risk sounding hollow. The lie of the land is changing.

By 397 a revolt in Africa led by the Roman commander and local prince, Gildo, had cut off the supply of corn to Rome, leaving the city close to starvation. It is a very different Roma who now meets the reader in what survives of Claudian's epic poem, *The War against Gildo,* her voice feeble, hair grey, eyes and cheeks sunken and her limbs, wasted. Her shield is unpolished and her spear rusted.[133] Rather than dash 'without delay' as she had done to Theodosius,[134] she can barely make it to Jupiter. 'If my walls deserved to rise by virtue of prophesies that will endure, if the Sibyl's predictions are unalterable, if you are not yet disapproving of the Tarpeian citadels, I come to you as a suppliant', she wheezes on bended knee.[135] Military victory is not what she seeks: Jupiter granted that in the past.[136] She needs food. Not only is she starving, but the River Tiber has broken its banks, 'threatening the very tops of the hills' ('summisque minatum collibus').[137] Not that floods were a rare occurrence in Rome: Tacitus describes a senatorial debate which demonstrates this, and Gregory of Tours will mention a serious one in 589 CE in which many ancient buildings are damaged.[138] It is that her hills are her last bastion. A few lines later, she drives this message home:

---

[131] Claud. *Cons. Olyb. et Prob.* 116: 'surguntque toris maioribus herbae'.

[132] Claud. *Cons. Olyb. et Prob.* 110–12:

> crescunt in cumulum strages vallemque profundam
> aequare iugis; stagnant inmersa cruore
> corpora . . .

[133] Claud. *De bello Gildonico* (*B. Gild.*) 17–25 (edition by Olechowska 1978). Note that Lucan's Roma (1.183–92) is also distressed at the prospect of civil war, her face sorrowful and her hair, white.

[134] Claud. *Cons. Olyb. et Prob.* 102:

> nec traxere moras, sed lapsu protinus uno,
> quem poscunt, tetigere locum.

[135] Claud. *B. Gild.* 28–31:

> si mea mansuris meruerunt moenia nasci,
> Iuppiter, auguriis, si stant immota Sibyllae
> carmina, Tarpeias si necdum respuis arces:
> advenio supplex . . .

[136] Claud. *B. Gild.* 31–4.

[137] Claud. *B. Gild.* 41–2: 'aut fluvium per tecta vagum summisque minatum | collibus . . .'

[138] Tac. *Ann.* 1.76, 79 and Gregory, *Histories* 10.1. For a full list, with sources, see Aldrete 2007: 242–3, and for modern floods in Rome, especially those of 1530 and 1557, Rinne 2010: 14–26.

quid mihi septenos montes turbamque dedistis,
quae parvo non possit ali? felicior essem
angustis opibus; mallem tolerare Sabinos
et Veios; brevior duxi securius aevum.
ipsa nocet moles. utinam remeare liceret
ad veteres fines et moenia pauperis Anci.

Why have you given me seven hills and a population which cannot be fed on little?
I would have been more fortunate with scantier power. I would have preferred to
tolerate the Sabines and Veientes. When I was smaller, I spent my days more safely.
My very mass harms me. Would that I could return to my former boundaries and
the walls of poor Ancus.[139]

After all these centuries, Rome's seven hills are still her achieved state or
contents, as critical to her as her people are. Whereas in Propertius she was
nourished by her hills ('septem urbs alta iugis'),[140] now they are a burden
and she is unable to nourish them. She is literally harmed by her bulk. She
looks back to a pre-Servian city as Rome's Augustan historians did, but to
regret, rather than celebrate, its expansion. In the next breath, she draws on
Virgil by asking Cybele to help her petition Jupiter:[141] 'and you, Cybele, if
you willingly sailed across the sea to exchange Ida for the hills of Rome and
bathe your Phrygian lions in the Almo instead, move now your son with
a mother's entreaties'.[142] *Aeneid* 6 is being evoked to stir the gods' and the
readers' sympathies.

By the end of the poem, Roma has been restored to her youthful self.[143]
Soon peace, however fleetingly, will be re-established. But Rome, the urban
capital, is still a world away from the imperial city of the first and second
centuries. Honorius and Stilicho's prolonged absence from Rome, along
with the rise of other western centres such as Milan and Ravenna, changes
the ways in which the emperor and the hills relate. They are no longer his as
they were Domitian's. Claudian writes: 'He [Stilicho] was always in camp,
very rarely in the city, and then only when the emperor summoned him with
anxious affection.'[144] He and his charge are no more at home there than

---

[139] Claud. *B. Gild.* 104–9.   [140] Prop. 3.11.57.   [141] Virg. *Aen.* 6.784–7.
[142] Claud. *B. Gild.* 117–20:

> tuque o si sponte per altum
> vecta Palatinis mutasti collibus Idam
> praelatoque lavas Phrygios Almone leones,
> maternis precibus natum iam flecte, Cybebe.

[143] Claud. *B. Gild.* 208–12.
[144] Claud. *De consulatu Stilichonis* (*Cons. Stil.*) 1.116–7:

> adsiduus castris aderat, rarissimus urbi,
> si quando trepida princeps pietate vocaret.

Propertius' 'stranger' who is shown the city in 4.1. Their initial alienation prompts a different response to and from the hills – one more akin to the views of later tourists.

Viewing Rome from the hills is the subject of Chapter 6; but for the moment it remains to be seen how imperial panegyric adjusts to accommodate Rome's estrangement, both from its ruler and from its past. In 400 CE Stilicho's victories are rewarded when he is elected consul. Claudian imagines the provinces of the Empire, each in female guise, gathering on the Palatine to have Rome ask Stilicho to take up office.[145] She succeeds and at the start of book 3, he finally enters the city: 'certainly Rome's *arces* have not received any general with greater magnificence'.[146]

> nonne vides et plebe vias et tecta latere
> matribus? his, Stilicho, cunctis inopina reluxit
> te victore salus! septem circumspice montes,   65
> qui solis radios auri fulgore lacessunt,
> indutosque arcus spoliis aequataque templa
> nubibus et quidquid tanti struxere triumphi.
> quantum profueris, quantam servaveris urbem,
> attonitis metire oculis. haec fabula certe   70
> cuncta forent, si Poenus adhuc incumberet Austro.

Do you not see both the streets hidden by the people and the roofs by women? Thanks to your victory, Stilicho, unexpected salvation has dawned on them all. Look around at the seven hills which challenge the rays of the sun with their sheen of gold, and the arches decked with spoils and the temples as high as the clouds and whatever building these great triumphs have generated. Measure with your astonished eyes how great a service you have performed and how great a city you have saved. All these things would certainly be the stuff of legend, if the African were still oppressing the south.[147]

The first thing that Stilicho is asked to look at lies hidden. Instead, it is the 'montes' that stand out, and in words which remind us of the exiled Ovid's image of Rome, 'the place of Empire and the god that surveys (*circumspicit*) the whole world from its seven hills (*de septem montibus*)'.[148] 'All these things

---

[145] Claud. *Cons. Stil.* 2.218–338.
[146] Claud. *Cons. Stil.* 3.30–1:

> non alium certe Romanae clarius arces
> suscepere ducem...

[147] Claud. *Cons. Stil.* 3.63–71.
[148] Ov. *Tr.* 1.5.69–70:

> sed quae de septem totum circumspicit orbem
> montibus, imperii Roma deumque locus.

would certainly be the stuff of legend', had Gildo's insurrection succeeded. But the implication is that they are already, the arches and temples that these hills carry rising apocalyptically to the sky, taking Ovid and Martial with them: 'from here it is possible to see the seven sovereign hills and get the measure of all of Rome'.[149] How much brighter do they have to shine before they combust? The magnitude of Stilicho's actions and the greatness of the city he has saved are still calculated in Martial's terms. The difference is that the hills are no longer regal as they once were: the regent's eyes are unaccustomed to them.

Some sixty lines later, and Stilicho is seen looking out over, and looking after, Rome, 'prospicere' being the verb that Lucan used to describe Jupiter's view of the city.[150]

proxime dis consul, tantae qui prospicis urbi,	130
qua nihil in terris complectitur altius aether,	
cuius nec spatium visus nec corda decorum	
nec laudem vox ulla capit; quae luce metalli	
aemula vicinis fastigia conserit astris	
quae septem scopulis zonas imitator Olympi;	135
armorum legeque parens quae fundit in omnes	
imperium primique dedit cunabula iuris.	
haec est exiguis quae finibus orta tetendit	
in geminos axes parvaque a sede profecta	
dispersit cum sole manus.	140

Consul, next in line to the gods, who takes care of/commands a view of such a great city, loftier than any other on earth that the air embraces; the eye cannot grasp its vast area, nor the heart its beauty, nor can any voice capture its praiseworthiness; a city which with its metallic light brings its rivalling heights to compete with the neighbouring stars; which with its seven hills imitates the zones of Olympus, mother of arms and of law which extends its empire to everyone and gave it as the cradle of the earliest justice. This is the city which, risen from narrow boundaries, has reached to both poles and starting from a small site, has dispersed its power as far as the sun reaches.[151]

Now that Stilicho has arrived, and Rome and imperial power have reconvened, the optimism is boundless. His gaze is that of a god. He has command over a city which is otherwise uncapturable. Not that this idea is new: the 'spatium' that no amount of looking can take in, and the beauty that

---

[149] Mart. 4.64.11–12:

> hinc septem dominos videre montis,
> et totam licet aestimare Romam.

[150] Luc. 1.195–6. See above, p. 82, n. 5.   [151] Claud. *Cons. Stil.* 3.130–40.

is beyond description, are the reasons why Augustus and his poets needed the seven hills in the first place – to delineate a capital which held sway from pole to pole. Recognizing this raises key questions about exactly what Balzac, Gibbon and Palmer see from their summits. Already the seven hills are less cultivated than we might expect – not a 'iugum' that boastfully beats at heaven's door, but 'scopuli' or 'rocks' of the kind that are so dangerous to Aeneas' ships in the *Aeneid*.[152] Rome no longer knocks as she did in Statius; she seeks to mimic Olympus. Centuries of praise poems have seen to that: Claudian has to top Statius, and Stilicho be given something wild for his colonial gaze to master.[153]

Claudian hopes that this peace will endure: 'you too, Rome, agitated by the civil discord of your people, more calmly lift up your now secure citadels'.[154] It is a wish prefigured in a panegyric of Theodosius written by Pacatus and delivered in Rome in 389 CE: 'you looked at these things from your hills, Rome, and sublime on your seven summits, you were borne higher with joy'.[155] These hills are still Rome's security. For Claudian, they function like ancestral jewels, looking after the city in her dotage.

ac velut officiis trepidantibus ora puellae	
spe propriore tori mater sollertior ornat	
adventiente proco vestesque et cingula comit	525
saepe manu viridique angustat iaspide pectus	
substringitque comam gemmis et colla monili	
circuit et bacis oncrat candentibus aures:	
sic oculis placitura tuis insignior auctis	
collibus et nota maior se Roma videndam	530
obtulit. addebant pulchrum nova moenia vultum	
audito perfecta recens rumore Getarum,	
profecitque opifex decori timor, et vice mira,	
quam pax intulerat, bello discussa senectus	
erexit subitas turres cunctosque coegit	
septem continuo colles iuvenescere muro.	535

And just as – when hope of a husband comes closer – a rather cautious mother with an anxious sense of duty does her daughter's make-up when the suitor comes

---

[152] Virg. *Aen.* 1.145.   [153] See below, p. 214.
[154] Claud. *De bello Gothico* 51:

> ipsa quoque internis furiis exercita plebis
> securas iam Roma leva tranquillior arces.

[155] *Pan. Lat.* 2 (12) 46.1: 'spectabas haec e tuis collibus, Roma, et septena arce sublimis celsior gaudio ferebaris'. See Nixon 1987 and Nixon and Rodgers 1994.

to visit, and often arranges her dress and her belt with her hand and defines her breast with green jasper, binds her hair with jewels, puts a necklace about her neck, and hangs glittering pearls from her ears, so Rome, to be pleasing to your sight, offers herself to be seen, more glorious with her hills increased, and bigger than the city you know. Her new walls, built recently when rumour was heard of the Getae's approach, added a beautiful face. And fear, architect of beauty, contributed to them and, by a wonderful quirk of fate, the shattering through war of the old age that peace had brought caused all those towers to rise quickly and compelled the seven hills to become youthful again by enclosing them in one, unbroken wall.

These lines are from Claudian's panegyric in praise of Honorius' sixth consulship in 404 CE, a work which we will be talking about in more detail later.[156] As Roma readies herself for the emperor's arrival, she is likened to a mother adorning her daughter to win a husband. In place of a pretty dress, necklace and earrings, she exploits her best assets, her 'colles', making them higher so as to attract admiring glances. The sense of restriction and circumference carried by the words 'cingula' (belt or girdle), 'angustat' (make narrow or restrain), 'substringit' (bind) and 'circuit' (encircle) is met by the hills which make her appear greater than she is known to be. Greater than she is? They had recently, we are told, been rejuvenated by restorations done to the Aurelianic wall which Claudian describes as giving a beautiful face to Rome's body.[157] But the cities of the present and past are still not commensurate: in stark contrast to Augustus' building programme, this adornment is rooted in alarm, not ambition.

For all that these restoration works help her cause, the cosmetic enhancement that results risks making Rome a willing conquest in an elegist's game of 'militia amoris'.[158] Any erotic undertones are enhanced when later in the poem the women of Rome are seen gazing at the newly arrived emperor, and in particular at his 'limbs which are green with the light reflected from the jewel-encrusted belt (*cinctus*) of the consul' and his jewel-clad neck.[159] It is a description which takes us back to the image of the girl being dressed by her mother, and one which enforces the sense of fetishization: Rome's

---

[156] A crucial companion to this poem is Dewar 1996.

[157] See Dey 2011: 100–1, 107–8 and 139–41.

[158] On the literary topos of love as warfare, see Spies 1930, Murgatroyd 1975, Kennedy 1993, especially 46–63, Gale 1997 and Davis 2006: 85–108.

[159] Claud. *Panegyricus de sexto consulatu Honorii Augusti* (*VI Cons. Hon.*) 560–4:

> conspicuas tum flore genas, diademate crinem
> membraque gemmato trabeae viridantia cinctu
> et fortes umeros et certatura Lyaeo
> inter Erythraeas surgentia colla smaragdos
> mirari sine fine nurus...

hills are not defences so much as baubles to be dangled in front of a suitor. Either that, or they are relics of former greatness. Honorius and Stilicho have to be actively encouraged to honour her as her previous rulers had done and in the process are rendered pilgrims.

Nothing can stop the sack of 410 CE, and further sacks, sieges and episodes of civil war. Although building in the city continues (the senator Cassiodorus, for example, writes a letter on behalf of the Gothic king Theoderic in 510–11 CE to command that the sewer system be repaired), her population is already low and her future in jeopardy. 'What other city could dare to compete with your heights (*culmina*), when not even your depths can find an equivalent?', asks Cassiodorus of Rome's sewers, describing them as 'rivers shut in as though by hollow *montes*'.[160] It is now the city's depths that are making the running and what is beneath the surface that signals greatness. In Emily Gower's words, the sewer is 'a substitute for more conventionally decorative and visible manifestations of the marvellous, nothing less than "a strange inversion"'.[161]

But it was not just invasion that threatened Rome's status as eternal city. Theodosius and Honorius were Christian, the latter was to be buried in a mausoleum built adjacent to the Constantinian Basilica of Old Saint Peter's.[162] For Christian poet Prudentius, Theodosius' Christianity had brought new life and light to the seven hills, allowing them to shine again as jewels should:[163]

In the grip of these rites, inherited from the origins of our ancestors, the palace of the highest empire was squalid, when an emperor, twice victorious with the slaughter of twin usurpers, looked back at the beautiful walls with his triumphant gaze. He saw a city besieged by black clouds in the darkness of obscure night; the thick mist blocked out the clear air from the seven hills (*septena ex arce*).[164]

Before that, they had been choked by the smog of pagan, sacrilegious activity. But for most people, it must have been increasingly difficult to believe that

---

[160] Cassiod. *Var.* 3.30.2: 'videas illic fluvios quasi montibus concavis clausos per ingentia signina decurrere . . . quae enim urbium audeat tuis culminibus contendere, quando nec ima tua possunt similitudinem reperire?'

[161] Gowers 1995: 25.   [162] Johnson 2009: 167–74.   [163] Prud. *Contra Symm.* 1.419–22.

[164] Prud. *Contra Symm.* 1.408–14:

en quibus inplicita squalebat regia summi
imperii tractis maiorum ab origine sacris,
cum princeps gemini bis victor caede tyranni
pulchra triumphali respexit moenia vultu.
nubibus obsessam nigrantibus aspicit urbem
noctis obumbratae caligine; turbibus aer
arcebat liquidum septena ex arce serenum.

the Rome they witnessed was a concentrated, cleaned up version of Virgilian Rome (its 'septem arces' boiled down into a 'septena arx'). Churches were being built in the Forum and on the hills and the effect on the visitor must have been similar to thirteenth-century Italian chronicler Jacobus de Voragine's description of Ephesus, when one of the 'Seven Sleepers of Ephesus' awakes after centuries of slumber:

> Coming timidly, therefore, to the gate of the city, he was extremely amazed on seeing the sign of the cross put up there. From there, proceeding to the other gate, when he discovered a similar cross, he marvelled beyond all measure, seeing all the gates with the sign of the cross upon them and the city, changed. And crossing himself, he returned to the first gate, thinking that he was dreaming. From there, strengthening himself and covering his face, he entered the city; when he came to the bread-sellers, he heard people speaking about Christ and, even more amazed, said, 'Why is it that yesterday no one heard Christ's name and now everyone acknowledges him? I think that this is not the city of Ephesus, because it was built differently, but I don't know another city such as this!'[165]

Postscript

For some, late antique Rome was similarly alien: the city which they walked with their pilgrim guides was a city of churches and catacombs. But for others, antiquity lived on: not only in the columns, inscriptions and sculpture, from which its Christian clothes were stitched, but, more holistically than that, in the Rome that these clothes now dressed – its topography, history and legends.[166] We have already seen how crucial the hills were in giving early antiquarians and historians the shape of ancient Rome and in channelling how they looked at the land. We have also seen how the first impressions of novelists including James, de Staël and Hawthorne were affected by them – not always positively as far as modern Rome was concerned. In between, poets continued to make use of them, as Propertius and Claudian had made

---

[165] *Jacobi a Voragine Legenda aurea vulgo historia Lombardica dicta: ad optimorum librorum fidem* (Grässe 1890), 436: 'veniens igitur timidus ad portam urbis valde miratus est videns suppositum signum crucis. unde pergens ad alteram portam, dum idem signum invenit, ultra modum miratus est videns omnes portas signo crucis apposito et mutatam civitatem. signansque se ad primam portam rediit existimans se somniare. unde se confirmans et vultum operiens urbem ingreditur et veniens ad venditores panum audivit homines loquentes de Christo et amplius stupefactus ait: "quid est", inquit, "quod heri nemo Christum audebat nominare, et tunc omnes Christum confitentur! puto, quod haec non est Ephesorum civitas, quia aliter aedificata est, sed aliam civitatem nescio talem."'

[166] On the importance of continuity and early imperial and late antique moves to preserve the monuments of pagan Rome, see Karmon 2011: 23–34.

use of them, to try to reconcile their understanding of ancient Rome with latter-day realities.

An excellent example, with which to end this chapter, is provided by sixteenth-century French tragic poet Robert Garnier (1544–90) and a section from the third act of his first tragedy, *Porcie,* written most probably in 1564 and published in 1568.[167]

O beau séjour natal esmerveillable aus Dieux,
O terre florissante en peuple glorieux,
Coustaux sept fois pointus, qui vostre teste aiguë   1015
Portez noble en palais jusque aux pieds de la nuë:
Soit où flanquez de tours vous honorez Jupin,
Dans un temple basti du roc Capitolin,
Soit où vous élevez en bosse Celienne,
En pointe Vaticane ou en Esquilienne: 1020
Soit où vous recourbez sous le faix Quirinal,
Sous l'orgueil Palatino ou sous la Viminal,
Joyeux je vous salue.

O, noble birthplace, held in awe by the gods,
o, land abundant in glorious people,
hills, seven times pointed, who hold your sharp head high
carrying noble palaces right up to the foot of the sky,
either flanked with towers, you honour Jove,
in a temple built of Capitoline rock,
or you rear up on Caelian heights,
on Vatican or Esquiline mounds,
Or you bend under the Quirinal's weight,
under proud Palatine or Viminal,
radiant, I salute you.

The Rome pictured here owes as much to the poetry of Horace and Statius as it does to that of Lucan and Seneca, which influences the play's overall form and content. The hills ('coustaux' for the modern 'coteaux') are described as nobly ('noble' for 'noblement') bearing their pointed head all the way to the sky and carrying the imperial palaces with them. They are then itemized as they were in regionary catalogues and post-classical texts, all members of the canon being present and correct, except that the Vatican has ousted the

---

167 Garnier 1999: vol. III, 1013–23. The edition of the text used here, complete with useful introduction and annotations, is Ternaux 1999. I thank Margaret Rigaud-Drayton for helping me make sense of the translation. Crucial context is provided by McGowan 2000: 272–82.

Aventine. The description is Mark Antony's and the play about the suicide of Porcia, wife of Caesar's assassin, Marcus Junius Brutus, defender of the Republic. Antony's joy notwithstanding, the city he sees is a city rent apart by violence, and Roman grandeur destined, or so we are told in the play's opening soliloquy, to fall flat on its back ('la Romaine grandeur tomber à la renverse').[168] Pride which is here positively associated with the Palatine will be the city's undoing.[169] His elevated prose is at odds with reality. The Fury's soliloquy ends with the ill that Cleopatra will cause.[170] After the events re-enacted in the play, Antony's relationship with her will bring civil war and accusations of betraying his Roman-ness.

The lessons are pointed, like the hills. The subtitle of the play read: 'French tragedy depicting the cruel and bloody season of civil wars in Rome: suitable and appropriate for seeing painted there the calamity of our time'.[171] As Garnier wrote, France was in the grip of its own civil conflict, wars of religion, which would leave hundreds dead and the monarchy temporarily weakened. For Garnier, a Catholic, the need to reassert the centrality of Rome in the wake of increasing antagonism from the Protestants was tantamount – going as far as to embrace the Vatican within the canon. The seven hills are his touchstone, an image of a glorious city in which the ruling elite (the palace), religion (the gods) and the people live together harmoniously, an image that endures as a kind of dream state against which to assess the different phases of Rome's urban and political aspirations and those of other capitals. Seen like this, the seven hills are not just about Rome's landscape, but about the iconic entity they help this landscape become, with all of the invincibility and longevity that this brings with it. They are a benchmark of what it means to be a city and of what a city has to lose. When Moscow and Durham boast of seven hills, they are trying less to oust Rome than to lay claim to cultural capital and future stability.

We have come a long way from Anchises' prediction that Rome would one day embrace seven hills within its walls. And yet in other ways, we have barely travelled: fulfilment of this prophecy still determines how we define what Rome is, above and beyond any temporal limits – not what Rome was like in 7 BCE or in 400 CE, but what it had to have to be Rome, even when barbarians and competing cities threatened its supremacy. In what follows we will look at how this written Rome intersects with the ways in which

---

[168] Garnier 1999: vol. I, 134.   [169] See Terneux 1999: 18–20.
[170] Garnier 1999: vol. I, 150: 'Et le mal qu'ourdira la Royne Egyptienne.'
[171] Terneaux 1999: 8 and McGowan 2000: 273: 'tragédie françoise, représentant la cruelle et sanglante saison des guerres civiles de Rome: propre et convenable pour y voir dépeincte la calamité de ce temps'.

artists represented the city. For them, there is need for a different kind of 'ongoing moment', one which is still and spatial rather than dynamic and temporal.[172] All views of Rome are shaped by the literary record. But like writers, artists are at greater liberty than scholars or map makers to use their imagination. They just use it differently. The next chapter explores the implications of having the seven hills oscillate in status from enduring idea to artwork.

---

[172] I owe the phrase the 'ongoing moment' to Geoff Dyer's 2005 book on photography, and the description of the difference between poetry and painting to Gotthold Ephraim Lessing's classic *Laokoon* essay of 1766.

| Painting by numbers

Rome contains in its walls ten or eleven hills which hug the Tiber tightly,
making it a rapid river and one which is deeply banked. These hills
appear to have been drawn by the genius of Poussin in order to give the
eye a pleasure which is serious and sort of funereal.

Stendhal (17 November 1827, published 1829: 127)[1]

The limits of representation

'Advertising is legalized lying.'[2] The poems of Virgil, Statius and Claudian
worked their magic in establishing Rome's hills as a topos. But they beg the
question: how does spin relate to reality? It is all very well to claim that their
praise, and Constantinople or Durham's borrowing, make Rome symbolic,
but Rome still exists. Whereas the Colosseum and imperial palaces are now
ruins and can be romanticized accordingly ('Let's go to the Capitoline. Let's
go to the Palatine. But what do we see here? Stop! Everything is old and in
ruin; and what about Rome? This is what she is, broken. Everything has had
its day'),[3] Rome's hills do not belong to the past in the same way, do not
inevitably evoke 'retrospective raptures'.[4] One has to climb them for that,
as we shall discover in the next chapter. What and how does one see, when
one looks not from, but for, the seven? Does one see as Stendhal sees – an
Arcadia of the kind painted by Poussin? Or can one be more objective? How
does the act of *visually* depicting the hills fit with the success of the literary
concept?

---

[1] 'Rome comprend dans ses murs dix ou onze collines qui serrent le Tibre de fort près et en font
un fleuve rapide et profondémont encaissé. Ces collines semblent dessinées par le génie du
Poussin, pour donner à l'oeil un plaisir grave et un quelque sort funèbre.'

[2] Attributed to English author H. G. Wells (1866–1946).

[3] Claude de Pontoux 1579: 148:

> Allons au Capitole, allons au Palatin . . .
> mais quoy que voyons nous icy nous arrestons,
> toute vieille ruine; et qu'est ce que de Rome,
> voilà que c'est, froissard, toute chose a son temps.

[4] See Henry James, above, p. 49.

Chapter 2's attempt to trace the *longue durée* of the concept and its relationship to the land inevitably introduced us to various views of the ancient and modern city. It highlighted the extent to which the visions of antiquarians, tourists and artists were influenced by the hills' reputation. But this is to assume that this influence plays out similarly in each case. 'We paint to ourselves the massive bulk of some castellated rock, whose commanding proportions and rugged grandeur admit of no material modification from the labours of men, and retain the same essential features through all changes of time . . . But how disappointing is the touch of reality', admitted American lawyer and author George Stillman Hillard in the middle of the nineteenth century.[5] Yet painting to oneself and painting a picture are not the same thing. Imagining the past in oil as Piranesi or Bartolomeo di Giovanni were to do is all very well, but what about committing the present to canvas? If Virgil were as influential here as he was for Antonio Loschi,[6] would the resulting Capitol be recognizable? And what about the relationship between past and present? Does the fusion of ancient and Renaissance buildings on Bufalini's map only work because they are in outline? If constancy or equivalence is what the concept of the seven hills provides, is it then impossible to paint the canon?

This question is made more pressing by the shortage of visual depictions of the canon and its members from antiquity. Not that there is anything especially surprising about this lack: although a fresco showing a bird's-eye view of an unidentified port city was discovered in excavations in the Baths of Trajan on the Esquiline in 1997, such images are unusual.[7] It is not simply that its Hellenistic architecture and single acropolis argue against its being Rome, but that to have rendered Rome as such would have been to render it an artwork, a fate preserved for conquered cities like the Parthian ones that grace the Arch of Septimius Severus in the Forum (Figure 5.1), or those that were held aloft as models in triumphal processions.[8] Livy tells us that Lucius Scipio had carried 134 replicas ('simulacra') of towns in his procession and Tacitus, that the triumph of Germanicus displayed 'spoils, captives, replicas

---

[5] Hillard 1853: 218.   [6] See above, p. 49.

[7] Now known as the 'città dipinta', the large fresco (almost 10 square metres) was discovered in a buried gallery beneath the baths and is probably Flavian in date. See Van der Meer 1998, La Rocca 2000 and 2001. On the representation of cities in the Roman Empire more broadly, see Gardner 1888, Rostovtzeff 1911 and Goodman 2007: 28–38.

[8] Arch of Septimius Severus: lower zone, right, Forum side, Edessa; Capitoline side, lower half, left, Seleucia, and right, Ctesiphon. On the bird's-eye view in Roman military art and in triumphal processions, Favro 2006: 21 and 25, and on coins in the East, Price and Trell 1977: 24 and 25.

Figure 5.1 Relief from Arch of Septimius Severus, Rome, showing the siege of Ctesiphon.

(*simulacra*) of mountains, of rivers, of battles'.[9] Here, foreign peoples and their environment are reduced in scale, rendered souvenirs or specimens.[10] Any hubris involved in playing god over nature is redirected in the service of conquest. Romans doing this to their own city would have been suicidal. Whereas Rome's poets could make the *montes* soar to the skies, artists would have been forced to strangle them. As architectural historian, Diane Favro has argued, 'such an animated, expansive urban form could not be fully captured by ancient representational techniques'.[11]

In Renaissance eyes, by contrast, the *montes* were objects of scholarly and aesthetic inquiry – samples of the species known as the eternal city. To make simulacra of them then was, in one sense, unproblematic. In practice, however, modelling ancient Rome was difficult: the texts of Varro and his successors, and fragments of brick and marble that had survived the centuries, were all that there was to put under the microscope and

---

[9] Livy 37.59.3: 'oppidorum simulacra centum triginta quattuor' and Tac. *Ann.* 2.41: 'vecta spolia, captivi, simulacra montium, fluminum, proeliorum'. See Beard 2007: 109.

[10] See S. Stewart 1984.

[11] Favro 2006: 33. Also relevant here is Edwards 1998: 238.

Figure 5.2 Wall painting from the *triclinium* of the House of M. Fabius Secundus, Pompeii. See also colour plate section.

set against the land. It was not just ancient images of the city that were lacking but images of individual hills: there were no ancient *vedute* to rival the landscapes of Poussin and Turner. Only the Palatine features in Roman wall painting – and this, an Augustan fresco not published until the beginning of the twentieth century (Figure 5.2).[12] Originally in the dining

[12] Pompeii, V. 4.13. Now in the Archaeological Museum, Naples: see e.g. Sogliano 1905; Pais 1905: 47; Dall' Osso 1906; Dulière 1979: vol. I, 110–13, vol. II, cat. no.137; Aichholzer 1983: cat. no. 143; Grandazzi 1986: 59–60; Gersht and Mucznik 1988: cat. no. 9; and Carandini and

room of the house of Marcus Fabius Secundus at Pompeii, it shows the foundation of Rome, from Mars's seduction of Vestal Virgin Rhea Silvia, to the suckling of her twin sons, Romulus and Remus, possibly on to her punishment and into the afterlife. A grassy hill rising above a river, with two temples, provides a backdrop which scholars have tied to specific elements of Rome's topography, some of these archaic (for example, the Lupercal and the Temple of Victory, which was at least ascribed to Evander, if built much later) and others, Augustan.[13] Which Palatine are we looking at? Is this even a valid question, given that different moments of the foundation-story are happening simultaneously within one frame, and that the panel is more obviously about the joys and perils of love between gods and mortals than it is the birth of a superpower? This painting is no more a snapshot of how the Palatine looked than it is about defining the urban.

More striking than this dearth of painted topography is the lack of person-ifications of the hills. In antiquity, mountains were not just the haunts of gods and nymphs. They were gods. From Homeric epic onwards, they were given human characteristics: the poetess Corinna tells how Helicon was defeated by Cithaeron in a singing contest presided over by the Muses.[14] And they were shown in art as personifications or piles of stones interchangeably.[15] Take Mount Argaeus (today Mount Erciyes) in Cappadocia, central Ana-tolia, the most frequently represented mountain in the whole of antiquity: more often than not it is shown as a cavernous, peaked mountain, sometimes topped with a star, circle or male figure; and occasionally, as a bearded per-sonification or deity (Figure 5.3).[16] Mount Tmolus, meanwhile, in Lydia, Asia Minor, is always a male figure, sometimes standing and sometimes seated – on one coin, on small rocks (Figure 5.4).[17] Ovid imagines him taking his seat on his mountain top and shaking his ears free of the trees. 'Looking out (*prospiciens*) far and wide over the sea, Tmolus stands stiffly, high and steep to climb, and stretched out on both sides reaches with one slope to Sardis and with the other to little Hypaepae.'[18] 'Prospicere' is the

---

Cappelli 2000: 167–76. A very simplified version of the same scene appears on an *opus sectile* panel, found in Bovillae and displayed in the Palazzo Colonna in Rome. Dated to the fourth century CE, this is less a landscape than a series of symbols, including the goddess Roma seated and surveying the action from a rocky outcrop. See Dulière 1979: vol. I, 188–90 and Carandini 2008: 17.

[13] See esp. T. P. Wiseman 1981 and Carandini 2008: 15–18.   [14] Page, *PMG* fr. 654.
[15] See 'Montes' in *LIMC* 8.1: 856–60.   [16] See 'Argaios' in *LIMC* 2.1: 584–6.
[17] See 'Tmolos' in *LIMC* 8.1: 44–5.
[18] Ov. *Met.* 11.157–8 and 150–2:

> nam freta prospiciens late riget arduus alto
> Tmolus in ascensu clivoque extensus utroque
> Sardibus hinc, illinc parvis finitur Hypaepis.

Figure 5.3 Coin from the reign of Commodus showing Mount Argaeus.

Figure 5.4 Coin from third century CE showing Mount Tmolus.

verb that Lucan and Claudian use as their Jupiter and Stilicho survey the city.

Rome's seven hills are not like Tmolus. Make any one of them too charismatic and it would threaten the canon's cohesiveness. Although 'Palatinus' has been attributed to a male figure on an Etruscan mirror and to more than one marble monument from the centre of Rome, all of them showing Romulus and Remus,[19] only some of these candidates are bearded as

---

[19] 'Palatinus', *LIMC* 7.1: 150–1. Identifications of the reclining youth on the fourth-century BCE mirror, supposedly found at Bolsena, range from Palatinus, a protective genius, Faustulus, the shepherd who finds the twins, to Hermes: see T. P. Wiseman 1995: 65–71, who argues that this mirror was made *prior* to the invention of the Romulus and Remus story in the third century.

Figure 5.5 Relief panel showing Caelian Jupiter, Hercules Julianus and the Genius Caelimontis.

mountain gods tend to be, and others, idealized youths. In these crowded scenes, and without identifying legends, it is impossible to be confident. A more obvious exception to the rule is provided by the Caelian Hill and a relief most probably dated to the late Antonine period, where the figures are labelled (Figure 5.5).[20] Caelian Jupiter is framed by two male figures, on his

[20] Today in the Palazzo dei Conservatori, Rome (inv. 1264, NCE 3022): Helbig (1899): vol. II, 1806 and *CIL* VI 334. See Colini 1944: 42–3; Palmer 1976: 47; Wrede 1981: 245, n. 133; Englen and Astolfi 2003: 150 and La Rocca *et al.* 2011: 293, no. 4.37. Although early interpretations identify Hercules Julianus with Didius Julianus, emperor for three months in 193 CE, the latest catalogue highlights how close his facial features are to those of Marcus Aurelius and asks us to be more cautious in putting the relief so late. In the line below their names are the words 'Anna sacrum', Anna perhaps the person dedicating the relief. It was not uncommon in late-first- and second-century Rome to commemorate one's loved one by a figure with portrait head and divine body. As to its find-spot, Palmer linked this to inscription *CIL* VI 377 = *ILS* 3051, and its reference to the Temple of Jupiter Fulgur and a shrine of the 'dei montenses', and he argued

Figure 5.6 The base of the Column of Antoninus Pius, 161 CE.

right a certain 'Hercules Julianus', and on his left the 'Genius Caelimontis', a bearded male who sits on rocks, leaning against a tree. While the tree may refer to the oak woods which Tacitus claimed had given the Caelian its original name of 'Querquetulanus',[21] 'Caelimontium' is the whole Augustan region of which the hill was only part. He directs our gaze towards Jupiter, who stands resplendent, the lower portion of a huge eagle still visible at his feet, and beyond him, towards a smaller male, *in formam deorum*, complete with the lion-skin, club and the apples of the Hesperides which are characteristic of Hercules. Just as god and demi-god vie with one another, so too the seated personification: is he or Jupiter Caelius better qualified as *genius loci*?[22]

Like the personification of the young Campus Martius in the famous relief of the apotheosis of Antoninus Pius and Faustina, the 'Genius Caelimontis' is the least active in the scene, not a character in the story, so much as a place holder (Figure 5.6).[23] The main flexing of muscles is between his standing

that all should be placed on the Quirinal. Most scholars prefer to put the Temple of Jupiter Fulgur on the Campus Martius, some associating it with Temple D in Largo Argentina: see L. Richardson 1992: 219.

[21] Tac. *Ann.* 4.65.   [22] On 'genii loci', see Serres 1991.   [23] Vogel 1973: 32.

Figure 5.7   Coin showing Roma seated on seven hills, 71 CE.

companions and the triad to which he belongs, suggestive of the different kinds of divinity that coexisted in the city. If any devotion to the Caelian hill is meant here, it is probably the sacrifices given by Varro and Festus' *montani*,[24] perhaps to the *dei montenses*.[25] As far as the seven-hills canon is concerned, Statius' *montes* may touch the sky, but it is Roma who does the knocking. She is the personification that matters. The goddess Roma holds the seven hills together, in the same way as they ground her.

Roma is fundamental to the two ancient images which do capture the seven hills and this goes some way towards explaining how a culture that generally avoided geographical features in state art was able to tackle them here. The first of these is a coin minted in Rome in 71 CE, with Vespasian shown side profile right on the obverse, and on the reverse, a magisterial Roma, staring in the same direction as the emperor but seated on seven rocks (Figure 5.7).[26] In contrast to the pebbles below Tmolus, or those that support the Tyche of Antioch (sometimes seven of them, but sometimes more than this), these are large mounds.[27] They are also a different species from those on earlier coins struck in Rome by Lucius Livineius Regulus in 42 BCE in honour of Mark Antony, and showing a figure, usually identified

[24]   See also *ILLRP* 698 = *CIL* I 1003 = VI 32455 = *ILS* 5428 and above, pp. 72–3. Note though that while Festus claims that all eight of the septimontium's *montes* received sacrifice, Antistius Labeo restricts this to two: the Palatine and Velia.
[25]   See Palmer 1976.   [26]   RIC II², 67, no. 108, and 73, no. 193.
[27]   BMC Lydia 324, 5. Plate 33.3. For coins of the Tyche of Antioch, see McAlee 2007. Also relevant here are the hills on which Cilicia sits: see e.g. the floor mosaic from the dining room on the House of Cilicia in the Norman University of Oklahoma, inv. M 126, A – Levi 1947: 57–9 and Huskinson 2002: 21–3.

Figure 5.8 Coin showing a seated Hercules (?), 42 BCE.

as Hercules from whom Antony claimed descent, again seated on stones (Figure 5.8).[28] This divergence puts them in a separate category; it has them stand up and be counted.

Below Rome and the seven hills is one word: 'Roma'. There is nothing odd in that: several Vespasianic issues label the goddess in this way, thereby distinguishing her from other seated deities such as Vesta, Concordia and Ceres.[29] Except that here it is rather redundant. In front of the hills is the she-wolf suckling the twins, and to the far right, at Rome's feet, the Tiber – human in form, tiny, his left arm mirroring her right so as to invite comparison between them. There are personifications and there are personifications, and he is dwarfed. He looks like every other river god. Worse than that, he is made to seem decorative. The hills, meanwhile, swell, fulfilling the function of the weapons on which Roma sometimes sits. There is no need for the statuette of Victory which she often holds in her hand.[30] The seven hills are her security blanket.

Of everything we have seen so far, this coin comes closest to making the poetic concept of the seven hills visual. It works because it is anonymous. No artist is claiming to capture the beauty or magnitude of the 'dominos montis' in metal. The claim is rather that these *montes* are kept in check by a goddess. She represents the city so that he does not have to. So why does

---

[28] For the coins of Regulus, see Grueber 1970, 578, nos. 4255 and 4256, Crawford 1974, 502, no. 494 2a and Walker and Higgs 2001: 238.

[29] See e.g. RIC II^2, 77, nos. 262–7, 259–61 and 118, no. 820.

[30] RIC II^2, 146, nos. 1206–7 and 1220–7.

Figure 5.9   Fragment of the 'Roma Monument', Corinth with Capitolinus Mons inscription.

not this image catch on?[31] The only comparable example is from Corinth in Greece, sculptural and probably second century. Found in fragments in 1927 in Byzantine walls on the northern part of the Lechaion Road which connected the city to the port, two blocks of grey-white marble with rough, cobbled surfaces preserve the names of the canonical seven (Palatinus mons, Esquilinus mons, collis Quirinalis (restored), Aventinus mons, collis Viminalis and Caelius mons on one, and Capitolinus mons repeated twice on the other, which would originally have been stacked on top) (Figures 5.9 and 5.10). Dowel holes in both blocks suggest they supported a statue. The logical conclusion is that this statue was Roma.[32]

It is no accident that Roma sits not on representations of the hills, but on a base which refers to them by name and by virtue of its uneven surface. Any

[31]   For more on the Vespasianic context of the coin, see above, Chapter 4.
[32]   The main publication of the monument is Robinson 1974. For the *editio princeps* of the inscription, Meritt 1927: 452 and, in more detail, Kent 1966: no. 352. Although Kent assumes that the texts belong to a series of statue bases, Robinson's argument for a single monument and statue of the goddess is convincing and now accepted. Kent also fails to record the Caelian inscription: Robinson 1974: 476; and on the restoration of 'collis Quirinalis': 479.

Figure 5.10 Fragment of the 'Roma Monument' with Collis Viminalis inscription.

similarities with the coin are superficial. Had the artist rendered its insignia in three dimensions, he would have had to decide how big to make the hills and how distinct from one another. What about the Capitoline, which is the smallest yet most important of the seven? What would be lost by modelling all of them on foreign soil? It would make Rome a 'simulacrum', or souvenir, of the kind carried in the Triumph, shrinking it to a status akin to a modern 'Lego Miniland' city – from 'caput mundi' to tourist attraction.

Instead, Rome's hills are made signs instead of symbols. Crucially, they remain text, and Latin text at that, closer to the versions of Augustus' *Res gestae* inscription (which were put up in temples in Asia Minor and which referred, in part, to the changing topography of the capital)[33] than to imperial portraits. These hills do not come to Corinth so much as transport the viewer to Rome, using subtler strategies than size to suggest a hierarchy between them: so 'Capitolinus mons' is the only legend to appear twice, on either side of the upper block. The sculpture itself, which may have been based on the cult statue in Hadrian's new temple of Venus and Roma in Rome,[34] is the only element which could qualify as a copy or an artwork. In contrast, the hills are a set of co-ordinates. They comment on Rome and on the personification of Rome, functioning a little like the labels on the

[33] Cooley 2009 and on the inscription's text as image, Elsner 1996.
[34] Robinson 1974: 483–4. On the temple, see above, Chapter 4, n. 20.

Pergamon frieze or the 'Apotheosis of Homer' relief, which use the nexus of art and text to question the ontology of the image.[35] The result is not a picture of the seven hills but a brainteaser: what does Rome mean to the Corinthians? Is it a place, a power, the gods they worship? How influential in reaching an answer was the entity that is the capital city?

It is impossible to say why Corinth, which became a Roman colony in or around 44 BCE, references the mother-ship in this unique way.[36] Although the city went on to hold a pre-eminent position in the province of Achaea and has yielded considerable evidence for the imperial cult in the first century CE, the presence of Roma is less well attested.[37] In the 70s CE she was included in the pediment of one of its temples and had appeared on a few Corinthian coins.[38] She is also the subject of a late-antique statuette found in 1999 in the Panayia Domus (Figure 5.11).[39] Perhaps the 'seven hills' monument was erected to commemorate the visit of Hadrian in 126 and/or 128/9 CE.[40] Perhaps, as I have suggested, its statue paid homage to his new temple. We can be clearer about why other cities might not have followed Corinth's example. Chapter 4 has already noted the difficulties caused for the capital by Roma's being a goddess of all lands and cities.[41] For these cities, this was an advantage: she could be theirs, even domesticated as a household miniature. Without the hills to put the viewer in their place, her presence spoke of integration.

The seven hills of Renaissance artists and patrons

We are so familiar with the area of the Palatine, the Aventine, and Celio in its present appearance that it becomes difficult for our minds to reconstruct its earlier aspect – an arid and deserted region of ancient remains, unkempt vineyards, malarial *villini*, and battered monastic foundations. But such was the landscape known to Poussin and to Claude, known also to Gaspar Van Wittel; and while we may mourn its loss, we may also salute the present appearance of these hills, which in their gentle and

---

[35] The Apotheosis of Homer relief: British Museum, London, inv. GR. 1819.8–12.1: see Newby 2007. And on art and text in Hellenistic art more broadly, Onians 1979: 95–118 and G. Zanker 2007.

[36] Note that Coarelli 1995: 176 sees this monument as referring to Corinth's own topography and organization.

[37] See Engels 1990: 101–2 and Bookidis 2005.

[38] Temple E in the Forum: Williams 1987 and Walbank 2003: 347. On the coins, see *Corinth* VI: 24, nos. 68–70 and Walbank 2003: 347–8.

[39] Stirling 2008, and for a possible fragment of a further monumental sculpture of Roma, S-158: *Corinth* IX: 67.

[40] J. Wiseman 1979: 507.   [41] Mart. 12.8.1–2.

Figure 5.11 Late antique statuette of Roma from the Panayia Domus, Corinth.

brilliant greenness, are apt to suggest a fragment of the Veneto posturing as an ideal and a better Rome, as a Rome of the northern imagination.[42]

By the sixteenth century, artists were making explicit claims about painting Rome's seven hills. Constantinople and Moscow had now borrowed

---

[42] Mulcahy's catalogue, *Rome: the Lost and the Unknown City (Roma Ignota e Perduta)* 1974, as cited in Rowe 1999: 132–3.

Figure 5.12   Nicolas Poussin, The Aventine as seen in *Studio di paese nella campagna romana.*

the byline as their own, making it less about Rome than about the ulti-mate cityscape. What does this cityscape look like? Some of the paintings of Poussin (Figure 5.12), Claude and Van Wittel aimed at reconstructing the ancient city (for example, Poussin's *The Rape of the Sabine Women*), others captured majestic Renaissance structures such as the Villa Medici on the Pincio, or the ruins of classical buildings, or mixed the real and the imaginary.[43] There was not one strategy for coping with the passage of time, but several.

Fast forward to 1978, and an exhibition organized by Incontri Inter-nazionali d'Arte in Rome's Trajan's Markets took a radical step, asking twelve international architects to imagine that time had stopped and his-tory had been suspended: *Roma Interrotta*, 'Rome Interrupted'.[44] The hiatus was made to coincide with the publication of Nolli's map in 1748 and the task was to extrapolate from its urban imprint to produce 'a plausible Rome, a city belonging to the category of the impossibly probable'.[45] An American

[43] For example, Nicolas Poussin, *The Rape of the Sabine Women*, 1637–8, oil on canvas, 159 x 206 cm, The Louvre, Paris, inv. 7290, and the lesser-known version by the same artist, 1633–4?, oil on canvas, 154.6 x 209.9 cm, The Metropolitan Museum of Art, New York, inv. 46.160; Claude, 1632, *A View in Rome*, oil on canvas, 60.3 x 84 cm, the National Gallery, London, inv. NG 1319 with its mix of accurate view and imaginary ruin; and Caspar van Wittel, *The Villa Medici and Garden in Rome*, 1685, 29 x 41 cm, Palazzo Pitti, Florence.

[44] Cerutti 1978. In 2008 the project was revived and inspired the theme of the Bienniale Architecture in Venice.

[45] Rowe 1999: 152.

team, led by Colin Rowe, was assigned a section covering the Palatine, Aventine and Caelian to conjure with, and they made up an authority, Father Vincent Mulcahy, to underpin their vision. The 'familiar', 'present' appearance of the hills, 'posturing as an ideal and a better Rome, as a Rome of the northern imagination' is Mulcahy's, and thus invented. Yet it is no more artificial than the images of its painters; in some ways, it is more believable. It toys with our sense of the visible, unforgettable and irrevocably unsalvageable.

Every act of committing the hills to canvas confronts these issues in ways which authors can escape. As we discovered in the previous chapter, while Rome's poets often invite their readers to look with them, they equally avoid describing the hills in detail. Martial's adjective 'sovereign' ('dominos') is about as graphic as it gets. Even when individual summits are concerned, more emphasis is given to how the Palatine and Capitoline might have looked in the past than to their current configuration. This is, in part, humility and the need for continuity: fulsome praise of the kind one finds about the Baths of Claudius Etruscus or Domitian's Palace would risk turning each hill into a budding Athos.[46] And it is in part a feature of writing: the sophistication of ekphrasis (literary description of an object) is not in the looking but in the interpreting.[47]

A possible exit route for artists is abstraction. And yet modern Rome is no keener than ancient Rome on rendering the seven hills ideogrammatically. There is nothing akin to the spiky logo of the 'Seven Hills of Edinburgh Race and Challenge' (Figure 5.13), nor to the seven gold domes and eagle which serve as the crest of the 309th Ordinance Batallion of the US army (commemorative of their role in the Rome–Arno campaign in World War II).[48] As far as visual shorthands for Rome are concerned, 'SPQR' or the Lupa Romana remain unchallenged.[49] Yet visit the city today and one sees the six-hilled crest and star of the House of Chigi everywhere (Figure 5.14), a nod not to Rome, but to the Tolfa Mountains in northern Latium and their alunite reserves which had made the family wealthy.[50] Its most ambitious member was Fabio Chigi, later Alexander VII (pope from 1655 to 1667),

---

[46] See Chapter 4, pp. 91–4. Also important here is Kaldellis 2007 on the ekphrastic poetry about the Baths of Zeuxippos in Constantinople.

[47] See Goldhill 2007.

[48] See www.seven-hills.org.uk/ (accessed on 22 January 2010) and Stein and Capelotti 1993: 292 and plate 88, no. 2.

[49] On the Lupa as icon, see Mazzoni 2010.

[50] Note too the three hills of the *rione* of Monti. For an introduction to the Chigi family and their impact on Rome's built environment, see Majanlahti 2005: 321–70. And on the urban development of Rome under Alexander VII, Habel 2002. Especially interesting here is the way

Seven Hills of Edinburgh
Race & Challenge

Figure 5.13 Official logo of the Seven Hills of Edinburgh Race and Challenge.

Figure 5.14 The six-hilled crest of the Chigi family, Porta del Popolo, Rome.

whose urban designs rivalled those of Sixtus IV and Sixtus V, and saw him similarly compared to Augustus, as well as to Domitian.[51] Controversially, he decided to live on the Quirinal, where – like Ustinov's Nero – he had a model of Rome which he enjoyed comparing with the view from his window.[52]

Here perhaps was an individual bold enough to write his name on the landscape. Soon the Chigi mountains were being referred to in word as well as image: 'Let the *montes* sustain peace for the people, and the *colles*, justice', reads the inscription on the façade of the church of Santa Maria della Pace, bringing them, the hills of Rome and of the Psalms together.[53] And soon artists could not resist further flattery by measuring his ambition against that of his namesake, Alexander the Great, and Mount Athos. Papal architect, Pietro da Cortona, has a demonstrative Deinocrates trying in vain to attract the pope's attention to the anthropomorphic landscape in front of them (topped with a Chigi star), only to be ignored in favour of the plans of a more modest-looking man, probably Cortona himself (Figure 5.15).[54] One of Cortona's pupils, Ciro Ferri goes further, having the pope himself take the place of the hill-enthroned automaton in a more crowded allegorical landscape (Figure 5.16). The legend reads: 'Alexander VII, Pontifex Maximus (or 'Pope') has been taken from the mountains of Siena to assume the uppermost command of the seven-hilled city.'[55] So integral is he that he has become the seventh and highest hill, the other six cowering in human form below him. Finally the hills are personified but at what cost, as they vie with each other for his attention?

in which Constantinople's appropriation of Rome and indeed the publication of Gilles' book (above, p. 22) shaped Alexander's vision.

[51] Venetian ambassador to the Papal States, Angelo Correr, 1660 (BAV, Chigi N. III. 80, fols. 3r–v, and BC, cod. 890, fol. 287v): 'ma i gusti del Papa in questo genere non si fermano nella sola amplificazione et abbellimento delle habitazione Pontifice mà suongano per tutta La Città, così che essendo entrato in pensiero d'abbellirla in quella guisa che già s'invaghirono di fare anche gl'Imperatori Romani Augusto, Domiziano e altri ... ' ('But the tastes of the pope in this regard do not stop in amplification alone and in the embellishment of the pontifical residence but resound through the whole city, so that he thinks that he is embellishing it in the same way as the Roman emperors, Augustus, Domitian and the others...').

[52] The gallery of the Palace 'domina tutta la nostra città di Roma' ('commands a view over all of our city of Rome') (Pallavicino 1840: 180). On the amount of time spent by Alexander watching the city, see Krautheimer and Jones 1975: 205, no. 72 (26 February 1657) and on the wooden model of the city, Neri 1878: 676.

[53] 'Suscipiant montes pacem populo et colles iustitiam.' See Bauer and Bauer 1980: 123, n. 49.

[54] Pietro da Cortona, preparatory study, inscribed at the top of the sheet, 'Alexandra Sept. [-] Pontifex [-] maximo', British Museum, Prints and Drawings, 1860,0616.27. For the final engraving by François Spierre, see British Museum, Prints and Drawings, V-9–21.

[55] Engraved by Chateau Giullaume (1655), after Ciro Ferri (Gabinetto delle Stampe, Istituto Nazionale per la Grafica, Rome, FC 117803, Volume 57N25). See Della Dora 2005: 504–6.

Figure 5.15 Pietro da Cortona, *Deinocrates Shows Alexander VII Mount Athos.*

By now, however, the seven hills had been firmly established as the subjects of antiquarian inquiry. Browse not only the ancient texts but any history or guidebook of the city and it was impossible to miss them. Even foreign authors, including Hoby and Garnier, were celebrating them.[56] It was not

---

[56] See Chapter 2, n. 99 and Chapter 4, n. 167.

Figure 5.16 Chateau Giullaume, after Ciro Ferri, *Allegorical Portrait of Alexander VII.*

simply that these texts needed maps and *vedute* to accompany them, but that the urban interventions of Sixtus V and Alexander VII were inspired by them, putting increased emphasis on the fact that the hills had always been there. Artists were as indispensable in keeping them there as ideograms were

Figure 5.17 Giovanni Battista Naldini (1537–91), *Vue de Rome, avec un personnage assis dessinant.*

insufficient. In introducing his *Roma Interrotta* competition and exhibition, mayor of Rome and art historian Giulio Carlo Argan wrote: 'Rome is an interrupted city because it has stopped being imagined and begun to be planned.'[57] Such criticism is less easily directed against the sixteenth to nineteenth centuries.

Many are the catalogues that show how Rome's artists grasped the nettle that is continuity within change. And how they were self-conscious about the need for imagination, even when purporting to record what they saw. Take the drawing by sixteenth-century Florentine artist Giovanni Battista Naldini (Figure 5.17), which shows a cowled artist, any artist, tools of his trade in hand, in the process of sketching the vista.[58] The key at the bottom of the picture shows that the Palatine is the main subject (labelled A), its ruined palaces more or less level with the Colosseum and the Church of Saints Giovanni e Paolo on the Caelian to the right, while the tree stump signals decay. Here is the Palatine that contemporary Blaise de Vigenère described as 'a desert, vague and uninhabited or, for the better, a simple

---

[57] In Cerutti 1978.
[58] *Vue de Rome, avec un personnage assis dessinant,* Louvre, Paris, inv. no. 11032, recto. See Sassoli 2000: 29, fig. 8.

retreat for sheep'.[59] Except that the artist does not look at it. It is not this he sketches, but something mysterious beyond the frame. Real Rome is inevitably elsewhere.

Elevation helps to make some sense of the jumble that is Rome; and we will be looking at scenes that foreground the advantages of viewing from the hills in the next chapter. These visions have come to shape expectations of the city as much as ancient literature has shaped them, and to aestheticize hills other than the canonical seven. Of the Pincio, for example, Nathaniel Hawthorne wrote: 'here are beautiful sunsets; and here, whichever way you turn your eyes, are scenes well-worth gazing at, both in themselves and for their historic interest, as any that the sun ever rose or set upon'.[60] Between them, these visions create a Rome which rubs up against the imperial capital of Virgil or Statius and the urban paradigm of Renaissance map-makers, a Romantic Rome, which can ultimately accommodate narratives like *The Marble Faun*, one which relates to their Romes as Evander's Rome relates to them, with as much purchase as it has to reality. This Romanticism emphasizes beauty and further charges Durham's rivalry with Rome and its desire to be a certain kind of city.

In the rest of this chapter, however, I want to focus on two visual case studies which claim to capture the canon in a more literal way than Ferri's image, case studies which subject the hills to a more intense scrutiny than we have seen thus far, a kind that is closer to the vision of Claude and van Wittel than to the Vespasianic coin or the monument from Corinth. The two are very different from one another. The first is a set of frescoes in the eponymous Sala dei Sette Colli of the Villa Giulia, built for Pope Julius III on the slopes of Rome's Monti Parioli between 1551 and 1555 and today home to the Etruscan collection of the National Museum (Figure 5.18). And the second, a set of thirty engravings, entitled *I Sette colli di Roma antica e moderna*, produced between 1827 and 1829. For all that the Napoleonic plans outlined by Rowe's Father Mulcahy were never realized, the French occupation of the city and the archaeological activity that went with it combined with broader shifts in the treatment of ancient artefacts to impact on the appearance and purpose of the latter's images. Napoleon never visited Rome, but this only fuelled his ambition: 'I am of the race of the Caesars', he claimed to Antonio Canova, 'and of the best of their kind, the founders.'[61] While the frescoes were primarily aimed at impressing Julius' friends and

---

[59]   Blaise de Vigenère 1586: col. 768: 'un désert vague et inhabité, ou pour le mieux une simple retraitte de brebailles'.

[60]   Hawthorne [1860] 2002: 79.

[61]   As cited by Driault 1917: 8: 'je suis de la race des Césars, et de la meilleure, de ceux qui fondent'.

Figure 5.18 The Villa Giulia, Rome.

bolstering his status, the engravings were for 'lovers and students of Roman antiquities, who labour all day long to trace exactly its vestiges consumed for the most part by time, or else confused and covered by modern buildings, very many of which are still torn apart and almost completely damaged by barbarian incursions'.[62] They had an explicitly didactic purpose; offered a different way of representing a different landscape. How does their Rome compare with the Rome of the frescoes, and each of these Romes with the Rome of the literary canon? What are the limits within which the artists are working? Are all of the members of the canon similarly treated? To what extent is this painting by numbers?

The frescoes in the 'Sala dei Sette Colli' are usually attributed to Urbino-born painter Taddeo Zuccaro (1529–66), though this is not without its problems. Whereas the scenes in the neighbouring 'Sala delle Virtù e Arti Liberali' are typical of his hand, those in the 'seven hills room' are not, and indeed were attributed by one eighteenth-century picture-restorer to

---

[62] Rossini 1829: preface: '. . . gli amatori e gli studiosi delle Romane antichità, i quali tutto giorno si affaticano per rintracciarne esattamente le vestigie nella maggior parte comsumate dal tempo, altre confuse, e ricoperte dai moderni edifizj, moltissime ancora dilacerate, e quasi totalmente guaste dalle incursioni dei barbari'.

Prospero Fontana, who worked at the villa from April 1553 to March 1555. Archival evidence suggests that Fontana at least co-ordinated the decoration, with several of his pupils working on the projects.[63] In 1935 the question of attribution was made more complicated by the discovery of a second set of frescoes of the same scenes, in a *studiolo* of the 'Appartamento di Giulio III', now the 'Appartamento della Guardia Nobile', of the Vatican's Belvedere Court.[64] Vasari records that it was here that Zuccaro enjoyed one of his earliest papal commissions.[65] But the style is more delicate than its equivalent in the villa.

In the villa the scenes are inserted into a frieze, high up in the largest of the three rooms along the front of the building on the *piano nobile*, off the annular corridor (Figure 5.19).[66] In the Vatican they are lower on the wall, in a room on the east side of the famous court, but they were painted over when Pius IV inherited the apartment, only to be revealed centuries later. Though we will sometimes draw attention to differences between them, the damage done to those in the apartment, and their inaccessibility today, make privileging the villa unavoidable.

In both sets, the basic story is the same. The traditional members of the canon are all there, each in its own frame (Figure 5.20); each of them asking to be read against the others, and perhaps too against its alter-ego across the Tiber. The location of the villa, just beyond the Aurelianic wall, on the very boundary between city and countryside,[67] already puts pressure on the idea of the urban epitomized by the hills. The Via Flaminia, onto which the estate had its urban entrance, was one of the busiest roads into Rome: for anyone who stopped at the villa, the frescoes functioned like a graphic version of Andrea Fulvio's poetry,[68] showing them the city's high points before they reached their destination. The view from the villa, however, across its vineyards to the river pointed the viewer in the direction of Julius III's other kingdom, the Belvedere, where a second version of the frescoes repeated the seven-hilled message. The canon still provided the frame for understanding what Rome was, but a frame which was now not a skeleton

---

[63] On these frescoes and the problems of attribution, see Della Seta 1918: 22–5; Gere 1965 and 1969; and Falk 1971: 128–31. More recently, they have been studied by Nova 1982 (doctoral thesis), published 1988 as part of a project on the artistic patronage of Julius III, Campitelli 1984, and mentioned by Jacks 1993: 232 and fig. 79 and M. B. Hall 2005: 216–18 and fig. 159. For Taddeo Zuccaro, see Acidini Luchinat 1998–9.

[64] First published in Biagetti 1936.

[65] Vasari, *Lives* 7.82. Important here is Ackerman 1954: 80–1, whose publication of the Cortile del Belvedere is still key reading.

[66] Nova 1982: 102 suggests that the room is an audience chamber.

[67] Coffin 1979: 150–73.   [68] See Chapter 2, n. 96.

Figure 5.19 Section of the frieze in the Sala dei Sette Colli, Villa Giulia, Rome.

on which the flesh of modern Rome could be hung so much as a pair of bookends. Between them, these opened a new space. Within this triangle (the villa, Vatican, Servian city) Rome is rearticulated.

In case there were any doubts about this rearticulation, the fresco-cycles have a further card to play: each includes an eighth hill in the shape of the villa itself, high on a verdant slope above the fountain which Julius had dedicated

Figure 5.20 The Esquiline panel, the Sala dei Sette Colli, Villa Giulia, Rome. See also colour plate section.

on the Via Flaminia (Figures 5.21 and 5.22). He had controversially diverted part of the Aqua Virgo (now the Acqua Vergine) which Statius had celebrated as supplying Claudius Etruscus' baths to serve his estate and, as an act of appeasement, had provided an outlet for the public.[69] The versions differ from each other in their detail. In the Vatican apartment the emphasis is on the estate's expansiveness and wildness; and in the villa itself, on the building's monumentality. Julius' name is this time writ large on the fountain which people and a dog stare at in wonder. But the approach to the villa is still sufficiently steep to make the image of the Esquiline pale in comparison (Figure 5.23). Julius has claimed that too – a fountain in the foreground (in a similar position to the fountain in the Villa Giulia panel) supporting the same heraldic device, the trimontium, that decorates the shields in the corners of the room (Figure 5.24).[70] As the two panels face up to each other, one on either of the room's short sides, with the Viminal, Quirinal and Palatine from left to right along the long external wall, and the Aventine, Capitoline and Coelius (*sic*) opposite them, they challenge each other for membership. As the setting of Nero's Domus Aurea (perhaps

[69] D'Onofrio 1957: 169 and Rinne 2010: 35 and 49–50. For Statius, see above, pp. 99–100.
[70] Further back in the scene are the so-called 'Trophies of Marius' which were soon to be moved to the Capitoline, but which were, until the end of the sixteenth century, part of a structure at the intersection of the Via Labicana and Via Tiburtina on the Esquiline. See Tedeschi Grisanti 1977, which reproduces the Vatican version of the Esquiline scene at the end of its preface by Salvatore Settis.

Figure 5.21   The Villa Giulia panel, the Sala dei Sette Colli, Villa Giulia, Rome. See also colour plate section.

Figure 5.22   The Villa Giulia panel, Julius III's apartment, Palazzo del Belvedere.

Figure 5.23 Close-up of the Esquiline panel, the Sala dei Sette Colli, Villa Giulia, Rome. See also colour plate section.

Figure 5.24 Julius III's heraldic device, the Sala dei Sette Colli, Villa Giulia, Rome. See also colour plate section.

Figure 5.25 The Esquiline panel, Julius III's apartment, Palazzo del Belvedere.

the terraced building with the golden doorframe on which the artist has imagined the Laocoon to be displayed), the Esquiline was the benchmark of palatial extravagance.

Needless to say, the panels play out differently at the villa from in the Vatican (Figure 5.25). Stay with the Esquiline for a moment, and we realize that the Laocoon statue, which had been discovered on the hill in 1506, had already been installed in the Belvedere courtyard (Figure 5.26).[71] There was little need for Julius III's heraldic device in the Vatican version when the scene's star attraction was now papal property outside the window. The courtyard linked the Vatican Palace with Innocent VIII's fifteenth-century villa, the first villa to be built in Rome since antiquity,[72] and was decorated with a fountain which was then responsible for similar 'sleeping nymph' fountains in the Villa Giulia itself and in the gardens of Angelo Colocci on the Pincio and of Cardinal Pia da Carpi's villa on the Quirinal.[73] The result

---

[71] The Laocoon group, of controversial date but usually assumed to be a Roman version of a Hellenistic original from as early as 200 BCE, is today in the Vatican Museum, inv. 1059. The literature on this statue and its influence is huge. Particularly relevant here are Bieber 1967, Settis 1999, Brilliant 2002 and the catalogue, *Laocoonte: alle origini dei Musei Vaticani* 2006.

[72] Ackerman 1954: 7–13.

[73] On the fountain, installed in 1512, see Brummer 1970: 154, and for its statue of Cleopatra/Ariadne, Haskell and Penny 1981: 184–7. For the influence of this fountain, see

Figure 5.26 The Laocoon group, from Marliani's *Urbis Romae topographia*, 1544: 89.

was a hall of mirrors: competitive sparks flashed back and forth between hilltop houses all over the city. The fact that the Villa Giulia, and all that it stood for, was included in both cycles meant that the Vatican Mount was finally, after centuries of drifting in and out of the canon, included also – together with Monti Parioli. The apparent claim was that Rome had embraced a hill for the first time since Servius Tullius.

MacDougall 1975 with a revised version in her book of 1994, and for the Villa Giulia in particular, Coffin 1979: 158–65 and 196–7 and 2004: 13.

Julius III was better qualified than most to make such a bold assertion. Born Giovanni Maria *de Monte*, he had an even stronger stake in mountains than the Chigi, something which had been celebrated since his coronation as pope in 1550.[74] The prologue of a comedy performed in honour of this event offers us a good example:

> nasce in questo terreno Romano un monte, che a poco a poco è venuto crescendo, et è arrivato a tanto altezza, che supera tutti gli alteri sette de assai, e s'è mostrato fin qui sì fruttuoso, et fecondo a questo Popolo, che il Tarpeo, e gli altri hanno havuta ragione, et hanno di rallegrarsi del surgimento di uno tanto Fratello, che hora è di loro diventato Signore.

> Rising in this Roman soil is a 'monte' which has grown little by little and arrived at such a great height that it very much surpasses all the other seven and has shown itself until now to be so fruitful and fertile to this people that the Tarpeian and the others were right and are right to rejoice in the rising of one such brother who now has become their Lord.[75]

It is a vision which only narrowly escapes casting Rome as Athos, and Julius as a flawed Alexander. And as time went by he was accused of spending too much time in his villa, of excessive luxury, and of improper relations with his adopted nephew, Innocenzo, who was referred to as his Ganymede.[76] Displaying an image of his villa next to the traditional seven certainly risked a reputation as a Suetonian tyrant. But did it clinch it? In the passage above, the seven hills remain intact as a group and rejoice, as Claudian's hills rejoiced at the election of Probinus and Olybrius to the consulship.[77] Rather than embracing an additional hill and changing Rome's essence, or indeed pushing one of the canon out as Alexander VII would do, Julius is perhaps better understood as pitting the idea of Rome as a city of seven hills against his villa, himself, his triple monticule. What are we to make of the rivalry?

---

[74] Nova 1988: 164: the emblem of the mount became an obsession during Julius III's reign.

[75] *Triomphante festa fatta dalli sig. romani per la creatione di P. Iulio III*, published by Cancellieri 1802: 502–4 and cited in Nova 1988: 164.

[76] On Julius' relationship with Innocenzo, whom he made a cardinal, see Burkle-Young and Doerrer 1997. It was a relationship which potentially exposed Julius to similar charges to those which the Christians weighed against Hadrian (whose villa was a model for Renaissance elites) and Antinous (see Lambert 1984, Vout 2007a and Rizzi 2010), and to Suetonius' accusations of Tiberius' depravity, hidden from view in his Villa Jovis on Capri (*Tib.* 43–5). For Innocenzo as Ganymede, Joachim Du Bellay 1555: sonnet 105.

[77] See above, p. 109.

Figure 5.27 The Quirinal panel, the Sala dei Sette Colli, Villa Giulia, Rome. See also colour plate section.

A closer look at the 'Sala dei Sette Colli' will allow us to determine the nature of these seven summits. We have already noted that the Esquiline and Villa Giulia scenes faced each other across the room – the Esquiline above the door into the Sala delle Virtù e Arti Liberali, and the Villa Giulia above the entrance to the bedroom with its frieze of Venus and the four seasons. All eight panels are in elaborate frames with their names on shields suspended by *putti*. But only the Esquiline, Villa, Capitoline and Palatine have golden frames with tiny faces in small roundels left and right, and of these only the first two have further putti embracing their nameplates. The other four hills are in purple settings with holes in place of cameos. Two pairs of gods, Neptune and Jupiter and Mars and Mercury, flank the Quirinal and Capitoline respectively (Figures 5.27 and 5.28).[78]

These discrepancies invite the viewer to think hard about the equivalence of the scenes. Were we right to privilege the Esquiline and Villa, when it is the Capitoline and Quirinal that have the divine sentinels, the first of these above the door onto the annular corridor and the other above the windows? In the villa panel, labourers are seen working, shovels in hand. Others carry what appears to be a sedan chair. Is that Julius himself who admires the fountain? Whatever the answer, the activity means that the villa will always just have been built, its finishing touches still about to be added. What of the famed seven hills? Which moment in their history is captured?

[78] On the inelegance of these gods, especially Jupiter, see Nova 1988: 154.

Figure 5.28 Jupiter from the frieze in the Sala dei Sette Colli, Villa Giulia, Rome.

Rather than show the construction of Michelangelo's Piazza del Campidoglio, which was ongoing at the time of the villa's decoration, the artist has chosen to go back to grass roots with the Capitoline (Figure 5.29). The hill is envisaged as two green summits, each topped with a different kind of building, on the left a round classical or Renaissance temple, iced with statuary, and on the right, a mediaeval brick tower. The valley between them creates a chiasmus at the centre of which is a colossal, white portrait bust, as large as the five human figures who populate the foreground. A staircase zigzags from them and the water below them up the mountain. Three goats gambol.

The likeliest reading of the human figures is that they refer to the story of Tarpeia.[79] According to the legend with which we are already familiar, she betrayed the Roman citadel to the Sabines and was crushed to death as a result. Here, four men in military dress approach a woman, who has been fetching water (Figure 5.30). The correspondence with Propertius' account is striking: 'Tarpeia would draw water from this spring for the goddess,

---

[79] Campitelli 1984: 203.

Figure 5.29 The Capitoline panel, the Sala dei Sette Colli, Villa Giulia, Rome. See also colour plate section.

Figure 5.30 Close-up of the Capitoline panel, the Sala dei Sette Colli, Villa Giulia, Rome. See also colour plate section.

and an earthenware pot weighed heavily on the middle of her head. She saw Tatius exercising on the sandy plain.'[80] In the poem she retreats to the northern summit of the Capitoline, where she realizes that she has fallen in love.[81] In Livy, by contrast, her betrayal stems not from love but from greed – which is perhaps why in the painting, she is resplendent in gold, like the material she covets, reaching out towards what appear to be Sabine bracelets.[82] The implication is that the steps lead to the *arx* or northern summit which later took the name 'Tarpeian'.[83]

If the tower is meant to suggest the Capitoline's fortified citadel, what about the other building? Is it – despite its discrepancy from numismatic images – the Temple of Jupiter Optimus Maximus, which Tarquinius Priscus is said to have vowed while battling the Sabines?[84] In the Vatican equivalent (Figure 5.31) it is replaced by the Church of Santa Maria in Aracoeli, which still stands on the *arx* today, while the mediaeval building is not a tower but a structure which has more in common with the Campidoglio's Palazzo Senatorio as it appears in a 1562 engraving by Flemish artist Hieronymus Cock (Figure 5.32).[85] Our versions, in contrast, are made to seem symbolic rather than specific, representative not of topographical detail but of the hill's historiographical phases: Rome's mythological beginnings at the base, the Middle Ages with its towers fortified by the Corsi family,[86] the Renaissance facelift. The tower and temple are turned into proto-follies, purpose-built for this landscape.

They are as figurative as the head in the centre, and this head is more enigmatic than its Vatican sibling. Most scholars have been keen to link it to the marble head of Constantine found in the Basilica of Maxentius in the Forum in the second half of the fourteenth century (Figure 5.33).[87] Although the head was not incorporated into Giacomo della Porta's fountain on the Capitoline until later in the sixteenth century, an earlier image by Dutch artist Maarten van Heemskerck shows it already on the floor of the cortile

---

[80] Prop. 4.4.15–17 and 19 and on the complexities of this passage, Heyworth 2007a: 447–9.

> hunc Tarpeia deae fontem libarat, at illi
>   urgebat medium fictilis urna caput.
> videt harenosis Tatium proludere campis.

[81] Prop. 4.4.29–30:

> et sua Tarpeia residens ita flevit ab arce
>   vulnera, vicinae non patienda Iovis:

[82] Livy 1.11.8.
[83] See Prop. 4.4.93: 'a duce Tarpeium mons est cognomen adeptus' (although note that Heyworth's text reads: 'a duce *turpe* Iovis mons est cognomen adeptus').
[84] Campitelli 1984: 203.   [85] See Pietrangeli *et al.* 1965: plate 15.
[86] Krautheimer 1980: 150–1 and 206.   [87] See Campitelli 1984: 203.

Figure 5.31 The Capitoline panel, Julius III's apartment, Palazzo del Belvedere.

Figure 5.32 Hieronymus Cock's engraving of the Campidoglio, showing the Palazzo Senatorio, 1562.

Figure 5.33 Head of Constantine, Collection of the Capitoline Museum, Rome.

of the Palazzo dei Conservatori when the frescoes were painted.[88] But if the purpose of having a sculpture in the painting was purely archaeological, then why not use the equestrian bronze of Marcus Aurelius which had been famous in Rome in the Middle Ages (first as a Constantine) and which by 1539–40 was already destined, much against Michelangelo's better judgement, to be the focal point of his piazza?[89] The head is less an antique statue than an apparition to enthrall the viewer.

The key to its meaning must lie in the hill's etymology. As we have observed, the Capitol was said to take its name from a human head that was unearthed during the digging of the foundations of Tarquinius' temple. This macabre discovery and the recent excavation of the portrait sculpture

[88] For the history of this head, which was originally identified as Apollo, see Stuart Jones 1926 5–6, *Cortile*, cat. no. 2, and for the drawing, Pietrangeli *et al.* 1965: plate 23.
[89] See Haskell and Penny 1981: 252–5.

Figure 5.34 The Viminal panel, the Sala dei Sette Colli, Villa Giulia, Rome. See also colour plate section.

converge and, with them, the antiquarian exercise of marrying new finds with ancient texts in an attempt to revive antiquity. Varro writes:

> Out of these, the Capitoline is so named, because here, when the foundations of the Temple of Jupiter were being dug, it is said that a human head was found. This hill was previously called the Tarpeian after the Vestal Virgin Tarpeia, who was killed there by the Sabines with their shields and buried. Of her name a memorial remains, namely that even now the cliff is called the Tarpeian Rock.[90]

The Capitoline panel tells of all these incarnations. The goats, meanwhile, add a further level: the southern summit was still 'Monte Caprino' in the sixteenth century.[91]

Are the other hills similarly rendered? In the case of the Viminal (Figures 5.34 and 5.35), a young male figure in a red tunic signals to a statue in the centre of the foreground. Nude, bearded and with a giant eagle at its feet, this statue is obviously Jupiter but less resonant as a recent find

---

[90] Varro, *Ling.* 5.41: 'e quis Capitolinum dictum, quod hic, cum fundamenta foderentur aedis Iovis, caput humanum dicitur inventum. hic mons ante Tarpeius dictus a virgine Vestale Tarpeia, quae ibi a Sabinis necata armis et sepulta: cuius nominis monimentum relictum, quod etiam nunc eius rupes Tarpeium appellatur saxum.'

[91] Krautheimer 1980: 285.

Figure 5.35 Close-up of the Viminal panel, the Sala dei Sette Colli, Villa Giulia, Rome. See also colour plate section.

than the head of Constantine or the Laocoon. Instead, its meaning seems to rest with Varro, who tells us that the hill gets its name from Jupiter Viminius (Jupiter who fosters the growth of twigs), who had an altar there.[92] Less easy to understand is the pool on the left, though it reminds the viewer that the ruins behind belong to the hill's most famous structure, the Baths of Diocletian. The statue, however, is the focal point – a signpost. So too the sculpture in the Quirinal panel (Figure 5.36). Damage done to its middle section does little to dent its legibility: Petrarch's 'naked giants',[93] the ancient statues of Castor and Pollux, which had stood there since the twelfth century if not since antiquity, dominate the scene – both with horses. They gave the hill its modern name of 'Horse Mountain' or Monte Cavallo.

Just as we are beginning to believe that etymology might be the unifying factor, the Aventine and Palatine take a different tack (Figures 5.37, 5.38 and 5.39), preferring plain and simple mythology. This is not surprising: the king of Alba Longa, Aventinus, is overly obscure to guarantee recognition, and Romulus and Remus, who appear with the she-wolf to the bottom right

---

[92] A point missed by Campitelli 1984. See Varro, *Ling.* 5.51: 'Collis Viminalis a Iove Viminio, quod ibi ara eius.'
[93] See Chapter 2, n. 89.

Figure 5.36 Close-up of the Quirinal panel, the Sala dei Sette Colli, Villa Giulia, Rome. See also colour plate section.

Figure 5.37 The Palatine panel, the Sala dei Sette Colli, Villa Giulia, Rome. See also colour plate section.

Figure 5.38 The Aventine panel, the Sala dei Sette Colli, Villa Giulia, Rome. See also colour plate section.

Figure 5.39 Close-up of the Aventine panel, the Sala dei Sette Colli, Villa Giulia, Rome. See also colour plate section.

of the Palatine panel, too iconic not to have a starring role. In the Aventine scene, a large male figure, naked except for a cloak, is seen dragging a large white cow by its tail into a cave. As with Tarpeia in the Capitoline panel, it is a close match for an image in Propertius book 4 – an image this time of

the legendary Cacus, stealing the cattle which Hercules had acquired in his tenth labour:

He, so that there would be no clear and obvious signs of theft, dragged the bulls backwards into the cave by their tails. But the theft was not unwitnessed by the god.[94]

Although Hercules' cultic activity was concentrated in the Forum Boarium, in the valley between the Aventine and Palatine, Virgil and Ovid identify Cacus with the Aventine, with early antiquarians unable to agree on which side of the hill to place his cave.[95] Not that our painting is concerned with the hill's ancient topography, any more than is that of the Palatine: while the latter includes ruins of the imperial palaces as well as the pristine Church of San Teodoro, the Aventine displays the Basilica of Santa Sabina on its summit. Instead, each of them incorporates iconic moments from Rome's legendary past (each rather self-contained towards the bottom corner of the frame), which function as the statue of Jupiter functions to advertise the hill's identity.

This leaves only the Caelian (Figure 5.40) – a scene which is curious for the absence of symbology: no statues or appeals to ancient texts – just buildings, with the Arch of Constantine and Septizodium on the right, the Colosseum on the flat in the foreground, and the Basilica of Santo Stefano Rotondo above. The roundness of these last two structures establishes an echo between the martyr church, which had yet to receive its graphic frescoes (see Figure 2.13), and the blood-soaked amphitheatre, which was beginning to be seen as a sacred site. Nowhere was the relationship of past and present so charged. Why dilute it with superfluous detail? To quote Martial on the Colosseum as one of the seven wonders: 'Fame will speak of one work in place of all.'[96]

---

[94] Prop. 4.9.11–13:

> hic, ne certa forent manifestaque signa rapinae,
>   aversos cauda traxit in antra boves.
> nec sine teste deo furtum est.

Also relevant here is Livy 1.7.

[95] For the Aventine, see Virg. *Aen.* 8.221 and 230–2 and Ov. *Fast.* 1.550–3:

> traxerat aversos Cacus in antra ferox,
> Cacus, Aventinae timor atque infamia silvae,
>   non leve finitimis hospitibusque malum.

[96] Mart. *Spect.* 1.8: 'unum pro cunctis fama loquetur opus.'

Figure 5.40 The Caelian panel, the Sala dei Sette Colli, Villa Giulia, Rome. See also colour plate section.

Only the Villa Giulia is labelled inside its panel (Figure 5.41), and this is revealing not only of Julius' name but of the date of his fountain's creation. It is also the only panel not to contain any ancient ruins or mediaeval buildings. All of the buildings are new, and the spades are indicative of construction rather than excavation. Any antiquities are well ordered and intact – resurrected on top of monumental structures or reframed within niches. The overall effect is similar to the imaginary setting of the Laocoon group, except that the damaged Acqua Vergine aqueduct is still working – water spewing from the mouth of the fountain's mask. Although there is also water in the fountain in the Esquiline panel, the aqueducts in the background of the scene lie broken.

Here, the relics which haunt the other panels, and the various relationships with the classical past that they embody (whether these relationships are based on a layered or palimpsestic model as in the Capitoline image, on a model of nostalgia as with the Viminal, of continuity as in the case of the Quirinal, or indeed a collector's or Christian perspective as with the Esquiline and Caelian respectively . . .), are repositioned and remade. As well as name and date, the fountain records a further detail, the words 'Pontifex Maximus' or 'head of the pontifical college', which we have already seen on Ferri's image, and which, on the one hand, refers simply to Julius'

Figure 5.41 Close-up of Villa Giulia panel, the Sala dei Sette Colli, Villa Giulia, Rome. See also colour plate section.

position as pope, and, on the other, to an office which had been made an imperial title under Augustus and went back as far as Romulus' successor, Numa. *Pontifex* literally means 'bridge builder' and suggests that he, like the seven hills, forges a link with the past, able in his villa to find a place for the antique that reanimates it, turning it from picturesque backdrop to part of the furniture, or – more than that – a marker not of what has been lost, but of what is to be gained – of status. The fountain's dedication fulfils the function of signature to make Pope Julius III mythographer.

The fresco-cycle does not reveal much more about the villa than the villa itself. Such were its statues, its setting and its view, that the archbishop of Uppsala in 1562 could describe it as an eighth wonder of the world.[97] But what it does reveal is Julius' vision of his villa, a vision which regarded it not as an expansion of or substitute for Rome, but as a microcosm of all that ancient Rome is and was, a better microcosm than the other Renaissance estates in and on the outskirts of the city (a better microcosm than the Vatican?).[98] The hills were perfect for this role: they provided coverage from

---

[97] Olaus Magnus 1562, *Historia de gentibus septem trionalibus*, as cited by Nova 1988: 95.

[98] For example, the Villa Madama on Monte Mario on the other side of the Tiber, begun by Raphael and completed in 1525 by Antonio da Sangallo the younger for Pope Clement VII: see Coffin 1979: 152.

Romulus and Tarpeia to the Julio-Claudian period to late antiquity and beyond, blending the pagan and Christian, myth and history, the real and the imaginary. They owed their appearance not to Michelangelo and the ongoing work on the Capitoline but to the work of Petrarch and Fulvio, and their interest in Varro, Virgil and Propertius, and in etymology. Reading the labels of any of these panels, the viewer is confronted with Montaigne's problem of what it means to know;[99] with the gap between the Rome they see on the walls, the Rome they see when they study Varro and Propertius, and the Rome they see from the windows. Which is more authentic? Each is being asked what Rome means to them, to turn the city from place to puzzle. The power of the Sala dei Sette Colli is that it dares to ask the question – and to ask it slightly differently from its Vatican counterpart. Julius understands that it is less important to provide an answer than it is to see that Rome is an intellectual problem.

Nineteenth-century ways of seeing

A systematic excavation and restoration of the main classical remains of the city was undertaken for the first time during the French occupation, 1809–14. Although the work was motivated by political and economic considerations, this was the beginning of archaeology in Rome.[100]

By the time we get to the first quarter of the nineteenth century and the publication of Luigi Rossini's engravings, the obsessions of antiquarians and papal collectors had long been enjoyed by a wider community of scholars and amateur enthusiasts. The Grand Tour had brought countless foreign aristocrats to Rome in search of cultural and real capital, accelerating the international trade in antiquities, casts and engravings. Competition for prime pieces increased the need for regulation of any digging done, and for information about where a sculpture had been discovered, with those from sites such as Hadrian's villa commanding especially high market value.[101] The popes remained the most powerful consumers – so much so that the expansion of the Vatican's Museo Clementino in the 1770s spurred

---

[99] See Chapter 2, n. 126.   [100] Ridley 1992: xix.
[101] Bibliography on the Grand Tour is formidable. For an overview, with a strong archaeological emphasis, see e.g. Bignamini and Wilton 1996 and Bignamini and Hornsby 2010. On the afterlife of Hadrian's villa at Tivoli, see MacDonald and Pinto 1995 and Lavagne and Charles-Gaffiot 1999. As a counterpoint, covering Renaissance engagement with ancient sculpture and its influence, are Barkan 1999 and Fusco and Corti 2007, and, for preservation strategies promoted by popes in Renaissance Rome, Karmon 2011.

a marked growth in the number of excavations. In 1777, for example, Scottish painter and dealer Gavin Hamilton was digging on the Palatine, and Don José Nicolás de Azara in the Villa Peretti on the Esquiline.[102] Three years earlier, Ludovico Mirri had unearthed painted rooms in Nero's Golden House, and in 1781 excavations in the Villa Palombara, again on the Esquiline, found the first known version of Myron's Discobolos or 'discus thrower'.[103]

Such activity needed scholarship to underwrite it and opened the door for a more empirical study of ancient artefacts and their find-spots. Classical literature was still crucial in identifying new works and linking them to specific artists, but the sheer number of pieces unearthed, displayed and published, meant that corpora of images could be established, and with them, chronologies, archaeologies even. Johann Winckelmann led the way here. Living and working in Rome for one of the greatest collectors, Cardinal Alessandro Albani, Winckelmann used his first-hand visual knowledge to help his patron augment his collection, and to revise his own magnum opus, the *Geschichte der Kunst des Alterthums*, or *History of the Art of Antiquity*, which he had started years before, working only from engravings. The 1764 edition's dearth of plates created the space for the soaring, subjective ekphrases for which Winckelmann is famed. But the book's framework was even more important than its descriptions. It constituted the first systematic attempt to root the production of ancient art and its changing style in a geographical, historical and political context. And it amounted to nothing less than the emergence of art history as a discipline.[104]

Not many of the artefacts that Winckelmann talked about had been made in Greece as he had assumed. Rather they were Roman versions – something which his friend Raphael Mengs had already suspected. Restoration too, though standard practice for any newly discovered antiquity, was a matter for debate. Collectors like Charles Townley refused pieces they thought had been inappropriately restored, while – by the time we come to the first volume of his *Specimens of Antient Sculpture... Selected from Different Collections in Great Britain*, published in 1809 – restoration was, in different ways, made a

---

[102] For Hamilton, see Amelung 1908: 448 and for the Villa Peretti – a site which became known as the 'Villa Negroni' – Buti 1778. For the later influence of the frescoes found there, see Joyce 1983, and on the Pompeian room at Ickworth House in particular, Moffitt 1983 and Amery and Curran 2002: 181.

[103] See Mirri and Carletti 1776 and Lanciani 1897: 160.

[104] See Potts 1994 with bibliography, and the new edition of the 1764 edition of the *Geschichte* by Malgrave 2006. Excellent on putting Winckelmann into a broader art historical and intellectual context is Prettejohn 2005: ch. 1.

feature of the engravings.[105] Desire for the antique and accurately recording the antique were becoming two sides of the same coin.

By 1827, when the first of Rossini's hills series was produced, Napoleon's troops have been and gone. The image that endures in the minds of the classicist is the Sèvres porcelain vase, showing the procession of Rome's most famous antiquities, the Laocoon group included, entering Paris in triumph under the Treaty of Tolentino.[106] But there is a more positive side to the French occupation. Under the guidance of papal antiquarian Carlo Fea, who had published his own important *Dissertazione sulle rovine di Roma* as an appendix to his 1783 French translation of Winckelmann's *Geschichte*, stricter rules governed the treatment of the city's past than ever before: all excavations had to be authorized, monuments protected at public expense, and no antiquities exported without a licence.[107] With the *Commission des Monuments* and *Commission des Embellisements* of 1810 and 1811, workers were contracted and key monuments cleared and restored, 'the Garden of the Capitol' and demolitions on the Palatine being seen as priorities.[108] Nero's Golden House too was much worked on, and the results published in Antonio de Romanis' *Le antiche camere esquiline* of 1822. At the same time, the proceedings of the *Pontificia Accademia Romana di Archeologia* and the *Bolletino of the Istituto di Corrispondenza Archaeologica* start up. As with Mussolini's projects, the emphasis on the classical meant the loss of much else: but archaeology had joined art history.

It is against this backdrop that Rossini (1790–1857) produced his hills ancient and modern.[109] Rossini began his training in Bologna under painter and set designer Antonio Basoli, and then he worked with Canova, but he has suffered subsequently, largely from following in the footsteps of Giovanni Battista Piranesi (1720–78). Piranesi's etchings (over a thousand of them in total) have come to define the eighteenth century's approach to antiquity, as well as to provide crucial information about how the many monuments he depicted looked prior to restoration in the nineteenth and twentieth centuries. We shall see Rossini negotiating a relationship with him. The figures in the foreground of his *vedute*, meanwhile, are the work of Trastevere-born engraver Bartolomeo Pinelli, who is known for his images of costumes and his illustrations of epic poetry.[110] In 1825 he too had

---

[105] Important here is the catalogue by Redford 2008. I owe this point to my doctoral student, Katie McAfee, whose forthcoming thesis has a chapter on the *Specimens*.
[106] The vase, made by Antoine Béranger in 1813 is 1.2 metres in height and today in the Musée National de Céramique, France: see Bourgeois 2008.
[107] See Ridley 1992.   [108] Ridley 1992: 52–71.
[109] See Cavazzi and Tittoni 1982 and Pirazzoli 1990: especially 165–97.
[110] See Pacini 1935, Incisa della Rocchetta 1956 and Fagiolo and Marini 1983.

Figure 5.42 Bartolomeo Pinelli, View of the Aventine.

produced a seven-hills series, his rendition of the Aventine rising from the Tiber rivalling Mantegna's 'Palatine' in its steepness (Figure 5.42). But these images lack the ambition of Rossini's. In what follows we take his *I sette colli di Roma antica e moderna con piante e restauri dei medesimi, e coi colli adiacenti* of 1829, which mixes views of and from the hills with sculptural fragments, maps, including pieces of the Marble Plan (discovered in 1562, after the Villa Giulia's frescoes are complete, and not exhibited until 1741, fifteen years after which Piranesi publishes the main fragments), and reconstructions based on texts and coins, to examine what these and the text on the plates and in the preface do to the way that the hills represent the city.[111]

Rossini is often seen as providing an accurate picture of post-Napoleonic Rome.[112] And a quick look at plate 7, a view of 'the Palatine and part of the

---

[111] The publication is itself an amalgamation and enlargement of two previous series by Rossini, the eight plates of his *Vedute dei sette colli di Roma con altre parti adiacenti ossia Roma antica e moderna* and the six of *Vedute adiacente i sette colli di Roma con un panorama preso in luogo ove si veggono tutti i monumenti antichi*, and has, in its first edition, thirty plates in total. A subsequent edition adds a further three, giving more of a starring role to the Vatican. See Cavazzi and Tittoni 1982: 101.

[112] A point well made by Ridley 1992 and his caption for plate 45: 'it is important to note the artist's license, since he is so often credited with exactness'.

Figure 5.43 Rossini's *Palatine and Part of the Roman Forum.*

Roman Forum, looking west from Capitoline mount, and precisely in the garden of the Convent of Aracoeli', demonstrates why (Figure 5.43).[113]

In this grandiose view, one can make out all of the ruins of the above-mentioned hill – on the side that faces towards the Capitoline and the Roman Forum. In there one also admires the ruins of the house of Tiberius, Augustus and of Caligula and on the top the remains of the library of Palatine Apollo. At the foot of the above-mentioned mount, one sees the remains of the temples of the Roman Forum and of the others right up to the Colosseum, and on the right hand one sees part of the Aventine hill and the tall tower of the Capitol that concludes this immense scene. The keys under the *veduta* indicate all of the aforementioned monuments.[114]

As we might expect from the title and explanatory text on the plate, the Palatine is numbered 1, but we have to search hard for its numeral, meeting

[113] As described in the 'Spiegazione delle tavole' section of the volume: 'altra veduta del Monte Palatino, e parte del Foro Romano presa a ponente sul Monte Capitolino, e precisamente nell'orto del Convento del Aracoeli'.
[114] 'In questa grandiosa veduta scorgonsi tutte le rovine del sudetto Monte dalla parte che riguarda in Capitolino, e il Foro Romano. Ivi ammiransi pure li ruderi della casa Tiberiana, Augustana, e di Caligola, e gli avanzi in alto della Biblioteca di Apollo palatino.
     A piedi poi del sudetto Monte si veggono i residui de' templi del Foro Romano e degli altri sino al Colosseo; e a mano dritta si scorge una parte del Monte Aventino, e la gran torre Capitolina che chiude questa immense Scena. Le chiamate sotto alla veduta indicano tutti li sudescritti monumenti.'

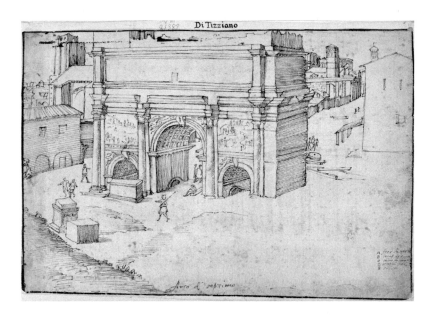

Figure 5.44 Giovanni Battista Naldini (1537–91), previously wrongly attributed to Titian, *Vue de l'arc de Septime Sévère.*

those which mark the Aventine and Caelian as we do so. Despite the weight of the prose, these and the Colosseum are but the backdrop to the Arch of Septimius Severus, the Column of Phocas behind it and, further to the right, the columns of the Temple of Saturn (labelled 20, and called the 'Temple of Concord', as it was until properly identified in 1834).[115] The setting of these structures bears witness to recent and radical archaeological activity.

Compare their appearance with an engraving of the Arch of Septimius Severus by Naldini and two engravings from Piranesi's *Vedute di Roma* series (1740s–1770s) (Figures 5.44–5.46), the first showing the Temple of Saturn, and the second a panoramic view of the Forum from a characteristically elevated viewpoint on or above the Capitol.[116] The modern buildings which crowd the temple's base have vanished from Rossini's image, and a road has been built to its left up to the Capitol – both initiatives accomplished by the French from 1810, before they turned their attention to the area around the column, and both emphasized here by the light shining through its columns

---

[115] Ridley 1992: 189.
[116] Ridley 1992: 194, plate 65, and 28, plate 6. On Piranesi's elevated viewpoint, see Watkin 2009: 31–3. And for Naldini, Louvre, Paris, D. A. G., inv. 11031, recto.

Figure 5.45 Piranesi's view of the Temple of Saturn.

Figure 5.46 Piranesi's panoramic view of the Forum.

Figure 5.47 Rossini's *Capitoline Hill.*

and by the horse and cart at the bottom of the slope.[117] The exposure of the arch is even more obvious, the retaining wall, built by Pius VII before his exile in 1809, encircling it like a frame so as to afford a similar perspective to the bird's-eye view of the Parthian cities on its piers (see Figure 5.1 on p. 123).[118] There can be no doubt that this is the nineteenth century, and that Rome has been tamed. Arguably the most important mound is the Forum, which gaze and pickaxe penetrate.

Yet something about the rhetoric of Rossini's text should make us hesitate. Its claims to encompass all of the ruins turn out to be typical. Take the next plate, a view of the Capitoline, taken from the top of the Palatine, or plate 17, a view of the Aventine (Figures 5.47 and 5.48): 'In this vast scene in which the eye can scarcely see all the objects that compose it, one can still see the remains of the Tabularium, on which is built the imposing Capitoline palace of the Senator' and 'In this view, we see all the ruins of the large Antonine baths of Caracalla and in the distance the whole of the Roman

---

[117] On the clearing of the temple, see Ridley 1992: 139–41 and 189–93, and, on the column, Ridley 1992: 123–6. In 1815, after Napoleon's fall, the Portuguese ambassador, the Comte de Funchal, began a private dig on the Clivus Capitolinus, the ancient approach to the Capitoline, and by 1817 the Duchess of Devonshire had funded further excavations around the Column of Phocas, which exposed the stepped pyramid at the base: Watkin 2009: 186–7.

[118] Ridley 1992: 36–38 and 139–40.

Figure 5.48　Rossini's *Aventine Hill.*

campagna.'[119] Or plate 12, the view of the Quirinal (Figure 5.49), 'In this immense scene, where the whole of the above-mentioned hill opens itself to view, I have tried to take the one point that I seemed to have found to give a general idea of the present state'.[120] By the time we reach his final four plates, not individual hills but his panorama of Rome ancient and modern (Figure 5.50), he has

tried to select a high point from which one should be able to see the whole of ancient Rome, given that modern things are on the whole of little interest to the lover of antiquity or to the foreigner. Therefore, I chose the tower of Santa Maria Nuova or Santa Francesca in Campo Vaccino adjacent to the Roman Forum and standing on its top I have portrayed it. In the foreground one sees all the ancient monuments of the aforementioned Forum and in the distance all the seven hills.[121]

---

[119] The explanatory text to plate 8 in the 'Spiegazione' section reads: 'In questa vasta Scena, in che l'occhio appena scorge tutti gli oggetti che la compongono, si vedono ancora gli avanzi del Tabulario, sul quale è fabricato il grandioso palazzo Capitolino del Senatore', and to plate 17: 'In questa veduta scorgonsi tutte le rovine delle grandi terme Antoniniane di Caracalla ed in distanza tutta la Campagna di Roma ...'

[120] 'In questa immensa scena ove scopersi tutto il monte suddetto, ho cercato prendere l'unico punto, che mi è sembrato trovare per dar un' idea generale dello stato presente ...'

[121] 'ho cercato di sciegliere un' altura in che si vedesse tutta Roma antica, essendo che le cose moderne poco più o meno interressano l'amatore dell'antichità, e lo Straniero. Dunque scelsi la torre di S. M. nuova o sia S. Francesca in Campo Vaccino; annessa al Foro Romano; e sulla cima di essa l'ho ritratto. In Avanti veggonsi tutti i monumenti antichi del detto Foro, e in distanza tutti i 7 Colli.'

Figure 5.49 Rossini's *Quirinal Hill.*

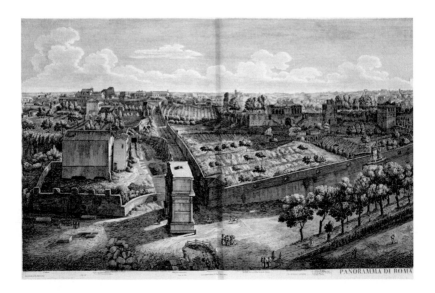

Figure 5.50 Rossini's *Panorama of Rome.*

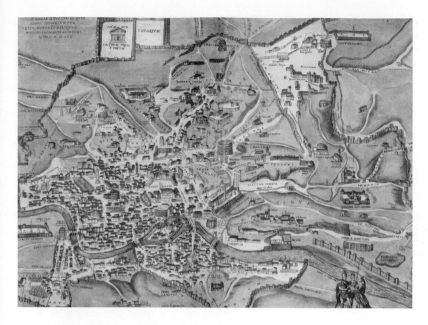

Figure 1.3 Bird's-eye view of ancient Rome by Pirro Ligorio, as printed in Braun and Hogenberg 1572–1617.

Figure 2.12 Section of Andrea Mantegna's *Martyrdom of St Sebastian*, 1480.

Figure 2.13 Fresco of Nero persecuting the Christians, Santo Stefano Rotondo, Rome.

Figure 2.14 Bartolomeo di Giovanni, *Rape of the Sabines*, 1488.

Figure 4.1 The goddess Roma as depicted in the Palazzo dei Congressi, EUR, Rome.

Figure 4.3 Pierre-Henri de Valenciennes, 1750–1819, *Mount Athos Carved as a Monument to Alexander the Great*, 1796.

Figure 5.2 Wall painting from the *triclinium* of the House of M. Fabius Secundus, Pompeii.

Figure 5.20 The Esquiline panel, the Sala dei Sette Colli, Villa Giulia, Rome.

Figure 5.21 The Villa Giulia panel, the Sala dei Sette Colli, Villa Giulia, Rome.

Figure 5.23 Close-up of the Esquiline panel, the Sala dei Sette Colli, Villa Giulia, Rome.

Figure 5.24 Julius III's heraldic device, the Sala dei Sette Colli, Villa Giulia, Rome.

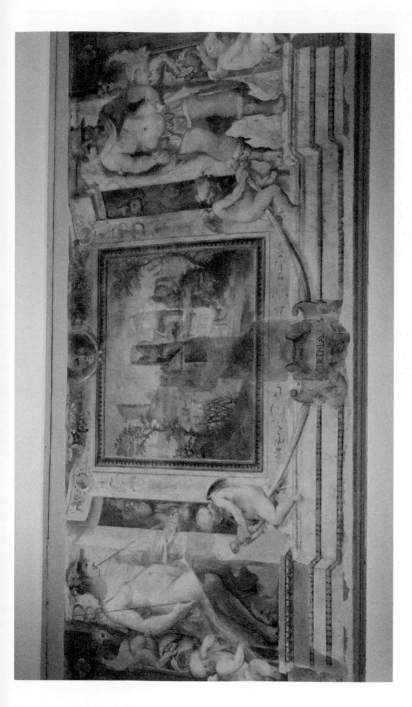

Figure 5.27 The Quirinal panel, the Sala dei Sette Colli, Villa Giulia, Rome.

Figure 5.29 The Capitoline panel, the Sala dei Sette Colli, Villa Giulia, Rome.

Figure 5.30 Close-up of the Capitoline panel, the Sala dei Sette Colli, Villa Giulia, Rome.

Figure 5.34 The Viminal panel, the Sala dei Sette Colli, Villa Giulia, Rome.

Figure 5.35 Close-up of the Viminal panel, the Sala dei Sette Colli, Villa Giulia, Rome.

Figure 5.36   Close-up of the Quirinal panel, the Sala dei Sette Colli, Villa Giulia, Rome.

Figure 5.37   The Palatine panel, the Sala dei Sette Colli, Villa Giulia, Rome.

Figure 5.38 The Aventine panel, the Sala dei Sette Colli, Villa Giulia, Rome.

Figure 5.39 Close-up of the Aventine panel, the Sala dei Sette Colli, Villa Giulia, Rome.

Figure 5.40 The Caelian panel, the Sala dei Sette Colli, Villa Giulia, Rome.

Figure 5.41 Close-up of Villa Giulia panel, the Sala dei Sette Colli, Villa Giulia, Rome.

Figure 6.6 John Robert Cozens (1782–3) *View of the Villa Lante on the Janiculum (Gianicolo), in Rome.*

Figure 6.9 Samuel Palmer, *The Golden City: Rome from the Janiculum.*

Figure 6.11 Samuel Palmer, *A View of Ancient Rome.*

Figure 6.12 Samuel Palmer, *A View of Modern Rome.*

Figure 5.51 Frontispiece to Rossini's *I sette colli.*

The agenda is less about accuracy than it is about capturing the whole of the (especially ancient) city.

Authors are still able to 'aestimare totam Romam' through its seven hills. What does this tradition look like? How does it look? How self-conscious is Rossini of marrying it (and the literature-inspired views of Julius III's frescoes and of artists such as Claude and Turner) with the more analytical gaze promoted by the clearance exercises of the French and ongoing excavation – not to mention Winckelmann's teleological narrative, and Nolli's map of 1748? The frontispiece of Rossini's hills collection already raises these issues (Figure 5.51). A banner bearing his name and the work's title is shown suspended between the 'Trophies of Marius'. Huge, formidable, frontal, these ancient marbles stand as gatekeepers to the volume as well as to the view on that particular page, which the volume's opening text describes not as the Roman Forum today, but as 'the Roman Forum imagined'.[122] Below the banner, and – less obviously – beyond the trophies to the far right and left of the image, are glimpses of a reconstructed Rome, complete with people, palaces, columns, triumphal arches topped with sculpture and an equestrian statue. Further down still, a block of tiny text expands on what we are

---

[122] 'In ondo a questa tavola si vede immaginato il Foro Romano.'

looking at: 'a little ideal view' ('una piccola veduta ideale') made up of the Forum, Palatine, Caelian, Esquiline, Capitoline, with its Temple of Jupiter, and below, the Arch of Septimius Severus, while a second block points to the Tarpeian Rock on the far right with its Temple of Juno Moneta. The hills crowd in. Although the explanatory description has already noted how the trophies (which we last saw on Julius' Esquiline panels) were moved to the Capitoline in 1590 and has called upon Piranesi and Winckelmann among others to debate their ancient history, the plate reiterates their position on the Capitoline, and their height ('sul Campidoglio alt. Met. 4.200'). Elevation is important (Figure 5.52). Up there, the view across the Campidoglio to the Forum is blocked by Palazzo Senatorio. Here, they offer a window onto the city.

They also set Rossini in direct competition with Piranesi, whose own engravings of the trophies appeared in 1753 as *I Trofei di Ottaviano Augusto*.[123] Four years later he had published his four-volumed *Le antichità romane* and had been made an honorary member of the Society of Antiquaries. Is Rossini's achievement comparable? In his preface he mentions Piranesi as he claims to present the hills in their actual state. And in his second plate (Figure 5.53) – *A General Plan Of Ancient Rome and its Seven Hills* – he explains that 'besides being the biggest, with the exception of that of Nolli, it contains all of the discoveries made right up to today, which have been exactly measured and placed in their respective places'.[124] Piranesi had collaborated with Nolli on his *Piccola pianta*, published in the same year as the cartographer's Great Plan, and had later used it as the basis for his own map of the city (his *Pianta di Roma e del Campo Marzo, c.* 1774).[125] It is tempting to see Rossini's mention of size as a challenge. Whereas Nolli's plan indexes ten ancient sites, Piranesi's version lists 402. Rossini's stress on the present day is a boast that his is an update.

Debts like this one pervade Rossini's images. In plate 4, for example, *Fragments Found on the Palatine*, and today in the 'Gran Sala' of Palazzo Farnese, are arranged on the page so as to afford a similar window onto the Circus Maximus as was given onto the Forum (Figure 5.54). 'In the middle of this plate, I have picturesquely imagined the Circus Maximus', writes Rossini.[126] His vision shares a lot with the illustrations in Onofrio Panvinio's

---

[123] Piranesi 1761, *Le rovine del Castello dell'Acqua Giulia*, followed.
[124] *Pianta generale di Roma antica, e dei sette colli*. In the explanatory text Rossini writes: 'Questa pianta, oltre all'essere la più grande, e tolta quella di Nolli, contiene tutte le scoperte fatte sino al di d'oggi, le quali sono state esattamente misurate e collocate ai luoghi respettivi.'
[125] See http://vasi.uoregon.edu/imagourbis.html (last accessed 25 January 2010) and Bevilacqua 1998: 83–96.
[126] 'Nel mezzo di questa tavola, ho immaginato pittorescamente il Circo Massimo.'

Figure 5.52 One of the so-called 'Trophies of Marius' on the balustrade of the Campidoglio.

De ludis circensibus, published posthumously in Venice in 1600 – highly appropriate given that Panvinio had been librarian of Alessandro Farnese (Figure 5.55).[127] Although he is keen in his preface to assert that he is leaving the origins, etymologies and position of the hills to others, if his images are to appeal to 'lovers and students of antiquity', as he hoped, then they have

---

[127] On Panvinio and his place in the antiquarian tradition, see Heenes 2003 with review by Vout 2006.

Figure 5.53 Rossini's *General Plan of Ancient Rome and its Seven Hills.*

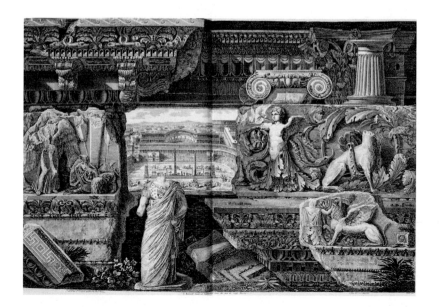

Figure 5.54 Rossini's *Fragments Found on the Palatine.*

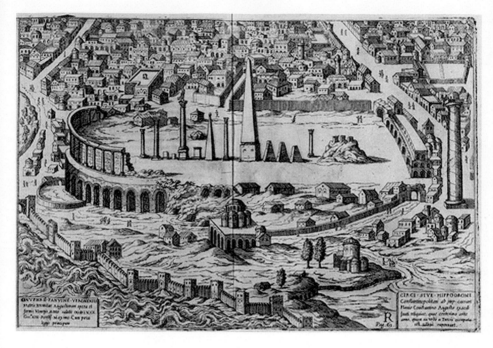

Figure 5.55 The hippodrome in Constantinople as seen in Onofrio Panvinio's *De ludis circensibus*, 1600.

to speak a familiar language. The next two plates (5 and 6), described as a *Plan of the Actual State of the Palatine and Forum* and *Restoration of the Palatine, Forum and Via Sacra* (or, as it is on the engraving itself, *Restoration of the Palace of the Caesars and the Roman Forum*) respectively, are, in a sense, companion pieces to the former. The accompanying text for the first of them cites Festus, Varro and Pausanias, as well as the reconstruction drawings of the palace by Veronese polymath Francesco Bianchini (1662–1729) and Panvinio's *De ludis circensibus*, and it boasts – a little like plate 2 – that it succeeds where even Leonardo Bufalini's plan of 1551 had failed. The second has a shorter explanatory text, drawing attention to the engraving's key, which identifies those buildings which appear neither on coins nor on the Marble Plan, fragments of which are laid out on the right but have been restored instead from their description in ancient texts; so, for example, 'the arch of Octavian Augustus, Pliny 36.5' and 'the Temple of Minerva, Martial 5.5'. Between the restorations are inset *vedute* of the Palatine's ruins and of the Forum with the half-buried Arch of Septimius Severus (Figure 5.56). Although the appearance of Rossini's plates does not depend on ancient

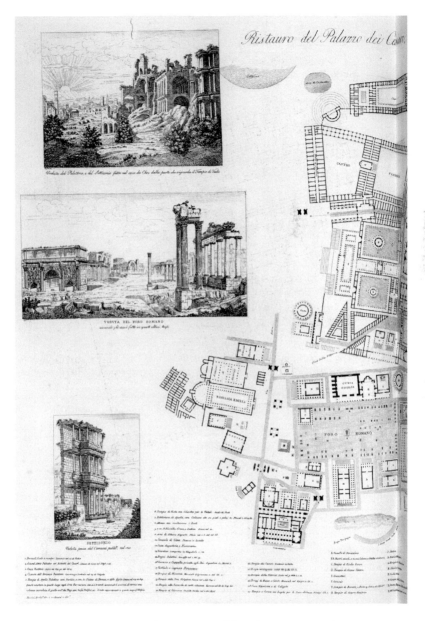

Figure 5.56 Section of Rossini's *Restoration of the Palatine, Forum and Via Sacra.*

Figure 5.57 Rossini's *View of the Palatine from the Aventine.*

and Renaissance literature in the way that the Villa Giulia's frescoes do, it still relies on it for affirmation. The hills' importance is there as much as in Rossini's meticulous reconstruction and recording. One never looks at Rome alone. As different ways of seeing come together on the page (the ekphrastic, antiquarian, ichnographic, pictorial), we get something of the 'vastness' that the individual cannot observe by himself, and a keener sense of the artist's perspective.

As was the case with Naldini's view of the Palatine, not seeing, and indeed realizing that one's understanding stems as much from expectation as from confrontation, weighs heavy in Rossini's work. In plate 3 (Figure 5.57), a view of the Palatine from the Aventine – from the 'only point from which one can see the whole hill with its superb ruins' – none of the figures in the foreground actually engages with the 'unique' vista.[128] On the hill opposite is the 'pulvinare' or royal box (number 3 on the engraving), from where, the key tells us, 'the emperors watched the spectacles of the Circus Maximus'.[129] But the thrills which captivated even Rutilius Namatianus have long gone, this demise, and the scene's emptiness, marked by the privileging of a lidless sarcophagus. Now the only sport is to watch women washing linen.

---

[128] 'Questo punto è l'unico ove si scuopre tutto il monte colle e sue superbe rovine'.
[129] 'Pulvinare ove gl' Imperatori vedevano li spettacoli del Circo Massimo'.

Figure 5.58 Rossini's *Viminal.*

Rossini is more explicit about his disappointment in the nineteenth-century Viminal (plate 20) (Figure 5.58): 'this hill offers rather barren views, being full of modern buildings. Its form is narrow, long, so unified and joined with the Quirinal and with the Esquiline that it is difficult for the eye to distinguish it alone, it being confused with the others.'[130] And he is just as honest about adapting the view of the Quirinal (see Figure 5.49 on p. 174) to fit his vision: 'the trees in the foreground have been added to avoid the odiousness of the roofs that do not belong to the above-mentioned hill'.[131] In one view of the Capitoline (plate 9), 'which is today totally full

[130] 'Questo monte offera vedute piuttosto sterili, essendo ripieno di fabriche moderne. La sua forma è stretta, e lunga, e talmente unita, e congiunta col Quirinale, e coll'Esquilino, che difficilmente lascia l'occhio il distinguerlo solo, essendo cogli altri confuso.' Rossini is not alone in singling the Viminal out. Joseph Forsyth 1835, writing about an excursion to Italy which he took in 1802–3, writes: 'The study of these antiquities leads you first to trace the figure, extent, mould, and distribution of the city. This you may begin on some eminence, as that denoted in the motto, now considered part of the Corsini garden; or on any of the towers that command all the hills. On each hill, except the Viminal, the most difficult of all, you will find one master object, as the Villa Medici on the Pincian, the Papal Palace on the Quirinal, the three basilicas on the Esquiline, Caelian and Vatican, etc, which will serve each as a point of general reference, and enable you to combine the perspective with the plan. You may then trace on foot the outlines of those hills, the successive boundaries of the Augustan regions, or the modern Rioni; and at last make the circuit of the inviolable walls.'

[131] Bottom right of the image itself, he writes: 'N.B. gli alberi avanti sono aggiunti per evitare l'odiosita dei tetti che non appartengono al sud.° Monte'.

Figure 5.59 *Another View of the Capitoline* by Rossini.

of modern buildings which do not allow us to see any ancient remnant' and taken from the bank of the Tiber, he legitimately narrows his focus to a specific moment in time, midday (Figure 5.59).[132] Boats scuttle across the river and people sit in the sunshine or promenade, some of them pausing to point to something beyond the frame. 'In this view, we see the whole of the pyramid', claims Rossini, as – despite, if not because of, the scene's everyday aspect – the Capitoline shifts in status from the 'metonymy of Rome itself' to a foreign symbol. Almost counterintuitively, prior knowledge of the Capitoline is what makes it seem alien: the watery landscape could almost be Venice.[133]

One further engraving is worthy of special mention, and this (plate 11) is the only full plate in the volume to imagine a scene at a specific historical moment (Figure 5.60). It is also the only one to declare that it shows but a section: its title, *Part of the Roman Forum and the Capitoline Hill with the Temple of Jupiter.*

---

[132] 'In questa veduta scorgesi bene tutta la piramide, che forma il sudetto Monte, il quale essendo in oggi totalmente pieno di fabriche moderne non lascia scorgere alcun avanzo antico; ma ciò non ostante forma una veduta sorprendente.'

[133] For Venice, see Tanner 1992.

Figure 5.60 *Part of the Roman Forum and the Capitoline Hill with the Temple of Jupiter* by Rossini.

The explanatory text reads: In this plate, one gets an idea of a terrible breakdown and of the burning of the aforementioned temple caused by Genseric the Vandal King, called to Rome by [Licinia] Eudoxia, widow of Valentinian III in 455. Instead of helping Eudoxia, this barbarian sacked Rome and robbed it of all of its most precious objects and led Eudoxia and lots of other great characters into slavery. The monuments placed on the Capitol are all imagined according to what the ancient authors clearly say, and those of the forum have been restored and placed prospectively in the place where ruins still remain.[134]

One also gets an idea of the loss of antiquity over time as the text below the picture explains how 'the whole thing is destroyed'.[135] Yet the intact arches, temples and columns, topped with statues, beg to differ. The Quirinal's Castor and Pollux, or figures very like them, grace the temple podium to the left. So animate are they and the other statues (several of them, Victory

---

[134] 'In questa tavola si dà un'idea del terribile guasto, e dell' incendio del suddetto Tempio dato da Genserico Re Vandalo, chiamato in Roma da Eudossia vedova di Valentiniano III nel' anno 455. Invece questo barbaro di soccorrere Eudossia saccheggiò Roma, e la derubò di tutti gli oggetti più preziosi, e condusse schiava la sullodata Eudossia con molti altri grandi personaggi. I Monumenti collocati sul Capitolino, sono tutti ideati secondo che ne hanno chiaramente parlato gli antichi scrittori; e quelli del Foro si sono restaurati, e collocati prospetticamente nel luogo ove rimangano ancora i ruderi.'

[135] 'Il tutto distrutto da Genserico Re Vandalo . . .'

and Roma with their arms aloft in triumph), that it is hard to tell them and the people apart. As the Vandals head towards the Capitol, blazing torches in hand, Rome's future and (future) past hang in the balance.

How do any of us plug the gap left by centuries of destruction? How many precious objects are lost to us for ever, and how many of them are further cast aside by our blindness to crucial evidence? Is every act of description preconditioned, and all retrospection fictional? Rossini's hills are a different species from those in Julius' frescoes, each of which existed in the space between two versions of the same image, and in the relationship of this space to real Rome and to an embedded textual tradition. Rather, all of them are sketched in several ways (as ancient and modern, *veduta* and plan, elevation and viewing platform), and these sketches, and the sources on which they are based, paraded and pitted against each other for all to contemplate. Rossini's engravings are neither statements nor puzzles: they do not say, 'solve me and you will understand the city'. The Renaissance had already given the hills that status. Their packaging turns them to arguments with a special take-home message: that representing Rome is always a rhetorical exercise and that the sense of 'all of ancient Rome' that he craves lies in the success of his persuasive strategies. The seven hills are less the subject of his series than they are its justification.

It matters little that this series includes the 'colli adiacenti' of the Vatican and Janiculum and Pincio (plates 23 to 25) in addition to the traditional seven. Their depictions are marked out, as the image of the Villa Giulia was marked out, by an absence of ruins. The view of the Janiculum is dominated by the Tiber, and the Pincio by Piazza del Popolo, with an accompanying text that emphasizes its recent restructuring by Giuseppe Valadier (Figure 5.61).[136] This simplicity or historical one-dimensionality reinforces the depth of tradition that informs the others: the sense in which the canonical hills are not just about the then and now but bring Varro, Martial, Biondo, Bufalini and Napoleon with them. They do not so much equal Rome as they did for their ancient authors. They offer a lens for looking at Rome, a Rome that is no longer lived in but is studied from afar, a Rome that has offered models for the plotting and planning of other cities. Exposing the artistic choices of these engravings, the Villa Giulia and the Vatican apartments alerts us to the artifice of every image of antiquity.

---

[136] The explanatory text starts: 'questa piazza cominciata da Pio VII . . .' ('this piazza, begun by Pius VII'); while beneath the engraving, attention is drawn to his architect, Valadier: 'L'Architettura tanto del Monte che della Piazza e' Opera dell' Illustre Archit.° Cav.^re Giuseppe Valadier.'

Figure 5.61 Rossini's *Pincio*.

Even a photograph has to choose its frame: we are all artists when we stand on the Capitoline or Caelian. As David Larmour and Diana Spencer write, 'when we think about "seeing" (the *gaze*) we are also making decisions about taxonomy, perspective, and value that have a significant impact on our *point of view* (where we think we are looking from, and how the singularity of our position relates to the dimensionality of the object of our gaze), and on our *perspective* (the act of capturing the object of our gaze within a mimetic reality in which vertical and horizontal axes are hugely significant, and the object is relationally experienced vis-à-vis our position)'.[137] In the next chapter we privilege one gaze in particular – that afforded by the hills – and the way in which seeing the city from above finds order, syncretism, in a single snapshot.

Often scholars speak of Rome as a palimpsest,[138] the truth of which lies in its layers. But from the vantage point of its hills, its coherence lies in the flattening and blurring of past and present produced by the overview; the sense of seeing not a city but an image of a city; of being filled with something more elemental than the process of intellectualization;[139] with the kind of awe that makes communion with the ineffable possible. Although artists

[137]   Larmour and Spencer 2007: 11.
[138]   See Gowers 1995: 23; Edwards 1996: 28; and Larmour and Spencer 2007: 3–4. And on the notion of palimpsests and landscape more generally, Bender 1993: 9.
[139]   De Bolla 2003: 2.

rarely risked reproducing this image until the sixteenth century, authors in antiquity were already keen to step outside their lived experience in order to throw Rome into relief. Rome as a city of seven hills was an exportable concept that supplied an enviable sense of circumference, stability and urban identity. It shaped political ambition, intimidated enemies and comforted the exiled Ovid. But – as we have begun to see with Rossini – Rome from its seven hills was crucial in reconnecting this concept with the land. Those in the thick of it have long gauged Rome's might *from* its hills, exploiting them as viewing platforms.

6 | On top of the world

I, therefore, strongly rate the panorama of the whole city where there is
such a large crop of towers and so many palace-buildings that no one has
succeeded in counting them. When from the slope of the hill I had seen
this city for the first time from afar, that saying of Caesar's, which he
uttered long ago when he had conquered the Gauls, flown across the Alps
and was greatly wondering at the walls of Rome, entered my stupefied
mind ...

Magister Gregorius, *Narratio de mirabilibus urbis Romae* 1[1]

Panoramas are powerful things. Early in the nineteenth century, in the dome
of London's Colosseum in Regent's Park (a building which was actually
modelled on the Pantheon) a painted panoramic perspectival view of the city
was installed, captured from the cupola of Saint Paul's Cathedral. Visitors
ascended to a viewing platform by means of a hydraulic lift and were
met by the illusion of looking out over London, the Colosseum included
(Figure 6.1).[2] It was heady stuff – 'exactly similar to ... looking from the top
of St Paul's, with this difference – that in the Coliseum you may command
a constantly clear atmosphere, and are spared the labour of mounting the
never ending stairs' – 'a view of the British metropolis without parallel'.[3]
Enthusiasm knew no limits. The urban jungle had become a toytown. One
could even see where one was standing.

For architectural historian Dana Arnold, panoramas like this one were
novel ways of representing the metropolis, linked to new conceptions of
space demanded of the city at the start of the nineteenth century.[4] And

[1] 'vehemencius igitur admirandam ce<n>seo tocius urbis inspectionem. ubi tanta seges
turrium, tot aedificia palatiorum, quot nulli hominum con | tigit enumerare. quam cum primo
a latere montis a longe vidissem, stupefactam mentem meam illud Caesarianum subiit, quod
quondam victis Gallis cum Alpes supervolaret inquid, magne miratus moenia Romae ...'
(edition by Rushforth 1919: 45).

[2] The Colosseum was demolished in 1875. See D. Arnold 2009, especially 340–5.

[3] *Mechanics' Magazine* 6: 155, and John Britton as cited in D. Arnold 2009: 345.

[4] It is true that panoramas of this kind – massive circular paintings, enhanced through an original
apparatus for viewing them – were patented and the word 'panorama' coined by
Newcastle-upon-Tyne-born painter Robert Barker in 1787: see Garrison *et al.* 2012. That said,

Figure 6.1 *Bird's-Eye View from the Staircase and the Upper Part of the Pavilion in the Colosseum, Regent's Park*, 1829.

she is obviously right to see Jeremy Bentham's Panopticon of 1791 as influential. His prison design enabled a guard in a central tower to watch all of the prisoners, unobserved, rendering him omniscient.[5] But for all that

painters had used the panoramic view before this. Helpful here is the catalogue accompanying a Yale Center for British Art show by Hyde 1985, and Oettermann 1997.

[5] Crucial here is the investment by Foucault 1977.

the Romans were reluctant to subject their own city to a 'città dipinta' treatment,[6] the advantages of the wide-angled, and indeed bird's-eye, view were not lost on them: Trajan's Column, for example, which was inaugurated in 113 CE and built to a height of 38 metres, offered an internal staircase and 360° viewing gallery over his Forum.[7] What better way to appreciate the emperor's impact on the city than from above it? Hills too, both within and beyond the city, played a fundamental part in enabling the viewer to confront its countless towers and buildings – and have done ever since, causing these hills to be terraced and planted into formal gardens. Why have a painted view of Rome on one's wall, when one could build a villa that would frame it from its windows? As Pliny the Younger says of his Tuscan estate: 'you would be delighted, if you looked out at the geography of this region from the mountain. For you would imagine that you were looking not at the land but at some image painted to the highest degree of beauty.'[8]

This chapter takes us back to Virgil, Martial and Claudian and forward to English landscape painter, Samuel Palmer (1805–81), to examine how Rome's hills, and the topos of viewing from these hills, have helped to bring coherence to Rome, turning its highs and lows into a steady state which can be apprehended, if not itemized – a 'collage city',[9] in which the pieces come together into a dazzling patchwork. Michel de Certeau expresses this idea very well in a passage which 9/11 makes all the more emotive:

To be lifted to the summit of the World Trade Centre is to be lifted out of the city's grasp. One's body is no longer clasped by the streets that turn and return it according to an anonymous law; nor is it possessed, whether as player or played, by the rumble of so many differences and by the nervousness of New York traffic. When one goes up there, he leaves behind the mass that carries off and mixes up in itself any identity of authors and spectators. An Icarus flying above these waters, he can ignore the devices of Daedalus in endless and mobile labyrinths far below. His elevation transfigures him into a voyeur. It puts him at a distance. It transforms the bewitching world by which one was 'possessed' into a text that lies before one's eyes. It allows one to read it, to be a solar Eye, looking down like a god. The elevation of

---

[6] See above, Chapter 5, n. 7.

[7] The column's inscription declares that it stands in place of a *mons*: see above, Chapter 4, n. 62. Note that the described and illustrated book on Rome by Guattani opens with Trajan's Column because of the view it affords – 1805: 7.

[8] Plin. *Ep.* 5.6.13: 'magnam capies voluptatem, si hunc regionis situm ex monte prospexeris. neque enim terras tibi, sed formam aliquam ad eximiam pulchritudinem pictam videris cernere.' See McEwen 2005, Du Prey 1994 and Chinn 2007.

[9] Rowe and Koetter 1978.

a sceptic and gnostic drive: the fiction of knowledge is related to this lust to be a viewpoint and nothing more.[10]

The distance from the Servian city of the Janiculum and other hills beyond the river makes, as we shall discover, the image that one commands from there distinct from that which one owns from the Capitoline or Palatine; and not just because every overview is different, but because from the Janiculum one can see 'the seven sovereign hills and get the measure of the whole of Rome'[11] whereas from the Capitoline one is on the crest of a wave which inevitably offers an alternative vista. One is literally on top of the seven hills, as Lucan's Jupiter was on top of them when he looked out from the Tarpeian Rock,[12] and can look down into the Forum with a depth of relief that is impossible from afar: 'I came to the Capitol and looked down on the other side. There before my eyes opened an immense grave, and out of the grave rose a city of monuments in ruins, columns, triumphal arches, temples and palaces, broken, ruinous but still beautiful and grand – with a solemn mournful beauty! It was the great apparition of ancient Rome.'[13] How are this view and act of viewing different from on the Pincio, where 'pictures will be stamped upon the memory, which will ever shed around them the serene light of undecaying beauty, never dimmed by disappointments, the burdens, the torpid commonplaces, and the dreary drudgeries of future years' (Figure 6.2)?[14] Looking from Rome's other hills, then from the seven, we will – like the visitors to London's Colosseum – have a clearer sense of our own position.

Villas and gardens

In a letter about the lax morals of the coastal town of Baiae on the Bay of Naples, where many elite Romans, including emperors, went to escape the frenzy of the capital city, Nero's tutor, the philosopher and playwright Seneca, tells of the importance of choosing a place to live which is healthy for the mind as well as the body. Gaius Marius, Pompey and Caesar may have built villas near Baiae but they 'set them on the very tops of the mountains (*summis iugis montium*)'.[15] He continues:

---

[10] De Certeau 1984: 92.   [11] Mart. 4.64.11–12.   [12] Luc. 1.195–6.
[13] Feminist writer Fredrika Bremer as cited in Hare 1923: 85.   [14] Hillard 1853: vol. I, 160–1.
[15] Sen. *Ep.* 51.11: 'illi quoque, ad quos primos fortuna populi Romani publicas opes transtulit, C. Marius et Cn Pompeius et Caesar extruxerunt quidem villas in regione Baiana, sed illas inposuerunt summis iugis montium' ('Also those to whom the good fortune of the Roman people first transferred state wealth, Gaius Marius, Gnaeus Pompey and Caesar, did indeed

Figure 6.2 View from the Pincio today.

videbatur hoc magis militare, ex edito speculari late longeque subiecta. aspice quam positionem clegerint, quibus aedificia excitaverint locis et qualia; scies non villas esse, sed castra.

This seemed more soldier-like, to look from above upon lands spread far and wide below. Look at the position they chose, and what kinds of structures they built and where. You will realize that they are not villas but camps.[16]

Seneca gives viewing from above a mastery akin to the god-like gaze described by de Certeau. He adds a strategic dimension to living on the hills – something more sustaining than clean air and peace and quiet – and not just the security of seeing for miles, but the luxury that comes from examining everything subordinate(d) below.[17] And he was not the only one.

build villas in the region of Baiae but they placed them on the highest ridges of the mountains'). See also *Ep*. 55.6–7 and Henderson 2004.

[16] Sen. *Ep*. 51.11.

[17] Also relevant here is Livy's description of the Macedonian king Philip V, Livy 40.21.2: 'cupido eum ceperat in verticem Haemi montis ascendendi, quia volgatae opinioni crediderat Ponticum simul et Hadriaticum mare et Histrum amnem et Alpes conspici posse: subiecta oculis ea haud parvi sibi momenti futura ad cogitationem Romani belli' ('the desire had seized him to climb to the top of Mount Haemus, because he had believed popular opinion that the Pontic and Adriatic Seas and the Hister River and the Alps could be seen simultaneously. These

Some scholars think that inter-urban visibility was important to the success of urban settlements in Baetica, Roman Spain (especially to those far from major centres).[18] This was not just about safeguarding one's territory, but about getting sufficient purchase on it to lay claim to it as one's home.

Pliny, this time of his Laurentine villa, south of Ostia, tells a similar story, stressing how the charm and advantage of the place lay not in the house's contents, but in its views of the sea and neighbouring villas.[19] His description of the dining room is fairly typical:

undique valvas aut fenestras non minores valvis habet atque ita a lateribus et a fronte quasi tria maria prospectat; a tergo cavaedium porticum aream porticum rursus, mox atrium, silvas et longinquos respicit montes.

On all sides, it has folding doors or windows which are no smaller than the doors and in this way, it looks out at the sides and the front as if over three separate seas. From the back, it looks over the inner court of the house, a portico, the courtyard, another portico and then the atrium, and behind them the woods and in the distance, the mountains.[20]

It is as though everything – as far as the eye can see – belongs to Pliny. Did elite housing on Rome's hills play to similar strengths? And if so, how did the dimensions of a city defined by the limits of human vision accord with the city of seven summits?

We have already noted that from the Republic to late antiquity those who could afford to do so lived on Rome's hills. 'My house', claimed Cicero, 'is in view of almost the whole city.'[21] It was not simply that Cicero could see the city from his windows, but that all of the city could see him. It makes sense that Augustus lived on the Palatine. His house may have been 'remarkable neither in roominess nor adornment', but it made up for this in visibility: it was as important that the people sensed his watching over them as it was that he appeared in the box in the arena. When he wanted to escape the public glare, he had to retire to a garret or retreat from Rome completely.[22]

---

landmarks, once laid out before him, would be of no small consequence for his plans about war with the Romans').

[18] Earl and Keay 2006. See also Arist. *Pol.* 1327a, and for a more general discussion of Latin authors and 'the survey from on high', Murphy 2004: 131–3.

[19] Plin. *Ep.* 2.17.1 to Gallus: 'desines mirari, cum cognoveris gratiam villae, opportunitatem loci, litoris spatium' ('You will cease to be amazed, when you have got to know the charm of the villa, the advantages of its situation and the expansive view of the shore').

[20] Plin. *Ep.* 2.17.5.

[21] Cic. *Dom.* 37.100: 'in conspectu prope totius urbis domus est mea'. No wonder that Clodius was so keen to demolish it! See Hales 2003: 42 and Ash 2007: 212–14.

[22] Suet. *Aug.* 72.1: 'aedibus ... neque laxitate neque cultu conspicuis'. Also 71.2–3. Important here is Favro 2005: 256: 'Under the Princeps a new urban node appeared atop the Palatine.'

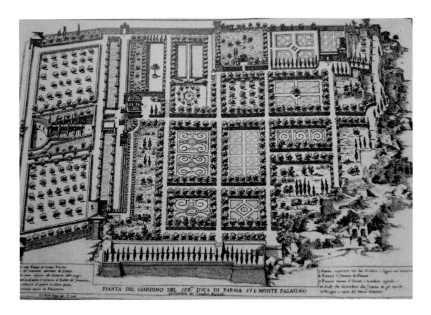

Figure 6.3 Plan of the Farnese Gardens (*c.* 1670) from Falda, Li giardini di Roma.

It also makes sense that Nero watched the fire of Rome from the tower of Maecenas on the Esquiline, a structure described by Horace as 'a mass close to the lofty clouds'.[23] His singing of the 'Sack of Troy' makes this view specifically 'teichoscopic', reminiscent of the perspective of the women in epic who watch the fighting from the battlements[24] – except that he is the enemy within, who had supposedly torched Rome to build a better one. The mere mention of Maecenas' name reminds the reader of Virgil and Horace, whom he sponsored, and the logic of the Augustan building programme. Nero commands the view to destroy it in an attempt to replace the 'eternal city' with a new metropolis.

The Farnese Gardens were the most famous Renaissance gardens to capitalize on this heritage. Created in the sixteenth century on the northern side of the Palatine, they overlooked the Forum, staking a claim to the imperial gaze of the Caesars (Figure 6.3).[25] 'There, one discovers all of

[23] Suet. *Ner.* 38. 2; Cass. Dio 62.18; Hor. *Carm.* 3.29.10: 'molem propinquam nubibus arduis'.

[24] Compare, for example, Hom. *Il.* 3.161ff. and Stat. *Theb.* 7.243–4. See Vessey 1973: 205–9, Fucecchi 1997, Scodel 1997, Salzman-Mitchell 2005, Scioli 2010 and Lovatt 2006 and forthcoming.

[25] For the Farnese and other gardens, see Coffin 1991 and the engravings in Falda 1640–78. Also important for the various views, plans and photographs it provides is Giess 1971 and specifically on the Farnese, Romanelli 1960.

Rome.'[26] But, as we have seen, other families preferred the less central summits – the Villa Giulia on Monti Parioli, Villa Madama on Monte Mario, and Villa Borghese on the Pincio. Not that there were not ancient gardens there also.[27] The first of Rome's great *horti*, the Horti Luculliani, created by Roman general and voluptuary Lucius Licinius Lucullus after his triumph in 63 BCE, and later imperial property covered the summit of the hill down to the Campus Martius. But they both were and were not part of Romescape. The sources' emphasis on Lucullus' eastern-inspired *luxuria* and on the empress Messalina's rapaciousness in wanting the gardens for herself stresses that they were a subversive space:[28] 'not an expression of political power, but an alternative to it'.[29] Was it as affirming of one's status and of Rome's to view from this liminal *belvedere*?

In the thick of it

We shall come back to the view from the Pincio presently, both the one which sees the city from the Villa Medici and the one which turns its back on the *centro storico* to look towards the Vatican. For all that Piazza del Popolo and Saint Peter's are an alternative, Christian Rome, it is a Rome that can be directly compared to the former, just as the artist of the Colosseum's panorama, Thomas Hornor, went on to publish a set of views of London, keen to compare it to Rome.[30] Down in the city, in contrast, in the Forum, for example, such detachment is, and was, impossible. French writer Émile Zola's reaction is not untypical: 'Spent the whole day in the ruins, an indigestion of ruins, which can evoke the grandeur of ancient Rome.' 'People walking around it look like ants.'[31] Nor is it unique to the modern period. In antiquity, most probably under Nero, Calpurnius Siculus has the rustic Corydon describe his experience of Rome as follows:

---

[26] According to one popular French guidebook by Deseine 1713: 'on y découvre tout Rome'.

[27] On the importance of green space in Augustan Rome, see Favro 2005: 251 and on ancient gardens in Rome more generally, Cipriani 1982, R. C. Häuber 1990, M. Cima and La Rocca 1998, Hartswick 2004, and C. Cima and Talamo 2008. See also George Vivian's *Views from the Gardens of Rome and Albano* 1848, which opens: 'These views, made during a residence at Rome in the years 1844, 1845 and 1846, have been arranged in the order of the hills from which they were taken.'

[28] Tac. *Ann.* 11.1; 11.32 and 37; Plut. *Luc.* 39 and 41; and Cass. Dio 60.27.3. See Broise and Vincent 1987, and the excavation reports in *MÉFRA* 1988, 1989, 1994 and 1995. On Messalina and the gardens, and the written import of *horti* more generally, see Beard 1998.

[29] Wallace-Hadrill 1998: 3 in the context of an argument about *horti* and Hellenization.

[30] D. Arnold 2009: 344.

[31] Zola 1893 as cited in Moatti 1993: 174.

vidimus in caelum trabibus spectacula textis   23
surgere, Tarpeium prope despectantia culmen...

qualiter haec patulum concedit vallis in orbem   30
et sinuata latus resupinis undique silvis
inter continuos curvatur concava montes:
sic ibi planitiem curvae sinus ambit harenae
et geminis medium se molibus alligat ovum.
quid tibi nunc referam, quae vix suffecimus ipsi   35
per partes spectare suas? Sic undique fulgor
percussit. stabam defixus et ore patenti
cunctaque mirabur necdum bona singula noram...

We saw the theatre rising to the sky with its interwoven beams, almost looking down
on the Capitoline's summit...

Just as this valley vanishes into a broad circuit and, curved at the side with sloping
forests on all sides, is bent hollow in the midst of unbroken hills, so there the fold of
the curved amphitheatre encircles the plain and the oval in the middle binds itself
with twin structures. Why now should I tell you things which we ourselves have
scarcely been able to see in their constituent details? So the splendour struck us from
all sides. I stood, transfixed, with my mouth agape, and I wondered at everything.
And not yet had I become acquainted with every individual marvel...[32]

In Corydon's eyes, the amphitheatre (probably the wooden one built by Nero
in 57 CE) is so huge as to rival the Capitoline, its banked seats enclosing
the arena as hills do a valley. Small wonder that he should be unable to take
it all in, or fail to know all of its details. A few lines later, a local who 'has
grown old in the city' claims that he too is still amazed. The word he uses,
'stupeo', means 'to be rendered senseless'.[33]

It is not only rustics whose vision fails them. When Constantine's son,
Constantius II (emperor from 337–61 CE), visits Rome for the first time in
357 CE, he is described by contemporary historian Ammianus Marcellinus
as moving through the city, where he is stupefied ('obstipuit') by what he
sees on every side and 'bound' or 'weakened' ('praestrictus') by the 'density
of the wonders' ('miraculorum densitate').[34] Ammianus continues:

---

[32] Calp. *Ecl.* 7.23–4 and 30–8. See Mayer 2007: 162–3.
[33] Calp. *Ecl.* 7.43–4:

> en ego iam tremulus iam vertice canus et ista
> factus in urbe senex stupeo tamen omnia.

[34] Amm. Marc. 16.10.13: 'proinde Romam ingressus imperii virtutumque omnium larem, cum
      venisset ad rostra, perspectissimum priscae potentiae forum, obstipuit, perque omne latus quo
      se oculi contulissent, miraculorum densitate praestrictus, allocutus nobilitatem in curia'
      ('Accordingly he entered Rome, the home of empire and of all virtues. When he had reached

deinde intra septem montium culmina, per acclivitates planitiemque posita urbis membra collustrans et suburbana, quicquid viderat primum, id eminere inter alia cuncta sperabat: Iovis Tarpei delubra, quantum terrenis divina praecellunt; lavacra in modum provinciarum exstructa; amphitheatri molem solidatam lapidis Tiburtini compage, ad cuius summitatem aegre visio humana conscendit; Pantheum velut regionem teretem speciosa celsitudine fornicatam; elatosque vertices qui scansili suggestu consurgunt, priorum principum imitamenta portantes, et urbis templum forumque Pacis, et Pompei theatrum et Odeum et Stadium, aliaque inter haec decora urbis aeternae. verum cum ad Traiani forum venisset, singularem sub omni caelo structuram, ut opinamur, etiam numinum assensione mirabilem, haerabat attonitus, per giganteos contextus circumferens mentem, nec relatu effabiles, nec rursus mortalibus appetendos.

Then, as he surveyed the sections of the city and its suburbs, positioned within the summits of the seven hills, across their slopes and on the level ground, he expected whatever he had seen first to stand out amidst everything else: the sanctuaries of Tarpeian Jupiter (they excel as much as divine things excel earthly things!), the baths, built to the scale of provinces, the mass of the amphitheatre, made solid by its Travertine stone structure, to whose top human vision can barely ascend; the Pantheon, like a rounded *regio* of the city, vaulted with a beautiful lofty dome, and the exalted heights which rise with platforms to which one can climb, carrying the likenesses of former emperors, and the Temple of Venus and Roma, the Forum Pacis, the Theatre of Pompey, the Odeum, Stadium and amongst these, the other adornments of the eternal city. But when he reached Trajan's Forum, a structure, unique under the whole heavens, as we believe, and wonderful even in the opinion of the gods, he stood still, amazed, turning his attention to the giant connecting buildings, which neither lend themselves to description nor could be imitated again by mortals.[35]

Constantius surveys the city by walking not on, but within, the summits of the seven hills, examining the sections and suburbs which are positioned on its slopes and flat surfaces. The designation of these sections as 'membra' or 'limbs' highlights how this way of seeing fragments the city's skeleton. Constantius has no sense of the whole, allowing whatever he sees first to distract him. He is constantly looking up, rather than down, as his gaze

the rostra, the most well-known forum of ancient power, he was amazed, and in every direction where his eyes had borne themselves, he was struck by the density of wonders and addressed the *nobiles* in the senate house'). For a detailed commentary, see de Jonge 1972: 125–32. Also relevant are Duval 1970; Matthews 1989: 231–5; M. Roberts 1988; Schmitzer 1999; and G. Kelly 2003, whose sophisticated discussion of the absence of Constantinople in Ammianus uses Rome as a counterpoint and stresses how Ammianus wrote 'in Rome and for Rome'. On Constantius' response to Trajan's Forum, see Edbrooke 1975 and G. Kelly 2003: 594–603.

[35] Amm. 16.10.14–15.

is drawn to things that tower above him. Everything swells, but in rivalry with each other – the Pantheon like a region of the city, the baths, like provinces, and the Colosseum, too big for the human eye to scale. The city is inflated into Rome as empire, then earth, then Rome as unquantifiable – growing bigger and bigger with each passing moment, until even one part of it, the Forum of Trajan, is so 'gigantic' or wild as to be unutterable and unreproducible. Where are Rome's urban limits now? The city has burst. Even the Roman emperor is aware of his incapacity.

Viewing from afar enabled the Romans to rise above this confusion and to make a virtue out of being barely able to see the details. It is a strategy that guide books still advocate today. The sense of 'seeing everything' ('pan' + 'horan' to give the ancient Greek etymology of 'panorama') is enough; stupefaction caused not by a single amphitheatre or by Trajan's Forum – something that would risk attaching the glory of Rome to a single act of manufacture, a single moment, that might make us feel inadequate by comparison – but by the whole. It matters little that ultimately 'totalising under the gaze is a dream of unity',[36] for dreams transform immediate surroundings as well as the dreamer, giving them powers denied to them in real life. Take this reaction to Rome from a tenth-century Islamic text: 'The inhabitants of Rome sent an envoy to accompany us to the city. On the way we climbed a hill, and there before us was a green expanse, as if of water. "God is great" we exclaimed . . . The guide smiled and said "What you are looking at is the roofs of Rome, which are sheathed throughout in metal."' The text goes on to enumerate the city's markets and bathhouses, as the regionary catalogues had done, but is no more accurate in the impression it gives than that first mirage of an oasis.[37] As Gregory recognizes when he recommends viewing the city from a hill, first impressions are worth their weight in gold: getting the measure of Rome need not demand precise counting.

English cleric Gregory, who visits Rome in the early thirteenth century, and these visitors three centuries earlier are probably on Monte Mario on the northern end of the Janiculum ridge, a hill which has given many travellers their first view of the city.[38] The speech which Gregory is inspired to cite is from Lucan's *Civil War* and elicited when 'from a lofty crag, he [Caesar] now caught sight of the city in the distance'.[39] 'In wonder, he addresses the walls of his Rome: "You, the abode of the gods, did men abandon you without

---

[36] J. Thomas 1993: 23.   [37] As cited in Purcell 1992: 426.   [38] See Rushworth 1919: 19.
[39] Luc. 3.88: 'excelsa de rupe procul iam conspicit urbem'.

being compelled by any war?" [40] Lucan's image of Jupiter looking out over the walls of the great city from the Tarpeian Rock was also Caesar's, at the moment when he crossed the Rubicon with his legion and cast the die to march on Rome. [41] Now he is the omniscient one. The emphasis on walls in both passages signals that Rome's defences will be breached. As Caesar gazes in wonder ('mirari'), Rome becomes his property ('suae') and soon 'he enters a city which is stupefied by fear'. [42] Gregory is filled with a similar confidence. A few lines later he is still standing there, admiring the city's 'incomprehensible beauty': 'although all of Rome is ruined, nothing whole is able to be made equal to it'. [43] From this elevated vantage point, Rome's power is fully realized – no matter how faded or ungraspable.

Getting the measure of the whole of Rome

Close reading of one of Martial's epigrams, written in praise of his friend's property on the Janiculum will make us more familiar with this vantage point and the Rome that it captures. As is the case with Pliny's villa, the appeal of the property is in the view: 'from here it is possible to see the seven sovereign hills and to *aestimare* the whole of Rome'. It is a boast that lives on in an inscription on the loggia of Giulio Romano's Villa Lante, built on the Janiculum in the first half of the sixteenth century – but this time in abbreviated form, without the summits which used to dominate: HINC TOTAM LICET AESTIMARE ROMAM (Figure 6.4). The implication is that the Janiculum itself has ousted them, an idea which chimes with the decoration in the rest of the villa, which emphasizes the hill's history and special relationship to the city. [44] This relationship was always unstable, with the hill precariously perched on the edge of city and canon. To read

---

[40] Luc. 3.90–1:

> miratusque suae sic fatur moenia Romae:
> 'tene, deum sedes, non ullo Marte coacti
> deseruere viri?'

[41] Luc. 1.195–6. See above, p. 82.

[42] Luc. 3.97–8:

> . . . sic fatur et urbem
> attonitam terrore subit . . .

[43] 'cuius incomprehensibilem decorem diu admirans deo apud me gratias egi, qui magnus in universa terra ibi opera hominum inaestimabili decore mirificavit. nam licet tota Roma ruat, nil tamen integrum sibi potest aequiperari.' With English edition by J. Osborne 1987.

[44] See, for example, the frescoes which were in the *salone* but are now in the Herziana, showing scenes pertaining to the hill, including the meeting of Saturn and Janus, who shake hands as though to cement the peace between the Janiculum and Capitoline communities.

Figure 6.4 Inscription on the loggia of the Villa Lante, the Janiculum, Rome.

the inscription, one has to turn one's back on Rome and face the house, while above the door the stucco work shows not Roma, or the Lupercal, but the enigmatic image of Diana of Ephesus (Figure 6.5). It is a move which the playful Martial would have applauded. As an eighteenth century watercolour by British artist John Robert Cozens shows, the villa towers over Rome like a sentinel (Figure 6.6).[45]

The modesty of the villa, today the home of the Finnish Institute, echoes that of its ancient counterpart. Martial's little poem about it is difficult, but repays citing in full.

Iuli iugera pauca Martialis
hortis Hesperidum beatiora
longo Ianiculi iugo recumbunt.

Indispensable here are O'Gorman 1971, Lilius 1981 and Steinby 1996. On the inscription itself and its relationship with Martial, see Kajava 2005 and 2006.

[45] John Robert Cozens (1782–3) *View of the Villa Lante on the Janiculum (Gianicolo), in Rome,* watercolour over traces of graphite on white laid paper, 25.3 | 36.8 cm, Metropolitan Museum of Art, New York, Rogers Fund 1967: 67.68.

Figure 6.5 Statue of Diana of Ephesus from Hadrian's villa at Tivoli.

alti collibus eminent recessus
et planus modico tumore vertex   5
caelo perfruitur sereniore
et curvas nebula tegente valles

Figure 6.6 John Robert Cozens (1782–3) *View of the Villa Lante on the Janiculum (Gianicolo), in Rome.* See also colour plate section.

solus luce nitet peculiari;
puris leniter admoventur astris
celsae culmina delicata villae.   10
hinc septem dominos videre montis
et totam licet aestimare Romam,
Albanos quoque Tusculosque colles
et quodcumque iacet sub urbe frigus,
Fidenas veteres brevesque Rubras,   15
et quod †virgineo cruore† gaudet
Annae pomiferum nemus Perennae.
illinc Flaminiae Salariaeque
gestator patet essedo tacente,
ne blando rota sit molesta somno,   20
quem nec rumpere nauticum celeuma
nec clamor valet helciariorum,
cum sit tam prope Mulvius sacrumque
lapsae per Tiberim volent carinae.
hoc rus, seu potius domus vocanda est,   25
commendat dominus: tuam putabis,
tam non invida tamque liberalis,

tam comi patet hospitalitate.
credas Alcinoi pios Penates
aut facti modo divitis Molorchi.   30
vos nunc omnia parva qui putatis,
centeno gelidum ligone Tibur
vel Praeneste domate pendulamque
uni dedite Setiam colono,
dum me iudice praeferantur istis   35
Iuli iugera pauca Martialis.

The few acres of Julius Martialis – more fortunate than the Gardens of the
Hesperides – lie on the long ridge of the Janiculum. High retreats stand out on
the hills; the summit, flat with a moderate crest, enjoys clearer sky and alone shines
with a light of its own, while mist covers the curved valleys. The delicate roofs of the
high villa rise gently towards the pure stars. From one side, you may see the seven
sovereign hills and get the measure of the whole of Rome; also the Alban hills and
the hills of Tusculum and whatever cool place lies near the city; ancient Fidenae
and little Rubriae and the fruit-bearing grove of Anna Perenna which rejoices in
virgin blood (?). From the other side, a traveller on the Via Flaminia and Via Salaria
is visible, though his chariot is silent in case the wheel is disruptive of sweet sleep
which neither the boatmen's commands nor the shout of the barge-pullers is strong
enough to break, although the Ponte Milvio is so close and keels glide smoothly
through the sacred Tiber. Its master commends this countryside to your care – or
rather, it must be called a town house. You will think it yours, so unbegrudging and
liberal is it and so open with kind hospitality. You would believe it the pious household of Alcinous or of the newly wealthy Molorchus. You now who think everything
small, tame icy Tiber or Praeneste with a hundred hoes, and give hanging Setia to a
single colonist, provided that I may prefer the few acres of Julius Martialis.[46]

The site is as small as the view is expansive: the opening words, 'just a
few acres', resurfacing in the last line of the poem to frame the window it
offers us. These 'iugera' share the same linguistic root as the long ridge or hill
('iugo') of the Janiculum (line 3), binding house and hill together as distinct
from the other promontories mentioned – the seven 'montes' and the Alban
or Tusculan 'colles'. Is the villa an urban dwelling ('domus') or 'countryside'
('rus') (line 25)? The 'retreats' or 'distances' ('recessus') separate it from the
city, allowing it to shine like a lantern over the misty valleys beneath it. As it
reaches up to the heavens, the activity below is made cool, calm and remote.

---

[46] Mart. 4.64. Most extensive on this poem is Fabbrini 2007: 1–57. Also of interest here is Rimell
2009 on the space of Martial's epigram, esp. 200–6 on pastoral space, and, on pastoral space
more generally, Purcell 1995: 159. For my own early analysis of this poem and an embryonic
attempt at a section of the Ammianus Marcellinus that follows, see Vout 2007b.

Figure 6.7 Giuseppe Vasi, *Prospetto del' alma città di Roma visto del Monte Gianicolo,* 1765.

Given this disinterest, it makes sense that the 1765 *Prospetto del' alma città di Roma visto del Monte Gianicolo* by Piranesi's tutor, Giuseppe Vasi should also have included the lines, 'HINC SEPTEM DOMINOS VIDERE MONTES | ET TOTAM LICET AESTIMARE ROMAM' on either side of the coat of arms of Charles III, to whom the view was dedicated (Figure 6.7). From Martial's Janiculum, the city of seven hills, surrounding region, roads and Tiber, are mappable.

From the Janiculum, the viewer controls the aperture. Travellers are consciously quiet (lines 18–24) in case they should disturb 'the dream', and those on the river and Milvian Bridge, powerless to penetrate the poet's sleep even though they seem so near. In this bubble, Martial feels at home, so much so that he thinks the house is his, and his friend, an Alcinous or Molorchus. Both of these mythological figures – one a king and the other a labourer – are renowned for their hospitality, the former, giving Odysseus the luxury to relate his travels. It is as though Martial too has been wandering but has reached a place where he can regroup. 'You will think the house yours', so unbegrudging and liberal is it (lines 26–7). But it is not the architecture or rich tapestries that do this, as they do in Alcinous' Palace in Homer, nor indeed the luxuriant gardens,[47] but the panorama that allows one's eyes to wander and one's mind to make up stories. The whole city plays to Martial's tune. Even the celebrated 'dominos montis' are possessed from here, subdued by the gaze of a new master.

Mention of Odysseus and Molorchus pits Homer against Callimachus. Molorchus carries with him memories of his appearance in Callimachus'

[47] Hom. *Od.* 7.78–132.

Aetia,[48] which had proved so influential in persuading poets to streamline the heaviness of epic into something lighter and more playful. Hence perhaps the 'delicate roofs' of Martial's lofty villa in line 10 (a deliberate contrast to the 'high-roofed', embellished palace of Alcinous in Homer?). Callimachus may also inhabit the Gardens of Hesperides in line 2, courtesy of his *Hymn to Demeter*,[49] and is writ large in Martial's 'iugera pauca' refrain: this is a poem about little measures, the 'iugera pauca Martialis'. Most critics assume this Martial to be the Lucius Julius Martialis of other poems.[50] But it is hard not to see it as working more personally also: you will think the house your own. This is potentially not just praise of a friend, but a clever authorial statement.

Miniaturizing Rome makes patron and author great. It is not just the seven sovereign hills which are encapsulated. 'Ancient Fidenae and little Rubriae' are also reduced – the 'long-established' or 'ancient' ('veteres') side by side with the 'little' or 'brief' ('breves'). And the 'hills of Alba and Tusculum' are combined with 'whatever cool place (*frigus*) lies near the city'. 'Frigus' is an odd word here, which pertains to an absence of strength or life – a 'torpor' or 'flatness' –, whereas 'sub urbe' literally means *beneath* the urban fabric. Rome is being compressed as we scan it from the Janiculum ridge – from world capital to epigram.

All of this is startlingly close to de Certeau and his 'bewitching world' made 'text', free from the rumblings of the New York traffic. And it is a view which continues to capture and to captivate. 'The view of Rome from the Janiculum includes all the rest of the city that Americans observed and described in the course of two centuries', writes William Vance of the nineteenth and twentieth century, as though the act of seeing becomes the stabilizing factor.[51] We see as they saw, just as the Villa Lante affords similar possibilities to Julius Martialis' villa. See the city from there today and the city seems almost tangible (Figure 6.8). The sense of distortion was ever thus and in this *mis*representation, each Rome made equal. This is the city of Samuel Palmer's *The Golden City: Rome from the Janiculum of 1873* (Figure 6.9)[52] with Saint Peter's to the left, Castel Sant' Angelo towards the

---

[48] At the beginning of book 3 of the *Aetia*: frs. 54–9. See Hollis 1986 and 1990, and Fabbrini 2007: 35–6, who develops the theme of hospitality and *paupertas* implicit in the parallel. Also relevant here is Stat. *Silv*. 3.1.29–33.

[49] Callim. 6.11–12. See Hopkinson 1984: 91.

[50] For example, *Epigrams* 12.34. See Citroni 1975: 326; Howell 1980: 328; and Shackleton Bailey 1993: vol. I, 53. Related to this is Fabbrini 2007: 50–7.

[51] Vance 1989: 404, although he also notes that, to his mind, this is a particularly twentieth-century phenomenon.

[52] Watercolour, gouache, pencil, black chalk, gum Arabic on paper, 51.4 x 71 cm, National Gallery of Victoria, Melbourne.

Figure 6.8 View from the Janiculum today.

Figure 6.9 Samuel Palmer, *The Golden City: Rome from the Janiculum.* See also colour plate section.

Figure 6.10　View of the Forum from the Capitoline today.

centre and the rest of the cityscape splayed out in the sunshine between the hills in the foreground and background. As in the epigram, 'iugera pauca' frame the scene. This is Rome – take her or leave her.

Framing a view from the Capitoline and Palatine

From the Capitoline, indifference is not an option (Figure 6.10).[53] 'Climbing the Campidoglio or Capitoline Hill, which has lured visitors to Rome since the days of the Caesars, still provides the best, most inspiring introduction to this dynamic city', claims a recent issue of the *Smithsonian Magazine*.[54] In 1843 John Murray's *Handbook for Travellers in Central Italy* advised: 'there is no scene in the world more magnificent than that commanded from this spot'.[55] Standing here, looking down towards the Colosseum, the

---

[53] Compare, for example, Hor. *Carm.* 3.29.11–12, which was highly influential on Mart. 4.64, and its advice to Maecenas to stop wondering at the smoke, riches and din of blessed Rome ('omitte mirari beatae | fumum et opes strepitumque Romae'). On the Esquiline, Capitoline and other central hills, one is very much in the thick of the action.

[54] Perrottet 2005.　　[55] Murray 1843: 268.

chaos of urban living subsides, the *fora* shrink, and one comes face to face
with antiquity. Is it recognizable? Is it the Forum that one sees in plate 7 of
Rossini, post the early eighteenth-century engravings, or in plate 11, where
it has yet to be destroyed by Vandal incursions? Is it what survives that
excites or what does not? What about the rest of the dynamic city? What
kind of introduction is this?

In another epigram Martial writes to another friend, Maximus, commenting on his many properties in the city with their competing vistas:

Esquiliis domus est, domus est tibi colle Dianae,
    et tua Patricius culmina vicus habet;
hinc viduae Cybeles, illinc sacraria Vestae,
    inde novum, veterem prospicis inde Iovem.
dic ubi conveniam, dic qua te parte requiram: 5
    quisquis ubique habitat, Maxime, nusquam habitat.

You own a house on the Esquiline, a house on Diana's hill, and the Vicus Patricius
too supports your roofs. From one, you command a view over the shrine of widowed
Cybele, and from another, that of Vesta; there you see the new temple of Jupiter,
and there, the old one. Tell me where I am to meet you. Tell me in which place I am
to seek you. He who lives everywhere, Maximus, lives nowhere.[56]

Scholars have worried about how three houses – on the Esquiline, Aventine
and Viminal (the Vicus Patricius being a street that ran from the Subura
to the Porta Viminalis) – can offer four competing prospects, with some
going as far as to suggest that the second couplet implies further properties
on the remaining seven summits.[57] But such rationalization, totalization
even, is not what this poem is about. Rather, the opposite, as the author
struggles to pin its addressee down to any one residence. One moment, his
house is on the Esquiline, and within the line, it is elsewhere, as competing
claims cancel each other out, making him nigh on homeless. Rome is not
brought together, as it was for Julius Martialis, but fractured, epitomized
first by one shrine, then the next, and by new-build, then ancient temple.
Maximus is just too big – he overreaches himself. In attempting to master
so many alternatives, he is master of none. The sense of having a grip on
Rome eludes him.

The view from the Capitoline is similarly partial and predisposed towards
one particular chapter of Rome's history, the Republic and Empire. Magnificent and inspiring it may be, but it is also elusive. As Janus Vitalis

---

56 Mart. 7.73.   57 L. Richardson 1980.

(1485–c. 1560), a priest of the papal court from Palermo, wrote, displaying his debt to Propertius as he did so:

qui Romam in media quaeris novus advena Roma
et Romae in Roma nil reperis media.

As a newly arrived visitor, you seek Rome in the middle of Rome and you find nothing of Rome in the middle of Rome.[58]

If Martial's looking for Maximus is hard, looking for Rome in Rome presents a real problem. Samuel Palmer explains:

I have had a hard grapple with ancient Rome – for I was determined to get the whole of the grand ruins, which I believe has not yet been done. I got a little pencil sketch of it from a window . . . then composed from it at home as I imagined it ought to come if all of it could be seen, and then worked the details from the tower of the Capitol where I saw everything – but 150 ft beneath me.[59]

Wholeness is again the aim, although this time ring-fenced as a complete picture of the past. What strategies does he adopt in his pictures to accomplish this?

Unlike his view from the Janiculum, entitled *The Golden city,* Palmer's watercolour from the Capitoline can only ever be, despite his best efforts, *A View of Ancient Rome* (Figure 6.11).[60] This Rome is but a blown up section of the former, no river, no hills, except those beyond – just the Forum out into the *suburbana.* It is not even ancient, the cupola of the Church of Saints Luke and Martina to the left of the cleared Arch cementing his modern perspective. This and other ruins punctuate an otherwise desolate space: if these represent the 'whole of the grand ruins', then one realizes how much has been lost. The grandeur of ancient Rome is in the size of the lacuna.

This loss is compensated for not by reconstruction, but by a pendant painting which was displayed with it at the Royal Academy in London in 1838 (Figure 6.12).[61] Entitled *A View of Modern Rome during the Carnival,* it takes not the Capitoline, but the Pincio as its vantage point, looking away from ancient Rome, across the expanse of Valadier's Piazza del Popolo with

---

[58] *Elogia* 1–2. See Mayer 2007: 166, and on Janus Vitalis, the Latin name for Giano Vitale de Palerme, within a broader sixteenth-century literary context, Skyrme 1982.

[59] 7 June 1838. See Lister 1974.

[60] Watercolor and gouache over graphite on buff paper laid down on board, 41.1 x 57.8 cm, Birmingham City Museums and Art Galleries. Also important here are the catalogue entries in Edwards and Liversidge 1996: nos. 29 and 30, pp. 109–12 and the essay by Liversidge in the same volume (38–52); Powell 1998: 28 and Barker et al. 2005: nos. 105a and 105b, pp. 180–2.

[61] Watercolour and bodycolour over pencil, on white paper, 41 x 57.6 cm, Birmingham Museums and Art Gallery, acc. no. 1946P16.

Figure 6.11 Samuel Palmer, *A View of Ancient Rome*. See also colour plate section.

Figure 6.12 Samuel Palmer, *A View of Modern Rome*. See also colour plate section.

its churches of Santa Maria dei Miracoli and Santa Maria in Montesanto to the left and that of Santa Maria del Popolo to the right, over the heads of classicizing statuary, towards Saint Peter's, which occupies the centre, like the Colosseum. Modern Rome is a Christian Rome – Vatican City. That said, in the foreground, winding its merry way towards the viewer, is a procession of carnival revellers. From the half-clad figures and winged 'Victory' leaning from the cart, to the cherubic boy with twin pipes on a goat, and the gay abandon of the leading figure with tambourine and mask-like face, everything about this line-up is pagan. This quality connects the two paintings, the past and the present, making the former and its Rome, for all of its partiality, half of a single entity. In the process, *A View of Ancient Rome* swells to be 'the whole of the grand ruins', the essence of the antique.

Seen like this, one can see why the Capitoline is 'endowed with something of the same qualities as Wells' Time Machine, rising as it does like an island of peace out of the student roar of Piazza Venezia in the heart of the city. It can lead us backwards by degrees through the centuries to the time when Rome first emerged from a collection of pastoral villages set upon seven hills.'[62] These degrees are crucial: what is important is not what one is seeing and not seeing, so much as whom one is viewing with. I have already mentioned Bracciolini and Gibbon. In the eighteenth century, Scottish antiquarians James Byres and Colin Morison, who specialized in tours for the English visitor, pointed out the main sites from the Capitoline, including the seven hills, before moving to the neighbouring Palatine. There, one of Morison's customers, James Boswell, was so inspired as to have resolved to speak in Latin.[63]

Virgil is as responsible for the premium of viewing from these hills as he is for the success of the 'seven-hills' concept. In book 8 of the *Aeneid* he has Evander show Aeneas the future site of Rome on a famous walk from the Ara Maxima in the Forum Boarium to his house on or near the Palatine. As soon as they enter the city Aeneas is described as wondering ('miratur') and turning his ready eyes all around as he is taken by the scene ('capitur locis').[64] The route that they take has proved difficult to

---

[62] Masson 1965: 19.   [63] Prown 1997: 95 and n. 20.
[64] Virg. *Aen.* 8.306–12:

> exim se cuncti divinis rebus ad urbem
> perfectis referunt. Ibat rex obsitus aevo,
> et comitem Aenean iuxta natumque tenebat
> ingrendiens varioque viam sermone levabat.
> miratur facilisque oculos fert omnia circum
> Aeneas, capiturque locis et singula laetus
> exquiritque auditque virum monumenta priorum.

reconstruct[65] but enables Evander to point out the Carmental Gate between the river and the Capitoline, Romulus' asylum on the Capitoline itself, the Lupercal on the slope of the Palatine and the Argiletum and 'fashionable Carinae' ('fashionable' being an adjective which collapses time by referring to the smart residential area it will become).[66] In the midst of this description, they go 'ad Tarpeiam sedem et Capitolia':

hinc ad Tarpeiam sedem et Capitolia ducit
aurea nunc, olim silvestribus horrida dumis.
iam tum religio pavidos terrebat agrestis
dira loci, iam tum silvam saxumque tremebant.   350
'hoc nemus, hunc', inquit 'frondoso vertice collem
(quis deus incertum est) habitat deus; Arcades ipsum
credunt se vidisse Iovem, cum saepe nigrantem
aegida concuteret dextra nimbosque cieret.
haec duo praeterea disiectis oppida muris,   355
reliquias veterumque vides monumenta virorum.
hanc Ianus pater, hanc Saturnus condidit arcem;
Ianiculum huic, illi fuerat Saturnia nomen.'

From here he leads them to Tarpeia's place and the Capitol – golden now, once bristling with woodland thorns. Already then the dire sanctity of the place used to terrify the fearful rustics; even then they trembled at the wood and at the rock. 'This grove', said Evander, 'this hill with its leafy summit is home to a god (though which god is uncertain); the Arcadians believe that they have seen Jupiter himself, when, as often happens, he shook the blackening aegis with his right hand and stirred up the clouds. Moreover, you see these two towns with their walls torn apart, the relics and monuments of men of old. This citadel father Janus built and that citadel, Saturn. Janiculum was the name given to former, and Saturnia, the name given to the latter.'[67]

('From there, with the sacred rites performed, they all return to the city. The king, weighed down with age went on his way and, as he walked, kept Aeneas next to him as his companion and his son and lightened the route with varied conversation. Aeneas is amazed and turns his eager eyes all around; and he is taken with the place and happily seeks out each individual thing and hears about the monuments of men of old.')

[65] On their route and its topography, see Warde Fowler 1918, Grimal 1948 and Gransden 1976. Also relevant here, and concentrating on the role of Evander, is Papaioannou 2003.

[66] Virg. *Aen.* 8.337–65 and, on the choice of sites to emphasize, Renaud 1990. On the contemporary import of the reference to the Carinae, see Edwards 1996: 32, and on the Carinae in the archaic period, Terrenato 1992. Also relevant here is Harrison 2006, who explores how the *Aeneid* and the buildings mentioned as newly built or restored by Augustus in his *Res gestae* intersect.

[67] Virg. *Aen.* 8.355–8.

The view that unfolds prompts walls to be torn down or dissolved, and towns to become accessible, however ancient they might be. Attention is drawn to the Temple of Saturn at the base of the hill and to the hill's former name, Saturnia. It is then directed to the Janiculum some 2,000 metres away on the opposite side of the river.

Some commentators have suggested that line 358 is interpolated,[68] leaving the reference to Janus above it applicable to a second shrine at the base of the Capitoline.[69] But this is to ignore the ways in which Aeneas and Evander's walk has motivated later visitors. Whether Virgil imagines them actually on the Capitoline, able to see for miles, or not,[70] their seeing is similar to the panoramic views that I have just been describing and has shaped the visions of Palmer, Byres and Morison, making them climb. So too Evander's house. Although there is some disagreement about whether it was on the Palatine or in the Forum, the sense of ascending implied by Virgil's use of the verb 'subibant' (literally, 'they came up to the house of humble Evander' (line 359)), together with the view of the Forum and Carinae it affords, has again proved influential.[71] Poggio Bracciolini's response is arguably impossible without him.

Her primeval state, such as she might appear in a remote age, when Evander entertained the stranger of Troy, has been delineated by the fancy of Virgil. This Tarpeian rock was then a savage and solitary thicket: in the time of the poet, it was crowned with the golden roofs of a temple . . . The hill of the Capitol, on which we sit, was formerly the head of the Roman empire, the citadel of the earth, the terror of kings . . . Cast your eyes on the Palatine hill, and seek among the shapeless and enormous fragments the marble theatre, the obelisks, the colossal statues, the porticoes of Nero's palace: survey the other hills of the city, the vacant space is interrupted only by ruins and gardens. The forum of the Roman people, where they assembled to enact their laws and elect their magistrates, is now enclosed for the cultivation of pot-herbs, or thrown open for the reception of swine and buffaloes.[72]

And Gibbon is not the only one to make the link between Virgil and viewing from above explicit. At roughly the same time as the publication of the

---

[68] See e.g. Pichon 1914.   [69] See e.g. Grimal 1945: 56.

[70] Although many scholars accept that Aeneas has his attention directed towards the Janiculum, most also agree (*contra* B. Tilly 1961: 385) that he and Evander do not climb the Capitoline: see, for example, Gransden 1976: 33.

[71] Virg. *Aen.* 8.359: 'talibus inter se dictus ad tecta subibant . . .' On Evander's house being in roughly the same place as the house of Augustus, see Warde Fowler 1918: 72; Gransden 1976: 30; Fordyce 1977: 246; and Richmond 1958. And for an alternative reading, tying it instead to the Regia in the Forum, Rees 1996. Relevant to Rees' arguments is Claudian's use of 'regia', below, pp. 216–17.

[72] Bracciolini as cited in Gibbon 1776–88: ch. 71 (edition by Bury 1900: vol. vii, 301–2).

Decline and Fall, German traveller Friedrich Leopold Stolberg reflected, 'There, repeatedly said I to myself, looking at the Mount Palatine, there must the good Evander have lived . . . We now ascend the highest hill [the Capitoline]' and in 1840 English poet Samuel Rogers:

. . . Climb the Palatine,
Dreaming of old Evander and his guest
Dreaming and lost on that proud eminence.[73]

Dreaming of Evander achieves the effect of Palmer's pendant paintings, making the 'golden present' and 'the bristling' past (or vice versa) two halves of a whole. It legitimates looking for Rome in, or directly above, Rome, by making the meeting of 'now' and 'then' overwhelm any resulting fragmentation of its territory. As we are about to discover, *Aeneid* 8 already inspires Claudian's account of Honorius' visit to the city. The value of the Capitoline and Palatine for perceiving Rome, past, present and future, gives the emperor the control that is denied to the experimental Maximus.

The imperial gaze

There has been a lot of work done recently on analysing the strategies adopted by European travellers to the Americas and to Africa in the nineteenth century, or indeed to Italy on the 'Grand Tour', for coping with and reliving the strange sights that confronted them – the emphasis being very much on the translation or taming of this strangeness under the banner of 'cultural imperialism'.[74] Mary Louise Pratt writes, 'Nineteenth-century travellers often used promontory views with pictorial conventions to present themselves as a "discoverer" who has the power/authority to elevate, if not to possess a scene.'[75] This kind of analysis makes us more conscious about what is happening in a text like Claudian's panegyric on the sixth consulship of Honorius, delivered in 404 CE probably in the audience chamber of the imperial palace.[76] This was not the first time that the young emperor had visited the city: he had accompanied his father, Theodosius, when an

---

[73] Stolberg 1796–7: 337 and Rogers 1840: 133.

[74] For the 'magisterial gaze', see Boime 1991; on the 'tourist gaze', Adler 1989 and Urry 1990; on the 'colonial gaze', Eeden 2004; and, in relation to the Grand Tour and to Italy, Pemble 1987 and Chard and Langdon 1996. Excellent are M. L. Pratt 1992, Wallach 1993, Nash 1996, and W. A. King 2004 and, for developing the difference between the gaze of the 'traveller' and that of the 'tourist', Buzard 1993.

[75] M. L. Pratt 1992: 205.   [76] Dewar 1996: xliv–xlv.

infant.[77] But the Empire was divided, and Honorius, as the ruler of the west, was based in Ravenna. It makes sense that Claudian chose to emphasize looking and measuring from the Palatine to enable Honorius and Rome to get to know one another.[78]

ecce Palatino crevit reverentia monti
exultatque habitante deo potioraque Delphis
supplicibus late populis oracula pandit
atque suas ad signa iubet revirescere laurus.
   non alium certe decuit rectoribus orbis
esse larem, nulloque magis se colle potestas   40
aestimat et summi sentit fastigia iuris;
attolens apicem subiectis regia rostris
tot circum delubra videt tantisque deorum
cingitur excubiis! iuvat infra tecta Tonantis
cernere Tarpeia pendentes rupe Gigantas   45
caelatasque fores mediisque volantia signa
nubibus et densum stipantibus aethera templis
aeraque vestitis numerosa puppe columnis
consita subnixasque iugis inmanibus aedes,
naturam cumulante manu, spoliisque micantes   50
innumeros arcus. acies stupet igne metalli
at circumfuso trepidans obtunditur auro.
agnoscisne tuos, princeps venerande, penates?

Behold, reverence for the Palatine Mount has increased: it rejoices in its native deity, spreads oracles far and wide to its suppliant people more powerful than those of Delphi and orders its own laurels to grow green again for the standards [of Rome].

    Certainly no other place was fit to be a home to the world's rulers; on no other hill does power more accurately get the measure of itself and perceive the heights of its supreme law. Lifting its head over the Forum with the rostra below it, the palace sees so many temples around it and is surrounded by such great shrines of the gods! It is pleasing to see below the Temple of the Thunderer the giants hanging from the Tarpeian Rock, and its engraved doors, and statues flying amid the clouds, and the air thick with thronging temples, bronzes planted on columns adorned with numerous prows, and shrines built on massive ridges, where the human hand

---

[77] As the poem itself makes explicit. See below.
[78] Excellent on this poem is the commentary by Dewar 1996. For its historical context, see Alan Cameron 1970 and Schmidt 1976 and for Claudian and representations of Rome, M. Roberts 2001 and Long 2004.

enhances nature, and countless arches glittering with spoils. The gaze is stupefied by the metallic blaze and, faltering, is blunted by the engulfing gold. Venerable Princeps, do you recognize your home?

Here, having introduced homecoming as his theme, the poet has his readers and listeners imagine themselves on the Palatine with Rome's rulers. In a move already familiar from Lucan, whose Caesar imagines Jupiter looking out from the Capitoline,[79] it is the palace itself and not a mortal agent who does the seeing. Later, Claudian will come even closer to Lucan as his Roma describes how she had long anticipated Honorius' arrival – 'for Jupiter to see from the Tarpeian Rock'.[80] But for the moment, all eyes are on the Palatine: 'on no other hill does power more accurately get the measure of itself'. The Latin for this phrase – 'se potestas aestimare' – takes us back to Martial and his measuring of Rome from the Janiculum – except that now it is not Rome that is measured, but power.[81] From this position, at the very heart of the city, Rome and watchtower, Rome and authority, are one. This is a narcissistic vision: the city's imperial power sees and feels ('sentit') the heights of its supreme sway, which is literally embodied in its structures ('fastigia' being the gables or pediments of a building as well as 'heights'). But still it strains for a better view: the palace ('regia') lifts its head above the parapet to render the rostra of the Forum abject beneath it.

'Regia' is a word which ranges in meaning from the abstract (royal power) to the concrete (palace) to the specific (a temple between the House of the Vestals and the Temple of Antoninus Pius and Faustina, which tradition attributed to King Numa). It was also used of the 'kingdom of heaven'. Here it embraces all of these nuances to make this vantage point more controlling. It also embraces the *Aeneid* and the house or 'regia' of Evander – a building with its own 'fastigia', which Virgil describes as belonging to a 'narrow roof' ('angusti subter fastigia tecti').[82] This poem represents an expansion of that vision. 'It is pleasing to see below' (or 'below the surface' – 'infra') shouts Claudian, rallying his readers to join him in his looking. The first thing we notice are the roofs ('tecta') of the Temple of Jupiter on the Tarpeian

---

[79] See above, p. 113.

[80] Claud. *VI Cons. Hon.* 374–5: 'iamque parabantur pompae simulacra futurae | Tarpeio spectanda Iovi' ('and already the models for the future triumphal procession were being prepared for Jupiter to see from the Tarpeian Rock').

[81] Although Dewar 1996 ad loc. sees 'se aestimat' as a simple stand-in for the passive, a move that is fairly common in spoken Latin of the time, this need not negate the impact of the sustained personification. He himself goes on to show how a second use of the verb by Claudian (*Theod.* pr. 11) reinforces the sense in which this measuring makes Rome the centre of the world.

[82] Virg. *Aen.* 8.366–7: 'dixit, et angusti subter fastigia tecti | ingentem Aenean duxit . . .' See Dewar 1996: ad loc.

Rock – another point of contact with Virgil – this time his 'Tarpeian place and Capitolium' ('Tarpeiam sedem et Capitolia').[83]

Competition between the Palatine and Capitoline was already there in Virgil,[84] but it had become a measure of a ruler's right to rule. So Statius of Domitian's palace:

tectum augustum, ingens, non centum insigne columnis,
sed quantae superos caelumque Atlante remisso
sustenare queant. stupet hoc vicina Tonantis
regia, teque pari laetantur sede locatum
numina (nec magnum properes ascendere caelum).

An august building, huge, outstanding not with a hundred columns but as many as would be able to support the immortals were Atlas to let go. The Thunderer's neighbouring palace views this building with amazement, and the gods are happy that you are established in a seat equal to their own (and you would not hurry to ascend to the great sky!)[85]

Here the Jupiter Temple is the 'regia' that stares in amazement – this time at Domitian's palace. Claudian reverses the trope to have this palace do the looking, claiming the expansiveness of its architecture for the view instead (so many shrines, so many deities...).[86] So commanding is this view that rather than render the hills equal as in the Statius poem, it has the Palatine tower above the Capitoline. Honorius wins outright where Domitian could only compete, and Claudian trumps Statius. We are reminded of Corinna's story about Mount Cithaeron's poetic victory over Helicon, which some scholars read as a statement of her rivalry with Pindar.[87]

The mastery offered by and from the Palatine is so well established that Rome does not shrink as from the Janiculum, but bloats below it: at the end of our looking, there are still 'countless glittering arches'. The Latin for 'glittering', 'micare', also means to 'dart about' or 'quiver with life'. Statues are not stilled, like Martial's travellers, but fly around ('volantia') in the midst of the clouds, temples throng together in the air and Rome's ridges or 'iugis', a word used by Virgil and Statius of its seven hills, are 'immanibus' or 'monstrous', made higher by human intervention. Unsurprisingly perhaps,

---

[83] Virg. *Aen*. 8.347: 'hinc ad Tarpeiam sedem et Capitolia ducit'.
[84] On the competition created by Augustus' development of the Palatine, see Favro 2005: 256 and 261.
[85] Stat. *Silv*. 4.2.18–22.
[86] Also relevant here is Dewar 1996: 91, who in commenting, on line 42 and 'attollens apicem', notes that Martial (8.36) uses 'apex' in relation to the roof of Domitian's palace.
[87] Page, *PMG* fr. 654, col. 1 = *P Berol*. 284. For ease of reference, see Campbell 1992: 27–9. The most persuasive advocate for reading Corinna's hills in this way is Clayman 1993.

the gaze gives up: it is powerless ('stupet') in the face of the blaze of metal; 'alarmed' ('trepidans') and 'blunted' ('obtunditur') by the overwhelming goldenness.

Nothing stands still long enough to offer itself to the ekphrastic exegesis of its author. This is not a panorama so much as pandemonium. It is like the frustration described by American writer Eleanor Clark in her wonderful book *Rome and a Villa*:

> Something, after all, is being presented to the glazed eyeball and paralyzed sense of the worrying traveler, who came most often not looking for Rome at all but for love . . . He sees a city of bells and hills and walls . . . an impossible compounding of time, in which no century has respect for any other and all hit you in a jumble at every turn; or roaring motors and other dreadful noises . . . It is all too much.[88]

Even the Temple of Jupiter reveals its delicately carved doors and hanging giants – the civilized and the wild within one frame: from the primordial past when the gods fought the giants, to the time of Romulus and Tarpeia, to the restorations of the temple by Domitian, complete with his gold-clad doors, which Stilicho will soon order to be stripped at the threat of Alaric's invasion.[89] This is the chaos that Honorius must rise to domesticate.

'Maxima Roma':[90] only an emperor can possess her. It is an act which makes both of them greater. Only as our vision falters is Honorius addressed directly: 'Do you recognise your home?' He can identify what is only a blur to mere mortals, can join the ranks of Rome's helmsmen ('rectoribus'). In that moment of acknowledgement, he too is recognized as venerable Princeps. When he was a child, continues Claudian, Honorius had accompanied his father to Rome so that, 'as her new heir, he might even then begin to grow accustomed to empire'.[91] Then he had 'wondered' ('miratus') at what she had to offer.[92] Only now, does he possess her and belong there. Mention of the *penates*, or household gods, again reminds the reader of Lucan's Caesar, who, having addressed the Thunderer, invokes the *penates* of the Julian

---

[88] E. Clark 1950: 17–18.   [89] Zos. 5.38.5. See Dewar 1996: ad loc.
[90] Prop. 4.1.1.   [91] Claud. *VI Cons. Hon.* 76: 'ut novus imperio iam tunc adsuesceret heres'.
[92] Claud. *VI Cons. Hon.* 54–5:

> hacc sunt, quae primis olim miratus in annis
> patre pio monstrante puer.

('these are the things which you wondered at long ago in your early years when, as a boy, you were shown them by your pious father').

family and, through this, of Roma herself, who later in Claudian's poem bemoans Honorius' absence by comparing the Tiber and the Rubicon.[93] Finally, he reaches Rome to assume his place on the Palatine. His power is not in the palace but in the capacity to come, see and conquer.

When next we hear of the Palatine, it is as the people pour onto the streets to acclaim Honorius emperor. This is a crucial next step. The Persian king, Xerxes, was famously criticized for watching a naval battle from on high.[94] There was always a danger that taking stock from above was misinterpreted as aloofness or cowardice.

omne Palatino quod pons a colle recedit
Mulvius et quantum licuit consurgere tectis,
una replet turbae facies: undare videres   545
ima viris, altas effulgere matribus aedes.

As one body, the crowd filled the whole area between the Ponte Milvio and the Palatine hill and as far up as it was possible to climb on the roofs. You could see the depths surging with men and the high buildings bright with women.

It is now Rome's population that throngs together causing the buildings to glitter. These people expand to fill every available space, both horizontally from the Milvian Bridge to the base of the Palatine, and vertically.[95] But as is the case with Trajan's Column, they can only climb so high. Far off the ground they may be, but their emperor is always bigger. Now we get the ekphrasis that has thus far been denied as one of the crowd, a young woman, likens the armour-clad horses of Honorius' procession to statues

---

[93] Luc. 1.196 and Claud. *VI Cons. Hon.* 363–5:

> . . . vetitumque propinqua
> luce frui, spatiis discernens gaudia parvis,
> torquebit Rubicon vicino numine Thybrim?

('Is it forbidden to enjoy a close encounter? Will the Rubicon, which keeps the object of joy distant from me by a small margin, torture the Tiber with the proximity of [an inaccessible] god?')

[94] Herod. 8.90.4, as is evoked in *Panegyric of Constantine Augustus* 10 (Nixon and Rodgers 1994: 310–11): 'spectavit ex edito monte Xerxes navale certamen; Augustus aliud agens vicit apud Actium; fuit etiam qui sublatus in scalas invicem nexas concurrentes eminus vidit exercitus, ut nec interesset periculo et adesset eventui' ('Xerxes watched the naval battle from a high mountain; Augustus won at Actium, while he was otherwise engaged; there was even one who, raised up on ladders fastened together, saw from on high his armies clashing so that he would not be involved in the danger and would be present at the conclusion').

[95] Dewar 1996: ad loc.

made by Hephaestus.[96] Now, once he and we have been introduced to the
city's magnitude, he can command the appropriate respect. It is a bit like
Aeneas' route to knowing Rome in the *Aeneid* – only when he has been
shown the seven citadels in book 6 and understands what Rome is, does
Virgil provide the thicker description of book 8, where again we are given
Evander's tour and then the details on the shield. By the poem's conclusion
Honorius has arrived – the Palatine is 'happy at the sight of a consul after
many ages'.[97] He is no longer a 'stranger' in a foreign land[98] but has had the
seven hills echo his title, 'Augustus'.[99]

Divine omniscience

The presence of the gods on Olympus means that the view from above had
long had the power to confer divine status. In the *Iliad* the immortals are not
just there on high but often watch the fighting. Zeus in book 8 is envisaged,
sitting 'among the mountain peaks, rejoicing in glory, looking upon the city
of the Trojans and the ships of the Achaeans', and later, 'looking down from
Ida'.[100] 'By placing the gods as spectators', wrote Dean Hammer of Homer
recently, 'the audience "is invited to share the focalization" of the gods, "and

---

[96] Claud. *VI Cons. Hon.* 569–74:

> ut chalybe indutos equites et in aere latentes
> vidit cornipedes: 'quanam de gente' rogabat
> 'ferrati venere viri? quae terra metallo
> nascentes informat equos? num Lemnius auctor
> indidit hinnitum ferro simulacraque belli
> viva dedit?' . . .

('As she sees the horsemen clad in metal and horses clothed in bronze, she asks, "From what
race do the iron men come? What land shapes horses born from metal? Has the god of
Lemnos [Hephaestus] imbued metal with neighing and given living statues for fighting?"')

[97] Claud. *VI Cons. Hon.* 643–4:

> consule laetatur post plurima saecula viso
> Pallanteus apex . . .

[98] Prop. 4.1.1.

[99] Claud. *VI Cons. Hon.* 616–17: 'unaque totis | intonat Augustum septenis arcibus echo!' ('An
echo intones "Augustus" from all seven hills together').

[100] Hom. *Il.* 8.51–2:

> αὐτὸς δ' ἐν κορυφῇσι καθέζετο κύδεϊ γαίων
> εἰσορόων Τρώων τε πόλιν καὶ νῆας Ἀχαιῶν.

And 11.336–7:

> Ἔνθά σφιν κατὰ ἶσα μάχην ἐτάνυσσε Κρονίων
> ἐξ Ἴδης καθορῶν . . .

('Then the son of Cronos, laying out the battle equally for them, looking down from Ida . . .')

at the same time to feel that it is only a partial appreciation of what is going on."'[101] This partiality puts us in our place. 'The individual spectator could not avoid being aware of his or her own position in this hierarchy.'[102]

Honorius is not the only emperor whose viewing makes him god-like. Domitian too is described by Statius as a god, looking forth upon the walls of Rome from the Alban hills (an allusion to his villa at Castel Gandolfo).[103] And a panegyric, written to celebrate the birthday of Maximian (Augustus from 286 CE) and dated to around 291 CE, has its honorand rival Roma in his command of the world's great mountains.

nunc autem, ut primum ex utrisque Alpium iugis vestrum numen effulsit, tota Italia clarior lux diffusa, omnibus qui suspexerant aeque admiratio atque dubitatio iniecta, ecquinam di de illis montium verticibus orirentur, an his gradibus in terras caelo descenderent.

But now when your divinity first shone out from both Alpine ridges, a clearer light spread over all of Italy and everyone who looked up was struck by admiration, and equally by uncertainty as to whether the gods were rising from those mountain crests or by these steps were descending from heaven to earth.[104]

A few paragraphs later, with the emperor installed in Milan, the goddess cannot resist weighing up the opposition.

ipsa etiam gentium domina Roma immodico propinquitatis vestrae elata gaudio vosque e speculis suorum montium prospicere conata, quo se vultibus vestris propius expleret, ad intuendum cominus quantum potuit accessit.

Even Rome herself, the mistress of nations, elated by excessive joy at your proximity and trying to command a view from the mirrors of her own mountains, so that she

---

[101]   Hammer 2002: 54. As Kearns writes 2004: 59: 'if we were thus to reduce the storylines of the *Iliad* and *Odyssey* to the bare essentials, the Gods would not have to feature at all ... [yet] without the Gods the epics would be quite different from the *Iliad* and *Odyssey* that we have, and surely also from the tradition that produced the poems ... Insofar as some concept of cause and effect is inherent in narrative, then, the divine must make its appearance.' See also Griffin 1980: 162: 'The Homeric epics are poems about the actions and doom of heroes, but we see everything in them falsely if we do not see it against the background of the gods ...' and Griffin 1978.

[102]   Edwards 2007: 54.

[103]   Stat. Silv. 5.2.168–71:

> sed quis ab excelsis Troianae collibus Albae,
> unde suae iuxta prospectat moenia Romae
> proximus ille deus ...

('But who is this that from the high hills of Trojan Alba, where that closest deity looks out on the walls of his own Rome nearby ...')

[104]   *Genethliacus of Maximian Augustus* 10.4 (Nixon and Rodgers 1994: 95).

might more closely take her fill of your physical appearance, advanced as near as she was able to have a look.[105]

Rome's desperation to see accords with what we have already experienced in Claudian – a city prepared to make its hills higher to get the emperor's attention.[106] But these hills are 'mirrors', imitative of the Alps, but also able to reflect imperial glory. This glare sheds light on one of the best-known sections of Ammianus' account of Constantius' entry into Rome: his gazing straight ahead like a cult statue.

We have already witnessed Constantius II's consternation at the buildings that he encountered on his route through the city. Faced with Trajan's Forum, 'all hope of trying anything of that kind is dashed to the ground'. Never again will it be imitated by mortal men.[107] After lengthy deliberation on what he might contribute to the cityscape, Constantius decides to erect an obelisk in the Circus Maximus, but description of this is withheld by Ammianus until the subsequent book and a section of text which struggles to stay focused on him or Rome. When it finally does return to Constantius' installation of the monument, this monument is referred to as a 'veritable mountain' ('mons ipse')[108] and the emperor seen replaying a version of what Rome's early kings did in adding a hill to the city – a sense which is intensified by his inevitable comparison with Octavian and his own father. Except that an obelisk is a foreign image. The moment it is erected by thousands of men, the orb on top is struck by lightning.[109]

This is hardly auspicious, especially given that Ammianus has already, on recounting Constantius' intention to enter Rome, told of his failure to add anything to the Empire:

nec enim gentem ullam bella cientem per se superavit, aut victam fortitudine suorum comperit ducum, vel addidit quaedam imperio, aut usquam in necessitat ibus summis primus vel inter primos est visus, sed ut pompam nimis extentam, rigentiaque auro vexilla, et pulcritudinem stipatorum ostenderet agenti tranquillius popolo, haec vel simile quicquam videre nec speranti umquam nec optanti. ignorans fortasse, quosdam veterum principum in pace quidem lictoribus fuisse contentos . . .

For neither did he overcome by himself any warring nation nor find out about any which had been conquered by the bravery of his own generals, nor did he add anything to the Empire, nor ever at times of greatest need, was he seen at the front of

---

[105] *Genethliacus of Maximian Augustus* 12 (Nixon and Rodgers 1994: 96).
[106] See Chapter 4, pp. 114–15.   [107] Amm. Marc. 16.10.15.
[108] Amm. Marc. 17.4.15. On the role of this obelisk in the text, see G. Kelly 2003: 603–6.
[109] Amm. Marc. 17.4.15.

the battle-line or among those at the front. But he sought to display an inordinately long procession, banners stiff with gold, and the beauty of his retinue to people who were living quite peacefully, neither expecting nor ever desiring to see this or anything like it. Perhaps he was ignorant of the fact that certain *principes* of old in times of peace had been happy to have had lictors...[110]

All is show, without substance. The reputation of every emperor resides in the gap between representation and reality, but for Ammianus' Constantius this gap is too wide and his displays of power are unconvincing.[111] When crises were at their height he was invisible, and when least expected he was there with a triumphal procession that was too extensive. Perhaps he was simply 'unknowing' ('ignorans'), muses our author. It is a suggestion that puts a different gloss on his arrival or *adventus* a section later.

This scene has become the classic example of late antique ceremonial.[112] Before he sees the city and its suburbs, he is ferried into Rome, impassive and immobile. Even his cavalrymen are likened to statues, polished by the famous Greek sculptor Praxiteles.

Augustus itaque faustis vocibus appellatus, non montium litorumque intonante fragore cohorruit, talem se tamque immobilem, qualis in provinciis suis visebatur, ostendens. nam et corpus perhumile curvabat portas ingrediens celsas, et velut collo munito, rectam aciem luminum tendens, nec dextra vultum nec laeva flectebat et (tamquam figmentum hominis) nec cum rota concuteret nutans, nec spuens, aut os aut nasum tergens vel fricans, manumve agitans visus est umquam.

And so, as he was being hailed Augustus with favourable shouts, he did not shudder at the thundering roar of the hills and shores, showing himself to be so big and so immobile as he seemed in his provinces. For he bent his body very low on passing through lofty gates and as though his neck were in a vice, he held the gaze of his eyes straight ahead and turned his face neither to right or left and (as if he were a statue of a man) neither did he nod when the wheel shook nor was he ever seen spitting or wiping or rubbing his face or nose or moving his hand.[113]

Rome is not the enemy, but Constantius seems set to terrify rather than to tame. It is as though he is working with the wrong parameters – so intent on seeming mightier than he is that he bends his head needlessly, overestimating his majesty. Although he is hailed 'Augustus', the presence of shores and hills together suggests that the latter are not the hills of Rome but landforms more suited to a bigger landscape. What works in the provinces does not work in the city and his impassivity becomes a problem. He is not

[110] Amm. Marc. 16.10.2.   [111] Matthews 1989: 234–5.
[112] See, for example, de Jonge 1972: 120; MacCormack 1972 and G. Kelly 2003: 598.
[113] Amm. Marc. 16.10.9–10.

godlike, as we might expect our *triumphator* to be,[114] nor even a cult statue. The text makes sure of that in an aside that describes him as being, 'like a statue *of a man*'. He and his Praxitelean horsemen are closer to the artworks that were brought into Rome after the conquest of Greece.[115] In contrast to Honorius, Constantius will never be curator of this city, but is fated/feted to remain an exhibit.[116]

Constantius does proceed to the Palatine, where he is said to enjoy 'longed-for pleasures'.[117] But Ammianus gives us no indication of what these are, preferring instead to dwell on the amazement that he feels when wandering through the Forum and then, in the section we have already looked at, within the seven hills. If we think about the Arch of Titus in the Forum: reliefs on either side of the passageway celebrate the joint triumph of Titus and Vespasian in the Jewish War of 71 CE, the spoils from the Temple of Jerusalem heaped high on one side and, on the other, Titus in a chariot being crowned by a winged Victory. But these are but the rehearsal for the scene above, that moment when Titus sheds his mortal coil and becomes a god.[118] Stand in the arch, and it is as though its ceiling has opened, sucking the emperor heavenwards (Figure 6.13). Now we see him, now we . . . it is hard not to feel that the coffering might close again, taking him away for ever as he rises high on the back of Jupiter's eagle; either that, or it will shatter, as the pair break the architectural frame that contains them. It is an appropriately odd image. Much of its power is inevitably in the emperor's bird's-eye view – in his capacity to survey us with divine detachment.

Compared with this, Constantius II is left clutching at straws, attempting to make mountains out of obelisks. Better to have identified a real *mons*, and to embrace vision as a means of social control, rather than keep his eyes fixed straight ahead of him. That the eyes of Claudian's poem function almost independently of Honorius reinforces the sense in which viewing from above offers detachment from the human experience, a detachment that lifts the viewer sufficiently far from the flux of collective activity to have him or her accept an imagined relationship with the land, a relationship that has little to do with gender or background. It is also why the human figures in landscape paintings like those by Palmer are so small. They are ciphers, not of a specific story but of a specific genre – the universalized

---

[114] Livy 10.7.10 for the triumphant general, decked out in the robes of Jupiter Optimus Maximus. And on the difficulties of reconstructing any kind of standard practice, Beard 2007: 225–33.

[115] For an excellent survey of these 'spoils', see K. E. Welch 2006 and Miles 2008.

[116] On Ammianus' description of Rome being that of a 'museum city', see Elsner 1998: 187.

[117] Amm. Marc. 16.10.13: 'in palatium receptus . . . laetitia fruebatur optata . . .'

[118] See Pfanner 1983: 76–9.

Figure 6.13 Relief of the apotheosis of Titus from the attic of the Arch of Titus.

experience that is viewing the land as landscape. Landscape is an artefact that encourages a different engagement with the land from living on it, invites a contemplation which makes the local alien. The ensuing need to familiarize oneself makes omniscience attainable.

Geographers have seen this 'landscape concept' as a fifteenth-century invention. For Denis Cosgrove, it is no accident that it coincides with capitalism and the rise in land as a valuable commodity. But the hills of Rome made it possible for ancient writers to realize this vision and, in the process, to turn their city into something tangible and reproducible – a cityscape with more immediate structure than any number of signposts or Augustan regions could supply. The landscape concept is about power, but not merely economic power. Whether they were on one of the seven summits, or in their friend's house on the Janiculum, this 'scape' gave them 'the presence

of a unifying principle... so that this part is perceived to carry the typical properties of the actually undivided whole'.[119] In this way Rome's hills became its footprint, and its eyes, mirrors even, able to reflect an image of the city back to itself and to other communities around the world – one reflection out of the miasma of overlapping, contradictory and personal pasts, a reflection eager to have us share in centuries of looking. As we look, we are confronted with a way of seeing the city, a city that is greater than our own peculiar standpoint. American writer Harold Bond encapsulates this sense of continuity and understanding: 'For nearly 3000 years, men had lived on these hills and in the valleys that I looked upon. Nor had they been, in their strife and turmoil, their loves and hates, much different from ourselves.'[120]

---

[119] Cosgrove 1984: 13.   [120] Bond 1964: 200.

7 | Signing off

What is one, who has received so much information about its hills, to expect from the city of Rome? You were thinking that I would write something big when I reached Rome. Perhaps I have procured prodigious material for future writing; but for now there is nothing which I dare begin, overwhelmed as I am by the miracle of such great sights and by the weight of wonder.

Petrarch, January–February, 1337 CE[1]

The history of an idea

Rome is a city built on volcanic plateaus composed of deposits from explosions in the Alban hills. It is also an imaginary city, composed of layer upon layer of construction: concrete structures such as the Colosseum collide with centuries of encounters to make Rome exemplary. The advantages of the site are obvious – the terrain provides hills for defence, proximity to the sea, a river for transport, and drinking water. Although there is archaeological evidence of earlier settlement, Rome's authors located the city's foundation in the eighth century BCE. Except that even then, Romulus and Remus occupied different hills, taking the auspices from the Palatine and Aventine and establishing the act of surveying from their summits: there was benefit to be derived from their conflict. It had to be hard to bring form and function to the land for this land to be worth something.

The foundation of Rome was worth killing for. Fratricide may seem an extreme starting point, even for a superpower, but it was no more than the aristocratic rivalries of the Republic demanded. Augustus' power and the power of empire depended on civil war as much as it did on Rome's victories against Parthia or Egypt – the popularity of the Lupercal image legitimated the fact that kin had died. But this was not a Greek tragedy: those aspects

[1] Petr. *Fam.* 2.14.103, to his patron, Cardinal Giovanni Colonna: 'ab urbe Roma quid expectet, qui tam multa de montibus acceperit? putabas me grande aliquid scripturum, cum Romam pervenissem. ingens michi forsan in posterum scribendi materia oblata est; in praesens nichil est quod incohare ausim, miraculo rerum tantarum et stuporis mole obrutus.'

had been played out already in the burning of Troy and the suicide of Dido. This was history: a writing of Rome which would define it against Greece for ever. Myths of origins gave the city its own 'back-catalogue' and prevented it from appearing an upstart.

The question then became how to get Romulus' Rome, as it came to be known, both to expand and to maintain its integrity. And the answer – to celebrate the realized city, as intended by Romulus and defined by Servius Tullius, as a city of seven summits. How these seven summits mapped onto the 'montes', seven or otherwise, of the 'Septimontium', and the 'Septimontium', onto Rome's proto-urban terrain, was a different question. But by the time that Varro was writing, these questions had merged to intensify the sense that the idea predated the city, rather than the other way round. Each of Romulus' successors is seen purposely to add a hill to steer the juggernaut towards its conclusion.

Arguments, ancient and modern, about which king did what make the seven hills more important – fundamental even to what Rome is, was and will be. They maintain the value of the land as it was first worked out in the arguments between Romulus and Remus. They also help to make each of these kings, some of them Sabine or Etruscan, Roman. And they help to integrate the Trojan Aeneas. In the process, the hills are made as academic as they are real, and Rome and Roman-ness described in the retrospective shaping of the landscape. This is particularly important at the end of the Republic. There has been a lot of work done recently on the ways in which Roman men were forced to perform their masculinity on the public stage in order to affirm their identity, but insufficient acknowledgement of the extent to which these performances relied on the land.[2] Claiming descent from Venus, for example, wrote one into a lineage which was both divine and earthly, taking one on a route from Troy via Carthage to Rome, and then, within Rome, to the Palatine of Evander, the Palatine of Romulus, the Palatine of the present. There had to be a way of reconciling competing claims and *degrees* of Roman-ness within the citizenship, of realizing a Roman-ness which could be shared and which rose above, and brought together, the most expensive tombs and the tallest houses. This was especially true once Augustus took the reins as 'primus inter pares'.

Augustus was only as great as the city and the Empire he ruled. The city and Empire were part of the same whole but were also separate entities: the second, Roman by design, and the former, Roman by default. Augustus'

---

[2] See, for example, Gunderson 2000 and (though second century CE in its focus) Gleason 1994. Also important in the emphasis it puts on place is Vasaly 1993.

urban reforms aimed at making the capital seem similarly intentional – grand and ordered enough to be a world city. But how could it be revamped without replacing everything it stood for and without making Rome's elite feel disoriented and disenfranchised? For all of the emphasis that modern scholarship puts on the gradual displacement of senatorial families from their homes on the Palatine, senatorial benefactions to the emperor, and the inscriptions that graced such monuments, gave the senate a new cohesion, against which Augustus defined his own evolving identity. It made them visible and authoritative as a group in a way different from before.[3] The question was how to project this symbiosis on a bigger scale: to take the grouping of senate, *populus* and Princeps that was writ large on the Forum's Arch of Augustus and apply it to the metropolis so that it should be theirs as well as his. Rome had to be worthy of Augustus' personal agenda but could not risk becoming an Athos.

The concept of the seven hills was perfect for this purpose, making all Romes equal to one another and to the Rome that was retro-conceived by Romulus. This is not to deny that the seven hills belonged to the Servian city east of the river and that Rome's built environment had long overreached it. Rather it is to understand how this Servian city was able to lend its legitimation to subsequent incarnations; how the idea of this city was sufficiently attractive to transcend any wall associated with it, and the land sufficiently hilly to have people continue counting. In time, this meant that the Janiculum and Vatican could be included, and what constituted the urban core recalculated without redefinition. And in the short term, it allowed Augustus to adorn the city as opposed to revise or expand it. Augustan reforms were all very well in bringing order to the urban landscape, but they involved a different kind of counting. His fourteen regions were not about defining the nature and limits of the city, but about structuring people's living in it.

The number seven, with all of the antiquity and mystery it implies, lent a universal significance to Rome's geography which made the city comprehensible to those beyond its boundaries. Poets from Virgil to Claudian developed this, using the hills to celebrate the power and permanence of the city, even after it has been seriously compromised by tyrants like Nero and by barbarians. Thebes had seven gates; Rome, seven hills; the world, seven wonders. Reiteration of the theme turned Rome into a cosmopolis and from cosmopolis into a city of legend. With each adjustment (whether *montes, colles, iuges*; whether qualified by adjectives such as 'septemgeminus' or 'septicollis'; with or without Roma, nymphs and other deities), the legend

---

[3] I owe this point to Amy Russell.

lived by being revisited. Poets pitted themselves against one another for a definitive version. The seven hills were the measure of Rome, of imperial power, poetic creativity and, later, threats of invasion.

Arguments about the membership of the canon followed. The identity of Rome's seven hills is incidental to the force of Virgil's or Statius' poetry. Or rather, it is fundamental on account of the poems' evasiveness. Either they deliberately raise the question, or they assume that everyone knew, in which case they create a club of initiates. Determining Varro's stake in this canon formation is as difficult as his writing. Undoubtedly committed to the number seven, he is also committed to making sense of the city by looking at its nomenclature. And it is this, and the influence of his text in Augustan and Renaissance Rome, rather than the success or failure of his project, that is crucial. His is a dissecting gaze – a way of seeing that is highly technical. He underwrites, or glosses, the efforts of these later poets by demonstrating that the city is only as great as its conceptualization.

Unsurprisingly, artists do not follow in these poets' footsteps. Not immediately at least – apart from those rare exceptions discussed, which render the hills more abstract. But the general unwillingness of ancient painters and sculptors to render Rome as they rendered conquered cities does not prevent us from thinking harder about what would have been lost had they tried to paint the seven hills as Palmer painted them, and indeed about how the relationship of concept and landscape is working. Visual representation changes the hills' status from a metaphor of indomitable Rome to an artwork akin to a 'copy' of the Laocoon or a portrait of Constantine. Had the hills been painted in antiquity, their power would have lain in their dissemination, and in a relationship between image and referent that concentrated on the present: how like, or unlike, was any one version of the hills to Rome's real hills? This comparison would have accented the Roman-ness of the originals but reduced them, and the city they stood for, to a single moment. It would have shifted the focus from idea to reality by raising the question of the genuine.

In the Renaissance, ancient Rome was a single moment – in contrast to the modern day. Distance framed it as a world to be intensively studied, a past life or alternative universe, which left only traces of its existence in the viewers' space. Could the seven hills serve as a bridge back to antiquity? Antiquarian writers such as Biondo certainly thought so, using them to map out the area of inquiry, and to get inside the ways in which Varro and contemporaries realized their relationship with the cityscape. Artists too were now attracted to the hills, excited by the challenges of pitting

vedute of the ruins against these reconstructions. Rome lay between them, as Julius III appreciated in offering not one, but two solutions, each of which pitted the ancient city against a Rome of his definition; the ancient city as encapsulated by the seven hills pitted against the ancient city encapsulated in the sculptures of villa and Vatican. Some fifteen hundred years after Statius and Domitian, Rome's most powerful individuals still rivalled the hills as the city's figurehead.

Gradually Rome ousted Venice as chief gatekeeper to the classical antique. As new finds surfaced, knowledge of this surface changed: ancient Rome existed in dimensions other than the literary imagination – in shards of pottery, statues, coins, inscriptions, the Marble Plan – and historical narratives were constructed to throw more impressionistic, timeless, images, like those on the walls of the Villa Giulia, into relief. Ruins and regions of the city were reidentified and reinvigorated. Visitors flooded in to see for themselves, confronting the gap between expectation and experience. Not all of them were as satisfied as Petrarch with what they found. Often the modern city seemed more alien than that emerging from the earth. But art appeased these visitors, fuelling a trade in engravings, including those of Pinelli and Rossini, which served as virtual Romes back home. This physicality turned Rome's landscape into an 'object of desire', whatever the reality.

Rossini's seven hills are as much about the views as they are about the escarpment. Not that *this* is new: Rome's hills were always a way of looking at the city in more ways than one – as subject and aperture. Looking down from the Palatine or across the river from the Janiculum offers different experiences. Yet each provides a sense of Rome that is denied to anyone on the Campus Martius or in the Forum. For all that artists working in ancient Rome avoided bird's-eye views of the capital, the city's authors were well aware of the mastery afforded by the overview. They understood the various ways in which it made the seething mass of Rome tangible, blurring its constituent parts (north or south of the river, inside or outside the walls, real, reconstructed, imaginary) into some sort of unity. The Farnese's terracing of the Palatine, the building of the Villa Lante, or indeed the decision in the fifteenth century to add a portico to the famous monastery of San Saba on the smaller of the Aventine's heights, exploited existing viewing axes (Figure 7.1),[4] while properties like the Villa Giulia created new ones.

---

[4] See C. M. Richardson 2003 for the prestige to be gained from this enhanced view over the Aurelianic wall and Porta Praenestina; and for the wonderful view of and from the Piccolo Aventino by French landscape painter Nicolas-Didier Boguet (born 1755), pencil, pen and grey ink, grey washes, caption in grey: BSR fol. 31, Hornsby 2002: 114–15.

Figure 7.1 View of and from the Piccolo Aventino by Nicolas Didier Boguet.

These vistas reinforce or challenge the idea of Rome, city of seven hills, and the totality it provides, while reasserting that totality is possible: why else did Henry James, de Staël and others describe what they could and could not see from their summits? Even today, one company offering its clients a Seven Hills Walking Tour, promises 'all of the city'.[5]

Antiquarianism, mapping, engravings and tourism combined to make Rome a model city. The building initiatives of Sixtus V, Napoleon and Mussolini were further enhanced by this status. As we have seen, the seven hills were as crucial to these initiatives as the writings of Augustan architect Vitruvius. Take Mussolini: excavating the hills from centuries of landfill was only part of the package. He did more than widen the road between the Palatine and Esquiline, creating parks on the Esquiline, a new street, villas and apartment blocks on the Aventine, and making the Capitoline 'stand out with renewed prominence'.[6] He referenced the seven hills in his Esposizione Universale di Roma project three miles south of Rome – an area originally planned for the world exhibition of 1942. EUR, as it is known today, is how urban Italy might have looked if Fascism had not fallen, and it pays homage to the eternal city at every turn. Inscribed on the monumental portico of the first building to be completed, the Palazzo degli Uffici's Hall of the Fountains, are the words: 'a third Rome which would spread over

---

[5] www.walkingrome.com/SEVEN_HILLS_T5_C1.html (last accessed 3 April 2011).
[6] Painter 2005 10 and 33. Also important here are Kostoff 1973 and Di Majo and Insolera 1986.

Figure 7.2 The Palazzo degli Uffici, EUR, Rome.

other hills, along the banks of the sacred river, even to the shores of the Tyrrhenian sea' (Figure 7.2).[7] Serious contenders to Rome needed their own hills to allude to their *alma mater*.

One of the aims of the Fascist regime was to give 'the sense of Rome' ('il senso di Roma') – 'sense' here meaning both 'sensation' or 'perception' and 'meaning'.[8] Is this what other cities are seeking in staking claims to seven summits? Not all of them can boast the continuum with Rome that Constantinople, Siena and Nîmes are celebrating. Nor are they, like Rome in Georgia, USA, named after their seven-hilled terrain. Their motivations are less obvious. Durham is a case in point: 'DURHAM, the capital of the county of Durham, is an ancient city, situated on seven hills, and surrounded by others more lofty, in a beautiful winding of the River Wear. Here are pleasant walks along the banks of the river, which are covered with woods, and edged with lofty crags. Around it are grown large quantities of the best mustard.'[9]

[7] *Opera omnia* 22.48 (after Mussolini's speech on 31 December 1925 on the Capitol): 'la Terza Roma si dilaterà sopra altri colli lungo le rive del fiume sacro sino alle sponde del Tirreno'.
[8] Bertilaccio and Innamorati 2004: 9.
[9] Barclay 1813: 287. I thank Tim Lambert for alerting me to the existence of this text as reproduced in the re-edition of Thomas Moule (1784–1851), *The Country Maps of England*, 1990.

There is nothing Roman about the town. Its most famous building, the Cathedral, is Norman. Stranger still – when the same nineteenth-century encyclopaedia gets to ROME, its seven hills are not even mentioned.

Rome's hills do not have to be made explicit. Cultural memory of lines such as 'city, high on seven hills, which presides over the whole world' and indeed Martial's view from the Janiculum inhabit the description of Durham,[10] turning it from straight description into something more emotive.[11] These associations make Durham a certain kind of city nonetheless – not simply a residential zone that means something to its inhabitants but one with a more universal appeal, a city worthy of our gaze. Suddenly the mundanities of mustard have greater *gravitas*: although in the eighteenth century Durham led the way in making English-style mustard,[12] its origins as a condiment lie in Roman literature.[13]

The modern metropolis of Seattle in Washington lacks even Durham's antiquity. Today its official nickname is 'the Emerald City', after its evergreen forests – a name which it received in 1982 in a competition run by its Convention and Visitors' Bureau.[14] Cities still see a benefit in branding themselves. But from early in the twentieth century it was also a city of seven hills and explicit parallels were drawn to Rome. DWEM mentality has not killed the concept completely. A public garden, opened in 2010, was named 'Seven Hills Park' by a group of first-grade children who took their inspiration from the proposed art element: seven boulders, designed not just to provide creative play and seating but to reference the hills of Seattle.[15] Even after the fashion for neoclassicism has faded, and the architecture of Greece and Rome has been appropriated by Mussolini, the seven hills can still bolster a community's sense of belonging. Any 'sense of Rome' here is less about antiquity than about urbanism. Statistics like total area or population density are suddenly too bland a measure. Seven hills are an alternative marker of civic identity.

And so we move from a home-grown image of Rome to an exportable concept. Worrying about when this first happened is, in a sense, superfluous: Rome both never and always already had seven hills. As experiences of Rome became more and more diverse, it became more and more important to insist that those who lived there and visited it enjoyed a shared experience of its place in history. Seven hills proved a suitably plural but confined

---

[10] Prop. 3.11.56.   [11] Mart. 4.64.11–26.   [12] *The Durham Times*, 7 September 2007.
[13] Antol 1999.   [14] Klingle 2007.
[15] See www.seattle.gov/parks/proparks/projects/7_hills_development.htm and the architects, Mithun: http://mithun.com/projects/project_detail/capitol_hill_park/ (both last accessed 3 April 2011).

focus upon which they could hang their encounter. They enabled Rome to accommodate the designs of Augustus and his successors – to change, yet remain the same city. As Christianity flourished and the Empire's powerbase shifted, they grew loftier still, insisting that Rome endured, continuing on into the Renaissance when scholars used them to help in their navigation of an otherwise alien landscape. Tourists too have found them indispensable and brought the concept back to their own communities to lend cohesion and aspirations to their cities.

Geography as history

The hills are not the only way to tell the story of the city of Rome. I could have taken a different concept, for example that of Rome as 'eternal city',[16] and traced that from its beginnings in the imperial period through to today. Or I could have examined a different element of the landscape – the Tiber and how it was represented in antiquity and, more recently, how its traffic, flooding, and embankment in the late nineteenth century changed its import and the feel of the city. But that would have felt parochial. In antiquity the Empire-wide significance of the river was swamped by the Nile, while wateriness has long been the preserve of Venice. The seven hills bring landscape and literature together on an international stage. Competition reinforces the idea that all imitations are inspired by a city that cannot be surpassed and so allows other cities to mount a challenge. The hills are rare in their capacity to bind Rome together, geographically as well as temporally. Plutarch writes,

For a city, like a living creature, is one continuous thing, and it does not cease to be itself through changes caused by age nor does it become one thing after another over time, but it is always in sympathy with and suited to itself and must take all the blame and gratitude for what it does or has done publicly as long as the association that creates it and binds it together carefully guards its unity. To make many or rather an infinite number of cities, separating them over time, is like making many men out of one man because he is now old but was younger before and a lad before that.[17]

---

[16] See K. J. Pratt 1965.
[17] Plut. *Mor.* 559A: ἓν γάρ τι πρᾶγμα καὶ συνεχὲς ἡ πόλις ὥσπερ ζῷον οὐκ ἐξιστάμενον αὑτοῦ ταῖς καθ᾽ ἡλικίαν μεταβολαῖς οὐδ᾽ ἕτερον ἐξ ἑτέρου τῷ χρόνῳ γινόμενον, ἀλλὰ συμπαθὲς ἀεὶ καὶ οἰκεῖον αὑτῷ καὶ πᾶσαν ὧν πράττει κατὰ τὸ κοινὸν ἢ ἔπραξεν αἰτίαν καὶ χάριν ἀναδεχόμενον, μέχρι ἂν ἡ ποιοῦσα καὶ συνδέουσα ταῖς ἐπιπλοκαῖς κοινωνία τὴν ἑνότητα διαφυλάττῃ. τὸ δὲ πολλὰς πόλεις διαιροῦντα τῷ χρόνῳ ποιεῖν μᾶλλον δ᾽ ἀπείρους ὅμοιόν

Figure 7.3 Banner advertising the Monti region of Rome with its three hills.

Diane Favro responds accordingly: 'As a container of collective memory, Rome could not be represented at one moment in its glorious history, like a fly in amber. Thus its image could not be reduced to a static panoramic urban icon.'[18] But she underestimates the power of the poets' hills, and of the view from their summits, to conjure up an image of the city which transcends its spatial and sequential remit. The concept of the seven hills is the closest the Romans come to creating a perceptible entity.

The concept of the seven hills forces us to look at Rome holistically. This is not to say that focusing in on a particular area or period is not also useful. Some of the best studies of the city's history and reception, for example Favro's own *The Urban Image of Augustan Rome*, Michael Herzfeld's recent *Evicted from Eternity: the Restructuring of Modern Rome*, which tells the story of the Monti region (Figure 7.3), Margaret McGowan's *The Vision of Rome in Late Renaissance France* or Jon Sachs' *Romantic Antiquity: Rome in the British Imagination 1789–1832* engage in detailed analysis of temporally defined material to explore how Rome was changed by practical or intellectual

ἐστιν τῷ πολλοὺς τὸν ἕνα ποιεῖν ἄνθρωπον ὅτι νῦν πρεσβύτερός ἐστι, πρότερον δὲ νεώτερος, ἀνωτέρω δὲ μειράκιον ἦν.
18 Favro 2006: 35.

investment.[19] But in doing this, these books foster a series of parallel worlds by cutting the cake differently: they are about imperial Rome, an alternative Rome, Rome of later European consciousness. All of them are variations on a theme which remains largely un-interrogated. What is this Rome that Renaissance France and eighteenth-century Britain are re-imagining, beyond its poems, Ciceronian prose, statuary, and toga plays? How does Augustan Rome relate to the Romes of Domitian, Honorius, Napoleon; and how does Monti, and the ancient Subura which it occupies, relate to the rest of Rome as it exists on the ground and in collective consciousness?

In this book I hope to have answered these questions. It is worth looking back on some of this. It has alerted us to the need to put Virgil's description of Rome into a broader context. Much ink has been spilled on both *Aeneid* 6 and *Aeneid* 8 but with insufficient awareness of the ways in which later poets such as Statius and Claudian have manipulated them. Just as a focus on Rome in the eighteenth-century imagination throws ancient Rome into relief, so too does Claudian's manipulation of the Augustan poets and Statius. If he can describe Rome in this way, when it is no longer the centre of the Empire and home of the emperor, what does this say about the relationship of representation and *Realien*, expectation even, at any period? Likewise Livy, Strabo and Dionysius of Halicarnassus: their reports of Rome's development make more sense once seven hills are seen as the end point. And Romulus, Remus, Aeneas and co-stars get to inhabit an arena which extends beyond Rome's archaic origins or indeed its re-foundation as a Principate. These sources are less about writing Augustan Rome than they are about writing a city.

Claudian's use of the hills also helps us to understand the tenor of Ammianus' account of Constantius. Again, as we appreciate exactly what it is about the emperor's vision that overwhelms him, a famous passage is thrown into relief; we appreciate why it is that Rome's elite, from senators and emperors to cardinals and popes, chose to live on the hills' summits. Art historians and geographers need to remember ancient literature's justification of these choices as they make statements about a new appreciation of the aesthetic nature of landscape in fifteenth-, sixteenth- or seventeenth-century Europe.[20] Roman historians need a keener awareness of how the

---

[19] Favro 1996, Herzfold 2009, McGowan 2000 and Sachs 2010.

[20] See e.g. K. Clark 1949, Gombrich 1953 and Cosgrove 1993. Excellent in critiquing the idea of landscape as a genre, specifically associated with western imperialism is Mitchell 1994. He prefers 'medium' to 'genre' and writes (p. 14): 'Landscape painting is best understood, then, not as the uniquely central medium that gives us access to ways of seeing landscape, but as a representation of something that is already a representation in its own right.'

construction of the emperor's image intersects with this landscape, and that of Rome with the Empire; how imperial power resides not only in the king's body, building, or his relationship with senate and people, but in his and his empire's relationship with the cityscape of Rome, how the capital is always pitted against the rest of the Roman world, and the Roman emperor's divine majesty is pitted against nature. It is against this background that Julius III's fresco-cycles come into their own: without careful consideration of the age-old value of the canon, these paintings can seem an exercise in vanity publishing.

Thinking hard about the problems of representing Rome from Varro and Cicero through to Rossini, Palmer and beyond has also demanded that we think harder about definition (and not just the definition of art vis à vis text). I mean this in two ways, the first of them pertaining to our own responses to Rome and where these come from, and the second, to what makes a city a city. We are used to signposts which announce our arrival in a place, and then scored-through signposts, announcing our departure. We are familiar with city maps, plotting our 'you are here'. But a city is always more than our coming and going, more than navigating through it. These are merely forays. Conquest comes from understanding that signs, maps and place names are strategies which make the land livable and that, in this respect, they are similar to myths of origins. Reconstructions of Rome's topography, and ongoing arguments about the Velia, are ways of seeing, not solutions.

Writing a history of Rome is an impossible task. It was never my intention to attempt such a history – rather to find a way of throwing centuries of attempts into relief; to make us more self-conscious of the sources with which we are working. Petrarch continues:

This one thing I must not be silent about: and it happens to be contrary to what you suspected. For you used to, I remember, discourage me from coming [to Rome] on these grounds above all, fearing that as the city's ruined appearance does not correspond with its fame and with my expectation received from books, my enthusiasm would slacken...[21]

The seven hills have proved invaluable in helping to process these discrepancies. They are somehow before time, beyond ruin and the vagaries of architectural taste, as pristine now as they were in antiquity. A paradigm.

---

[21] Petr. *Fam.* 2.14.104: 'unum hoc tacitum noluerim: contra ac tu suspicabaris accidit. solebas enim, memini, me veniendo dehortari, hoc maxime praetextu ne, ruinose urbis aspectu famae non respondente atque opinioni mea ex libris conceptae, ardor meus ille lentesceret...'

They are not only illustrative of the eternal city, able to bridge its various incarnations, but provide a framework within which other cities' ambitions are formulated and against which they are measured. The seven hills are not, like the Colosseum, an attribute of Rome. The seven hills are Rome's signature.

References

Acidini Luchinat, C. (1998–9) *Taddeo e Federico Zuccari: fratelli pittori del cinquecento*. 2 vols. Milan.

Ackerman, J. S. (1954) *The Cortile del Belvedere*. Vatican City.

Adams, J. N. (2003) *Bilingualism and the Latin Language*. Cambridge.

Adler, J. (1989) 'Origins of sightseeing', *Annals of Tourism Research* 16: 7–29.

Ahl, F. M. (1971) 'Lucan's *De incendio urbis*, *Epistulae ex Campania* and Nero's ban', *Transactions of the American Philological Association* 102: 1–27.

(1985) *Metaformations: Soundplay and Wordplay in Ovid and Other Classical Poets*. Ithaca.

Aichholzer, P. (1983) *Darstellungen römischer Sagen*. Vienna.

Aldrete, G. S. (2007) *Floods of the Tiber in Ancient Rome*. Baltimore.

Amelung, W. (1908) *Die Sculpturen des Vatikanischen Museums*. Vol. IV. Berlin.

Amery, C. and B. Curran (2002) *The Lost World of Pompeii*. London.

Amin, A. and N. Thrift (2002) *Cities: Reimagining the Urban*. Cambridge.

Ammannati, G. (2011) 'Il papiro di Servio Tullio (P. Oxy. 2088): una nuova interpretazione', *Materiali e discussioni per l'analisi dei testi classici* 66: 93–120.

Ammerman, A. (2006) 'Adding time to Rome's *imago*', in L. Haselberger, and J. Humphrey (eds.) *Imaging Ancient Rome: Documentation, Visualization, Imagination. Proceedings of the Third Williams Symposium on Classical Architecture, Held at the American Academy in Rome, the British School at Rome, and the Deutsches Archäologisches Institut, Rome, on 20–23 May 2004*. Portsmouth, RI: 285–96.

Ampolo, C. (1981) 'La città arcaica e le sue Feste. Due ricerche sul Septimontium e sull' equus October', *Archeologia Laziale* 4: 23–240.

Anderson, A. M. (1922) 'Edinburgh in the latter half of the eighteenth century', *Juridical Review* 34: 136–51.

Anker, A. (1996) 'Il Pape e il Duce: Sixtus V's and Mussolini's plans for Rome, capital of the world', *Journal of Urban Design* 1.2: 165–78.

Antol, M. N. (1999) *The Incredible Secrets of Mustard*. New York.

Arce, J. (1999) 'El inventario de Roma: curiosum y notitia', in W. V. Harris (ed.), *The Transformation of Urbs Roma in Late Antiquity* (*Journal of Roman Archaeology*, Suppl. ser. 33), Portsmouth, RI:15–22.

Arnaldez, R. (1961) *De opificio mundi, introduction, traduction et notes*. Paris.

Arnold, D. (2009) 'Panoptic visions of London: possessing the metropolis', *Art History* 32.2: 332–50.

Arnold, T. (1840) *History of Rome*. London.

Ash, R. (2007) 'Victim and voyeur: Rome as a character in Tacitus' *Annals* 3', in D. Larmour and D. Spencer (eds.), *The Sites of Rome: Time, Space, Memory*. Oxford: 211–38.

Augenti, A. (1996) *Il Palatino nel medioevo*. Rome.

Aune, D. E. (1998) *Revelation 17–22*. Nashville.

Baier, T. (1997) *Werk und Wirkung Varros im Spiegel seiner Zeitgenossen: von Cicero bis Ovid*. Stuttgart.

Baldovin, J. F. (1987) *The Urban Character of Christian Worship*. Rome.

Balina, M. (2007) 'Ancient Rome for little comrades: the legacy of classical antiquity in Soviet children's literature', in D. Larmour and D. Spencer (eds.), *The Sites of Rome: Time, Space, Memory*. Oxford: 323–52.

Balland, A. (1984) 'La *casa Romuli* au Palatin et au Capitole', *Revue des études latines* 62: 57–80.

Balty, J. (1977) *Mosaïques antiques de Syrie*. Brussels.

Balty, J. Ch. (1960) 'Études sur la Maison Carrée de Nîmes', *Latomus* 47: 59–73.

Balzac, J.-L. G. de (1665) *Les oeuvres de Monsieur de Balzac*. Paris.

Barclay, J. (1813) *Barclay's Universal Dictionary*. London.

Baring-Gould, S. (1897) *A Tale of Nimes in AD 213*. New York.

Barkan, L. (1999) *Unearthing the Past: Archaeology and Aesthetics in the Making of Renaissance Culture*. New Haven.

Barker, E. B., C. Harrison and W. Vaughan (eds.) (2005) *Samuel Palmer 1805–1881: Vision and Landscape*. London.

Barnes, T. J. and J. S. Duncan (1992) *Writing Worlds: Discourse, Text and Metaphor in the Representation of Landscape*. London.

Bartelink, G. J. (1965) *Etymologiserung bij Vergilius*. Amsterdam.

Barton, T. (1994) *Ancient Astrology*. London.

Bassett, S. (2004) *The Urban Image of Late Antique Constantinople*. Cambridge.

Bauer, G. and L. Bauer (1980) 'Bernini's organ case for S. Maria del Popolo', *The Art Bulletin* 62.1: 115–23.

Baxa, P. (2004) 'Piacentini's window: the modernism of the Fascist master plan of Rome', *Contemporary European History* 13.1: 1–20.

(2010) *Road and Ruins: the Symbolic Landscape of Fascist Rome*. Toronto.

Beard, M. (1998) 'Imaginary *horti*: or up the garden path', in M. Cima and E. La Rocca (eds.), *Horti Romani: atti del convegno internazionale Roma, 4–6 maggio 1995*. Rome: 23–31.

(2007) *The Roman Triumph*. Cambridge, MA.

Bell, A. J. E. (1997) 'Cicero and the spectacle of power', *The Journal of Roman Studies* 87: 1–22.

Bender, B. (ed.) (1993) *Landscape: Politics and Perspectives*. Providence and Oxford.

Bergin, T. G. and A. S. Wilson (1977) *Petrarch's Africa*. New Haven.

Bergmann, M. (1977) *Studien zum römischen Porträt des Dritten Jahrhunderts n. Chr*. Bonn.

Berman, D. W. (2002) '"Seven-gated" Thebes and narrative topography in Aeschylus' *Seven Against Thebes*', *Quaderni urbinati di cultura classica* 71: 73–100.

Bertilaccio, C. and F. Innamorati (2004) *EUR SpA e il patrimonio di E42: manuale d'uso per edifici e opere*. Rome.

Bevilacqua, M. (1998) *Roma nel secolo dei lumi*. Naples.

Biagetti, M. (1936) 'Monumenti, musei e gallerie pontificie nel anno accademico 1935–6, III. Relazione, 1935–6', *Rendiconti della Pontificia Accademia di Archeologia, Roma* 12: 351–95.

Bialik, H. N. and Y. H. Rawnitzky (1992) *Book of Legends/Sefer Ha-Aggadah: Legends from the Talmud and Midrash*. New York.

Bieber, M. (1967) *Laocoon: the Influence of the Group since its Rediscovery*. Detroit.

Bignamini, I. and C. Hornsby (2010) *Digging and Dealing in Eighteenth Century Rome*. New Haven.

Bignamini, I. and A. Wilton (1996) *The Grand Tour: the Lure of Italy in the Eighteenth Century*. London.

Biguzzi, G. (2006) 'Is the Babylon of *Revelation* Rome or Jerusalem?', *Biblica* 87: 371–86.

Biondo, F. (1474) *Italia illustrata*. Rome.

  (1510) *Blondi Flauii Forliuiensis De Roma instaurata libri tres*. First published 1444–6. Venice.

Birley, A. R. (1999) *Septimius Severus*. London.

Bispham, E. (2006) '*Coloniam deducere*: how Roman was Roman colonization during the middle Republic?', in G. Bradley and J.-P. Wilson (eds.), *Greek and Roman Colonization: Origins, Ideologies and Interactions*. Cardiff: 73–160.

Blondin, J. E. (2005) 'Power made visible: Pope Sixtus IV as *urbis restaurator* in quattrocento Rome', *The Catholic Historical Review* 91.1: 1–25.

Boatwright, M. T. (2000) *Hadrian and the Cities of the Roman Empire*. New Haven.

Bohn, J. (1845) *The Historical Works of the Venerable Bede*. London.

Boime, A. (1991) *The Magisterial Gaze: Manifest Destiny and American Landscape Painting c. 1830–1865*. Washington.

Bollansée, J. (1999) 'Fact and fiction, falsehood and truth. D. Fehling and ancient legendry about the seven sages', *Museum Helveticum* 56: 65–75.

Bond, H. L. (1964) *Return to Cassino*. New York.

Bookidis, N. (2005) 'Religion in Corinth: 146 BCE to 100 CE', in D. N. Schowalter and S. J. Friesen (eds.), *Urban Religion in Roman Corinth: Interdisciplinary Approaches*. Cambridge, MA: 141–64.

Bourgeaud, P. (1987) 'Du mythe à l'idéologie: la tête du Capitole', *Museum Helveticum* 44: 86–100.

Bourgeois, B. (2008) 'The French Laocoon', in P. Curtis and S. Fecke (eds.), *Towards a New Laocoon*. Leeds: 25–8.

Boyle, A. J. (2003) *Ovid and the Monuments: a Poet's Rome*. Bendigo.

Bracciolini, P. (1993) *De varietate fortunae edizione critica con introduzione e commento a cura di Outi Merisalo*. First published 1430. Helsinki.

Brandes, W. (2003) 'Sieben Hügel: Die imaginäre Topographie Konstantinopels zwischen apokalyptischem Denken und moderner Wissenschaft', *Rechts-geschichte: Zeitschrift des Max-Planck Instituts für europäische Rechtsgeschicte 2*: 58–71.

Braun, G. and F. Hogenberg (1572–1617) *Civitates orbis terrarum*. Cologne.

Brilliant, R. (2002) *My Laocoön. Alternative Claims in the Interpretation of Artworks*. Berkeley and London.

Broise, H. and J. Vincent (1987) 'Recherches sur les jardins de Lucullus', in *L'urbs: espace urbain et histoire (Ier siècle av. J.-C.-IIIe siècle ap. J.-C.). Actes du colloque international de Rome (8–12 mai 1985)*. Rome: 747–61.

Brummer, H. (1970) *The Statue Court in the Vatican Belvedere*. Stockholm.

Buchheit, V. (1965) 'Tibull II 5 und die *Aeneis*', *Philologus* 109: 104–20.

Burkert, W. (1972) *Lore and Science in Ancient Pythagoreanism*. New Haven.

Burkle-Young, F. A. and M. L. Doerrer (1997) *The Life of Cardinal Innocenzo del Monte, a Scandal in Scarlet*. New York.

Busine, A. (2002) *Les Sept Sages de la Grèce antique. Transmission et utilisation d'un patrimonie légendaire d'Hérodote à Plutarque*. Paris.

Buti, C. (1778) *Pitture antiche della Villa Negroni*. Rome.

Buxton, R. (1992) 'Imaginary Greek mountains', *Journal of Hellenic Studies* 112: 1–15.

(2009) *Forms of Astonishment: Greek Myths of Metamorphosis*. Oxford.

Buzard, J. (1993) *The Beaten Track: European Tourism, Literature, and the Ways to Culture, 1800–1918*. Oxford.

Cairns, F. (1979) *Tibullus: a Hellenistic Poet at Rome*. Cambridge.

(2003) 'Propertius 3.4 and the *Aeneid* incipit', *Classical Quarterly* 53.1: 309–11.

Calvino, I. (1972) *Invisible Cities*. Turin.

Calvo, F. (1527) *Antiquae urbis Romae cum regionibus simulachrum*. Rome.

Cameron, Alan (1970) *Poetry and Propaganda at the Court of Honorius*. Oxford.

(1983) 'The foundation of Constantinople: myths, ancient and modern', *Abstracts of Papers, Ninth Annual Byzantine Studies Conference, Nov. 4–6, 1983*. Durham: 33–4.

Cameron, Averil (1993) *The Later Roman Empire: AD 284–430*. Cambridge, MA.

Campbell, D. A. (1992) *Greek Lyric*, vol. IV: *Bacchylides, Corinna, and Others*. Cambridge MA.

Campitelli, G. A. (1984) 'Fregio raffigurante vedute di Roma', in *Oltre Raffaello: aspetti della cultura figurativa del cinquecento Romano / [Roma] Villa Giulia [ecc.] Maggio–Iuglio 1984*. Rome: 200–5.

Cancellieri, F. (1802) *Storia de' solenni possessi de sommi pontefici*. Rome.

Capanna, M. C. and A. Amoroso (2006) 'Velia, Fagutal, Oppius. Il periodo archaico e le case di Servio Tullio e Tarquinio Prisco', in *Workshop di archeologia classica* 3: 87–111.

Carafa, P. (1993) 'Il Tempio di Quirino: considerazioni sulla topografia arcaica del Quirinale', *Archeologia classica* 45.1: 119–43.

Carandini, A. (1997) *La nascita di Roma: dèi, lari, eroi e uomini all'alba di una civiltà.* Turin.

(2004) 'Tra Palatino e valle del Colosseo: nuovi dati', in *Workshop di archeologia classica.* Vol. I. Pisa.

(2007) *Cercando Quirino: traversata sulle onde elettromagnetiche nel suolo del Quirinale.* Turin.

(2008) *La casa di Augusto: dai 'Lupercalia' al Natale.* Bari.

(2011) *Rome: Day One,* translated by S. Sartarelli. New Jersey.

Carandini, A. and R. Cappelli (2000) *Roma: Romolo, Remo e la fondazione della città.* Milan.

Carnochan, W. B. (1987) *Gibbon's Solitude. The Inward World of the Historian.* Stanford.

Cassola, F. (2002) 'Bilancio conclusivo', in L. Polverini (ed.) *Aspetti della storiografia di Ettore Pais. Università degli Studi di Perugia. Incontri perugini di storia della storiografia antica e sul mondo antico.* Vol. VII. Naples: 327–39.

Castagnoli, F. (1951) 'Roma Quadrata', in G. E. Mylonas (ed.), *Studies in Archaeology Presented to David Moore Robinson.* St. Louis: 389–99.

Cavazzi, L. and M. E. Tittoni (1982) *Luigi Rossini incisore. Vedute di Roma 1817–1850.* Rome.

Cecamore, C. (2002) *Palatium: topografia storica del Palatino tra 3 Sec. a. C. e 1 Sec. d. C.* Rome.

Ceen, A. (1989) 'Piranesi and Nolli: *imago urbis Romae*', in *Piranesi: Rome Recorded, Catalog of the Exhibition of Piranesi's Vedute di Roma at the Arthur Ross Gallery.* Pennsylvania.

(2000) 'Giambattista Nolli', in E. P. Bowron and J. J. Rishel (eds.), *Art in Rome in the Eighteenth Century.* Philadelphia: 137–9.

Célié, M., P. Garmy and M. Monteil (eds.) (1994) 'Enceintes et développement urbain: Nîmes antique des origins au 1er s. ap. J.-C.', *Journal of Roman Archaeology* 7: 383–96.

Ceresa, M. (2004) 'Andrea Fulvio erudito; antiquario e classicista', in S. Colonna (ed.), *Roma nella svolta tra quattro e cinquecento.* Rome: 143–9.

Cerruti, M. (1978) *Roma Interrotta: mostra organizzata dagli Incontri Internazionali d'Arte: Roma, Mercati di Traiano, Maggio-Giugno 1978.* Rome.

Certeau, M. de (1984) *The Practice of Everyday Life.* California.

Chard, C. and H. Langdon (1996) *Transports: Imaginative Geographies 1600–1830.* New Haven.

Chéhab, M. H. (1958–9) *Mosaïques du Liban.* Paris.

Chinn, C. M. (2007) 'Before your eyes: Pliny *Epistulae* 5.6 and the ancient theory of ekphrasis', *Classical Philology* 102.3: 265–80.

Christie, N. (2006) *From Constantine to Charlemagne: an Archaeology of Italy AD 300–AD 800.* Farnham.

Christol, M. (1996) 'Nîmes dans les sources antiques', in J.-L. Fiches and A. Veyrac (eds.), *Nîmes.* Paris: 58–60.

Cima, C. and E. Talamo (2008) *Gli horti di Roma antica*. Rome.

Cima, M. and E. la Rocca (eds.) (1998) *Horti Romani atti del convegno internazionale Roma, 4–6 maggio 1995*. Rome.

Cipriani, G. (1982) *Horti Sallusatiani*. Rome.

Citroni, M. (1975) *Valerii Martialis Epigrammaton Liber 1*. Florence.

Clark, E. (1950) *Rome and a Villa*. New York.

Clark, K. (1949) *Landscape into Art*. London.

Clarke, J. (2003) *Looking at Laughter*. Berkeley, Los Angeles and London.

Clayman, D. L. (1993) 'Corinna and Pindar', in J. Farell and R. M. Rosen (eds.), *Nomodeiktes: Studies in Honor of Martin Ostwald*. Ann Arbor: 633–42.

Clayton, P. A. and M. Price (1988) *The Seven Wonders of the Ancient World*. London.

Coarelli, F. (1988) 'Rom. Die Stadtplanung von Caesar bis Augustus', in M. Hofter (ed.), *Kaiser Augustus und die verlorene Republik*. Mainz: 68–70.

(1993) 'Argei, sacraria', in E. M. Steinby (ed.), *Lexicon topographicum urbis Romae*. Rome. Vol. I: 120–5.

(1995) 'Vici di Ariminum', in R. Bedon and P. M. Martin with C. M. Ternes (eds.), *Mélanges Raymond Chevallier*. Vol. II. Tours: 175–80.

(1997) *Il Campo Marzio*. Rome.

(1999) 'Septimontium', in E. M. Steinby (ed.), *Lexicon topographicum urbis Romae*. Rome. Vol. IV: 268.

(2007) *Rome and Environs: an Archaeological Guide*. Berkeley, Los Angeles and London.

Coates-Stephens, R. (1996) 'Housing in early medieval Rome, 500–1000 AD', *Papers of the British School at Rome* 64: 239–59.

(1998) 'The walls and aqueducts of Rome in the early middle ages, AD 500–1000', *The Journal of Roman Studies* 88: 167–78.

(2004) *Porta Maggiore, Monument and Landscape: Archaeology and Topography of the Southern Esquiline from the Late Republican Period to the Present*. Rome.

Coffin, D. R. (1979) *The Villa in the Life of Renaissance Rome*. New Jersey.

(1991) *Gardens and Gardening in Papal Rome*. New Jersey.

(2004) *Pirro Ligorio: the Renaissance Artist, Architect, and Antiquarian with a Checklist of Drawings*. Philadelphia.

Coleman, K. M. (1988) *Statius*, Silvae IV. Oxford.

(2006) *M. Valerii Martialis*, Liber spectaculorum. Oxford.

Colini, M. (1944) 'Storia e topografia del Caelio nell' antichità', *Atti della Pontificia Accademia Romana di Archeologia: Memorie* 7: 18–45.

Collart, J. (1954) *Varron: de lingua Latina, Livre V*. Paris.

Coogan, R. (1983) *Babylon on the Rhone: a Translation of Letters by Dante, Petrarch, and Catherine of Siena on the Avignon Papacy*. Madrid.

Cooley, A. (2009) *Res gestae Divi Augusti*. Cambridge.

Cornell, T. J. (1995) *The Beginnings of Rome: Italy and Rome from the Bronze Age to the Punic Wars (c. 1000–264 BC)*. London.

Cosgrove, D. (1984) *Social Formation and Symbolic Landscape*. New Jersey.

(1993) *The Palladian Landscape: Geographical Change and its Cultural Representations in Sixteenth-Century Italy.* Leicester.

Cosgrove, D. and S. Daniels (eds.) (1988) *The Iconography of Landscape: Essays on the Symbolic Representation, Design and Use of Past Environments.* Cambridge.

Costenza, M. E. (1910) *Petrarch's Letters to Classical Authors.* Chicago.

Coxe, H. (1818) *A Picture of Italy.* London.

Craddock, P. B. (1984) 'Edward Gibbon and the ruins of the Capitol', in A. Patterson (ed.), *Roman Images.* Baltimore: 63–82.

Crawford, M. H. (1974) *Roman Republican Coinage.* Cambridge.

Cuomo, S. (2001) *Ancient Mathematics.* London.

Curran, J. (2000) *Pagan City and Christian Capital: Rome in the Fourth Century.* Oxford.

Dalby, A. (2000) *Empire of Pleasures: Luxury and Indulgence in the Roman World.* London.

Dall' Osso, L. (1906) 'Il quadro sulle origini di Roma recentemente scoperto a Pompei', *Nuova antologia*: 293–304.

Daniels, S. (1993) *Fields of Vision: Landscape Imagery and National Identity in England and the United States.* Princeton.

D'Anna, G. (1992) 'Una breve divagazione sui sette colli di Roma', *Strenna dei Romanisti* 53: 149–58.

Davis, P. J. (2006) *Ovid and Augustus: a Political Reading of Ovid's Erotic Poems.* London.

De Bolla, P. (2003) *Art Matters.* Cambridge, MA.

DeBrohun, J. B. (2003) *Roman Propertius and the Reinvention of Elegy.* Michigan.

Della Dora, V. (2005) 'Alexander the Great's mountain', *The Geographical Review* 95: 489–516.

(2008) 'Mapping a holy quasi-island: Mount Athos in early Renaissance isolarii', *Imago mundi* 60.2: 139–65.

Della Seta, A. (1918) *Museo di Villa Giulia.* Rome.

Delle Corte, F. (1970) *Varrone, il terzo gran lume romano.* Florence.

Del Lungo, S. (2004) *Roma in età carolingia e gli scritti dell'Anonimo augiense Einsiedeln, Bibliotheca Monasterii ordinis sancti Benedicti, 326 [8 nr. 13], IV, ff. 67v-86r.* Rome.

Den Boer, W. (1954) *Laconian Studies.* Amsterdam.

De Sanctis, G. (1907) *Storia dei Romani: la conquista del primato in Italia.* Vol. I. Rome.

Deseine, F. J. (1713) *L'ancienne Rome.* Leiden.

Dewar, M. (1996) *Claudian,* Panegyricus de sexto consulatu Honorii Augusti. Oxford.

Dey, H. W. (2011) *The Aurelian Wall and the Refashioning of Imperial Rome, AD 271–855.* Cambridge.

Diels, H. (1904) 'Laterculi Alexandrini aus einem Papyrus ptolemäischer Zeit', *Abhandlungen der königlich preussischen Akademie der Wissenschaften*: 1–16.

Di Gioia, V. (2004) *L'Aventino: un colle classico tra antico e moderno.* Rome.

Di Majo, L. and I. Insolera (1986) *L'EUR e Roma dagli anni trenta al duemila*. Bari.

Dölger, F. (1937) 'Rom in der Gedankenwelt der Byzantiner', *Zeitschrift für Kirchengeschichte* 56: 1–42.

Dombart, T. (1967) *Die sieben Weltwunder des Altertums*. Munich.

D'Onofrio, C. (1957) *Le fontane di Roma*. Rome.

Donovan, J. (1842–4) *Rome Ancient and Modern and its Environs*. Rome.

Dotti, U. (ed.) (2002–) *Francesco Petrarca*, Familiarum rerum libri. Paris.

Driault, É. (1917) 'Rome et Napoléon', *Revue des études napoléoniennes* 20: 5–43.

Du Bellay, J. (1555) *Les regrets*. Paris.

Dulière, C. (1979) *Lupa Romana. Recherches d'iconographie et essai d'interpretation*. 2 vols. Brussels and Rome.

Dunbabin, K. M. D. (1999) *Mosaics of the Greek and Roman World*. Cambridge.

Duncan, J. (1990) *The City as Text: the Politics of Landscape Interpretation in the Kandyan Kingdom*. Cambridge.

Duncan, J. and N. Duncan (1988) '(Re)reading the landscape', *Environment and Planning: Society and Space* 6: 117–26.

Du Prey, P. de la R. (1994) *The Villas of Pliny from Antiquity to Posterity*. Chicago.

Duval, Y. M. (1970) 'La venue à Rome de l' Empereur Constance II en 357 d'après Ammien Marcellin xvi 10, 1—20', *Caesarodunum* 5: 299–304.

Dyck, A. R. (2008) *Catilinarians*. Cambridge.

Dyer, G. (2005) *The Ongoing Moment*. New York.

Earl, G. and S. Keay (2006) 'Structuring of the provincial landscape: the towns in central and western *Baetica* in their geographical context', in G. Cruz Andreotti, P. Le Roux and P. Moret (eds.), *La invención de una geografía de la peninsula Ibérica*, vol. II: *La época imperial*. Madrid: 305–58.

Edbrooke, R. O. (1975) 'Constantius II and Hormisdas in the Forum of Trajan', *Mnemosyne* 28: 412–17.

Edmunds, L. (2009) 'Horace's Priapus: a life on the Esquiline (*Sat.* 1.8)', *Classical Quarterly* 59.1: 125–31.

Edwards, C. (1996) *Writing Rome: Textual Approaches to the City*. Cambridge.

(1998) 'Imaginaires de l'image de Rome ou comment (se) représenter Rome?', in C. Auvray-Assays (ed.), *Images Romaines*. Paris: 239–51.

(2003) 'Incorporating the alien: the art of conquest', in C. Edwards and G. Woolf (eds.), *Rome the Cosmopolis*. Cambridge: 44–70.

(2007) *Death in Ancient Rome*. New Haven.

Edwards, C. and M. Liversidge (eds.) (1996) *Imagining Rome: British Artists in the Nineteenth Century*. London.

Eeden, J. van (2004) 'The colonial gaze: imperialism, myths, and South African popular culture', *Design Issues* 20.2: 18–33.

Ekschmitt, W. (1984) *Die Sieben Weltwunder. Ihre Erbauung, Zerstörung und Wiederentdeckung*. Mainz.

Elsner, J. (1994) 'Constructing decadence: the role of Nero as imperial builder', in J. Elsner and J. Masters (eds.), *Reflections of Nero: Culture, History and Representation*. Chapel Hill: 112–27.

(1996) 'Inventing imperium: texts and the propaganda of monuments in Augustan Rome', in J. Elsner (ed.), *Art and Text in Roman Culture*. Cambridge: 32–54.

(1998) *Imperial Rome and Christian Triumph: the Art of the Roman Empire*. Oxford.

(2006) 'Perspectives in art', in N. Lenski (ed.), *The Cambridge Companion to Constantine*. Cambridge: 255–77.

Engels, D. (1990) *Roman Corinth: an Alternative Model for the Classical City*. Chicago.

Englen, A. and F. Astolfi (2003) *Caelius I: Santa Maria in Dominica, San Tommaso in Formis e il Clivus Scauri*. Rome.

Erkell, H. (1981) 'Varroniana', *Opuscula Romana* 16: 51–7.

(1985) 'Varroniana, II: studi topografici in Varro, *De lingua Latina* v, 45–50' *Opuscula Romana* 15: 55–65.

Erskine, A. (1995) 'Rome in the Greek world: the significance of a name', in A. Powell (ed.), *The Greek World*. London: 368–87.

Evans, H. B. (1997) *Water Distribution in Ancient Rome*. Michigan.

Fabbrini, D. (2007) *Il migliore dei mondi possibili: gli epigrammi ecfrastici di Marziale per amici e protettori*. Florence.

Fagiolo, M. and M. Marini (eds.) (1983) *Bartolomeo Pinelli (1781–1835) e il suo tempo. Catalogo della mostra tenuta a Roma nel 1983. Roma, Rondanini*. Rome.

Falda, G. B. (1640–78) *Li giardini di Roma*. Rome.

Falk, T. (1971) 'Studien sur Topographie und Geschichte der Villa Giulia in Rom', *Römisches Jahrbuch für Kunstgeschichte* 13: 101–78.

Fantham, E. (1997) 'Images of the city: Propertius' new-old Rome', in T. N. Habinek and A. Schiesaro (eds.), *The Roman Cultural Revolution*. Cambridge: 122–35.

Fauno, L. (1548) *Delle antichità della città di Roma*. Venice.

(1549) *De antiquitatibus urbis Romae ab antiquis novisq[ue] auctoribus exceptis, et summa brevitate ordineq[ue] dispositis per Lucium Faunum*. Venice.

(1552) *Compendio di Roma antica*. Venice.

Favro, D. (1996) *The Urban Image of Augustan Rome*. Cambridge.

(2005) 'Making Rome a world city', in K. Galinsky (ed.), *The Age of Augustus*. Cambridge: 234–63.

(2006) 'The iconicity of ancient Rome', *Urban History* 33.1: 20–38.

Feeney, D. C. (1986) 'History and revelation in Vergil's underworld', *Proceedings of the Cambridge Philological Society* 32: 1–24.

Fehling, D. (1985) *Die sieben Weisen und die frühgriechische Chronologie. Eine traditionsgeschichtliche Studie*. Bern.

Fentress, E. and A. Guidi (1999) Review of A. Carandini, *La nascita di Roma*, *Antiquity* 73: 463–7.

Ficacci, L. (2006) *Piranesi: the Etchings*. Cologne.

Filoche, C. (2007) *L'intertexte virgilien et sa réception: écriture, récriture et réflexivité chez Virgile et Rutilius Namatianus / textes rassemblés par Christina Filoche*. Dijon.

Fischer von Erlach, J. B. (1712) *Entwurff einer historischen Architectur*. Leipzig.

Fitzgerald, W. (2007) *Martial: the World of Epigram.* Chicago and London.

Foeller-Pituch, E. (2003) 'Henry James' cosmopolitan spaces: Rome as global city', *The Henry James Review* 24.3: 291–7.

Fontanella, F. (2007) *A Roma / Elio Aristide; traduzione e commento a cura di Francesca Fontanella; introduzione di Paolo Desideri.* Pisa.

Fordyce, C. J. (1977) *P. Vergili Maronis* Aeneidos, *Libri VII–VIII / with a commentary by C. J. Fordyce; introduction by P. G. Walsh; edited by John D. Christie.* Oxford.

Forsyth, J. (1835) *Remarks on Antiquities, Arts, and Letters, during an Excursion in Italy, in the Years 1802 and 1803.* London.

Foucault, M. (1977) *Discipline and Punish: the Birth of the Prison,* trans. A. Sheridan. New York.

Fox, M. (1996) *Roman Historical Myths: the Regal Period in Augustan Literature.* Oxford.

Francino, G. (1588) *Le cose maravigliose dell'alma città di Roma.* Rome.

Fraschetti, A. (1984) 'Festa dei monti, festa della città', *Studi storici: rivista trimestrale dell' Istituto Gramsci, Roma* 25: 37–54.

(1990) *Roma e il principe.* Bari.

(1996) 'Montes', in E. M. Steinby (ed.), *Lexicon topographicum urbis Romae.* Rome. Vol. II: 282–4.

(2002) *Romulo, il fondatore.* Rome and Bari.

(2005) *The Foundation of Rome,* translated from the Italian by Marian Hill and Kevin Windle. Edinburgh.

Frey, W. H. and Z. Zimmer (2001) 'Defining the city', in R. Paddison (ed.), *Handbook of Urban Studies.* London: 14–35.

Frézouls, E. (1987) 'Rome ville ouverte: refléxions sur les problèmes de l'expansion urbane d'Auguste à Aurélien', in *L'urbs: espace urbain et histoire (Ier siècle av. J.-C.–IIIe siècle ap. J.-C.). Actes du colloque international de Rome (Rome, 8–12 mai 1985).* Rome: 373–91.

Fridh, A. (1987) 'Three notes on Roman toponomy and topography', *Eranos* 85: 115–33.

(1990) 'Esquiliae, Fagutal and Subura once again', *Eranos* 88: 139–61.

(1993) '*Mons* and *collis*', *Eranos* 91: 1–12.

Fuchecchi, M. (1997) *Una guerra in Colchide. Valerio Flacco,* Argonautiche *6,1–426.* Pisa.

Fulvio, A. (1513) *Antiquaria urbis.* Rome.

(1517) *Illustrium imagines.* Rome.

(1527) *Antiquitates urbis.* Rome.

Funiciello, R. and C. Caputo (2006) 'Giovan Battista Brocchi's Rome: a pioneering study in urban geology', in G. B. Vai and W. G. E. Caldwell (eds.), *The Origins of Geology in Italy.* Colorado: 199–210.

Furno, M. and M. Carpo (2000) *Leon Battista Alberti,* Descriptio urbis Romae. Geneva.

Fusco, L. and G. Corti (2007) *Lorenzo de' Medici, Collector of Antiquities: Collector and Antiquarian.* Cambridge.

Gale, M. (1997) 'Propertius 2.7: *militia amoris* and the ironies of elegy', *The Journal of Roman Studies* 87: 77–91.

Gamucci, B. (1565) *Libri quattro dell'antichità della città di Roma.* Venice.

Gardner, P. (1888) 'Countries and cities in ancient art', *Journal of Hellenic Studies* 9: 47–81.

Garnier, R. (1999) *Porcie: tragédie; édition critique, établie, présentée et annotée par Jean-Claude Ternaux.* First published 1568. Paris.

Garrison, L., S. Erie, V. Hunt, P. West and A. Anderson (2012) *Panoramas 1787–1900: Texts and Contexts.* London.

Gärtner, H. A. (2002) 'Der *Eucharisticos* des Paulinus von Pella: Bemerkungen zu einem autobiographischen Gedicht der Spätantike', in D. Walz (ed.), *Scripturus vitam: lateinische Biographie von der Antike bis in die Gegenwart. Festgabe für Walter Berschin zum 65. Geburtstag.* Heidelberg: 673–80.

Gasparro, G. S. (1985) *Soteriology and Mystic Aspects of the Cult of Cybele and Attis.* Leiden.

Geiger, J. (1998) 'Hebdomades (binae?)', *Classical Quarterly* 48.1: 305–9.

Gelsomino, R. (1975) *I sette colli di Roma.* Rome.

(1976a) 'Varrone e il Septimontium: una polemica', *Giornale italiano di filologia* 28: 324–331.

(1976b) 'Varrone e i sette colli di Roma, II', *Atti Congr. studi varroniani*: 379–88.

Gere, J. A. (1965) 'The decoration of the Villa Giulia', *Burlington Magazine* 107.745: 199–206.

(1969) *Taddeo Zuccarri. His Development Studied in his Drawings.* London.

Gersht, R. and S. Mucznik (1988) 'Mars and Rhea Silvia', *Gerion* 6: 115–33.

Giavarini, C. (1998) *Il Palatino: area sacra sud-ovest e Domus Tiberiana.* Rome.

(2005) *The Basilica of Maxentius: the Monument, its Materials, Construction, and Stability.* Rome.

Gibbon, E. (1776–88) *Decline and Fall.* 6 vols. London.

(1896–1900) *The History of the Decline and Fall of the Roman Empire*, ed. J. B. Bury. 7 vols. London.

Gibson, R. K. (2003) Ars amatoria: *Book Three.* Cambridge.

Giedion, S. (1982) *Space, Time and Architecture.* First published 1941. Cambridge, MA.

Giess, H. (1971) 'Studien zur Farnese-Villa am Palatin', *Römisches Jahrbuch für Kunstgeschichte* 13: 179–230.

Gilles, P. (1561) *De topographia Constantinopoleos.* Lyons.

Giora, Z. (1988) 'The magical number seven', in R. Dàn (ed.), *Occident and Orient: a Tribute to the Memory of Alexander Scheiber.* Leiden: 171–8.

Gjerstad, E. (1962) *Legends and Facts of Early Roman History.* Lund.

Gleason, M. (1994) *Making Men: Sophists and Self-Presentation in Ancient Rome.* Princeton.

Glinister, F. and C. Woods with J. A. North and M. H. Crawford (eds.) (2007) *Verrius, Festus, and Paul: Lexicography, Scholarship and Society*. London.

Goldhill, S. D. (2001) *Being Greek under Rome: Cultural Identity, the Second Sophistic and the Development of Empire*. Cambridge.

(2007) 'What is ekphrasis for?', in S. Bartsch and J. Elsner (eds.), *Essays on Ekphrasis* (Special issue of *Classical Philology* 102): 1–19.

Gombrich, E. (1953) 'Renaissance artistic theory and the development of landscape painting', *Gazette des Beaux-Arts* 41: 335–60.

Goodman, P. J. (2007) *The Roman City and its Periphery: from Rome to Gaul*. London.

Gossage, A. J. (1955) 'Two implications of the Trojan legend', *Greece and Rome* n.s. 2: 72–81.

Gow, A. S. F. and D. L. Page (1965) *The Greek Anthology. Hellenistic Epigrams*. Cambridge.

Gowers, E. (1995) 'The anatomy of Rome from Capitol to Cloaca', *The Journal of Roman Studies* 85: 23–32.

Graf, F. (2000) 'The rite of the Argei', *Museum Helveticum* 57.2: 94–103.

Grandazzi, A. (1986) 'La localisation d'Albe', *Mélanges de l'École française de Rome. Antiquité* 98: 47–90.

(1991) *Le fondation de Rome: réflexion sur l'histoire*. Paris.

(1993) 'La Roma Quadrata: mythe ou réalité?', *Mélanges de l'École française de Rome. Antiquité* 105: 493–545.

(1997) *The Foundation of Rome: Myth and History*, trans. by J. M. Todd. Ithaca and London.

Gransden, K. W. (1976) Aeneid, *Book VIII*. Cambridge.

Grässe, J. G. Th. (1890) *Jacobi a Voragine Legenda aurea vulgo historia Lombardica dicta*. Bratislava.

Green, S. J. (2004) *Ovid,* Fasti *I: a Commentary*. Leiden.

Griffin, J. (1978) 'The divine audience and the religion of the *Iliad*', *Classical Quarterly* 28.1: 1–22.

Grilli, A. (1979) 'Sul numero sette', in *Studi su Varrone, sulla retorica, storiografia e poesia Latina*. Reiti: 203–19.

Grimal, P. (1945) 'La colline de Janus', *Revue archéologique* ser. 6, 23: 56–87.

(1948) 'La promenade d'Evandre et Enee à la lumière des fouilles récentes', *Revue des études anciennes* 50: 348–51.

Grimm, J. and W. Grimm (1854–1960) *Deutsches Wörterbuch*. Leipzig.

Grueber, H. A. (1970) *Coins of the Roman Republic in the British Museum*, vol. I: *Aes rude, aes signatum, aes grave, and Coinage of Rome from BC 268*. London.

Grundmann, S. (2007) *The Architecture of Rome: an Architectural History in 402 Individual Presentations*. First published 1998. Fellbach.

Guattani, G. A. (1805) *Roma: descritta ed illustrata*. Rome.

Guidobaldi, F. (1986) 'L'edilizia abitativa unifamiliare nella Roma tardoantica', in A. Giardina (ed.), *Società romana e impero tardantico*. Rome and Bari: 165–237.

(1999) 'Le domus tardoantiche di Roma come sensori delle trasformazioni culturali e sociali', in W. Harris (ed.), *The Transformation of Urbs Roma in Late Antiquity*, (*Journal of Roman Archaeology, Suppl. ser.* 33). Portsmouth, RI: 53–68.

Gunderson, E. (2000) *Staging Masculinity: the Rhetoric of Performance in the Roman World.* Michigan.

Gurval, R. A. (1995) *Actium and Augustus: the Politics and Emotions of Civil War.* Ann Arbor.

Habel, D. M. (2002) *The Urban Development of Rome in the Age of Alexander VII.* Cambridge.

Hales, S. (2003) *The Roman House and Social Identity.* Cambridge.

Hall, E. (1988) 'When did the Trojans turn into Phrygians? Alcaeus 42.15', *Zeitschrift für Papyrologie und Epigraphik* 73: 15–18.

Hall, M. B. (2005) *Rome.* Cambridge.

Hammer, D. (2002) *The* Iliad *as Politics: the Performance of Political Thought.* Oklahoma.

Hardie, P. (2007) 'Poets, patrons, rulers: the Ennian traditions', in W. Fitzgerald and E. Gowers (eds.), *Ennius Perennis: the* Annals *and Beyond* (*Cambridge Classical Journal,* Suppl. vol. 31). Cambridge: 129–44.

Harding, C. H. B. and S. B. Harding (1898) *The City of Seven Hills: a Book of Stories from the History of Ancient Rome.* London.

Hare, A. J. C. (1923) *Walks in Rome (including Tivoli, Frascati and Albano).* First published 1871. London.

Harris, R. (1997) 'Varro on linguistic regularity', in R. Harris and T. J. Taylor, *Landmarks in Linguistic Thought,* vol. I: *The Western Tradition from Socrates to Saussure.* 2nd edn. London: 47–59.

Harris, W. V. (1999) 'Introduction: Rome in late antiquity', in W. V. Harris (ed.), *The Transformation of Urbs Roma in Late Antiquity* (*Journal of Roman Archaeology* Suppl. ser. 33). Portsmouth, RI: 9–14.

Harrison, S. (2006) 'The epic and monuments: interactions between Virgil's *Aeneid* and the Augustan building programme', in M. J. Clarke, B. G. F. Currie and R. O. A. M. Lyne (eds.), *Epic Interactions: Perspectives on Homer, Virgil, and the Epic Tradition Presented to Jasper Griffin by Former Pupils.* Oxford: 159–85.

Hartnell, B. J. (1964) 'The significance of seven', *Pegasus* 1: 15–20.

Hartswick, K. J. (2004) *The Gardens of Sallust: a Changing Landscape.* Austin.

Haselberger, L. (2002) *Mapping Augustan Rome.* Portsmouth, RI.

(2007) *Urbem adornare: die Stadt Rom und ihre Gestaltumwandlung unter Augustus = Rome's Urban Metamorphosis under Augustus,* Eng. trans. of the main text by Alexander Thein. Portsmouth, RI.

Haselberger, L. and J. Humphrey (eds.) (2006) *Imaging Ancient Rome: Documentation, Visualization, Imagination. Proceedings of the Third Williams Symposium*

on *Classical Architecture, Held at the American Academy in Rome, the British School at Rome, and the Deutsches Archäologisches Institut, Rome, on 20–23 May 2004.* Portsmouth, RI.

Haskell, F. and N. Penny (1981) *Taste and the Antique: the Lure of Classical Sculpture 1500–1900.* New Haven and London.

Hastings, M. and E. Hodder (1936) *The Seven Sovereign Hills of Rome.* New York.

Häuber, C. (2005) 'Das Archäologische Informationssystem "AIS ROMA": Esquilin, Caelius, Capitolium, Velabrum, Porta Triumphalis', *Bullettino della Commissione Archeologica Comunale di Roma* 106: 9–60.

Häuber, C. and F. X. Schütz (2006) 'Das Archäologische Informationssystem ROMA: Antike Straßen und Gebäude aus Sollis Romkarte iin modernen Stadtgrundiß', in L. Haselberger and J. Humphrey (eds.) *Imaging Ancient Rome: Documentation, Visualization, Imagination. Proceedings of the Third Williams Symposium on Classical Architecture, Held at the American Academy in Rome, the British School at Rome, and the Deutsches Archäologisches Institut, Rome, on May 20–23, 2004.* Portsmouth, RI: 253–69.

Häuber, R. C. (1990) 'Zur Topographie der Horti Maecenatis und der Horti Lamiani auf dem Esquilin nach Rom', *Kölner Jahrbuch* 23: 11–107.

Hawthorne, N. (2002) *The Marble Faun.* First published 1860. Oxford.

Hazlitt, W. (1995) *Classical Gazetteer.* London.

Heather, P. J. and D. Moncur (2001) *Politics, Philosophy, and Empire in the Fourth Century: Select Orations of Themistius.* Liverpool.

Heenes, V. (2003) *Antike in Bildern: Illustrationen in antiquarischen Werken des 16. und 17. Jahrhunderts.* Stendal.

Heiken, G., R. Funiciello and D. De Rita (eds.) (2005) *The Seven Hills of Rome: a Geological Tour of the City.* New Jersey.

Hekster, O. (2002) *Commodus: an Emperor at the Crossroads.* Amsterdam.

Helbig, W. (1899) *Fuhrer durch die offentlichen Sammlungen klassischer Altertumer in Rom.* Vol. II. Leipzig.

Henderson, J. (2004) *Morals and Villas in Seneca's Letters: Places to Dwell.* Cambridge.

Herzfeld, M. (2009) *Evicted from Eternity: the Restructuring of Modern Rome.* Chicago.

Heyworth, S. J. (2007a) *Cynthia: a Companion to the Work of Propertius.* Oxford.
(2007b) *Sexti Properti Elegos.* Oxford.

Hicks, P. (2003) 'Alberti's *Descriptio urbis Romae*', *Albertiana* 6: 205–15.

Hillard, G. S. (1853) *Six Months in Italy.* Boston.

Hobsbawm, E. and T. Ranger (1983) *The Invention of Tradition.* London.

Hoby, T. (1902) *The Travels and Life of Sir Thomas Hoby, Kt. of Bisham Abbey, Written by Himself, 1547–1564.* London.

Holland, L. A. (1953) 'Septimontium or Saeptimontium?', *Transactions of the American Philological Association* 84: 16–34.
(1961) *Janus and the Bridge.* Rome.

Hollis, A. S. (1986) 'The composition of Callimachus' *Aetia* in the light of P. Oxy. 2258', *Classical Quarterly* 36: 467–71.

(1990) *Callimachus*: Hecale. Oxford.

Hölscher, T. (2000) 'Augustus und die Macht der Archäologie', in F. Millar and A. Giovannini (eds.), *La revolution romaine après Ronald Syme. Bilans et perspectives* (Entretiens sur l'Antiquité classique 46). Geneva: 237–81.

Homo, L. (1921) *La Rome antique: histoire - guide des monuments de Rome: depuis le temps les plus reculées jusqu'à l'invasion des barbares.* Paris.

Hopkins, K. (1983) *Death and Renewal: Sociological Studies in Roman History.* Vol. II. Cambridge.

Hopkinson, N. (1984) *Callimachus*: Hymn to Demeter. Cambridge.

Hornsby, C. (2002) *Nicolas-Didier Boguet (1755–1839): Landscapes of Suburban Rome/Disegni dei Contorni di Roma.* Rome.

Hoskier, C. (1928) *The Complete Commentary of Oecumenius on the Apocalypse.* Ann Arbor.

Howell, P. (1980) *A Commentary on Book One of the Epigrams of Martial.* London.

Hubert, É. (1990) *Espace urbain et habitat à Rome du X siècle à la fin du XIII siècle.* Rome.

Hughes, J. (2005) 'Simulacra gentium: personifications of provinces, peoples, cities and regions in the art of the Roman Empire'. PhD thesis, The Courtauld Institute, London.

Humphries, M. (2003) 'Roman senators and absent emperors in late antiquity', *Acta ad archaeologiam et artium historiam pertinentia* 17 (n.s. 3): 27–46.

Hunter, R. (2006) *The Shadow of Callimachus: Studies in the Reception of Hellenistic Poetry at Rome.* Cambridge.

Huskinson, J. (2002) 'Three Antioch dining rooms', *Mosaic* 29: 21–3.

Hutchinson, G. (2006) *Propertius: Elegies Book IV.* Cambridge.

Hyde, R. (1985) *Gilded Scenes and Shining Prospects: Panoramic Views of British Towns 1575–1900.* New Haven.

Igolen, J. (1935) 'Les anciennes fortifications de Nîmes', *Mémoires de l'Académie de Nîmes* 1933–5: 67–132.

Ijsewijn, J. (1997) *Coryciana.* Rome.

Incisa della Rocchetta, G. (1956) *Bartolomeo Pinelli.* Rome.

Jacks, P. J. (1990) 'The *Simulachrum* of Fabio Calvo: a view of Roman architecture all'antica in 1527', *The Art Bulletin* 72.3: 453–81.

(1993) *The Antiquarian and the Myth of Antiquity: the Origins of Rome in Renaissance Thought.* Cambridge.

Jaeger, M. (1998) *Livy's Written Rome.* Ann Arbor.

James, H. (1995) *Italian Hours.* First published 1909. London and New York.

Janin, J. R. (1950) *Constantinople byzantine.* Paris.

Johnson, M. (2009) *The Roman Imperial Mausoleum in Late Antiquity.* Cambridge.

Jones Hall, L. (2004) *Roman Berytus: Beirut in Late Antiquity.* London.

Jonge, P. de (1972) *Philological and Historical Commentary on Ammianus Marcellinus XVI*. Groningen.

Jordan, H. (1871) *Topographie der Stadt Rom im Alterthum*. Berlin.

Joyce, H. (1983) 'The ancient frescoes from the Villa Negroni and their influence in the eighteenth and nineteenth centuries', *The Art Bulletin* 65.3: 423–40.

Jullian, C. (1920) *Histoire de la Gaule*. Vol. V. Paris.

Kajava, M. (2005) 'La Villa Lante al Gianicolo e la villa di Giulio Marziale', in T. Carunchio and S. Örmä (eds.), *Villa Lante. Storia della fabbrica e cronaca degli abitatori*. Rome: 11–18.

(2006) 'Hinc totam licet aestimare Romam', *L'Orecchio di Giano*: 5.

Kaldellis, A. (2007) 'Christodoros on the statues of the Zeuxippos baths: a new reading of the ekphrasis', *Greek, Roman and Byzantine Studies* 47: 361–83.

Karmon, D. E. (2011) *The Ruin of the Eternal City: Antiquity and Preservation in Renaissance Rome*. Oxford.

Kearns, E. (2004) 'The gods in the Homeric epics', in R. Fowler (ed.), *The Cambridge Companion to Homer*. Cambridge: 59–73.

Kelly, C. (1999) 'Empire building', in G. Bowersock, P. Brown and O. Grabar (eds.), *Late Antiquity: a Guide to the Postclassical World*. Cambridge, MA: 170–95.

Kelly, G. (2003) 'The new Rome and the old: Ammianus Marcellinus' Silences on Constantinople', *Classical Quarterly* 53.2: 588–607.

Kennedy, D. F. (1993) *The Arts of Love: Five Studies in the Discourse of Roman Love Elegy*. Cambridge.

Kent, J. H. (1966) *Corinth: the Inscriptions 1926–1950*. New Jersey.

King, R. (1990) 'Creative landscaping: inspiration and artifice in Propertius 4.4', *The Classical Journal* 85: 225–46.

King, W. A. (2004) 'Through the looking glass of silver springs: tourism and the politics of vision', *Americana* 3.1. www.americanpopularculture.com/journal/articles/spring_2004/king.htm.

Kirkham, V. and A. Maggi (eds.) (2009) *Petrarch: a Critical Guide to the Complete Works*. Chicago.

Klingle, M. W. (2007) *Emerald City: an Environmental History of Seattle*. New Haven.

Kobovy, M. and Y. Psotka (1976) 'The predominance of seven and the apparent spontaneity of numerical choices', *Journal of Experimental Psychology: Human Perception and Performance* 2: 291–4.

Kostof, S. (1973) *The Third Rome, 1870–1950: Traffic and Glory. An Exhibition Organized by the University Art Museum, Berkeley, in Collaboration with the Gabinetto Fotografico Nazionale, Rome*. Rome.

(1992) *The City Assembled: Elements of Urban Form through History*. Boston.

Krautheimer, R. (1980) *Rome. Profile of a City 312–1308*. New Haven.

(1983) *Three Christian Capitals: Topography and Politics*. Berkeley and London.

Krautheimer, R. and R. B. S. Jones (1975) 'The diary of Alexander VII: notes on art, artists and buildings', *Römisches Jahrbuch für Kunstgeschichte*. 15: 199–233.

Kunze, M. (ed.) (2003) *Die Sieben Weltwunder der Antike. Wege der Wiedergewinnung aus sechs Jahrhunderten.* Mainz.

Lafitau, J. F. (1724) *Moeurs des sauvages ameriquains comparées aux moeurs des premiers temps.* Vols. I–II. Paris.

Lambert, R. (1984) *Beloved and God: the Story of Hadrian and Antinous.* London.

Lanciani, R. (1897) *The Ruins and Excavations of Ancient Rome.* London.

(1899a) *The Destruction of Ancient Rome.* New York.

(1899b) *Pagan and Christian Rome.* New York.

Lançon, B. (2000) *Rome in Late Antiquity,* trans. A. Nevill. Edinburgh.

Langdon, M. K. (1999) 'Classifying the hills of Rome', *Eranos* 97: 98–107.

Lanzillotta, M. A. (1996) *Contributi sui* Mirabilia urbis Romae. Genova.

La Penna, A. (1951) *Properzio. Saggio critico seguito da due ricerche filologiche.* Florence.

Larmour, D. and D. Spencer (eds.) (2007) *The Sites of Rome: Time, Space, Memory.* Oxford.

La Rocca, E. (2000) 'L'affresco con veduto di città dal colle Oppio', in E. Fentress (ed.), *Romanization and the City: Creation, Transformations, and Failures* (*Journal of Roman Archaeology,* Suppl. ser. 38). Portsmouth, RI: 57–71.

(2001) 'The newly discovered city fresco from Trajan's baths, Rome', *Imago mundi* 53: 121–4.

La Rocca, E. and C. P. Presicce with A. Lo Monaco (2011) *Ritratti. Le tante facce del potere.* Rome.

Laureys, M. (1995) *Ioannes Caballinus,* Polistoria de virtutibus et dotibus Romanorum. Stuttgart.

(1997) 'Between *Mirabilia* and *Roma instaurata*: Giovanni Cavallini's *Polistoria*', in H. Ragn Jensen, M. Pade and L. W. Petersen (eds.), *Avignon and Naples Italy in France – France in Italy in the Fourteenth Century* (Analecta Romana Instituti Danici, Suppl. 25). Rome: 100–15.

(2006) 'Das alte und das neue Rom in Andrea Fulvios *Antiquaria urbis*', in M. Disselkamp, P. Ihring and F. Wolfzettel (eds.), *Das alte Rom und die Neue Zeit. La Roma antica e la prima età moderna.* Tübingen: 201–20.

Lavagne, H. and J. Charles-Gaffiot (1999) *Hadrien: trésors d'une villa impériale.* Milan.

Leonhardt, J. (2001) *Jewish Worship in Philo of Alexandria.* Tübingen.

Lessing, G. E. (1766) *Laokoon: oder über die Grenzen der Malerei und Poesie.* Stuttgart.

Levi, D. (1947) *Antioch Mosaic Pavements.* New Jersey.

Levick, B. (1965) 'Two inscriptions from Pisidian Antioch', *Anatolian Studies* 15: 53–62.

(1967) *Roman Colonies in Southern Asia Minor.* Oxford.

(1999) *Vespasian.* London.

Lhommé, M. K. (2007) 'Varron et Verrius au 2ème siècle après J.-C', in F. Glinister and C. Woods with J. A. North and M. H. Crawford (eds.), *Verrius, Festus and Paul: Lexicography, Scholarship, and Society.* London: 33–47.

Lightfoot, J. L. (2007) Oracula Sibyllina. The Sibylline Oracles: *With Introduction, Translation, and Commentary on the First and Second Books*. Oxford.

Lilius, H. (1981) *Villa Lante al Gianicolo. L'Architettura e la decorazione pittorica*. Rome.

Lister, R. (ed.) (1974) *The Letters of Samuel Palmer*. 2 vols. Oxford.

Long, J. (2004). 'Claudian and the city: poetry and pride of place', in W.-W. Ehlers (ed.), *Aetas Claudianea: eine Tagung an der Freien Universität Berlin vom 28. bis 30. Juni 2002*. Munich: 1–15.

Lønstrup, G. (2009) 'Normativity and memory in the making: the seven hills of the "new" and "old" Rome', in A.-C. Jacobsen (ed.), *The Discursive Fight over Religious Texts in Antiquity*. Aarhus: 85–109.

Looney, D. (2009) 'The beginnings of humanistic oratory: Petrarch's coronation oration', in V. Kirkham and A. Maggi (eds.), *Petrarch: a Critical Guide to the Complete Works*. Chicago: 131–40.

Lorenzatti, S. (1990) 'Vicende del tempio di Venere e Roma nel medioevo e nel rinascimento', *Rivista dell'Istituto Nazionale di Archeologia e storia dell'Arte* 13: 119–38.

Lovatt, H. V. (2006) 'The female gaze in Flavian epic: looking out from the walls in Valerius Flaccus and Statius', in R. R. Nauta, H.-J. van Dam and J. L. Smolenaars (eds.), *Flavian Poetry* (*Mnemosyne* Suppl. 270). Leiden: 59–78.

(2007) 'Statius, Orpheus and the post Augustan *vates*', *Arethusa* 40.2: 145–63.

(forthcoming) *The Epic Gaze*. Cambridge.

Lugli, G. (1943) 'Il solco primigenio della Roma Quadrata', *Capitolium* 18: 203–10.

Lumsden, A. (1797) *Remarks on the Antiquities of Rome and its Environs*. London.

Lynch, K. (1961) *The Image of the City*. Cambridge, MA.

MacCormack, S. (1972) 'Change and continuity in late antiquity: the ceremony of "Adventus"', *Historia* 21.4: 731–52.

MacDonald, W. L. and J. A. Pinto (1995) *Hadrian's Villa and its Legacy*. New Haven and London.

MacDougall, E. B. (1975) 'The sleeping nymph: origins of a humanist fountain type', *The Art Bulletin* 57.3: 357–65.

(1994) *Fountains, Statues and Flowers: Studies in Italian Gardens in the Sixteenth and Seventeenth Centuries*. Washington.

Maier, J. (2007) 'Mapping past and present: Leonardo Bufalini's plan of Rome (1551)', *Imago mundi* 59.1: 1–23.

Majanlahti, A. (2005) *The Families Who Made Rome: a History and a Guide*. London.

Malgrave, H. F. (ed.) (2006) *Johann Joachim Winckelmann*, History of the Art of Antiquity. Los Angeles.

Mansuelli, G. A. (1941) *Ariminum (Rimini): Regio VIII, Aemilia*. Rome.

Marder, T. A. (1978) 'Sixtus V on the Quirinal', *Journal of the Society of Architectural Historians* 37.4: 283–94.

Marliani, G. B. (1534) *Topographia antiquae Romae: libri septem*. Lyon.

(1544) *Urbis Romae topographia*. Rome.

Marsh, D. (2002) 'Leon Battista Alberti at the millennium', *Renaissance Quarterly*. 55.3: 1028–37.

Martin, R. P. (1993) 'The Seven Sages as performers of wisdom', in C. Dougherty and L. Kurke (eds.), *Cultural Poetics in Archaic Greece*. Oxford: 108–28.

Martinez, A. G.-T. (2002) *Rutilio Namaciano. El retorno. Geográfos latinos menores*, Madrid.

Masson, G. (1965) *The Companion Guide to Rome*. London.

Mastrocinque, A. (1993) 'Roma Quadrata', *Mélanges de l'École française de Rome. Antiquité* 110.2: 681–97.

Matheson, S. B. (1994) *An Obsession with Fortune: Tyche in Greek and Roman Art*. New Haven.

Matthews, J. (1990) *Western Aristocracies and Imperial Court, AD 364–425*. First published 1975. Oxford.

(1989) *The Roman Empire of Ammianus Marcellinus*. London.

Mauro, L. (1558) *Delle antichità di Roma*. Venice.

Mayer, R. (2007) 'Impressions of Rome', *Greece and Rome* 54: 156–77.

Mayernik, D. (2003) *Timeless Cities: an Architect's Reflections on Renaissance Italy*. New York.

Mazzoni, C. (2010) *She-Wolf: the Story of a Roman Icon*. Cambridge.

McAlee, R. (2007) *The Coins of Roman Antioch*. Lancaster.

McEwan, I. K. (2003) *Vitruvius: Writing the Body of Architecture*. Cambridge, MA.

(2005) 'Housing fame: in the Tuscan villa of Pliny the younger', *Res* 27: 11–24.

McGowan, M. (1990) 'Contradictory impulses in Montaigne's vision of Rome', *Renaissance Studies* 4: 392–409.

(2000) *The Vision of Rome in Late Renaissance France*. New Haven and London.

McLynn, N. B. (1995) 'Paulinus the impenitent', *Journal of Early Christian Studies* 3.4: 461–86.

Meer, L. B. van der (1998) 'L'affresco sotto le terme di Triano del Colle Oppio, Roma. Necropolis: realtà e progetto', *Oudheidkundige mededeelingen van het Rijksmuseum van Oudheden te* Leiden 78: 63–73.

Mellor, R. (1978) 'The dedications on the Capitoline hill', *Chiron* 8: 319–33.

(1981) 'The Goddess Roma', *Aufstieg und Niedergang der römischen Welt* 2.17.2: 950–1030.

Meneghini, R. and R. Santangeli Valenzani (2004) *Roma nell' altomedioevo. Topografia e urbanistica della città dal V al X secolo*. Rome.

Meritt, B. D. (1927) 'Excavations at Corinth, 1927', *American Journal of Archaeology* 31: 450–61.

Merlin, A. (1906) *L'Aventin dans l'antiquité*. Paris.

Meskell, L. and R. Preucel (2004) *Companion to Social Archaeology*. Oxford.

Middleton, R. (1996) *The Idea of the City*. Massachusetts.

Mignone, L. M. (2010) 'The Republican Aventine'. PhD thesis. Columbia University.

Miles, M. M. (2008) *Ancient Art as Plunder: the Ancient Origins of Debate about Cultural Property*. Cambridge.

Miller, G. A. (1956) 'The magical number seven, plus or minus two: some limits on our capacity for processing information', *Psychological Review* 63.2: 81–97.

Minor, H. H. (1999) 'Mapping Mussolini: ritual and cartography in public art during the second Roman empire', *Imago mundi* 51: 147–62.

Mirri, L. and G. Carletti (1776) *Le pitture delle Terme di Tito*. Rome.

Mitchell, W. J. T. (ed.) (1994) *Landscape and Power*. Chicago.

Moatti, C. (1993) *In Search of Ancient Rome*. London.

Moffitt, J. F. (1983) 'The poet and the painter: J. H. W. Tischbein's "Perfect Portrait" of Goethe in the Campagna (1786–87)', *The Art Bulletin* 65.3: 440–55.

Mols, S. T. A. M. (1997) 'Filosofen Te Kakken Gezet? Geschilderde Filosofen Portretten in Ostia', *Lampas* 30.4–5: 360–71.

Momigliano, A. (1963) 'An interim report on the origins of Rome', *The Journal of Roman Studies* 53: 95–121.

Mommsen, Th. (1887) *The History of Rome*. Ithaca.

Monssen, L. H. (1982) 'The martyrdom cycle in Santo Stefano Rotondo, part one', *Acta ad archaeologiam et artium historiam pertinentia* 2.2: 175–319.

   (1983) 'The martyrdom cycle in Santo Stefano Rotondo, part two', *Acta ad archaeologiam et artium historiam pertinentia* 2.3: 11–106.

Montaigne, M. de (2003) *De la vanité*. First published 1588. Paris.

Morgan, Lady (1821) *Italy*. London.

Morgan, L. (1999) *Patterns of Redemption in Virgil's* Georgics. Cambridge.

Murgatroyd, P. (1975) '*Militia amoris* and the Roman elegists'. *Latomus* 34: 59–79.

Murphy, T. (2004) *Pliny the Elder's* Natural History: *the Empire in Encyclopedia*. Oxford.

Murray, J. (1843) *Handbook for Travellers in Central Italy*. London.

Mussolini, B. (1930) 'Il Piano Regolatore di Roma', *Opera omnia*, vol. xxiv, ed. E. and D. Susmel. Florence: 269–70.

Nagy, B. (1985) 'The Argei puzzle', *American Journal of Ancient History* 10.1: 1–27.

Najbjerg, T. and J. Trimble (2004) 'Ancient maps and mapping in and around Rome – a review of E. Rodríguez-Almeida, *Formae urbis antiquae. Le mappe marmoree di Roma tra la Repubblica e Settimio Severo*', *Journal of Roman Archaeology* 17: 577–83.

   (2005) 'The Severan Marble Plan since 1960', in R. Meneghini and R. Santangeli Valenzani (eds.), *Formae urbis Romae: nuovi frammenti di piante marmoree dallo scavo dei fori imperiali* (*Bullettino della Commissione Archeologica Comunale di Roma*, Suppl. 15). Rome: 75–101.

Nardini, F. (1666) *Roma antica*. Rome.

Nash, C. (1996) 'Reclaiming vision: looking at landscape and the body', *Gender, Place and Culture* 3: 149–69.

Neri, A. (1878) 'Saggio della corrispondenza di Ferdinando Raggi agente della Repubblica Genovese a Roma', *Rivista Europea* n.s. 5: 657–95.

Nevola, F. (2007) *Siena: Constructing the Renaissance City*. New Haven.

Newby, Z. (2007) 'Reading the allegory of the Archelaos relief', in Z. Newby and R. Leader-Newby, *Art and Inscriptions in the Ancient World*. Cambridge: 156–78.

Newlands, C. (2002) *Statius' Silvae and the Poetics of Empire*. Cambridge.

Nicassio, S. V. (2005) *Imperial City: Rome under Napoleon*. Chicago.

Nichols, F. M. (1887) *Mirabilia urbis Romae; The Marvels of Rome*. London.

Nixon, C. E. V. (1987) *Pacatus, Panegyric to the Emperor Theodosius*. Liverpool.

Nixon, C. E. V. and B. S. Rodgers (1994) *In Praise of Later Roman Emperors: the Panegyrici Latini*. Berkeley, Los Angeles and London.

Norden, E. (1990) *Varro's Imagines*. Berlin.

Nova, A. (1982) 'Artistic patronage of Pope Julius III/1550–1555: profane imagery and buildings for the De Monte family in Rome'. PhD dissertation, The Courtauld Institute, London.

(1988) *The Artistic Patronage of Pope Julius III (1550–1555): Profane Imagery and Buildings for the De Monte Family in Rome*. New York.

O'Brian, K. (1997) 'Gibbon's prospects: rhetoric and empire at the end of *The Decline and Fall*', in D. Womersley with J. Burrow and J. Pocock (eds.), *Edward Gibbon: Bicentenary Essays*. Oxford: 235–52.

Oechslin, W. (1982) 'Dinocrates and the myth of the megalomaniacal institution of architecture', *Daidalos* 4: 7–26.

Oettermann, S. (1997) *The Panorama: History of a Mass Medium*. New York.

Ogilvie, R. M. (1977) 'Review of Remo Gelsomino, *Varrone e i sette colli di Roma*. Rome', *Classical Review* 27: 281–2.

O'Gorman, J. F. (1971) 'The Villa Lante in Rome: some drawings and observations', *The Burlington Magazine* 113.816: 133–8.

O'Hara, J. J. (1996) *True Names: Vergil and the Alexandrian Tradition of Etymological Wordplay*. Ann Arbor.

Olechowska, E. M. (ed.) (1978) *Claudii Claudiani De bello Gildonico*. Leiden.

Oliver, J. H. (1953) *The Ruling Power. A Study of the Roman Empire in the Second Century after Christ through the Roman Oration of Aelius Aristides*. Philadelphia.

Olsen, D. J. (1986) *The City as a Work of Art: London, Paris, Vienna*. New Haven.

Olwig, K. (1996) 'Rediscovering the substantive meaning of landscape', *Annals: Association of American Geographers* 83: 1–17.

O'Neill, K. (1995) 'Propertius 4.4: Tarpeia and the burden of aetiology', *Hermathena* 158: 53–60.

Onians, J. (1979) *Art and Thought in the Hellenistic Age: the Greek World View 350–50 BC*. London.

Orwell, S. and I. Angus (eds.) (1968) *The Collected Essays, Journalism and Letters of George Orwell*, vol. I: *An Age Like This, 1920–1940*. London.

Osborne, J. (1987) *The Marvels of Rome*. Toronto.

Osborne, R. and C. Vout (2010) 'A revolution in Roman history?', *The Journal of Roman Studies* 100: 233–45.

Pacini, R. (1935) *Bartolomeo Pinelli e la Roma del suo tempo*. Rome.

Packer, J. E. (1997) *The Forum of Trajan in Rome: a Study of the Monuments*. Berkeley, Los Angeles and Oxford.

Painter, B. W. (2005) *Mussolini's Rome: Rebuilding the Eternal City*. New York.

Pais, E. (1898) *Storia di Roma*. Rome.

(1905) *Ancient Legends of Roman History*. London.

Palladio, A. (1554a) *L'antichità di Roma*. Rome.

(1554b) *Descritione de le chiese, stationi, indulgenze e reliquie de Corpi Sancti, che sono in la città di Roma*. Rome.

Pallavicino, P. S. (1840) *Della vita di Alessandro VII*, vol. II. Prato.

Pallotino, M. (1960) 'Le origini di Roma', *Archeologia classica* 12: 1–36.

Palmer, R. E. A. (1970) *The Archaic Communities of the Romans*. Cambridge.

(1976) 'Jupiter Blaze: gods of the hills, and the Roman topography of *CIL* VI 377', *American Journal of Archaeology* 80: 43–56.

Palombi, D. (1997) *Tra Palatino ed Esquilino: 'Velia', 'Carinae', 'Fagutal': storia urbana di tre quartieri di Roma antica*. Rome.

(2006) 'Vecchie e nuove immagini per Roma augustea: *flavus Tiberis e septem colles*', in L. Haselberger and J. Humphrey (eds.), *Imaging Ancient Rome: Documentation, Visualization, Imagination. Proceedings of the Third Williams Symposium on Classical Architecture, Held at the American Academy in Rome, the British School at Rome, and the Deutsches Archäologisches Institut, Rome, on 20–23 May 2004*. Portsmouth, RI: 15–29.

Panvinio, O. (1570) *Le sette chiese principali di Roma*. Rome.

Papaioannou, S. (2003) 'Founder, civilizer and leader: Vergil's Evander and his role in the origins of Rome', *Mnemosyne* 61: 680–702.

Papi, E. (1995) 'Domus: M. Aemilius Scaurus', in E. M. Steinby (ed.), *Lexicon topographicum urbis Romae*, Rome. Vol. 2: 26.

Pappalardo, U. and A. Capuano (2006) 'Immagini della città nella pittura romana', in L. Haselberger and J. Humphrey (eds.), *Imaging Ancient Rome: Documentation, Visualization, Imagination. Proceedings of the Third Williams Symposium on Classical Architecture, Held at the American Academy in Rome, the British School at Rome, and the Deutsches Archäologisches Institut, Rome, on 20–23 May 2004*. Portsmouth, RI: 75–90.

Paradisi, D. (2004) *Il Campidoglio: storie, personaggi e monumenti del mitico colle di Roma*. Rome.

Paratore, E. (1975) 'Recensione a Gelsomino, *Varrone e i sette colli di Roma*', *Rivista di cultura classica e medioevale* 17: 181–205.

Patterson, J. R. (2000) 'On the margins of the city of Rome', in V. M. Hope and E. Marshall (eds.), *Death and Disease in the Ancient City*, London: 85–103.

Pavolini, C., 2006. *Archeologia e topografia della Regione II (Celio). Un aggiornamento sessant'anni dopo Colini*. Rome.

Pelc, M. (2002) *Illustrium imagines: Das Porträtbuch der Renaissance*. Leiden.

Pemble, J. (1987) *The Mediterranean Passion*. Oxford.

Pensabene, P. (2002) 'Venticinque anni dei ricerche sul Palatino: i santuari e il sistema sostruttivo dell' area sud-ovest', *Archeologica classica* 53: 65–136.

Perrottet, T. (2005) 'The glory that is Rome', *Smithsonian Magazine* October.

Pfanner, M. (1983) *Der Titusbogen*. Mainz.

Piazza, C. B. (1694) *Hieroxenia overo sagra pellegrinazione alle sette chiese di Roma, con le due d'antichissima divozione, che fanno le nove chiese*. Rome.

Picard, Th. (1902) 'Notes sure le vieux Nîmes', *Revue du Midi* 32.2: 341–80.

Pichon, R. (1914) 'La promenade d'Évandre et d'Énée au VIIIéme livre de l'Éneide', *Revue des études anciennes* 16: 410–16.

Pierre, DBC (2004) 'Moving on seamlessly', *Guardian*, September 1.

Pietrangeli, C., A. Ravaglioli and A. Petrucci (eds.) (1965) *Il Campidoglio: storia ed illustrazioni del Colle Capitolino, dei monumenti, degli edifici e delle raccolte storiche ed artistiche*. Rome.

Pingaud, L. (1872) *Africa*. Paris.

Pinto, J. (1976) 'Origins and development of the ichnographic city plan', *Journal of the Society of Architectural Historians* 35.1: 35–40.

Piranesi, G. B. (1756) *Le antichità romane*. Rome.

　　(1761) *Le rovine del castello dell' Acqua Giulia*. Rome.

Pirazzoli, N. (1990) *Luigi Rossini*. Rome.

Plaidy, J. (1958) *Madonna of the Seven Hills*. New York.

Poe, J. P. (1978) 'The Septimontium and the Subura', *Transactions of the American Philological Association* 108: 147–54.

Poe, M. (2001) 'Moscow, the Third Rome: the origins and transformations of a pivotal moment' *Jahrbücher für Geschichte Osteuropas* 49.3: 412–29.

Porte, D. (1985) *L'étiologie religieuse dans les Fastes d'Ovide*. Paris.

Potts, A. (1994) *Flesh and the Ideal: Winckelmann and the Origins of Art History*. New Haven.

Poucet, J. (1960) 'Le Septimontium et la Succusa chez Festus et Varron. Un problème d'histoire et de topographie romaines', *Bulletin de l'Institut historique belge de Rome* 32: 25–73.

　　(1967) 'L'importance du terme *collis* pour l'étude du développement urbain de la Rome archaïque', *L'Antiquité classique* 36: 99–115.

　　(1985) *Les origines de Rome: tradition et histoire*. Brussels.

Powell, C. (1998) *Italy in the Age of Turner: 'The Garden of the World'*. London.

Pratt, K. J. (1965) 'Rome as eternal', *Journal of the History of Ideas* 26.1: 25–44.

Pratt, M. L. (1992) *Imperial Eyes: Travel Writing and Transculturation*. London.

Pressly, W. L. (1995) 'On classic ground: James Barry's "memorials" of the Italian landscape', *Record of the Art Museum, Princeton University* 54.2: 12–28.

Prettejohn, E. (2005) *Beauty and Art: 1750–2000*. Oxford.

Price, M. J. and B. L. Trell (1977) *Coins and their Cities: Architecture on the Ancient Coins of Greece, Rome, and Palestine*. London.

Prown, J. D. (1997) 'A course of antiquities at Rome', *Eighteenth-Century Studies* 31.1: 90–100.

Purcell, N. (1992) 'The city of Rome', in R. Jenkyns (ed.), *The Legacy of Rome: a New Appraisal*. Oxford: 421–53.

(1995) 'The Roman villa and the landscape of production', in T. J. Cornell and K. Lomas (eds.), *Urban Society in Roman Italy*. New York: 151–80.

Putnam, M. C. J. (2001) *Horace's* Carmen saeculare: *Ritual Magic and the Poet's Art*. New Haven.

Rasch, J. (1984) *Das Maxentius-Mausoleum an der Via Appia in Rom*. Mainz.

Rea, J. A. (2007) *Legendary Rome: Myth, Monuments and Memory on the Capitoline and Palatine*. London.

Reader, J. (2004) *Cities*. London.

Rebert, H. F. (1925) 'The Velia: a study in historical topography', *Transactions of the American Philological Association* 56: 54–69.

Redford, B. (2008) *The Dilettanti: the Antic and the Antique in Eighteenth Century England*. Los Angeles.

Rees, R. (1993) 'Images and image: a re-examination of Tetrarchic iconography', *Greece and Rome* 40.2: 181–200.

(1996) 'Revisiting Evander at *Aeneid* 8.363', *Classical Quarterly* 46.2: 583–6.

Regn, G. and B. Huss (2009) 'Petrarch's Rome: the history of the *Africa* and the Renaissance project', *Modern Language Notes* 124.1: 86–102.

Renaud, C. (1990) 'Studies in the eighth book of the *Aeneid*; the importance of place'. PhD dissertation. The University of Texas at Austin.

Richardson, C. M. (2003) 'The housing opportunities of a renaissance cardinal', *Renaissance Studies* 17.4: 607–27.

Richardson, L. (1980) 'Two topographical notes', *American Journal of Philology* 101.1: 53–6.

(1992) *A New Topographical Dictionary of Ancient Rome*. Baltimore and London.

Richmond, O. (1958) 'Palatine Apollo again', *Classical Quarterly* n.s. 8: 180–4.

Ridley, R. T. (1989) 'The fate of an architect: Apollodorus of Damascus', *Athenaeum* 67: 551–65.

(1992) *The Eagle and the Spade: Archaeology in Rome during the Napoleonic Era*. Cambridge.

Riedweg, C. (2002) *Pythagoras: Leben, Lehre, Nachwirkung, Eine Einführung*. Munich.

Rimell, V. E. (2009) *Martial's Rome: Empire and the Ideology of Empire*. Cambridge.

Rinne, K. W. (2010) *The Waters of Rome*. New Haven.

Ritschl, E. (1877) *Opuscula philologica*. Vol. III. Leipzig.

Rizzi, M. (2010) *Hadrian and the Christians*. Berlin.

Robbins, F. E. (1921) 'The tradition of Greek Arithmology', *Classical Philology* 16.2: 97–123.

Roberts, J. M. (2005) *The Seven Hills*. New York.

Roberts, M. (1988) 'The treatment of narrative in late antique literature: Ammianus Marcellinus (16.10), Rutilius Namatianus and Paulinus of Pella', *Philologus* 132: 181–95.

(2001) 'Rome personified, Rome epitomized: representations of Rome in the poetry of the early fifth century', *American Journal of Philology* 122.4: 533–65.

Robinson, H. S. (1974) 'A monument to Roma at Corinth', *Hesperia* 43.4: 470–84.

Rodríguez-Almeida, E. (1981) *Forma urbis Marmorea. Aggiornamento generale 1980.* Rome.

(1993) 'Carinae' in E. M. Steinby (ed.), *Lexicon topographicum urbis Romae.* Rome. Vol. I: 239–40.

(2002) *Formae urbis antiquae. Le mappe marmoree di Roma tra la Repubblica e Settimio Severo.* Rome.

(2003) *Terrarum dea gentiumque: Marziale e Roma, un poeta e la sua città.* Rome.

Rodwin, L. and R. M. Hollister (1984) *Cities of the Mind: Images and Themes of the City in the Social Sciences.* New York.

Rogers, S. (1840) *Italy: a Poem.* London.

Romanelli, P. (1960) 'Horti palatini Farnesiorum', *Studi Romani* 8: 661–72.

Roscher, W. H. (1904) *Die Sieben und Neunzahl im Kultus und Mythus der Griechen.* Leipzig.

Rose, G. (1993) *Feminism and Geography: the Limits of Geographical Knowledge.* Cambridge, Oxford and Boston.

Rossini, L. (1829) *I sette colli di Roma antica e moderna con piante e restauri dei medesimi, e coi colli adiacenti: [con un panorama . . . con le respettive medaglie edi i frammenti della pianta antica di Roma esistente nel Museo Capitolino, in fine con una breve descrizione storico-antiquaria, e col testo degli antichi scrittori messi a'piedi d'ogni restauro].* Rome.

Ross Taylor, L. (1934) 'New light on the history of the secular games', *American Journal of Philology* 55: 101–20.

Rostovtzeff, M. I. (1911) 'Die hellenistisch-römische Architekturlandschaft', *Mitteilungen des Deutschen Archäologischen Instituts, Römische Abteilung* 26: 1–186.

Rothwell, K. S. (1996) 'Propertius on the site of Rome', *Latomus* 55: 829–54.

Rowe, C. (1999) *As I Was Saying: Recollections and Miscellaneous Essays.* Vol. III. Massachusetts.

Rowe, C. and F. Koetter (1978) *Collage City.* Cambridge, MA.

Rushworth, G. McN. (1919) '*Magister Gregorius de Mirabilibus urbis Romae*: a new description of Rome in the twelfth century', *The Journal of Roman Studies* 9: 14–58.

Rykwert, J. (1976) *The Idea of a Town: the Anthropology of Urban Form in Rome, Italy and the Ancient World.* New Jersey.

Sablayrolles, R. (1981) 'Espace urbain et propagande politique: l'organisation du centre de Rome par Auguste (*Res Gestae*, 19 à 21)', *Pallas* 17: 59–77.

Sachs, J. (2010) *Romantic Antiquity: Rome in the British Imagination, 1789–1832.* Oxford.

Sallares, R. (2002) *Malaria and Rome: a History of Malaria in Ancient Italy.* Oxford.

Salzman-Mitchell, P. B. (2005) *A Web of Fantasies: Gaze, Image and Gender in Ovid's Metamorphoses.* Columbus, OH.

Sandbach, F. H. (1962) 'Some problems in Propertius', *Classical Quarterly* 12: 263–76.

Santangeli Valenzani, R. (2000) 'Residential building in early medieval Rome', in J. Smith (ed.), *Early Medieval Rome and the Christian West. Essays in Honour of Donald A. Bullough*. Leiden and Boston: 101–12.

(2004) 'Abitare a Roma nell' alto medioevo', in L. Paroli and L. Vendittelli (eds.), *Roma dall' antichità al medioevo*, vol. II: *Contesti tardoantichi e altomedievali*. Rome: 41–59.

Sassoli, M. G. (2000) *Roma Veduta: disegni e stampe panoramiche della città dal XV al XIX secolo*. Rome.

Schama, S. (1995) *Landscape and Memory*. London.

Schmidt, P. L. (1976) *Politik und Dichtung in der Panegyrik Claudians*. Constance.

Schmitzer, U. (1999) 'Guiding strangers through Rome – Plautus, Propertius, Vergil, Ovid, Ammianus Marcellinus and Petrarch', *Electronic Antiquity* 5.2.

Schöffel, C. (2002) *Martial Buch 8. Einleitung, Text, Übersetzung, Kommentar*. Stuttgart.

Scioli, E. (2010) '*Incohat Ismene*: the dream narrative as a mode of female discourse in epic poetry', *Transactions of the American Philological Association* 140.1: 195–238.

Scodel, R. (1997) 'Teichoscopia, catalogue, and the female spectator in Euripides', *Colby Quarterly* 33.1: 76–93.

Scriba, F. (1995) *Augustus im Schwarzhemd: Die Mostra Augustea della Romanità in Rom, 1937/38*. Frankfurt.

Serres, M. (1991) *Rome: the Book of Foundations [Rome: le livre des fondations. Paris, 1983]*, trans. F. McCarren. Stanford.

Settis, S. (1999) *Laocoonte: fama e stile*. Rome.

Shackleton Bailey, D. R. (1993) *Martial*, Epigrams. Cambridge, MA.

Sharp, S. (1766) *Letters from Italy, Describing the Customs and Manners of That Country in the Years 1765, and 1766: To Which is Annexed, an Admonition to Gentlemen Who Pass the Alps, in their Tour through Italy*. London.

Sherk, R. K. (1988) *The Roman Empire: Augustus to Hadrian*. Cambridge.

Simon, E. E. and L. H. Primavera (1972) 'Investigation of the "Blue Seven" phenomenon in elementary and junior high school children', *Psychology Reports* 31: 128–30.

Simpson, J. (2005) 'Subjects of triumph and literary history: Dido and Petrarch in Petrarch's *Africa* and *Trionfi*', *Journal of Medieval and Early Modern Studies* 35.3: 489–508.

Skutsch, O. (1961) 'Enniana IV', *Classical Quarterly* 11.3–4: 252–67.

Skyrme, R. (1982) 'Quevedo, Du Bellay, and Janus Vitalis', *Comparative Literature Studies* 19.3: 281–95.

Smith, C. J. (1996) *Early Rome and Latium: Economy and Society c. 1000 to 500 BC*. Oxford.

(2006) *The Roman Clan: the Gens from Ancient Ideology to Modern Anthropology*. Oxford.

Smith, R. R. R. (1997) 'The public image of Licinius I: portrait sculpture and imperial ideology in the early fourth century', *The Journal of Roman Studies* 87: 170–202.

Smith, W. (1854) *Dictionary of Greek and Roman Geography*. London.

Snodgrass, A. (1985) Review of Symeonoglou, *The Topography of Thebes*, in *Times Literary Supplement* 27, December 1985.

Sogliano, A. (1905) in *Notizie degli scavidi antichità*: 85–97.

Solmsen, F. (1961) 'Propertius in his literary relations with Tibullus and Vergil', *Philologus* 105: 273–81.

Spentzou, E. (2005) 'The female sound of silence: Ovid and the heroines in exile', in R. Ancona and E. Greene (eds.), *Gendered Dynamics in Latin Love Elegy*. Baltimore: 318–40.

Spies, A. (1930) *Militat omnis amans*. Tübingen.

Stäel, G. de (1998) *Corinne*. First published 1807. London.

Stafford, E. and J. Herrin (eds.) (2005) *Personification in the Greek World*. Aldershot.

Stamper, J. W. (2005) *The Architecture of Roman Temples: the Republic to the Middle Empire*. Cambridge.

Stein, B. J. and P. J. Capelotti (1993) *US Army Heraldic Crests: a Complete Illustrated History of Authorized Distinctive Unit Insignia*. Columbia.

Steinby, E. M. (ed.) (1993–2000) *Lexicon topographicum urbis Romae*. 5 vols. Los Angeles.

(ed.) (1996) *Ianiculum - Gianicolo: storia, topografia, monumenti, leggende dall' antichità al rinascimento*. Rome.

Stendhal, H. B. (1829) *Promenades dans Rome*. Vol. I. Paris.

Stewart, P. C. N. (2003) *Statues in Roman Society: Representation and Response*. Oxford.

Stewart, S. (1984) *On Longing: Narratives of the Miniature, the Gigantic, the Souvenir, the Collection*. Durham, NC.

Stirling, L. M. (2008) 'Pagan statuettes in late antique Corinth: sculpture from the Panayia Domus', *Hesperia* 77: 89–161.

Stolberg, F. L. (1796–7) *Travels through Germany, Switzerland, Italy, and Sicily*. London.

Stone, M. (1999) 'A flexible Rome: Fascism and the cult of *romanità*', in C. Edwards (ed.), *Roman Presences: Receptions of Rome in European Culture, 1789–1945*. Cambridge: 205–20.

Stremooukhoff, D. (1953) 'Moscow, the Third Rome: sources of the doctrine', *Speculum* 28: 84–101.

Stuart Jones, H. (1926) *A Catalogue of the Ancient Sculptures Preserved in the Municipal Collections of Rome: the Sculptures of the Conservatori*. Oxford.

Swain, S. (1996) *Hellenism and Empire: Language, Classicism, and Power in the Greek World, AD 50–250*. Oxford.

Symeonoglou, S. (1985) *The Topography of Thebes from the Bronze Age to Modern Times*. New Jersey.

Tanner, T. (1992) *Venice Desired*. Oxford.

Tarpin, M. (2002) *Vici et pagi dans l'occident romain*. Rome.

Tedeschi Grisanti, G. (1977) *I 'Trofei di Mario': il ninfeo dell'Acqua Giulia sull'Esquilino*. Rome.

Terneux, J.-C. (ed.) (1999) *Robert Garnier, Porcie: tragédie*. Rome.

Terrenato, N. (1992) 'Velia and Carinae: some observations on an area of archaic Rome', *Papers of the Fourth Conference of Italian Archaeology* 3–4: 31–47.

Thomas, J. (1993) 'The politics of vision and the archaeologies of landscape' in B. Bender (ed.), *Landscape Politics and Perspectives*. Oxford: 19–48.

Thomas, R. F. (ed.) (2011) *Horace, Odes: Book IV and the* Carmen saeculare. Cambridge.

Thompson, L. L. (1984) 'Domitianus Dominus: a gloss on Statius *Silvae* 1.6.84', *American Journal of Philology* 105: 469–75.

Tilly, B. (1961) *The Story of Pallas*. Cambridge.

Tilly, C. (1984) *Big Structures, Large Processes, Huge Comparisons*. New York.

Tolliver, W. (2000) *Henry James as a Biographer: a Self among Others*. London.

Tomei, M. A. (1994) 'A proposito della Velia', *Mitteilungen des Deutschen Archäologischen Instituts, Römische Abteilung* 101: 309–38.

Toynbee, J. M. C. (1934) *The Hadrianic School: a Chapter in the History of Greek Art*. Cambridge.

(1947) 'Roma and Constantinopolis in late-antique art from 312 to 365', *The Journal of Roman Studies* 37: 135–44.

Trimble, J. (2007) 'Visibility and viewing on the Severan Marble Plan', in S. Swain, S. Harrison and J. Elsner (eds.), *Severan Culture*. Cambridge: 368–84.

Tucci, P. L. (2006) 'L'Arx Capitolina, tra mito e realtà', in L. Haselberger and J. Humphrey (eds.), *Imaging Ancient Rome. Documentation, Visualization, Imagination. Proceedings of the Third Williams Symposium on Classical Architecture, Held in Rome at the American Academy in Rome, the British School at Rome, and the Deutsches Archäologisches Institut Rome, on May 20–23 2004*. Portsmouth, RI: 63–74.

Urry, J. (1990) *The Tourist Gaze*. California.

Valentini, R. and C. Zucchetti (1940) *Codice topografico della città di Roma*. Rome.

Vance, W. (1989) *America's Rome*, vol. II: *Catholic and Contemporary Rome*. New Haven.

Varène, P. (1992) *L'enceinte gallo-romaine de Nîmes*. Paris.

Vasaly, A. (1993) *Representations: Images of the World in Ciceronian Oratory*. Berkeley and Oxford.

Vassiliev, A. (1883) *Anecdota Graeco-Byzantina*. Moscow.

Vermaseren, M. J. (1977) *Cybele and Attis: the Myth and the Cult*. London.

Vermeule, C. C. (1959) *The Goddess Roma in the Art of the Roman Empire*. Cambridge, MA.

Vessey, D. (1973) *Statius and the* Thebaid. Cambridge.

Vigenère, B. de (1586) *Traicté des chiffres ou secrètes manières d'écrire*. Paris.

Visser, R. (1992) 'Fascist doctrine and the cult of Romanità', *Journal of Contemporary History* 27.1: 5–22.

Vivian, G. (1848) *Views from the Gardens of Rome and Albano.* London.

Vogel, L. (1973) *The Column of Antoninus Pius.* Cambridge, MA.

Vout, C. (2006) 'Review of Heenes, *Antike in Bildern*', *Journal of Hellenic Studies* 126: 226–7.

   (2007a) *Power and Eroticism in Imperial Rome.* Cambridge.

   (2007b) 'Sizing up Rome or theorising the overview', in D. Larmour and D. Spencer (eds.), *The Sites of Rome: Time, Space, Memory.* Oxford: 295–322.

   (2009a) Review of S. Dillon and K. E. Welch, *Representations of War in Ancient Rome*, in *Art History* 32.1: 186–92.

   (2009b) Review of M. M. Miles, *Art as Plunder: the Ancient Origins of Debate about Cultural Property*, in *The Journal of Roman Studies* 98: 273–4.

Walbank, M. E. H. (2003) 'Aspects of Corinthian coinage in the late 1st and early second centuries A.C.', in C. K. Williams and N. Bookidis (eds.), *Corinth the Centenary 1896–1996.* Athens: 337–50.

Walker, S. (2000) 'The moral museum: Augustus and the city of Rome', in J. Coulston and H. Dodge (eds.), *Ancient Rome: the Archaeology of the Eternal City.* Dublin: 61–75.

Walker, S. and P. Higgs (2001) *Cleopatra of Egypt: From History to Myth.* London.

Wallace-Hadrill, A. (1998) '*Horti* and Hellenization', in M. Cima and E. La Rocca (eds.), *Horti Romani: atti del convegno internationzale Roma, 4–6 maggio 1995.* Rome: 1–12.

   (2008) *Rome's Cultural Revolution.* Cambridge.

Wallach, A. (1993) 'Making a picture of the view from Mount Holyoke', in D. C. Miller (ed.), *American Iconology: New Approaches to Nineteenth-Century Art and Literature.* New Haven: 80–91.

Warde Fowler, W. (1918) *Aeneas at the Site of Rome: Observations on the Eighth Book of the Aeneid.* Oxford.

Ward-Perkins, B. (1984) *From Classical Antiquity to the Middle Ages: Urban Public Building in Northern and Central Italy AD 300–850.* Oxford.

Watkin, D. (2009) *The Roman Forum.* London.

Weeks, S. (1962) 'Kampala: profile of a city', *Africa Today* 9.8: 6–8.

Weisweiler, J. (2010) 'Aristocratic rivalry in late antique Rome'. PhD thesis. Cambridge.

Welch, K. E. (2006) '*Domi Militiaeque*: Roman domestic aesthetics in the republican period', in S. Dillon and K. E. Welch (eds.), *Representations of War in Ancient Rome.* Cambridge: 91–161.

Welch, T. (2005) *The Elegiac Cityscape: Propertius and the Meaning of Roman Monuments.* Ohio.

Whitmarsh, T. (2001) *Greek Literature and the Roman Empire: the Politics of Imitation.* Oxford.

Wilamowitz-Möllendorff, U. von (1891) 'Die Sieben Thore Thebens', *Hermes* 26: 191–242.

Wilkens, I. J. (1991) *Where Troy Once Stood: the Mystery of Homer's* Iliad *Revealed.* London.

Wilkins, A. S. (1898) 'Pais's *Storia di Roma'*, *Classical Review* 12: 12: 419–22.

Wilkins, E. H. (1953) 'Petrarch's coronation oration', *Publications of the Modern Language Association* 68.5: 1241–50.

Williams, C. K. (1987) 'Corinth, 1986: east of the theater', *Hesperia* 56: 3–27.

Wiseman, J. (1979) 'Corinth and Rome I: 228 BC–AD 267', *Aufsteig und Niedergang der römischen Welt* 2.7.1: 438–548.

Wiseman, T. P. (1979) 'Topography and rhetoric; the trial of Manlius', *Historia* 28: 32–50.

(1981) 'The Temple of Victory on the Palatine', *The Antiquaries Journal* 61: 35–52.

(1995) *Remus: a Roman Myth.* Cambridge.

(1998) 'A stroll on the rampart', in M. Cima and E. La Rocca (eds.), *Horti Romani: atti del convegno internazionale Roma, 4–6 maggio 1995.* Rome: 13–22.

(2000) Review of A. Carandini, *La nascita di Roma*, in *The Journal of Roman Studies* 90: 210–12.

(2009) *Remembering the Roman People: Essays on Late-Republican Politics and Literature.* Oxford.

Wissowa, G. (1904) 'Septimontium und Subura', *Gesammelte Abhandlungen zur römischen Religions- und Stadtgeschichte.* Munich: 230–52.

Wolff, E. (ed.) (2007) *Rutilius Namatianus, Sur son retour.* Paris.

Wolfgang, M. (1988) 'Poetisch-mythologische Realität in De reditu suo des Rutilius Namatianus', in M. von Wissemann (ed.), *Roma renascens. Beiträge zur Spätantike und Rezeptionsgeschichte. Ilona Opelt von ihren Freunden und Schülern zum 9.7.1988 in Verehrung gewidmet.* Frankfurt: 235–56.

Wrede, H. (1981) *Consecratio in Formam Deorum: Vergöttlichte Privatpersonen in der römischen Kaiserzeit.* Mainz.

Wylie, J. W. (2007) *Landscape.* London.

Yarbro Collins, A. (1984) 'Numerical symbolism in Jewish and early Christian apocalyptic literature', *Aufsteig und Niedergang der römischen Welt* 2. 21.2: 1221–87.

Zanker, G. (2007) *Modes of Viewing in Hellenistic Poetry and Art.* Madison.

Zanker, P. (1987) *Augustus und die Macht der Bilder.* Munich.

Zawadzka, A. (2002) 'Roma Quadrata e il significato dell'aggettivo quadratus', *Appunti Romani di Filologia* 4: 55–60.

Zeleznikar, A. (2002) *Rome Explorations: the Ancient Rome Walking Tour.* Victoria, Canada.

Zolfanelli, C. (1884) *I sette colli.* Rome.

Index of principal passages discussed

General index

Achaea 133
  and the Achaeans 220
Aemilius Paullus, Lucius 82
Aemilius Scaurus, Marcus 32
Aeneas 19, 57, 75, 83, 220, 228
  and the Palatine 32, 211
  and the shield of the *Aeneid* 75, 220
aestimare 199
Africa 110
Agrippa *see* Vipsanus Agrippa, Marcus
Alaric 109, 218
Alban hills 19, 32, 203, 221, 227
Albani, Alessandro 166
Alberti, Leon Battista 43
Alcinous 203–4
Alexander
  the Great 91, 138, 151
  VII 136, 151
Alexandria 64, 96, 109
Allia, battle of 65
Almo 111
Alps 109, 188, 221
alunite 136
Ammianus Marcellinus 196–8, 222–4, 237
Anchises 75, 83, 119
Anio 99
Anthemius 27
Antioch 129
Antipater 64
Antiquaries, Society of 176
Antoninus Pius 30, 104, 128
Antony, Mark 65, 90, 119, 129
Aonia 101
Apollo 32, 95
Aqua
  Marcia 99
  Virgo (Acqua Vergine) 99, 146, 163
aqueducts 8, 32, 46
Ara
  Consi 76
  Maxima 76, 211
  Pacis 66
Arcadia 102, 121

arces 30, 75, 84, 89, 96, 112, 116
archaeology 14, 76, 142, 165–7
Ardea 50
Argaeus, Mount 125
Argan, Giulio Carlo 141
Argei 71
Argiletum 212
Ariminum (modern Rimini) 29
Aristides, Aelius 67, 104
Aristotle 62
Arno 136
Arnold, Dana 188
Arsilli, Francesco 31, 37
arx 22, 82; *see also* Capitoline
Athena 26
Athens 57, 103
  acropolis of 82
  Olympeion at 103
Athos, Mount 91, 136, 151, 229
Atticus 68, 82
Augustine 108
Augustus 32, 75, 90, 107, 227
  and the changing cityscape 9–10, 13, 17, 80, 82, 228, 235
  and the *Res gestae* 132
  and the seven hills of Rome 10, 13
  and the temple of Apollo 41
  arch of 179, 229
  as a new founder 66, 80, 87
  as god 98
  as model 55, 77, 138, 164, 194
  as Octavian 65
  house of 32, 86, 193
  Mons 91
  Primaporta statue of 105
Aurelian 5
Aurelius, Marcus 157
Aventine 22, 34, 43, 78, 119, 227
  and its etymology 71
  and its Temple of Diana 41, 95, 208
  and the *plebs* 10, 32
  as outside the *pomerium* 23
  in the frescoes of the Villa Giulia 159
  in the modern period 232

Printed in the United States
By Bookmasters